AFFECTIVE TRAJECTORIES

RELIGIOUS CULTURES OF AFRICAN AND AFRICAN DIASPORA PEOPLE

Series editors: Jacob K. Olupona, Harvard University; Dianne M. Stewart, Emory University; and Terrence L. Johnson, Georgetown University

The book series examines the religious, cultural, and political expressions of African, African American, and African Caribbean traditions. Through transnational, cross-cultural, and multidisciplinary approaches to the study of religion, the series investigates the epistemic boundaries of continental and diasporic religious practices and thought and explores the diverse and distinct ways African-derived religions inform culture and politics. The series aims to establish a forum for imagining the centrality of Black religions in the formation of the "New World."

AFFECTIVE TRAJECTORIES
RELIGION AND EMOTION IN AFRICAN CITY-SCAPES

HANSJÖRG DILGER,
ASTRID BOCHOW,
MARIAN BURCHARDT,
and MATTHEW
WILHELM-SOLOMON,
editors

DUKE UNIVERSITY PRESS Durham and London 2020

© 2020 Duke University Press

Printed in the United States of America on acid-free paper ∞
Designed by Aimee C. Harrison
Typeset in Adobe Caslon Pro and Myriad Pro
by Copperline Book Services

Library of Congress Cataloging-in-Publication Data
Names: Dilger, Hansjörg, editor.
Title: Affective trajectories : religion and emotion in African cityscapes /
Hansjörg Dilger, Astrid Bochow, Marian Burchardt, and Matthew
Wilhelm-Solomon.
Description: Durham : Duke University Press Books, 2020. | Series:
Religious cultures of African and African diaspora people | Includes
bibliographical references and index.
Identifiers: LCCN 2019023966 (print)
LCCN 2019023967 (ebook)
ISBN 9781478005490 (hardcover)
ISBN 9781478006268 (paperback)
ISBN 9781478007166 (ebook)
Subjects: LCSH: Cities and towns—Religious aspects—Christianity. |
Cities and towns—Africa. | Psychology, Religious—Africa. | Emotions—
Religious aspects—Christianity.
Classification: LCC BR1360 .A435 2020 (print) | LCC BR1360 (ebook) |
DDC 200.96/091732—dc23
LC record available at https://lccn.loc.gov/2019023966
LC ebook record available at https://lccn.loc.gov/2019023967

Cover photograph: Marisa Maza

CONTENTS

ACKNOWLEDGMENTS

This volume was developed from selected papers from the conference "Spirit and Sentiment: Affective Trajectories of Religious Being in Urban Africa," which was held at Freie Universität Berlin on May 28–30, 2015. The conference was organized by the editors of this volume on behalf of the research network Religion, AIDS, and Social Transformation in Africa (RASTA). The conference was cosponsored by the research project "Salvaged Lives: A Study of Urban Migration, Ontological Insecurity, and Healing in Johannesburg," based at the African Centre for Migration and Society, University of the Witwatersrand, in collaboration with the Institute of Social and Cultural Anthropology at the Freie Universität Berlin and funded by the Volkswagen Foundation Knowledge for Tomorrow—Cooperative Research Projects in Sub-Saharan Africa Programme.

The editors would like to thank the keynote speakers of the Berlin conference, Filip De Boeck and Rijk van Dijk, whose interventions informed the debates in the volume. We also would like to thank the following institutions and individuals for their invaluable support in the development and final production of this volume: Kulturwissenschaftliches Kolleg Konstanz for funding the proofreading of the manuscript before submission; Karoline Buchner for formatting the chapters, communicating with contributors, and preparing the manuscript for submission; Robert Parkin and Zoe Goldstein for language editing; and the three external readers for their highly insightful comments on the volume. We are extremely grateful to Miriam Angress at Duke University Press for her facilitation of the contracts and production; and the series editors Jacob Olupona, Dianne Stewart, and Terrence Johnson, who showed tremendous interest in this book project from its very beginning.

INTRODUCTION AFFECTIVE TRAJECTORIES IN RELIGIOUS AFRICAN CITYSCAPES

HANSJÖRG DILGER, MARIAN BURCHARDT,
MATTHEW WILHELM-SOLOMON,
and ASTRID BOCHOW

This volume is the first of its kind to focus comparatively on the multiple articulations between the varied affective and emotional states of people living in and beyond urban Africa, on the one hand, and the religious practices, ideas, and infrastructures present in African cities that impact them, on the other. In an important sense, the affective and emotional dynamics in urban Africa,[1] and the social, political, and material configurations that sustain—or are sustained by—them, are bound up with religion, its politics of collective aspirations and presence in public spaces, as well as its material practices.

In this volume, we envisage the intertwining of religion, affect, and emotion in African cityscapes and, more specifically, the ways in which religious symbols and rites structure—and are reworked through—embodied and affective relationships with urban materialities and power relations, on five levels. First, religious ideas and practices offer affective regimes that regulate the hermeneutics of the self; second, religion allows people to encode their emotional states in moral and/or spiritual terms that shape their maps of meaning and guide their actions; third, religion supplies affective forms of belonging that are often simultaneously localized and transnational, and thus forge new notions of emplacement; fourth, religion produces ritual spaces for catharsis, peace, and elation and hence offers an outlet for the discord and anxiety of city life, though religious groups and rituals also foster aggression toward those considered to be outside their moral order; and fifth, religious communities often provide concrete material, emotional, and organizational support and care to those living in precarious and dangerous situations.

In order to explore these various intertwinings between affect, emotion, and religion in urban African settings, the volume engages with two bodies of literature that have not yet been systematically applied to the analysis of religious practices in African cityscapes and beyond. First, the volume builds on the literature on affect, emotion, and sentiment that has flourished in the social sciences and cultural studies in recent years, and whose analytical potential for the field of religion still needs to be fully explored—not only in Africa but also in other parts of the world. Second, it connects the literature on affect, emotion, and sentiment—and the way in which it has been applied by individual authors to the study of religion so far (e.g., Riis and Woodhead 2010; Herbrik and Knoblauch 2014; Scheer 2015)—to the exploration of the diverse religious, symbolic, social, political, and material mediations of urban space in Africa and beyond.

Taken together, these two bodies of literature inform our notion of affective trajectories, which we consider central for thinking about how the affective and emotional dimensions of religious ideas, practices, and materialities coalesce to shape specific urban environments in contemporary Africa and beyond, and how they are simultaneously shaped by them. We argue that scholars of religion should focus more systematically on the ways in which theoretical notions of affect, emotion, and sentiment can be applied when exploring religious lives in the cityscapes of global Africa, which today extend far beyond the "narrow" confines of the continent, and how they provide unique entry points for analyzing the entwinement between religion, affect, emotion, and sentiment in the twenty-first century.

AFFECT, EMOTION, AND SENTIMENT IN THE STUDY
OF RELIGION IN AFRICA: A BLANK SPOT

The dynamics of affect, emotion, and sentiment powerfully mold the experiences and social practices of people living in urban Africa, as well as African migrants who have moved to the urban centers of Europe, North America, and other parts of the world (Cole and Groes 2016). For instance, the lives of Africans in urban environments have been shaped by regional and civic conflicts; the desires and pervasive pains induced by neoliberal market-oriented reforms; large-scale urban-rural and transnational migrations; the rapid demolitions, dispossessions, and constructions of urban and (post)colonial change; and high levels of unemployment, poverty, and epidemic illness. Taken together, these various processes challenge not only the imagination of African urbanites when navigating these often highly strenuous conditions in the creation of coherent lives but also the imagination of scholars to develop new understandings of these dynamics (Förster 2016), not least with regard to the conceptual and methodological repertoires that we apply when we research and represent the highly diversified experiences and responses of African urbanites in relation to these dynamics.

As this volume shows, moving into and residing in the vital and economically, ethnically, socially, and religiously diverse urban centers of the continent and its diasporas often triggers—and is triggered by—states of anxiety, insecurity, and fear, as well as feelings of excitement and hope, for instance, for a better life or for socioeconomic liberation. In this regard, life in urban African settings implies the reorganization of social relations and individual subjectivities, thereby giving rise to new understandings and practices of citizenship, self, and personhood, but also to sensations of marginality and exclusion and the anxieties of leading a "good life" in precarious environments. In addition, urban centers, and the opportunities and risks that living in them implies, provide spaces for sensations of pleasure, love, care, and intimacy, as well as experiences of suffering, alienation, and emotional drama.

Despite the pervasive presence of affect, emotion, and sentiment in the lives of African urbanites, the affective experiences of African cityscapes are often subordinated to a focus on macroeconomic, demographic, and political forces. Consequently, Edgar Pieterse emphasizes "the importance of reading the affective functions of popular practices, because it is only through the redeployment of such registers that one can begin to fathom what is going on in the real city, and potentially animate a resonant engagement with the city" (2011, 18). Nevertheless, an approach to the affective dimensions of African urbanisms—and particularly their relationship to religious practices—has thus far been largely absent in the literature.

This blank spot in the scholarly literature tends to ignore the fact that it is not only Pentecostal churches that incite a wide range of affective and emotional sensations among their members in the context of highly charismatic church services and collective healing prayers (Pype 2015). Indeed, emotions are part and parcel of the repertoires of other religious traditions, including Islam and other Christian denominations. These other religious traditions have also articulated very specific scripts on how their adherents are to experience and express emotional states with regard to love, sexuality, and ritual (Corrigan 2008) or their personal relationship with God (Gade 2008). At the same time, in African cities and their diasporic counterparts, people's religiously mediated affective and emotional states cannot be thought of independently of the social relations, material infrastructure, and configurations of power that have structured urban life in and beyond Africa over the last decades.

This volume does not aim to define a rigid framework for the study of affect, emotion, and sentiment in African cityscapes, especially as there is no consensus in the theoretical literature on how to define and distinguish these concepts; indeed, they are often used in interchangeable ways (see, e.g., Palmer and Occhi 1999, 12). In a similar vein, the contributors to this volume each formulate a specific understanding of affect, emotion, and sentiment, which are—and *need* to be—deeply situated in their respective research constellations and in relation to the particular conceptual arguments they make.

Against this background, this introduction aims to outline, above all, an "intellectual space" (Meyer 2009, 2) that emphasizes the importance of studying the dynamics of affect, emotion, and sentiment in relation to religious discourses, practices, and materialities in urban Africa from various disciplinary, regional, and thematic perspectives. Furthermore, the conceptual framework of "affective trajectories" that we outline here aims to formulate a mediating position between the various approaches to the study of affect, emotion, and sentiment—as we summarize them in the following two sections—in relation to urban African religion(s). Such an analytical framework highlights the need to formulate precise conceptual understandings of affect, emotion, and sentiment, and how they entwine with religion and the urban, without losing sight of ethnographic specificities and the conceptual subtleties that their exploration requires.

Significantly, we also recognize that in much Enlightenment-inspired thinking, key notions that are touched upon in this volume, such as "religion" and "affect," have been encased in conceptual binaries (such as affect, emotion, and sentiment vs. reason and intellect; body vs. mind; nature vs. culture; time vs. space). In line with postcolonial criticism, in this volume we seek to unsettle the hierarchical organization of these binaries and the privilege typically accorded to one side of them. Going beyond this criticism, we also highlight that conceptual dyads such as affect and reason, or body and mind, emerge through dialectical processes of coconstitution.

Pentecostal pedagogies that posit believers' emotions as the subject of conscious cultivation and training are a good illustration of this point (see Cazarin and Burchardt, this volume), as is the rationalization of sentiment among Pentecostals in the context of rural-to-urban migration in Botswana (see van Dijk, this volume).

AFFECT, EMOTION, AND SENTIMENT SHAPE— AND ARE SHAPED BY—RELIGION

In the wider social science and cultural studies literature, a significant corpus of studies has formulated the assumption that a fundamental distinction needs to be made between "affect" as a form of preconscious experience that establishes a largely unstructured and embodied relationship between individuals and the social and material world, on the one hand, and "emotion" as the culturally and socially mediated articulation of this experience, on the other. According to this perspective, a close relationship exists between affect and emotion, in that the former designates an intensification of bodily states that makes individuals act or relate to their surroundings in particular ways (Massumi 2002), while the latter translates this experience into the domains of language, cognition, and other modes of representation (Lutz and Abu-Lughod 1990).

While "emotions" are often thought of as the social and cultural coding of the inchoate experience that "affect" comprises, it would be misleading to think of emotion *as* affect: "It is better to think of emotion as that which follows affect once the moment is gone, and the 'affected' person finally becomes aware of the experience, framing it discursively" (Bialecki 2015, 97). In other words, while emotions describe the bodily and mental reactions of the subject toward events or encounters including pain, fear, anger, or pleasure, they also involve complex "judgments" (R. Solomon 1995), "perceptions" (W. James 2013), and "apprehensions of the world" (Sartre and Streller 1962, 9), and thus already contain an element of *reflexivity*. Emotions may also be an expression of ethical values and normative assumptions if they convey a person's or group's sentiments that something is fundamentally right or wrong.[2] Taken in this way, emotions can be regarded as complex "bio-cultural" formations (Röttger-Rössler and Markowitsch 2009), which comprise both cognitive elements and bodily sensations (Ahmed 2013, 5). It also becomes clear that this conception of emotion and affect goes beyond the Cartesian notion of "ratio" versus "emotions," "body" versus "mind," or the "individual" versus the "collective."

Recent social scientific studies have consequently moved beyond the individualistic perspective of the psychology-driven "emotion and affect studies" of earlier decades and have emphasized that affect and emotion are always embodied in the relationships between individuals and their wider social and material environments. Thus while Michelle Rosaldo (1984, 143) described emotions as "embodied thought" as early as 1984, it was only more recently that social scientists have shown how emotions are performed and enacted in relation to discursive frameworks and power configurations (Röttger-Rössler 2004; Riis and Woodhead 2010), as well as the social context at large (Lyon 1995).

As Riis and Woodhead (2010, 10) have argued for the domain of religion, for instance, it is through particular "emotional regimes" that religious communities shape their members' emotional and affective lives. In this sense, religion is the context not only for the regulation, cultivation, and disciplining of emotional states but also for their transformation (11). Riis and Woodhead also stress that the embodiment of such emotional regimes is not a passive process, as the members of religious groups are actively engaged in learning the "emotional repertoires" (11) of their respective social environments. Nor are such embodiments permanent or unchangeable, as emotional regimes "educate and structure sensibility not only in relation to daily tasks and duties, but across the life course, and they help in the navigation of its transitions and crises" (11).

In recent years, anthropological and sociological scholars of affect and emotion have adopted an increasingly broad perspective of "the social" in their research and have shown that environments are shaped not only by people's relationships with their fellow human beings but also by their interactions with the wider material and nontangible world. Especially in the context of "affect studies," these uses of affect have been informed by the philosophy of Deleuze and Guattari (1994, 169), who conceived of "affects" as "the nonhuman becomings of man" and "affection" as a form of corporeal relation to other bodies (Deleuze 1990, 218). Brian Massumi has elaborated on these ideas, arguing that affects are "basically ways of connecting, to others and to other situations" (2015, 6). According to his perspective, affects involve flows and networks between human and nonhuman actors, and "although affect is all about intensities of feeling, the feeling process cannot be characterized as exclusively subjective or objective: the encounters through which it passes strike the body as immediately as they stir the mind" (x).

In recent years, philosophical conceptions of affect and affection have been explored anthropologically in different ways. Elizabeth Povinelli (2011), for instance, has related these conceptions to the survival of marginalized populations under late liberalism and neoliberalism and has argued that an affective force is always one of *potentiality*—an articulation of endurance and striving. Kathleen Stewart (2007, 9–10) has embedded the study of affect within everyday events and experiences and explores how "ordinary affects" elicit transient, or unexpected, forms of sociality and trajectories. Finally, Sara Ahmed argues that affects and emotions circulate between humans and objects rather than residing within the subject: "Emotions are both about objects, which they hence shape, and are also shaped by contact with objects" (2013, 7). Ahmed thus moves away from an intrapsychic understanding of affect to an affective economy of the circulation of objects that attaches "affective value" to materialities and signs. Moreover, she links her reflections on the affective economy of emotions to material histories of social and political inequality in which emotions evolve. Through history, specific objects obtain "affective values," linking past and present suffering and inequalities (11).

While affect and emotion are always embedded in larger social and material environments and their histories, they are also a direct reflection of the moral and ethical values that guide a person's ways of being-in-the-world. According to Throop (2012, 158), the notion of "moral sentiments" helps us to explore how affective sensibilities and values shape our attention to the world we live in. It also highlights how value sentiments are simultaneously integrated into the larger political histories and configurations that govern people's lives (cf. Stoler 2004). Throop suggests that these embodied ways of being-in-the-world become subject to ethical reflection, especially in "moments of destabilization" and at times of heightened social and cultural rupture (Throop 2012, 158; see also Zigon 2007). In contrast to short-term emotional states and sensations, sentiments can therefore be conceived of as "emotional dispositions" (Reihling 2014, 33), which "refer to an individual's conscious anticipation of an event and justify the appearance of a corresponding response" (32). Furthermore, sentiments have been understood as the "conventionalized" form of representing affective and emotional responses—such as in literature and poetry—which "contributes to . . . representations that are tied to morality, which is ultimately tied to politics in its broadest sense" (Abu-Lughod 1988, 34).[3] Given the ambiguous potential of moral sentiments in times of social and political transformation, it is crucial to explore not only how sentiments cultivate our attitudes toward and practices of a "good life" (Robbins 2013a) but also how *resentment*—that is, sensations of rage, anger, bitterness, and frustration—becomes central in situations of injustice and injury (Fassin 2013).

With reference to the topic of this edited volume, a relational concept of affect, emotion, and sentiment (cf. Reihling 2014; Röttger-Rössler and Slaby 2018) concerns the various materialities and technologies—and all types of sensational forms (Meyer 2010)—that mediate religious expressions in urban space, such as (sacred) objects, (visual and sonic) media, language, text, and infrastructure. Informed by sociological theories of embodiment and the anthropology of the senses, scholars have analyzed, for instance, how religious groups use sound, images, and iconography to appeal to the sensual capacities of urban audiences and to engage their believers' imagination of the extraordinary (Oosterbaan 2009; Meyer 2008; Hirschkind 2001). They have also explored the conflicts that arise due to competition over sonic and iconic representations of different religious communities in urban space (Brennan 2010) and the idea that materialities are not simply "carriers" of affective and emotional codes but have the visual, aural, and haptic power to affect human and nonhuman beings on multiple levels (Scheer 2012; Larkin 2013; Pype 2015). They also stress that settings of mobility and migration can enhance emotional sensations of alienation and (failed) belonging in particular ways, as migrants can be faced not only with the challenge of (re)connecting to their places of origin but also with a host society that confronts them with political and bureaucratic barriers, as well as with a lack of empathy (Svašek 2010).

Again, religious communities contribute to the production of affective belonging and orientation in such settings of globalization and marginalization through, for instance, the provision of rituals and prayers for dynamics of emplacement (Dilger, Kasmani, and Mattes 2018; Englund 2002) or suffering bodies (Mossière 2007a). Religious affectivities thus transform the experience of social exclusion and marginalization and therefore have the potential to invert (or at least question) historical power relations. This holds true despite the fact that religious practice itself is embedded in relations of power, as has been shown meticulously in the history of Christianity in Africa (cf. Comaroff 1985). Religious teachings too have ambivalent effects: they enable members to move up socially by opening new emotional fashions and worldviews (Miescher 2005; van Dijk 2009), but they also forge new forms of social exclusion and inequality (Meyer 1998b).

As we have shown so far, the links between religion, emotion, affect, and sentiment are collectively authorized and subjectively felt, but one of the major arguments of this book is that they acquire particular qualities and cultural force in urban spaces. In this line of thinking, we follow Simmel's ([1903] 2006) pathbreaking insight that cities are sites of condensation, acceleration, and intensification and are constituted by spatialities and materialities that shape people's affective relations. We suggest that this conceptualization helps us to understand how cities mediate people's religious experiences and expressions. In pursuing this argument, we expand on the burgeoning field of studies on religion in urban space, and point to their shortcomings.

We intervene in these debates with two arguments. First, we contend that in many studies on religion and urban space, just as in urban theory more generally, affect, emotion, and sentiment have not received sufficient attention. Indeed, we argue that emotional dynamics are in fact central to understanding how urban space enables and constrains lived religions—and how it is simultaneously shaped by them. Second, we argue that religion affects—and is affected by—the city. Religious beliefs motivate urban dwellers to engage in practices that result in ideational-material assemblages that we call cities (Farías 2011; McFarlane 2011). Conversely, cities shape religion by confronting people with the need to permanently adapt their forms of religious belonging and worship to fluctuating urban circumstances and the often ephemeral nature of city life resulting from mobility (Burchardt and Höhne 2015; De Boeck and Plissart 2004). In order to appreciate the relevance of these arguments in the African context, a more precise understanding of the nature of urbanization in Africa is necessary.

The emergence of towns and urban centers in Africa significantly preceded European colonialism. These precolonial urban forms, along with those developed in parallel to but not by European colonists, included a diverse array of settlements, including Tswana "agro-towns," the intricate and vast constructions of Great Zimbabwe; Mbanza Kongo, a trading center (also for the slave trade) of the Kongo Kingdom; the Asante settlements of West Africa; Gondar, built by the Ethiopian emperor Fasilidas in the late seventeenth century; and Islamic cities such as Cairo; among many others (Freund 2007). As Bill Freund (2007) has meticulously documented in *The African City: A History*, the colonial city then took several forms, involving the imposition of colonial administrative and labor regimes onto existing settlements, but also the establishment of entirely new cities. Colonial towns and cities were often divided into spaces of prosperity and abandonment, but these divisions were also continually subverted and challenged by indigenous populations (Fanon 1961; Freund 2007).

The most rapid period of urbanization, however, has been during the postcolonial period. Pieterse and Parnell (2014) have characterized this as "Africa's urban revolution" in their edited book of this title. In the first chapter of their book, Pieterse and Parnell note, drawing from data from the United Nations Department of Economic and Social Affairs (UN DESA), that as of 2011, the continent was 40 percent urbanized, expanding from around 14 percent in 1950. They characterize the specific dynamics of African cities as relating to high levels of inward and circular migration; the emergence of porous peri-urban edges; the political emphasis on key cities; high levels of informal organization; overlapping systems of land tenure and power; and high levels of poverty.

Characterizations of African urbanism have often been caught between, on the one hand, dystopian imaginations of out-of-control African slums and related Marxist-inspired analyses of continual economic exclusion and immiseration (Murray 2011; Davis 2006); and, on the other, those that emphasize the agency and creativity of African urbanites—though recent analyses have attempted to move beyond these binaries (Harrison 2014; Mbembe and Nuttall 2008; Rizzo 2017; Robinson 2010; De Boeck and Baloji 2016; Simone 2008). Throughout Africa, urbanization has been characterized by continual processes of "accumulation by dispossession" (Harvey 2008). However, these processes have been driven not simply by capitalist development but also by the dynamics of postcolonial politics, land tenure and legal-political contestations, along with modernist visions for the postcolonial city (De Boeck 2013). Sometimes dispossession has been directly driven by party politics—for instance, in the case of Zimbabwe's Murambatsvina started in 2005, the clearance of informal settlements was aimed as a direct attack against urban opposition to Mugabe's government (Potts 2006). Furthermore, in spaces throughout Africa, enclave-style development with areas developed for the rich and conspicuous consumption have continued to produce further displacement and exclusion (Beall, Crankshaw, and Parnell 2002; Freund 2007).

The dynamics of contemporary migration and enforced displacement have powerfully shaped African cities (Kihato 2013; Landau 2009; Nyamnjoh 2006). In spite of their associated hardships, these processes have also contributed to the "Afropolitan" and transnational dimension of these spaces and their attendant cultural, symbolic, and semiotic density and vitality (Mbembe and Nuttall 2008; Quayson 2014). Simone (2008) and others have emphasized the ability of urban dwellers to improvise and continually generate new alliances and identities in order to navigate the city. Some observers furthermore have theorized the power of new mediascapes and technologies in shaping African cityscapes (Larkin 2004; Meyer 2015). Finally, the influence of religious forms and architectures has been particularly prominent in configuring African urban centers in recent decades (Burchardt and Becci 2013; De Boeck 2013; Landau 2009; Wilhelm-Solomon et al. 2016). In developing these themes in this volume, the emphasis on religion and affect does not entail a retreat into focusing only on passions and interiority, but rather on the ways in which the urban environment affects, debilitates, and capacitates urban dwellers. It is the relationship between urban spaces, mobilities, and mediascapes, and the intimate social and religious experiences of urban dwellers that this volume aims to explore.

Adopting this approach requires both elaborating on and also departing from the well-trodden paths of urban theory, particularly those relating to the production of urban spaces. These theories, though powerful and influential, have been limited in their theorizations both of religion and also of affect, emotion, and sentiment—and particularly the connections between them. Henri Lefebvre's writings have been hugely influential in urban theory and may serve to illustrate our first point. Although Lefebvre frames the "right to the city" as a "cry and a demand" (1996, 158), his work on urbanism and the production of space provides little theorization of the relation between religion and emotion. The closest he comes is in his writing on "rhythmanalysis," where he notes of his imagined figure of the rhythmanalysist in the Mediterranean city that he wanders the street with "his thoughts and emotions, his impressions and his wonder" (228–229). He also relates his notion of the study of rhythms explicitly to religious rituals and their "irruption and also their intervention in everyday life" (235). However, in his proposed methodology, and in his notion of the "(co-)production of space," anything like *affect* as a prediscursively felt and sensory apprehension of the city is never fully realized. Although the notion of the production of space thus remains a powerful idea for apprehending the structuring of the urban, it requires supplementation when theorizing the intimate and affective engagement with cities.

For the purposes of this volume, we engage the notion of space to refer to networks of sites in which humans and things are specifically emplaced

(Löw 2001). Such emplacements, like their articulations in people's momentary perceptions, past memories, and future imaginations, mark and punctuate spaces (Berberich, Campbell, and Hudson 2013). This also implies that people are not alone and above other beings in creating spaces but are always, as Ingold's "dwelling perspective" suggests, "in an active engagement with the constituents of his or her surroundings" (2005, 5). To this conceptualization, we add two central theoretical insights. First, the networks of sites that make the city always also include places beyond the city (such as "the rural," "the global," or the reference to "history"). The "urban proper" thus contains within it "other spaces," as Foucault ([1967] 1984) insisted. Second, the relations between the places within a network of sites are established through people's movements, mobilities, and imaginations. Cities are infrastructures of circulation that facilitate the movement of people, ideas, and things between sites. We suggest that circulations take place on territories that are in some way always religiously marked; albeit not all social groups are able to effect such markings in the same way, and perceive and interpret them differently. People circulate between places with religious meanings, and it is imperative to explore how the meanings actually influence their movements along with their emotive and affective experiences of urban space.

In addition, engaging analytically with urban space benefits from the notion of scale (Brenner 2001) that addresses the hierarchical arrangements of urban centers in an interconnected world, as well as the internal diversity of urban spaces with their "hot spots" and "dead zones" (van Dijk 2011). Consequently, in this volume cities are considered spaces of intensification (Debord 1967) configured around spatial mobilities, risks, and opportunities, as well as "vulnerable and often invisible infrastructures [which] impose their own spatial and temporal logic on the city" (De Boeck 2012). At the same time, cities also become spaces of "ontological insecurity" (Giddens 2004), where the vagaries and fragilities of urban centers threaten their inhabitants' sense of identity and coherence, challenging their social, spiritual, and moral beings in highly gendered and embodied ways (Mukonyora 2007). Again, religious practices that originate from the fields of Christianity, Islam, and African or other forms of "traditional" religion help to overcome these states of insecurity and establish affective and emotional belonging in the context of highly fluid urban environments (Wilhelm-Solomon, Kankonde, and Núñez 2017).

With regard to the specific role of religion in the production of cityscapes, finally, this volume is informed by the burgeoning literature on religion and urban space that has demonstrated how religion and urban environments are mutually shaped (Becker et al. 2013; Burchardt and Becci 2013; Wilhelm-Solomon et al. 2016). On the one hand, urban processes shape religious identities, forms of belonging, and religious aspirations and practices (van der Veer 2013; Dilger 2017). Chiefly, cities affect religion by casting religious communities and their forms of sociality within particular spatial regimes and by contributing to the territorialization of religious categories (Hervieu-Léger 2002). These regimes also involve questions around places of worship as key sites for organizing religious communities, celebrating togetherness through shared religious rituals, and expressing and consuming religious aesthetics through forms of "architectural registration" (Knowles 2013, 656) or decoration, especially in the context of festivals and ceremonies (Garbin 2013). On the other hand, religious communities and traditions shape cities and urban space in invisible and visible ways. They contain the imaginaries and ideas on the basis of which people make urban worlds and relate to the city. But they also often leave durable infrastructural and architectural imprints, whereby notions of the divine are materially mediated. In addition, in highly mobile African cities, life is characterized by new kinds of religious sociality that enable emotional, financial, and ritual support that often goes far beyond the role of kin and family networks and ties (Akyeampong 1996; Dilger 2007, 2014).

While we value this research, we nevertheless argue that there is a need to better understand how affect, emotion, and sentiment shape the nexus of religion and urbanism, as scholarly understandings have thus far remained limited. It is clear that for diaspora communities and migrants in African cities, religion contributes to notions of "home-making" (Adogame 1998; Eade 2012; Olupona and Gemignani 2007) or "place-making," by which Vásquez and Knott (2014, 326) understand articulations of dwelling, building, and inhabiting (see also Dilger, Kasmani, and Mattes 2018). Such practices engage with spatial regimes and reconfigure the ways in which religious lines of difference are mapped onto urban territories and spaces, thereby producing particular "topographies of faith" (Becci, Burchardt, and Casanova 2013). At the same time, religious actors and institutions connect these topographies to novel forms of religious popular culture (e.g., speaking, singing, dancing, praying, and dressing) (Schulz 2012), which also shape notions of home and feelings of belonging. Similarly, entrepreneurial religious individuals and organizations produce new forms of entertainment, for instance, through commercialized purchased artifacts of popular music (de Witte 2012) or the burgeoning video film industry (Meyer 2015).

In brief, throughout the early twenty-first century, religious practices, and the sensational forms they produce (Meyer 2011), have shaped the lives of urban African populations through emotional styles and fashions that become sources for identification, imagination, and desire in highly volatile urban settings. Next to Christianity and Islam, this also holds true for revitalized forms of "traditional" healing and religion in the city, such as the urban Marabout in Senegal who are increasingly popular among urban professionals (Gemmeke 2008), as well as globalized forms of African traditional religions (Olupona 2008). Similarly, herbal "Eastern" medicines such as Ayurvedic remedies or traditional Chinese medicine have moved increasingly into East and West Africa (Hsu 2009) to become part and parcel of the professional aspirations of urban medical entrepreneurs, as well as the spiritual-therapeutic (and affective) trajectories of African urbanites.

AFFECTIVE TRAJECTORIES: TEMPORALITY, SOCIOSPATIALITY, AND REASON

In this volume, we conceive of affective trajectories as highly diversified forms of sensation, which point to the dissolution and opening of human experience in the context of religious ritual and practice into its surrounding (urban) forms. Anthropologically and sociologically, this represents a concern with affect, emotion, and sentiment "as a space of potentiality where new forms of life can emerge" (Povinelli 2011, 105). The authors in this collection are thus interested in exploring how such potentialities unfold—and how they are modulated, experienced, and embodied—in specific religious settings, as well as with regard to the wider everyday lives of African urbanites. As proposed in Stewart's (2007) notion of "ordinary affects," the chapters explore the scenes, anxieties, and problems that are connected with everyday living in African urban settings, and the affective and emotional experiences and potentially religiously informed ideas and practices that are opened up.

The "affective arrangements" (Slaby, Mühlhoff, and Wüschner 2017, 6) that result from such potentialities are always highly situated and contingent, though their particular trajectories are never merely coincidental and are thus open for analysis and representation. In this regard, we move beyond studies of affect, which argue that affective states are always only unstructured and inchoate and thus ultimately nonrepresentational and nonrepresentable. As Wetherell has argued, affect is both represented and triggered by discourse, and "talk, body actions, affect, material contexts and social relations assemble *in situ*" (2013, 351).

Following these observations, with this volume we intend to provide an integrative space that accommodates insights from poststructuralist thought on affect (Massumi 2015; Stewart 2007), as well as concerns with the cultural coding and ordering of emotions (Scheer 2012; Reckwitz 2012). Our guiding concept of "affective trajectories" is indeed meant to highlight the fact that experiences of urban space involve a wide register of affects, emotions, and sentiments—often at the same time. In other words, "affective trajectories" are pathways through space-time in which affects, emotions, and sentiments are mobilized simultaneously and in coconstitutive ways. And insofar as they represent different modalities of affecting and being affected, each of these terms has a particular analytical potential necessary for understanding the complex nature of religiosity in urban Africa. Significantly, in this context, religion is not construed in opposition to rationality, knowledge, and intellect but provides spaces in which knowledge is embodied, affects are ordered, and so on.

With the notion of "affective trajectories," we also introduce a theoretical concept that captures analytically the relationship between religion, affect, emotion, sentiment, and urban forms. In particular, we seek to address the various forces of affecting and being affected as they are shaped by—and simultaneously co-shape—the nexus of temporality and spatiality in the religious lives of individuals and communities; that is, the ways in which people's movements and mobilities are inscribed in their biographical becoming and, conversely, the ways in which life courses always unfold in spaces. An affective trajectory is thus a mode of articulating time-space coordinates that involves memories of the past as well as imaginations of the future. It includes, for instance, the traces of the former presences of people and of encounters between believers, gods, and spirits in urban space (Selim 2018, 110–13; Dilger, Kasmani, and Mattes 2018, 109). Affective trajectories are therefore mutually interconnected series of emplacements whereby the networks between people, religious forces, and material places are constantly established, dissolved, and remade.

As the chapters in this volume show, there are in particular three dimensions that shape and reshape the relationships between religion, affect, emotion, and sentiment in urban settings. First, the chapters stress that affective trajectories extend across different time spans and account for the fact that imaginations related to historical sites and figures may also shape the religious practices and ideas in contemporary African cityscapes. Take, for instance, the wanderings and travels of Johane Masowe in the 1930s, which led the prophet far beyond colonial Zimbabwe into the wider southern African region; the routes he and his followers took have left traces on the morphology of the urban landscapes they passed through and have continued to shape the imaginations of the Masowe Apostles religious group—and their sense of belonging on the margins of Harare—until today (Mukonyora, this volume). In a similar vein, the affective expressions and experiences among Botswana's urban middle classes have to be understood through the colonial and postcolonial histories of Christian moral education and how religiously informed ideas of the family and class-based belonging have been shaped across generations and under shifting political and economic conditions (Bochow, this volume). Such ethnographic accounts highlight the historicity of affect, emotion, and sentiments by showing that affective arrangements "emerge out of multiple formative trajectories . . . [and] might be cautiously considered as 'conservation devices' in which histories of interaction and of collective habituation have become sedimented, so that the ongoing affectedness that transpires within the arrangement is a differential reenactment of past processes" (Slaby, Mühlhoff, and Wüschner 2017, 6).

Histories of affect comprise not only long-term historical processes but also biographical trajectories, which become embodied in specific affective and emotional (Beatty 2014) practices, situations, and experiences. Thus, as Kathleen Stewart notes, "the affective subject is a collection of trajectories and circuits" (2007, 59), becoming legible only in relation to a person's past experiences and practices, which culminate in specific modalities of being-in-the-world. As the chapters in this book show, such embodiments of affect, in being rooted in a person's history, can include the process of "becoming Muslim" in the zongos (Muslim wards) of Ghana (Pontzen), the conversions of young men in Cape Town to Pentecostalism (Reihling), and the affective journeys of patients on the West African coast (Lange, all in this volume).

In all these instances, it thereby becomes clear that the biographically rooted embodiment of affecting and being affected is rarely restricted to the individual's situation alone but is always a critical articulation of larger social, economic, political, and religious configurations. Thus the process of becoming Muslim in urban Ghana is a conflicted one, as the affective regimes of prayer mediate not only the individual emergence of the self within a wider transnational community of believers but also—and simultaneously—an articulation of dissent with alternative practices of being and becoming Muslim in the migratory contexts of the urban zongo. Similarly, the affective conversions of the young men in Cape Town are entwined with particular mobilities and emotional maps of the city and include in several instances the renunciation of "the evil forces of gangsterism and drugs." Finally, the patients' narratives on the West African coast are not only stories of affective (re)orientation and (re)connection in the search for healing and well-being but also—and simultaneously—a direct reflection of what the neoliberalized health systems in this region are *not* able to offer their citizens. All of these examples demonstrate that affects and emotions are not just "placed" in individuals but have to be read as distinct forms of collective mobilization and attachment (Ahmed 2013), as well as powerful articulations of discontent, anger, and frustration in settings of inequality and injustice (cf. Fassin 2013).

Second, the chapters in this volume draw attention to the way in which affective trajectories and potentialities are always embedded in—and co-shape—larger social, political, and material configurations and arrangements in specific urban settings. Thus, it is only in the context of collectively experienced sensations and affective potentialities that people are motivated to make decisions and act on their environments, which are modified and transformed in the process. Furthermore, it is only in the interactions with the specific conditions and materialities of urban spaces that the dynamics of affection "transfigure" (cf. Riis and Woodhead 2010, 11) the emotional lives of African urbanites in relation to religiously sustained ideas, practices, and paraphernalia. As van Dijk shows in his chapter in this volume, urban settings in Africa amplify the potential for mutual affection in that processes of urbanization have become essential for shaping the sentiment of sophistication among Pentecostal professionals, as well as for evoking particular desires for knowledge and distinction among the growing middle classes in Africa's cityscapes. Similarly, Lambertz explores how transnational religious forms and trajectories in Kinshasa become articulated with local spaces through religious ceremonies, and enmeshed in affective idioms and spatial practices that are closely entwined with local political histories and institutional practices.

With regard to the specific role of religion in the formation of affective cityscapes, it is thus important to emphasize that religious collectives do not enforce emotions, affect, and sentiment in uniform ways, but that they rather provide affective orientations and potentialities that are enacted and embodied along highly situated paths. Furthermore, while most of the contributors focus on one specific religious or denominational framework (Christian, Muslim, "traditional," or new spiritual movements), it should be remarked that most urban centers on the African continent (and in its diasporas) are shaped by the co-presence of a wide range of internally diversified and partly contested religious traditions and practices.

In this volume, it is primarily the chapters by Ibrahim and Wilhelm-Solomon that adopt an explicitly comparative perspective on these processes, looking at more than one religious form and congregation, and exploring how affective urban landscapes are configured in the context of religiously diverse settings. Thus Ibrahim explores how both Christian and Muslim congregations in Abuja become "sites of divine encounters," and how the affective attractions and practices of religious groups have become inscribed in the infrastructural setup of the "city of dreams." In Johannesburg, on the other hand, the lens of affect and religion illuminates how marginalized urban populations both experience and coproduce urban spaces in the interstices of larger-scale urban change and how in this process they engage in "affective regenerations" by referring to both Pentecostal, mainline Christian, and ancestral idioms and practices (Wilhelm-Solomon).

Third, and importantly, our notion of affective trajectories is also meant to unsettle and challenge time-honored dualistic philosophies in which emotion, affect, and sentiment are opposed to reason and intellect. Such binaries and traditions of thought have been particularly problematic in African contexts. Especially during the colonial period, but also subsequently, the accounts of Westerners—both nonacademic and academic—have often portrayed Africans' beliefs and forms of behavior as driven by emotions and entrapped in the immediacy of an ahistorical, unending present. Collective practices in the field of religion and politics were typically categorized as "delusional" (Comaroff and Comaroff 1987, 203) and viewed as expressions of irrationality and primordial attachments and drives (cf. Evans-Pritchard 1965).

Racist stereotyping has thus been part and parcel of earlier Western thinking on the role of emotions in Africans' lives. Postcolonial theorists such as Fanon have also worked to develop social and psychological approaches that take into account the effects of violence on the psyches of the colonized, without resorting to individualized models of therapeutic treatment (Akyeampong 2015; Fanon 1961). According to Fanon, colonial readings of subjects' emotional and affective states are direct reflections of relations of hierarchies and power within the colonial setup. We firmly wish to situate our approach to affect, emotion, and sentiment within the formation of colonial and postcolonial urban spaces. Fanon's analysis points out the interconnections of affective states and conditions of violence, exclusion, and struggle. In this regard, our approach here attends to the constant dialectic between affective and emotional experiences and practices and the spatial and structural conditions in which they emerge: of course this is not to preclude the analysis of particular modes of critical thought as they surface from these struggles, or to reduce Africans to affective or emotional conditions.

Our account unsettles the binaries underlying these traditions of thought, especially by highlighting how emotions—and religious "ways of knowing" (Peek 1991)—have been shaped through forms of intellectualism, learning, and trained reflection during the colonial and postcolonial periods. In many parts of Africa, the spheres of traditional healing and religion, as well as the highly diversified articulations of Christianity, Islam, and other religious (or spiritual) movements and traditions, are prime reserves of intellectual development. For instance, van Dijk (2015a) has observed how Pentecostalism has been characterized by high degrees of intellectual production, the emergence of new public intellectuals, and the flourishing of new literary genres, all of which are geared toward the shaping and legible rendering of emotional lives in social contexts such as kinship, family, and sexuality. In this volume, Cazarin and Burchardt explore how the notions of "emotional repertoire" and "regime" prove especially apt to capture both the similarities and the differences in the rules relating to feelings that Pentecostal pastors aim to teach in vastly different diasporic contexts: both concepts are tied to the fact that pastors engage systematically with the urban domain in terms of moral geographies that believers have to navigate successfully.

In this sense, it behooves us to emphasize that, from an anthropological and sociological perspective, religiously inspired emotions are not so much opposed to intellectualism and practices of reflexive cultivation as evolving in a dialectical relationship with them. Urban conglomerates and their religious articulations, in both Africa and its diasporic extensions, do not assemble erratically acting crowds; on the contrary, they prove to favor intellectualist versions of religion and spirituality that collapse the presumed dichotomy between reason and emotion, religion and science, nature and culture, body and mind, feeling and cognition. Affective trajectories, while shaped by the unintentional force of affect, are not amorphous and irrational, but indeed structured and intelligible. As Alessandro Gusman reminds us in his chapter, however, rendering affective trajectories intelligible requires a high degree of reflexivity and laborious efforts on the part of the researchers to unearth shared grounds of intersubjectivity, especially in contexts of forced migration and extreme violence.

AFFECT, EMOTION, AND SENTIMENT IN RELIGIOUS
AFRICAN CITYSCAPES: THE CONTRIBUTIONS

The chapters in this volume are all based on original ethnographic research—carried out by anthropologists, sociologists, and a scholar of Christian theology—and focus on the ways in which religion, affect, emotion, and sentiment are intertwined in people's lives in African cities and their diasporic counterparts. While there is a certain bias within the volume with regard to the strong focus of the chapters on (neo-Pentecostal) Christianity, and with only one chapter explicitly looking at Islam, this is reflective of existing scholarship, where research on neo-Pentecostalism has flourished within the broader study of Christianity in Africa (Meyer 2004a), and less attention has been paid to the study of Islam and "African traditional religion."[4] This being said, this volume includes chapters that explore situations of religious diversity *beyond* neo-Pentecostal religious practice (Wilhelm-Solomon, Ibrahim, Lange, Bochow) or that focus explicitly on "Islam" (Pontzen), "African traditional religion," and its relation to African Independent Churches (Mukonyora), and new spiritual movements in urban Africa (Lambertz).

Taken together, the chapters show how new conceptual perspectives can be formulated regarding the articulation of religious lives, and the ways in which they shape—and are shaped by—affect, emotion, and sentiment in urban settings in Africa and the African diaspora. Furthermore, the chapters in this book explore how experiences and practices of affect, emotion, and sentiment can be studied and represented ethnographically, as these areas of research are, by definition, difficult to access through a sole focus on language or text (Mattes, Kasmani, and Dilger 2019). In this latter regard, the scholars in this volume train attention to the ways in which affect, emotion, and sentiment are encapsulated in religious practices and materialities, as well as the various material and infrastructural forms that life in urban settings in Africa and their diasporic counterparts entails. They also reflect on the ways in which, as researchers, they themselves became implicated in the wider web of affective and emotional states and practices produced by the different relationalities in their field sites (Davies 2010; Stodulka 2015).

The chapters in the volume are organized into three thematic parts. The first part, entitled "Affective Infrastructures," explores the ways in which the materiality of the urban form can be an affective force. The infrastructures of African cities and their diasporic counterparts produce and elicit emotional responses and ritual cleansings and offer sites of catharsis, haunting, fear, disorientation, and hope. The contributors explore the diverse ways in which the spiritual, religious, and emotional are interpenetrated with the structures of the city—its streets, buildings, populations, and media. If, as Simone (2008) argues, "people are infrastructure" and infrastructure must be viewed in its social and relational aspects, then we argue that infrastructure also has an affective force that is imminent in the social and religious life of the city. Infrastructures also include more ephemeral forms such as soundscapes and mediascapes (Quayson 2014), which evoke particular sensorial and aesthetic experiences of religiously diverse cities (Meyer 2011).

Matthew Wilhelm-Solomon, in his opening chapter on the "dark buildings"—unlawfully appropriated buildings in inner-city Johannesburg—develops the concept of affective regenerations. These entail "the processes through which interpersonal relations and practices, enmeshed in the materiality of the city, are the source of the renewal of urban life and survival in the face of trauma, dereliction, and abandonment." He argues that religious symbols and rites drawn from both Christian and ancestral idioms structure affective relationships with urban spaces and are also reworked through material practices. Affective regenerations indicate some of the processes through which marginalized inner-city populations attempt to deal with the traumas and dislocations of urban life. The concept of affective regenerations is viewed in counterpoint to conceptions of urban regeneration founded on large-scale state-driven and private sector–driven schemes.

Isabel Mukonyora's contribution deals with the "urban wilderness" of Harare during the late 1990s, a time of major social and political upheaval in Zimbabwe. Based on a case study of the Masowe Apostles, an African Independent Church that does not use written texts, her chapter argues that colonial and postcolonial experiences of displacement have led to affective ritual engagements at the margins of the city as a way "to control anger, fear, and sadness associated with marginality in society and based on the belief that the healing power of the Holy Spirit is all around the sacred sites for prayer." The uninhabited urban fringes of the city thus become material spaces through which spiritual idioms of dispossession are projected and felt. The urban wilderness becomes both a material symbolic universe in which difficult human "conditions of injustice, sickness, and general misfortunes" are articulated, and a space where redemption is sought through the emotional connection with God.

Murtala Ibrahim explores how religiously diverse practices and material forms in Abuja mold into—and are simultaneously shaped by—the affective urban landscape that has become known as "the city of dreams" in

Nigeria. In this context, the public sphere of the city becomes a stage for various forms of religious expression and practices that comprise the use of media (images and sound), as well as specific modes of praying and ritual performance. Drawing on his fieldwork among both Christian and Muslim congregations, Ibrahim paints a complex picture of the similarities and differences that shape the ways in which religious spaces provide opportunities for affective participation and belonging, as well as for the correlating modes of aesthetic expression and experience.

Rijk van Dijk's contribution concludes this part by observing processes of sophistication as a central aspect of urban life, on the one hand, and of the development of Christianity, especially Pentecostalism, on the other, in contemporary Africa. More specifically, he explores religious sophistication in terms of the particular ways in which Pentecostals draw on scientific knowledge to arrive at a deeper understanding of human life. Building on his long-term ethnographic involvement with Christians in Malawi, Ghana, and Botswana, van Dijk draws our attention to facets of urban life, such as the emphasis on beauty and new forms of conspicuous consumption, that have rarely been viewed as linked to religion, and to how urban contexts are often seen to amplify religious experiences. Importantly, he theorizes these observations through the notion of sentiment, which means a set of enduring dispositions of collectivities that articulate persons, bodies, and polities.

The diversity of urban life in Africa and its diaspora is mirrored by a multiplicity of religious practices, beliefs, spirits, and religious institutions and authorities that have shaped people's journeys to, and aspirations regarding, cities on the continent and abroad. The importance of geography as well as social mobility for understanding religious practices and beliefs has long been noted in the anthropology of the urban (cf. Schildkrout 1970; Akyeampong 1996), and traveling spirits and ritual practices represent powerful spiritual sources in people's quests for healing and relief across urban and rural settings (Luedke and West 2006; Hüwelmeier and Krause 2010). Spirits, rituals, and religious practices, even if imported from a "foreign culture," establish a sense of "home" (Mohr 2012) and represent important sources of comfort, but also emotional and spiritual insecurity (Hüwelmeier and Krause 2010; van Dijk 2009). The second part, entitled "Emotions on the Move" (cf. Svašek 2010), asks how traveling religious practices and beliefs, and the affective and emotional forces they imply, contribute to novel forms of attachment and place-making and their respective contestations in African cities and the diaspora.

Isabelle Lange's chapter looks at the different affective possibilities that chronic surgical patients traverse in their quest for healing in the spatial (physical and imagined) triangle of their rural and urban networks, as well as the treatment opportunities of a Christian "mercy ship" offering its services in ports along the West African coast. Her argument draws on Vigh's concept of "social navigation" and explores how West African men and women engage in "affective journeys" that arise out of—and simultaneously co-shape—the uncertainties, anxieties, and hopes associated with their suffering. At the same time, she describes how these navigations lead to the formation of new, or the modification of old, attachments and networks of support—with relatives, healing and treatment collectives, religious congregations—as the patients struggle to inhabit and overcome the liminal spaces between illness and wellness.

Like Lange, Peter Lambertz deals with transnational religious connections, in his case the Église Messianique Mondiale (EMM), a transnational Japanese spiritual movement, in Kinshasa. Lambertz explores the spiritual geography of cleansing ceremonies, or *nettoyage,* as they form an affective engagement with urban spaces, including the "spiritual atmospheres" of markets and squares, of Kinshasa. Lambertz proposes the concept of at*touch*ment to analyze the affective dimensions of engaging with urban spaces in a manner in which the symbolic and sensory are enmeshed in spatial practice. Developing this, he also argues that the EMM's practice and philosophy deploy "a reflexive theory of sentiment and affective behavior as a core theoretical grid to explain . . . the vicissitudes of city life." His chapter thus explores how analytical conceptions of emotion and affect can be articulated in relation to urban spaces, as well as to local languages and categories.

The chapter by Rafael Cazarin and Marian Burchardt focuses on the emotional dynamics of Pentecostal social life in Nigerian and Congolese diaspora communities in Bilbao in northern Spain and Johannesburg in South Africa. The authors argue against an understanding of emotions as spontaneous, unmediated inner representations of experiences and focus instead on the ways in which emotions are bodily states that are learned, inculcated, and cultivated. Building on a close reading of the life stories and biographical narratives of Pentecostal pastors who fashion self-images as emotional teachers, their chapter is based on the conceptual distinction between emotional regimes and emotional repertoires. The former refers to sets of feeling rules that circulate through transnational Pentecostal public spheres, while the latter means the regulated ways in which pastors draw on and improvise with emotional regimes in their attempts to grapple with the predicaments of migrants in specific urban settings.

The third part, entitled "Embodiment, Subjectivity, and Belonging," shows how religion becomes a source of identification and belonging in the materially, socially, and spiritually often insecure social worlds of African cityscapes, with their highly dynamic landscapes of religious actors, institutions, and practices offering meaning and spiritual orientation. Partially informed by a historical perspective, the chapters show that messages of salvation, healing, holiness, and piety, as well as their reinterpretation of evil forces, spirits, or witchcraft, are often accompanied by attempts to shape or even discipline people's visions of family life, community, and alternative forms of care for others, as well as care of the self and the body, including sexuality, emotionality, and intimacy (Miescher 2005; Ojo 1997). Furthermore, they highlight how affective and emotional styles that are closely connected to the embodiment of religiously informed codes and norms have become intertwined with processes of social class formation and emerging cosmopolitan lifestyles.

In his chapter, Benedikt Pontzen analyzes the zongos—wards of Muslim immigrants from the north—in the Asante towns of southern Ghana. In these wards, daily prayers, or *salat*, form an "affective regime" through religion, which operates through an encoding of daily life, rendering it meaningful through Islamic practice and symbolism. It is from these practices, and the affective and emotional states they induce, Pontzen argues, that a Muslim sense of self emerges. The practices of the salat, its "cycle of postures, gestures, and recitations," produce an embodied and affective relationship with God, strengthening ties of solidarity among the worshippers and locating them as a distinct community. However, the salat also opens up a space for religious dissent; thus it both mediates divisions within the local migrant community of the zongos and produces relations with a transglobal Islamic community.

Astrid Bochow builds on Sara Ahmed's theory of the cultural politics of emotions and explores how Christians in urban Botswana have ascribed shifting emotional and moral meanings to the family throughout the twentieth and early twenty-first centuries. In particular, she shows that Christian moral education shaped the ambitions and desires, as well as the anxieties, of different generations of urban professionals with regard to their marriages and reproductive lives in specific ways. Furthermore, she describes how recent socioeconomic transformations, along with the drastic morbidity and mortality rates associated with HIV/AIDS, have become intertwined both with new opportunities for religious and professional belonging and with the cutting of family ties in the wake of growing socio-economic pressures.

Alessandro Gusman's chapter centers on the question of what it takes to explore religion and emotions in the contexts of forced displacement and extreme violence. He does so by focusing on the experiences of Congolese refugees who have resettled in the Ugandan capital city of Kampala, and on the meanings of belonging to one of the many Congolese Pentecostal churches. Despite their relief at having escaped the violence, for Gusman's interlocutors, many of whom have been traumatized by their experiences of war, the city is initially a place of radical insecurity and solitude. Subsequently, Christian beliefs in salvation and practices of prayer acquire dramatic importance for these refugees as they reconstitute their lives. Gusman highlights the need to take seriously the hermeneutic limits that can emerge in ethnographic encounters of this kind. In order to tackle these limits, he reengages with phenomenological traditions in social theory and argues that emotions play a central role in the working of intersubjectivity as the basic condition for understanding experience.

Hans Reihling's contribution also examines processes of urban religious subject formation and explores how the emotions involved in concepts of masculine subjectivity are revisited in processes of religious conversion. His ethnography is set in a specific urban environment, namely, one that encompasses the crime-ridden streets of Cape Town's townships. In order to examine the links between masculinity and the transposition of emotional dispositions, Reihling discusses the case of gangsters becoming born-again Christians by being drawn into evangelical crusades on the street. He observes that conversion to Christianity is but one of the few institutional avenues available to young men who wish to leave the deadly world of gangsterism and the drug economy, and he astutely describes what it takes to engage in this route. Specifically, while these young men had previously trained themselves to keep their emotions under control in order to survive life as a gangster, conversion enables and sometimes forces them to temporarily embrace their emotionality and vulnerability.

NOTES

1. When we refer to "urban Africa" in this introduction, this also includes those urban contexts beyond the African continent in which a significant number of people with an African migratory or diaspora background live and engage with different types of religious practices, ideas, and materialities.

2. Compare Williams (2011, 13) regarding how ethics are rooted in sentiments.

3. Such an approach echoes Radcliffe-Brown's theory of social sentiments, which he defines as "organized systems of emotional tendencies centered around some object" (1922, 324fn1). In this way, sentiments "serve to regulate the conduct of individuals in conformity with social needs" and "are affected by social values, which in turn are reflected in legends and ceremonials" (Palmer and Occhi 1999, 3).

4. Only recently has more attention been paid to the explicit study of religious diversity in rural and urban Africa, most notably with regard to the dynamics of Christian-Muslim encounters (see Soares 2006; Janson and Meyer 2016; Dilger and Schulz 2013; for urban contexts, see Dilger 2014, 2017).

PART I AFFECTIVE INFRASTRUCTURES

1 AFFECTIVE REGENERATIONS
INTIMACY, CLEANSING, AND MOURNING IN AND AROUND JOHANNESBURG'S DARK BUILDINGS

MATTHEW WILHELM-SOLOMON

This chapter traces how, in inner-city Johannesburg, experiences of loss and renewal, despair and hope, intimacy and friendship are not interior or private states but part of what I term "affective regenerations" within the city. This concept entails that these experiences and their affective intensities are part of the coproduction of urban spaces; religious rituals contain and give form to these through rites of cleansing, prayer, and gathering. The rooms, pavements, and stairwells of Johannesburg hence have an affective force as sites of the condensation and dissolution of social relations. Furthermore, affective relations are formed through the political, juridical, and spatial forms of the city, producing sites of both abandonment and the potential for social renewal (Povinelli 2011; Biehl 2013).

This chapter draws on ethnographic fieldwork conducted in unlawfully occupied buildings—known as "dark buildings" in street vernacular and as "bad buildings" or "hijacked buildings" in political, media, and policy discourse—and their surroundings in deindustrialized areas of Johannesburg between 2011 and 2016. Many of these buildings are in states of severe infrastructural decay, without electricity or sanitation, or at best with illegal electricity and water connections, and their passages, courtyards, and stairwells are frequently filled with detritus and stagnant water. Yet they are home to thousands of urban residents, many of them migrants both from rural South Africa and from other African countries who are trying to find a decent and dignified life in the city and lay claim to Johannesburg's promise of work and prosperity.

However, Johannesburg remains a "city of extremes" (Murray 2011) characterized by dramatic inequalities of class and race, which have been only partly eroded in the postapartheid era. Private-sector developers manage over forty thousand housing units in the inner city,[1] yet there is a major lack of affordable accommodation for very low-income households (earning below R3200, around $220 per month),[2] and migrants face additional barriers of access to accommodation, including discrimination and lack of documentation (Misago and Wilhelm-Solomon 2016; RebelGroup 2016). Unlawful occupations, or dark buildings, are the result of capital disinvestment from the inner city, along with a chronic shortage of low-cost accommodations, a situation intensified by inward migration. Both the inner city and its suburbs are characterized by high levels of private security, as well as multiple and plural religious processes and "enchantment" (Katsaura 2016) that shape and reshape urban space (Wilhelm-Solomon et al. 2016). In this chapter, I explore how religious rituals and rites, including cleansing ceremonies and funeral rites encompassing both Christian and ancestral idioms, are examples of affective responses to urban insecurities.

In exploring these themes, I aim to engage a central problem in this volume, as presented in the introduction—the relation between affect, urban space, and religion. Edgar Pieterse has argued, with regard to African urbanisms, for "the importance of reading the affective functions of popular practices, because it is only through the redeployment of such registers that one can begin to fathom what is going on in the real city, and potentially animate a resonant engagement with the city" (2011, 18). An emphasis on affect also "enables a more empowered and differentiated conception of agency in which all people become more 'autonomous' and proactive actors in the construction of their lives and socialities" (17). In developing these concerns in this chapter, I argue that it is important to consider religion as part of the array of popular practices concerning theories of affect.

Such theories, developed in particular from the work of Spinoza as read by Deleuze, have emphasized the embodied and relational dimension of affect: emotional states arise from, and are part of, the ways in which bodies affect and are affected by their surroundings and webs of relationality (Ahmed 2004; Stewart 2007; Povinelli 2011; Massumi 2015; Deleuze 1990). In this sense, affect designates the relatedness of emotional and experiential states to a material and social terrain. My concept of "affective regenerations" therefore aims to identify specific relations to urban space, involving processes of social renewal, that offer a counterpoint to conceptions of urban regeneration being driven by private-sector developments or state planning projects (Leary and McCarthy 2013). In light of the concerns of this volume, I view affect as constituting the relation between interior and symbolically and ritually coded emotional states and urban infrastructures. Furthermore, as Deleuze (1990) notes, the politics of affect operates through the ways forms of action are enabled, coded, and constricted. My concern here is with the ways in which urban infrastructures and exclusions are experienced, reworked, and symbolized in ways that may not enter the formal domains of municipal governance and civic politics, and in which religious ritual plays a key role.

The term "affective regenerations" refers to the processes through which interpersonal relations and practices, enmeshed in the materiality of the city, are the source of the renewal of urban life and survival in the face of trauma, dereliction, and abandonment. Affective regenerations involve both the passive processes through which urban dwellers are subjected to wider movements of urban change and also how they seek to shape their personal and social renewal in response to these processes. The politics of affective regenerations may be found in the ways they constitute experiences of debilitation and capacitation in the urban terrain and how these are formed within wider juridical, economic, and spatial processes. The concept of affective regenerations is not a theory of religious ritual per se, although religious rites are part of them. Religious rites, in this chapter, are hence discussed as part of a wider set of affective relations through which urban dwellers experience and seek to compose and calm unsettled urban spaces. In this sense, the rites of spatial cleansing discussed here are attempts at affective regenerations, but they also arise from the prediscursive and not explicitly ritualized affective experience of urban space.

This approach poses a conceptual difficulty regarding how to relate affect to religion. The anthropology of religion in recent decades has often been oriented around a tension between two concerns: the first has been an understanding of religion as a set of cultural symbols that aim both to establish "long-lasting moods and motivations in men" and to align these moods with an objective sense of cosmic order (Geertz 1973, 90). The second has been an attempt to account for religious experience in terms of the relation between the "self" and the "sacred" (Csordas 1994b). I follow Comaroff (2012, 6) in moving away from a Geertzian approach and understanding religion as embedded in "particular social-historical formations" and the "social and material grounding" of everyday life. Given that affect encompasses experiences and practices that include though exceed the discursive and symbolic dimensions of religion, it is necessary here to move beyond symbolic analysis.

However, a phenomenological account of religious "experience," in spite of its important emphasis on embodiment, is also limited in that it lacks analysis of the ways in which religion is implied in the production of sociospatial relations—concerns central to the study of affect. Asad advances, for instance, that "the connection between religious theory and practice" involves "constructing religion in the world (not in the mind)" (2009, 38); however, his approach remains on the level of hermeneutics and moral discourse.[3] An affective encounter with religion must encompass materiality and embodiment in the production of urban space. The approach I take here—without attempting to advance a unifying definition of religion—is to analyze religious symbols and rites through the ways they alter, code, and give form to the affective intensities of urban life through the invocation, incarnation, or expulsion of a transcendental presence, be that of God, spirits, ancestors, ghosts, or Satan, for instance. However, these symbols and rites are also transformed by these affective relations with urban space. Affective regenerations hence encompass religious symbols and rites through the recomposing and containment of disordered urban spaces (cf. De Boeck and Baloji 2016, 295).

This chapter first provides a background, reflexive, and methodological account of the research process, then provides a theoretical discussion of how the concept of affective regenerations is situated in relation to both urban theory and existing theories of affect; finally, it provides ethnographic case studies of three unlawful occupations, Diamond Exchange, Cape York, and The Station (the latter is pseudonymized as it was still occupied at the time of writing). The chapter thus draws on ethnographic fieldwork conducted between 2012 and 2016, through which the concept is elaborated. In particular, the chapter explores the ways in which Christian rituals, rooted in both Methodist and Pentecostal rites, along with those of ancestrality, are invoked in cleansing ceremonies and funeral rites in the city.

ENCOUNTERING THE AFFECTIVE CITY

Analyses of postapartheid Johannesburg can broadly be characterized as, on the one hand, concerned with the continued material and racial divides of apartheid (Murray 2011; Beall, Crankshaw, and Parnell 2002) and, on the other, with emergent forms of migration, belonging, consumption, and conviviality in the "Afropolis" (Mbembe and Nuttall 2008; Landau 2009; Wanjiku Kihato 2014), though recent work has attempted to reconcile these approaches (Harrison 2014; Winkler 2013). Johannesburg remains an extraordinarily unequal and racially divided city, one in which the spatial and racial segregation of apartheid persists but has been reshaped to an extent by the emergence of the black middle class, along with intense inward migration, particularly into the inner city (Harrison 2014).

South Africa has among the highest number of asylum seekers in the world. According to the United Nations Refugee Agency, in 2017, there were more than a million pending asylum applications and 121,645 refugees in South Africa.[4] However, Stupart (2016) has questioned these data, arguing that asylum seekers whose cases were rejected, resolved, or are no longer pending were not removed from the statistics, and there are likely fewer than 400,000 pending asylum applications. After 2005, political and economic turmoil in Zimbabwe, characterized by widespread political persecution, decline in agricultural production, and hyperinflation, led to intense migration into South Africa. In 2008, anti-immigrant violence spread through Johannesburg and nationwide, leading to more than sixty deaths and the displacement of 100,000 people (Landau 2010).

In spite of large-scale private and public-private housing developments in Johannesburg, workers and traders operating informally are widely excluded from access to decent and secure living conditions with basic services and amenities (Charlton 2014; Tissington 2013). In the inner city many migrants find themselves living alongside poor South Africans in unlawfully occupied buildings known as "dark buildings" in street vernacular and "bad buildings" or "hijacked buildings" in policy documents. They are subject to extraordinarily poor living conditions, general daily violence, evictions, deportations, and existential insecurity.

The "dark" itself is a powerfully affective force in Johannesburg, as elsewhere. Residents of the inner city, including those in the occupied buildings themselves, widely refer to occupied buildings using the grammatically informal *'mnyama'indawo*, which can be literally translated as a "dark place" in isiZulu and isiNdebele. Umnyama and its related noun isinyama have connotations of both literal darkness and misfortune (Zulu and Wilhelm-Solomon 2015). The "dark," a reference to both a developmental failure and a site of spiritual insecurity (cf. Ashforth 1998; De Boeck 2009), involves an affective disordering, both for those who live in unlawful occupations without electricity or basic services and in the wider sense of an unknown and disturbing presence that requires containment.

The dark buildings are widely associated across different races and classes with the "crime and grime" of the city. Although some of the unlawfully occupied buildings serve as bases for violent criminal activity, they are also homes to informal workers, the unemployed, the disabled, and beggars, who cannot afford or access decent living spaces in the city. Nonetheless, a discourse of fear among the middle classes, particularly "the fear of the vagrant, or the out-of-place black person, the person who does not seem to have much of a reason to be there" (Nevin 2014, 196), is pervasive in driving urban regeneration schemes in the city. It is no wonder that a newly gentrified area in the city calls itself a "place of light" (Nevin 2014) and that innovative street lighting was a central part of the property developer's urban "regeneration" strategy and promotion campaign. It must be noted, however, that fear of the dark buildings and their associations with crime cross different classes and races and are grounded in both real threats (in cases in which criminal groups operate from them) and imagined ones.[5]

While the former white suburbs have become partly mixed-race areas, areas like the inner city—formerly a center for both white residents and commerce—are inhabited by predominantly black residents, including relatively high densities of foreign nationals. New Doornfontein, the primary area in which I conducted my research, exemplifies this situation. According to 2011 census data, the percentage of noncitizens living in the inner-city wards in which I conducted most of this research was just over 27 percent compared with just over 10 percent in the city as a whole,[6] a percentage affirmed by a 2015/2016 study by the Gauteng City Region Observatory (GCRO), which found that 26.2% of inner-city residents were cross-border migrants (Skosana, 2017).

AFFECTIVE DESUBJECTIVIZATION

As a white middle-class South African, I was entering a space in which my race marked me out, even though the area of New Doornfontein is only a few minutes' drive from my family home in a suburb bordering on the inner city. Johannesburg is the city of my birth and where I have spent most of my life, and yet my engagement with the city as an anthropologist involved a profound reorientation and reshaping of my position within it, as I entered spaces where few white or black suburbanites venture. When I first visited a dark building, my overwhelming sense was one of fear. Over the years of doing research in these spaces, and as my relationships have changed, the sense of fear has receded and been replaced by other emotional states, such as anxiety, amusement, sorrow, and frustration. My relationship with these sites has been shaped and mediated by my own alliances, friendships and intimacies, and informal exchange relationships. Although my race and class position shaped my responses to the field sites, the dark buildings are also a source of fear for many city residents across race and class. This is based both on the imaginary that surrounds these spaces and on the fact that, at least in some of them, criminal gangs do operate, even though they are mostly a minority of the population.

I have worked at times with a research assistant and translator (herself a Zimbabwean migrant and former inhabitant of an occupied building, who wishes to remain unnamed), but mostly unaided in the sense of meeting with people, sharing meals or tea with them, participating in shared events (parties, funerals, meetings, court cases), and also visiting Zimbabwe in 2016, where I met some of those with whom I have conducted research in Johannesburg and their families. Sometimes I have relied on formal and recorded interviews, but for the most part I draw on field notes and informal conversations. The relations of intimacy are still, however, structured and unequal due to my different class and race position in the city in contrast to those of my informants.

While I am not, and never will be, a part of the "community" in which I conduct research (the word itself veils complex networks of alliances), the experience of my research and the themes I explore here are ones in which I too am affectively immersed. For instance, these affective relations surface in the guarded intimacy of research relations, in experiences of anxiety (say, in cases of the deportation or eviction of those I know), or in a shared sense of sorrow in cases when friends die, or their relatives do. I do not claim to share the same affective worlds as my interlocutors, but I certainly cross the threshold of my own familial and friendship relations, rooted in my having grown up, studied, and worked in the city. Hence, there is a process of disorientation and desubjectivization that takes place in anthropological fieldwork. Anthropology, then, in my view, is a form of (un)becoming that opens up a kind of affective hinterland between self and other (cf. Biehl and Locke 2010). I share proximate spaces and visions with those I engage with, a shared sense of exposure, but one which is not equally distributed (Butler 2004). I do not spend my nights in the dark buildings, I can retreat to the safety of a suburban home; I am not subject to deportation or continual police harassment; and although I am exposed to crime, I am not exposed to the same degree. And yet my research engagement demands a different vision of what urban regeneration means to most of those of my race and class position—the pervasive rhetoric of "cleaning the city" or "reclaiming" it for middle class unsettles me. It demands critique, a rethinking of the language of urban regeneration. Developing the concept of affective regeneration is part of this project, one that is both intimate in the sense it concerns the spaces I share, work in, and live in, and analytic in that it requires a separation and distance.

AFFECTIVE REGENERATIONS: A CONCEPTUAL DISORIENTATION

There are two prominent strands of urban theory in relation to which this chapter can be framed. The first is that of the production of space and the right to the city (Lefebvre 1991, 1996; Harvey 2008). This approach has emphasized the social embeddedness of space within a materialist dialectic, together with continued processes of class-based exclusion and political claims. A second line is the so-called assemblage theory (Farías 2011; McFarlane 2011), which draws on actor-network theory developed by Bruno Latour and emphasizes the interconnectedness of human and nonhuman actors, along with the Deleuzian approach that has explored the affective dimension of embodied relations and emphasizes complex processes of (de)territorialization. It is from the latter that this chapter develops its approach, while retaining the concern with the processes of displacement and debilitation analyzed by the former (see also Burchardt and Becci 2013; Malcomess and Wilhelm-Solomon 2016).

Following Pieterse (2011), I aim to provide an empirically grounded account of urban regeneration—one that is embedded in lived social experiences but that also retains a concern with the materiality of the city and its processes of exclusions. I argue that an affective approach offers a way of accounting for embodied and lived experiences of urban space in relation to a shifting and precarious urban terrain. If, as Vigh (2009) has argued, "social navigation" requires establishing subjective coordinates within a landscape that is itself in motion, then an affective approach indicates the relation between embodied experience and a terrain subject to collapse, instability, and dislocation, as well as the potentiality for new forms of subjectivity and social relations.

Affects, then, are both corporeal orientations in webs of uncertain relations and unstable infrastructure, and the forms of temporal experience these generate and open up (Deleuze 1990; Massumi 2015). These orientations encompass coordinates near and far, mundane and ancestral, religious and infrastructural, and relations with both the living and the dead (Wilhelm-Solomon 2017). Hence, affect encompasses the ways in which bodies are cast adrift in streams of material and social flows that are only partially registered cognitively and emotively in particular spaces and moments. The implications of this for urban theory are significant in that this approach provides a way of connecting the emotive and intimate experiences of individuals with wider processes of material change and structural forces. In this sense, affective regenerations indicate how wider-scale forces of urban change affect the lives of inner-city residents and how social relations and intimacies coalesce as a response to these. Recalling Simone's (2004) conception of "people as infrastructure," affective regenerations are a way of thinking about these intertwined material and social attempts at urban renewal. The concept calls attention to the ways in which inner-city residents survive and endure in the face of continued dislocation and social abandonment.

Affective regenerations may not bring about wide-scale social or political change or spatial productions; they may simply be the ways in which inner-city residents survive and endure the troubles and sorrows of urban life and the ways social relations are re-formed under conditions of extreme stress. To make this claim is not to argue that poor residents of the inner city do not hope for or desire the benefits of state and private-sector regeneration schemes: safe and secure accommodation, access to urban markets, leisure commodities, and so on. However, these benefits are often foreclosed to them due to a lack of formal and stable work and, in the case of undocumented migrants, a lack of documentation. Nor do I wish to argue that, foreclosed from the benefits of urban development, there is simply a retreat to tradition or ritual as a source of social regeneration. Certainly, the use of religious rites as a way to come to terms with the adversities of the city is not merely the domain of the poor, but crosses racial and class divides in the city (Katsaura 2016). My point is, rather, that the relationship with the city's transformations, along with urban insecurities, involves an affective relation with its materiality. Affective regenerations indicate the intimate and social responses of marginalized urban communities as a form of survival and re-orientation in the wake of social and spatial dislocations.

And what is the role of religion in this? The importance of religious ritual, and particularly mourning rites, in theorizing social regeneration is well rehearsed in the anthropological literature. As Bloch and Parry have argued in relation to funerary rites, "'Good' death not only promises a re-birth for the individual but also a renewal of the world of the living; while 'bad' death represents a loss of regenerative potential" (1982, 16). Religious rites play an important part in affective regenerations in that they provide a way of containing and giving form to the emotive and affective disorders that trauma causes. However, I do not treat religious symbols and rites as discrete discursive and cognitive structures; rather, they shape affective relationality and are reworked in material practice. As I show later, rituals of cleansing are central to affective regenerations in cleansing certain spaces and sites of misfortune.

Affective regenerations indicate a particular relation to urban spatiality in which religion plays a powerful, though not totalizing, role. Religious rites form a significant part of how urban residents in cities like Johannesburg and elsewhere compose and claim the urban environment in a way that is not easily assimilated into a formal politics of the right to the city (Lanz 2013; Burchardt and Becci 2013; Wilhelm-Solomon et al. 2016). However, my argument is slightly different here. In the sense that affect is both anterior to discourse and ideas and saturates these, affective regenerations both elicit and encompass formalized and ritualized responses. They indicate the surging forth (Stewart 2007) of spatially specific intensities, which hence require a formal ritualized response. Of course these immediate and affective experiences, and the responses to them, are always intertwined both spatially and temporally. Hence the spatial and embodied character of affective regenerations is central here. Urban spaces acquire an affective force that elicits plural responses and the reworking of religious ritual. Gordillo (2014, introduction) draws attention to the "ruptured multiplicity that is constitutive of all geographies as they are produced, destroyed and remade," processes that produce an affective multiplicity. In this sense, affective regenerations are generative in that the force of dislocation requires a response and opens up a space of potentiality; they are regenerative in the sense that they involve a reclaiming and reconfiguring of particular rites and traditions. The affective force of grief or mourning, for instance, invokes a multiplicity of experiences and responses: funeral rites that blend Christian and ancestral idioms cannot be reduced to the "syncretism" of different traditions but rather constitute a mode of becoming in which diverse sites are connected and webs of relations are localized in relation to experiences of trauma. In the following case studies, I will explore these relations between the affective force of certain urban spaces and the ritualistic responses they elicit.

Diamond Exchange was an unlawfully occupied building in the inner city from which residents were evicted in late 2013; it was a space in which hundreds of residents lived, mostly asylum seekers, in conditions of extreme precarity (Fassin, Wilhelm-Solomon, and Segatti 2017; Wilhelm-Solomon 2015). The residents were violently evicted by a private security company called the Black Bees in late 2013. I conducted research both within the building and with several of its residents in the years following their eviction. The committee and leadership of the building, unique in my experience, were composed primarily of women—shebeen (informal bar) matrons, domestic workers, a subcontracted cleaner, and an informal trader, among others. They were labeled by others in the building the "petticoat government." I will discuss some of the relations of three women: Chihera, an informal Zimbabwean trader; Panashe, a Zimbabwean-born domestic worker with South African citizenship; and Linda, a South African cleaner.

In Diamond Exchange, relations of interpersonal intimacy were formed through wider experiences of gendered precarity (cf. Butler 2004). The women in the building, some of whom formed relationships with criminals, did so in response to conditions of social abandonment in which neither the government nor economic forces provided them with any form of care or protection. This is not to say that gendered violence was accepted without contestation. Women frequently intervened in cases where other women were being beaten, attempting to protect one another and occasionally trying to bring in the police. Forms of sociality and intimacy were structured around birth and death: birthday parties, for instance, were common forms of celebration where shared contributions were made for food and beer.

In a context of high levels of gender-based violence, the committee of women leading Diamond Exchange was often undermined and dismissed as a "petticoat government." In addition, conflicts between the women also proved corrosive. One particularly significant argument, for instance, was whether to agree to the property company's offer that residents pay a rental of 750 rands (around $50) a month. Disputes within the committee and the lack of support from the occupants more widely led to the occupants losing their legal support and being unable to prevent their eviction. What was striking to me, however, was not the recurrence of these fights but the resilience of intimate friendships among women that enabled them to withstand even fierce conflicts. The members of the petticoat government of Diamond Exchange remained friends, even though their conflicts had in part led to their being unable to oppose eviction. The affective regenerations of Diamond Exchange involved the continual resilience of relations of care in spite of precarity and conflict, as well as the spiritual need to cleanse and purify the building.

One example, recounted to me by different sources in the building, is telling in this regard. At Diamond Exchange, two deaths were to shake the community, causing celebration but also terror and social division. In the first, in late 2012, a well-known criminal—not a resident of the building, but someone who regularly robbed its residents outside the local tavern—ran into the building to evade the police. He climbed out one of the windows, trying to hide from the police, but fell to his death on the garbage-cluttered balcony several floors below. The corpse was collected to be taken to the mortuary, but the man's family did not undertake the physical and ritualistic cleansing at the site of his death. The bloodstains remained on the balcony for several weeks. The balcony was one of the access points to one of the two taps in the building, which served several hundred people, but the residents now stopped using that tap. An air of anxiety set in, and residents reported feeling the hair on their heads prickle when they passed that floor. They only started using the tap again once the rains had come and washed away the bloodstains. Two months later, in early 2013, another man fell to death on the balcony in what appeared to be a suicide after a domestic fight—the latter event was considered linked to the misfortune of the first. The residents of Diamond Exchange who stayed behind felt the building required cleansing of its aura of death. Many reported experiences of disquiet and being watched. Bishop Paul Verryn, the prominent leader of the Central Methodist Mission, a refuge for asylum seekers in the city, was brought in by the petticoat government to cleanse the building with holy water, while members of the congregation carried palm leaves. After the cleansing, according to residents, the experiences of haunting quieted down.

As Gastón Gordillo has argued, haunting "is not reducible to narratives articulated linguistically; it is rather an affect created by an absence that exerts a hard-to-articulate, non-discursive, yet positive pressure on the body thereby turning such an absence into a physical presence that is felt and that thereby affects" (2014, ch. 1). The hauntings of the inner city were part of the ruptured multiplicity of space, the layering of violence that was irreducible to formal histories or narratives. Hauntings of those who had died untimely deaths, whether from violence, fire, or HIV/AIDS, were reported in several of the buildings in which I worked (Wilhelm-Solomon

2015; Wheeler 2012). Such hauntings reveal the ways in which social histories of trauma and violence become spatially localized and require affective regenerations.

Cleansing the streets in inner-city Johannesburg is a response not only to specific traumatic events but also to a more generalized sense of misfortune that pervades life in the city. Each year at Easter, many Methodist congregations in the city observe an early morning ritual called *imvuselelo* in isiZulu and isiNdebele (which translates as "waking," "rebirth," or "revival," though this is also the term used for "regeneration"). I attended one of these services at a Methodist church in the postindustrial south of the city in 2014, in the year after the eviction, with Chihera and Linda, formerly of the petticoat government. The entire hall was very dark, and only a few candles beside the altar were lit. Pastors and some women dressed in red garments were at the front conducting blessings, and throughout the hall in the darkness was the sound of prayers, groans, and wails. After some time, these suddenly were transformed into a hymn, a change that was very powerful, as if the weight of suffering had been lifted from the hall. After that the procession went out into the street, and we followed. The service went on for a while, the pastors shouting in a manner that was almost violent, and then we walked down the road to where some homeless people were living on the street. The pastors prayed for the homeless, saying that Satan had put them on the street when they had come to the city to look for work. One of the homeless men remained hidden in his blanket, while another lowered his head almost in shame. Across from the homeless an electricity box was steaming, electric wires were burning orange in the early light, and a large black mark had scorched the wall. We returned to the church, and the congregation scattered after some final prayers. The services indicated that experiences of misfortune, poverty, and homelessness are understood by many as a form of spiritual disorder that becomes spatialized and contaminates the general urban surroundings. However, these rites of purification cannot be seen outside the daily experiences of misfortune, care, and renewal.

In early 2016, almost three years after the eviction, I visited Panashe in her rented space in a shared room in the inner city—a space that she struggled to afford. At the time Panashe was suffering from uterine cancer and had started chemotherapy. Next to her bed, alongside her medications—I was to discover she was also HIV positive and on antiretrovirals—was the blue bottle I recognized from the Revelation Church of God, a new prophetic evangelical church. Each Wednesday, members of the church would come to visit her in her room and pray with her. The landlady would not allow Panashe's daughter to stay with her, and so the daughter had to stay in a distant township on the outskirts of Johannesburg. I visited Panashe with Chihera and Linda. Panashe, very thin and frail, said to us as she lay on her bed, "I would not be like this if it were not for the eviction." I understood her to be speaking of her solitude in the room, that she was forced to live far from her daughter and outside the caring and affective relationships she had had in Diamond Exchange. As Didier Fassin has argued, experiences of illness become tied up with personal biographies and "events inscribed in situations of poverty and relations of power" (2007, 225). In the same ways, larger-scale processes of urban change such as eviction are felt at a deeply affective level. As Fassin also argues, "The body is a presence unto oneself and unto the world, embedded in a history that is both individual and collective" (175). For Panashe, her experience of cancer became bound up with her experiences of eviction and dislocation. Panashe died a few weeks after I last saw her.

The poignancy of Panashe's illness and death, which she herself associated with the experience of eviction, was that, in spite of the residents' disputes over how to defend themselves against eviction, the intimacies of this time endured: the women, now living in disparate locations, one an undocumented Zimbabwean, another an isiZulu woman, and Panashe herself, who was born in Zimbabwe, still retained relations of care. These enduring relations of care are part of the affective regenerations of the city—they involved visiting one another, bringing food, sharing stories, and praying with one another. I was not able to attend Panashe's funeral because I was traveling, but only a few days before she died, I awoke from a terrible dream of her death, literally in a sweat and feeling a sense of terror, and later I felt deep sorrow at the news of her death. The affective becoming of the anthropologist is one of a truncated intimacy, disrupted by distance, both physical and of the ethnographic process, its condition one of only partially ritualized mourning. To mourn, through the idioms of those both intimate and other, is perhaps the unbecoming of the anthropological process. Maybe writing then becomes a proxy, a form of ritual for this truncated intimacy, for a community in which one is only peripherally a part. I was told about the funeral by Chihera over WhatsApp. In spite of her protestations that she was a South African, Panashe's body was returned to her "ancestral" home in Bulawayo.

The story of Cape York is one of how a dark building comes into being.[7] It is not a story of a grand hijacking but one of gradual dereliction. In it, the loss of basic services—water, electricity, security—opened up the possibility of other threats both physical and otherworldly: the threat of violence, but also of malevolent spirits and ghosts. The building, which was owned by the Banco de Mozambique, housed the Mozambican consulate until 2011. In 2011 the consulate moved out and rented two floors of the building to the International Federation of People with Blindness and Albinism (IFPAB), an association led by an albino Pentecostal pastor. Its members were mainly migrants and asylum seekers from southern Africa, particularly Zimbabweans, who were forced into begging for a livelihood in the inner city. Inside Cape York they ran a school and housed offices and living spaces for the blind, the disabled, and people with albinism. When the group moved into Cape York, they had to do a cleansing ceremony, as they found *muthi* in the building that could be used both for medicinal purposes and for malevolent practices (Ashforth 2005), and also what they thought could be human bones on the floor—alleged signs of witchcraft and misfortune. In order to cleanse the building they held an all-night prayer vigil led by the pastor, and he and other pastors went through the building, anointing it with holy oil. At first, the building was perceived as safe by IFPAB, and they set up their offices and even a crèche in the building.

The building was managed in a quasi-formal manner whereby the property management company operated it but others, including the former caretaker, took control of the lower floors of the building and were renting them out illegally. Rates were not paid and in 2012 the water and electricity were cut, and Banco de Mozambique had lost control of the building.

The building did not lose its associations with misfortune for those I spoke to, and people told me about a car accident on the corner and several untimely deaths that occurred in the building. The building was also considered as a place of threat of misfortune and pain, a *gahena*, or "hell," in the words of one inner-city resident.

In the early hours of Saturday August 3, 2013, a fire tore through its upper levels. When I visited the building shortly afterward, the walls of the upper levels were blackened by the fire. Four people were thought to have died in the fire, including a young child. On the upper floor, where members of the IFPAB lived, I found a group huddled around. It was cold, and wind blew through the cracked windows where the flames had curled up while the group took shelter from the fire. The group were in a state of confusion and fear. The explanation they first gave me for the fire was that a man who wanted to kill his partner for cheating on him had firebombed the room. The group also recounted how part of the blame for the fire lay with the building management and municipality, which had cut off the water supply, so residents could not put out the fire. However, one woman I spoke to said, "Satan is at large here" and speculated that satanic spirits were at work. She also speculated that the deaths of the mother and child in the fire were unsettling and suggested malevolent spirits at work. It could, she explained, be the work of *ngozi*, a Shona term for a vengeful spirit (Fontein 2015, xv), who, according to Zimbabweans, often manifests itself in the form of fire. The others concurred that this was a possibility. An elderly blind musician, Edward Mavura,[8] explained that ngozi could be the work of a family seeking revenge for murder: they could light a fire over the grave of the dead and send the spirit to seek revenge. The woman beside him explained that a tree could be planted over the grave of the dead, and when the petals began to fall, three people would die. The group felt that the spirits of the dead in the building needed to be prayed for, but they were anxious, as the families of the deceased had not communicated with the remaining residents of the building.

For the group, the fire represented the final unraveling of what had been a place of refuge and intimacy. Staying with IFPAB in the inner city, even under poor conditions, was a period of transitory happiness for Mavura, the blind musician. "I was happy beyond belief," he told me. It was the place where he met his partner, a blind woman who also lived in the building. He had met her and composed a love song, which he sang to her. Even under dire conditions and in spaces of dereliction and physical incapacitation, there are still capacities for love, intimacy, and creativity. Meeting with the blind and disabled, and identifying now as blind, Mavura had ironically found a sense of belonging and refuge in the city. It is precisely this that is the paradox of dark buildings—they offer spaces of refuge and intimacy for those who are generally excluded from the city's formal housing markets and from stable employment.

I also spoke to two women who had been living on the floor that was burned. They too were Zimbabwean migrants who, they told me, survived on petty theft in the inner city. Their story was different from the dominant explanation of the lovers' quarrel: they recounted that there had been a rental dispute when an isiZulu gang had tried to force Zimbabwean residents on the floor to pay them rent. When the residents refused, according to the women, the gang firebombed the floor. Having nowhere to stay, the women returned to the building but now lived in fear. One said that she had been walking up the stairs with her child, who told her that he had seen the child who had died standing on the stairwell. Stories of haunting were widespread in the dark buildings of the inner city, the hauntings of those who had died "unnatural" deaths from violence, illness, or accident. The study of Cape York illustrates how a dark building may be a site of intense affective experiences: fears of misfortune and violence, but also sites of affiliation, music, and love. Religious rites and cleansing played a role in demarcating such a space, making it inhabitable and giving it a sense of "home" even in a transient sense.

In the wake of the fire, a dispute between Zimbabwean and isiZulu recyclers over extracting copper wires and other metals from the wreckage led to at least two murders in the building. Rumors among residents recounted how one of the murdered men had his lips and genitals cut off and was dumped in the garbage. The fire had elicited tensions and continuing violence that ran along ethnic and nationalist lines but were thought by some residents to have had overtones of witchcraft.

The building itself had become entangled in the complex politics of urban regeneration and divisions, which included property developers and municipal officials. One of the largest companies in Johannesburg, the Affordable Housing Company, had taken the owners of Cape York, Banco de Mozambique, along with the City of Johannesburg, to court for neglecting the building and to have it cleaned up. Renny Plitt, the CEO of the Affordable Housing Company, a prominent developer, was quoted in the media as saying, "We are also in the process of launching a damages claim against the bank for about R2.4 million. We have had to empty out the apartments in our redeveloped building that faces Cape York. Also, the crèche in our building was forced to close by the Education Department as a result of the stench and rats."[9] In the same article he exclaimed: "People living in the hijacked building throw human waste, rotting food, dirty water and other rubbish out of the windows. The outside of the building and all the fire escapes are piled high with rubbish."

Title deeds of the building show that in 2014 Cape York was purchased by a company called Mark of the Divine, run by an Ethiopian man, for R9.2 million (around $643,000). However, it was later alleged that this transaction was fraudulent and the Banco de Mozambique was trying to claim back the building.[10] This form of real estate speculation, in which occupied buildings are traded, along with contestations over ownership and title

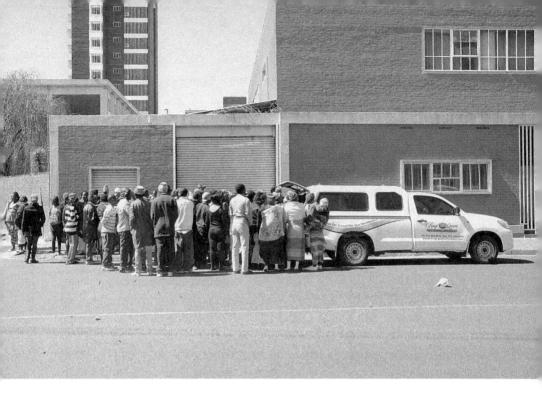

FIGURE 1.1 Mourners conduct a street-cleansing ceremony at the site of a murder and next to a newly gentrified area. Photo by Matthew Wilhelm-Solomon.

deeds, is common in the inner city. The affective force of fire and dereliction elicit multiple responses encompassing an array of actors and forces. In Cape York we see the contrasting dynamics of private-sector regenerations encounter affective regenerations inasmuch as they concern the lived experiences and security of the same spaces. Furthermore, this is not to place affect and emotion solely on the side of those who live in dark buildings: emotion is invoked by different actors, including property developers, as well as those who live in dark buildings—an act of coding, the affective responses to the instability and politics of urban infrastructures.

THE STATION (ROSEMARY'S STORY)

A few bricks lie on the pavement outside a dirty-brown warehouse, beside a corrugated iron garage door and the white stripes of burglar bars. It is October 2014. The warehouse borders the Jeppe Police Station, the main police station in the area, which became a site of refuge after the anti-immigrant violence of 2008 and in whose basement migrants are now regularly confined, awaiting deportation. A little down the road across Albertina Sisulu Avenue is the Zebra Bar, adorned with the stuffed heads of animals. Across the street, the facade of a building adorned in multicolored letters advertises the site as one of the inner city's new urban renewal projects, Maboneng or "place of light," a place of galleries, coffee shops, and loft conversions.

Pedestrians pass the bricks, hardly noticing them. The bricks seem like the rubble left over by construction workers, but if one looks more closely, one can see the brown stains that mark the paving and tar around them, like the contours of lakes on a concrete grid. Those who pass the bricks do not even look at them as they walk by, on their way to work, or in search of work, to the police station or home. The violence these bricks memorialize is almost entirely erased; they are, like the lives they mark, the banal leftovers of ceaseless demolition and reconstruction.

The murder took place only days earlier, at the site marked by the bricks. A young man I shall call David had been collecting beers with a friend for his mother Rosemary's shebeen, an illegal bar in a nearby building, when they were attacked and David shot. Mourning for the young man in the building he had lived in went on all week. I went one night with Bishop Paul Verryn to Rosemary's room, and I was struck by the intensity of grief, by the proximity of bodies and voices, by songs and alcohol, by the uncontainable energy of loss and grief that seemed to take people to a precipice of near madness. Rosemary, whom I had not seen since the murder, sat in the corner of the room surrounded by women, lost in her grief, as Verryn said prayers for her murdered son.

A few days later, a large crowd gathered at the site of the strewn bricks. They came along with the young man's body, which was being carried in a coffin in the back of a Toyota Hilux serving as a hearse for the King's and Queen's funeral parlor, where a nondenominational Christian service had been held. The van had stopped at The Station, where David's clothes were collected. Rosemary sat in the back of the van, her face contorted by grief. After the ceremony the group collected clothes and dust from Rosemary's room, before moving to the site of the murder. David's cousin, dressed in a gray suit, prayed and cleaned the tar at the site of the murder with a brush made of grass thatch while the crowd sang. He collected the bloodstained dirt from the site and placed it with the body. It was an act of cleansing, of calling the spirit from the site of death to travel with the body on the long journey back to Zimbabwe, to his ancestral home; if these rites are not performed, the spirit can remain unsettled, itinerant, causing misfortune to strangers and kin alike.

Kennedy Chinyowa (2001, 5) explains that in Shona funerary rites, in cases of mysterious deaths, the spirit requires cleansing and rehabilitation through rituals such as *kutora mudzimu* (taking the spirit home) or *kudzora mudzimu* (returning the spirit). David's funerary rites can also be referred to as a *kutakura mudzimu* (to carry the spirit).[11] But other words, which I did not understand at the time, were also spoken as David's brother washed the stale blood from the pavement. As I learned only a year after the death, the spirit was also invoked to return as an ngozi to avenge the murder.

A year after the murder, when a memorial service was once again held in Rosemary's room, Rosemary and her partner, Farai, had still not learned of any developments in the case, and the murder file was being archived. Rosemary and Farai decided to do something that they had been considering for a while, which was to save money for a traditional healer in Harare, who said he could tell who David's murderers were. Rosemary had already visited the healer once, and he had told her that members of David's family on the paternal side were responsible for the murder through witchcraft, but they told me they wanted to know who pulled the trigger. Farai explained that, since the police had failed, this was the only recourse left for their investigation, though they never managed to pay the full amount to find out who the actual murderer was. Rosemary told me that every time she had to walk past the site of the murder, "bad memories" returned.

More than a year later, I visited the site of her son's burial at a rural homestead in Gutu, Zimbabwe. The homestead consisted of a few clay and brick houses far off the road. It was surrounded by red wild grasses and gardens of okra, sun-stunted maize, beans, and pumpkins. Rosemary's son had been buried in a mound beneath a leafless wild peach tree alongside his aunt, who had died of AIDS, and his grandfather. Rosemary had returned to the site to arrange for cement and bricks to be put over the grave. She knelt beside the grave and wailed with pain, her voice emanating from her frail frame, her dreadlocks hanging over her face. Afterward she told me that it was healing to visit the grave and that her son must know "she was there." She would arrange for the elders and councilors of the village to be there for the burial. The affective force of loss, grief, and memory is something felt as a deep and overwhelming pain and stress. Rosemary smoked marijuana heavily to calm her "stress," but the affect of loss is also something that overflows interiority, overflows borders, and is intensified in certain sites—the room in which the loved one, the site of the murder, the ancestral home.

Affective regenerations indicate the ways in which wider processes of urban change—the drive for private-sector investment, evictions, policing—which are widely conceived of by the state and private actors as part of "urban regeneration," are part of processes of capacitation and decapacitation affecting the ability of urban dwellers to act, live, and endure meaningfully in the city. Affective regenerations indicate the ways in which interpersonal forms of social renewal are enmeshed in, and formed in response to, wider processes of urban change and the materiality of the city. As I have argued in this chapter, intimacy and mourning are integral to affective regenerations. In line with the concerns of this volume, I have aimed to show how religion ritualizes and codes affective relations within urban space. In this, religious rites form a powerful role in social responses to the debilitating affects of marginalization and trauma in Johannesburg.

The stories of Diamond Exchange, Cape York, and The Station, and of Panashe, Rosemary, and others, reveal how personal and social renewal is formed in relation to urban spaces and their attendant dislocations. Affective regenerations are integral to the will to live under conditions of social abandonment (Biehl 2013; Povinelli 2011). Religious rites—cleansing ceremonies, prayers, and funerary rites—are an important part of this, but they must be viewed in relation to the wider affective experiences of the city.

The pervasiveness of experiences of illness, dislocation, haunting, and fear of the unsettled dead frequently elicits the need for cleansing ceremonies aimed at placating unsettled spirits and protecting against misfortune. These rites of cleansing draw both on rituals linked to ancestral religions and on diverse forms of Christianity, including mainline churches such as the Methodist Church, along with neo-Pentecostal movements. These rituals not only invoke the interrelationality among migrant residents of the city but also have an important affective role in containing and calming the experiences of insecurity and violence in urban space. Funeral rites in the inner city, where a wider diasporic community gathers in the rooms of the deceased to sing hymns and comfort the bereaved, are a form of gathering that creates a sense of belonging among groups scattered throughout the city, and even beyond. The affective force of loss becomes spatially localized through ritual: ceremonies of cleansing and mourning do not permanently calm and contain loss or haunting. The absence of those who have died continues to exert an affective force to gather and haunt, while it is also a source of sociality and intimacy.

The politics of affective regenerations may be viewed as a stabilization and containment of affective intensities—experiences of hope, desire, fear, and loss. Rituals of cleansing and catharsis, of calming and containment, are modulated through the material forms and rituals of the city on multiple levels—from intimate experiences of hope and loss, to responses to large-scale urban regeneration schemes and evictions. The politics of urban affect involves forms of capacitation and debilitation, the opening and foreclosing of certain possibilities of movement and experience (cf. Livingston 2005). Religiosity and religious rites channel, contain, and localize these affective intensities. These rites are distributed and disrupted by wider-scale processes of urban change: property-market speculation, criminality, migration, and dispossession. The coproduction of the city (Lefebvre 1991) also involves and produces a multiplicity and densification of affective relationships that are contained and intensified through ritual activity. Affective regenerations are hence integral to the ways in which inner-city residents survive and relate to urban spaces, even though they are not necessarily tied to formal movements pressing for the "right to the city."

The force of intimacy, friendship, and attachment resides not only in personal emotion but also in the movements, capacities, and relations in which the possibility for intimacy opens up—this opening up and potential for renewal is what I refer to as affective regeneration. In the dark buildings the capacities for personal intimacy often coalesce around traumatic events and bodily debilitation—yet these far from exhaust their potential. Friendships form in the routine day-to-day rituals of life in the city—trading, drinking, eating, and praying—but also in moments of affective intensity, such as at funerals, in sickness, or in mourning. Anthropology here is also an affective relationship: it is an undoing—a displacement—of one's own subjectivity. Perhaps the labor of writing—in making present those who have passed, who have shared their words and stories with me, and whose voices remain on recorded files on the computer or in traces in my notebooks, or merely in memory—is also an affective regeneration of sorts.

NOTES

Acknowledgments: The research and writing for this chapter were supported by the Volkswagen Foundation Knowledge for Tomorrow—Cooperative Research Projects in Sub-Saharan Africa Programme as part of the project entitled "Salvaged Lives: A Study of Urban Migration, Ontological Insecurity, and Healing in Johannesburg," which also supported my editorial work on this book. The project was hosted by the

African Centre for Migration and Society at the University of the Witwatersrand, in collaboration with Professor Lorena Núñez and Peter Kankonde there, and also in collaboration with Professor Dr. Hansjörg Dilger of the Institute of Social and Cultural Anthropology, Freie Universität Berlin. The writing of this chapter was completed while I was based at the Department of Social Anthropology at the University of the Witwatersrand. Elements of this chapter were reworked from my articles "Dispossessed Vigils" (Wilhelm-Solomon 2015) and "The Ruinous Vitalism of the Urban Form" (Wilhelm-Solomon 2017). I would also like to thank the coeditors of this volume and the anonymous readers for their insightful comments on the chapter, Adriana Miranda da Cunha for her support in the research and writing process, and all of those who shared their lives and stories in the research process.

1. https://www.jpoma.co.za/about/ (accessed June 16, 2019).

2. Calculated at the approximate exchange rate of June 6, 2019, as are the other conversions in this chapter.

3. I am indebted to Marian Burchardt for this point.

4. UNHCR, "Population Statistics: Data Overview," last updated May 19, 2017, http://popstats.unhcr.org/en/overview (accessed June 15, 2017). A screenshot of this date is available at www.evernote.com/shard/s256/sh/f3321ec9-f34c-44fd-b79f-832d365066ed /988155fb8f2dbef5919b7ab826d40bbc (last accessed June 23, 2019).

5. After the writing of this chapter, the newly elected Democratic Alliance mayor and well-known businessman Herman Mashaba initiated a campaign of "shock and awe" against so-called hijacked buildings involving increased police and immigration raids on the buildings. See www.bloomberg.com/news/articles/2017-08-14/johannesburg -mayor-insists-on-shock-and-awe-plan-for-city (accessed January 20, 2017).

6. I generated and analyzed these data through the Statistics South Africa interactive site: http://interactive2.statssa.gov.za/webapi/jsf/dataCatalogueExplorer .xhtml (accessed June 15, 2017). The data analyed are for Johannesburg Wards 60 and 123, where most of the research was carried out. They should not be generalized to the inner city as a whole. A screenshot of the data can be found at www.evernote.com /shard/s256/sh/9ec06989-d50b-4c71-8cf3-145ddbcc7c59/d8922576ebb0242f92ec4ea 106816154 (accessed June 15, 2017). A ward map of the areas can be found at www .demarcation.org.za/index.php/gauteng/gp-prov-wards2010/jhb/6842-jhbward-123-1 /file (accessed June 15, 2017).

7. After this chapter was completed, in June 2017, a second fire hit Cape York as the result of a faulty generator, leading to four deaths and the closure of the building.

8. While the names in this chapter are primarily pseudonyms, Edward Mavura requested and gave informed consent for his real name to be used.

9. www.iol.co.za/news/crime-courts/fatal-hijacked-building-blaze-sparks-anger -1557553 (accessed February 8, 2018).

10. http://www.iolproperty.co.za/roller/news/entry/joburg_hijacked_building _saga_continues (accessed June 23, 2019).

11. Thank you to Dr. Obvious Katsaura of the Department of Sociology, University of the Witwatersrand, for clarifying this for me.

2   EMOTIONS AS AFFECTIVE TRAJECTORIES OF BELIEF IN MWARI (GOD) AMONG MASOWE APOSTLES IN URBAN ZIMBABWE

ISABEL MUKONYORA

This chapter shows how Shona-speaking Christians who are popularly known as Masowe (Wilderness) Apostles view Mwari (God) as an all-powerful sentient being with Eyes (Maziso), Ears (Nzewe), Mouth (Muromo), and Voice (Izwi) (Daneel 1970a, 24) and the point of origin of the elements of nature upon which all sentient beings depend as living creatures. As highlighted in Karanga myths of creation collected by Aschwanden (1989, 11–48), Mwari is identified with elements of nature which scientists say support life on earth, from water, wind, dirt, the sun, and the origins of sentient beings on earth. In Masowe Apostles' religious language for revelation, Mwari becomes known through divine wisdom and healing Izwi (Voice), associated with gospel stories of the Holy Spirit. In other words, God is part of this world and, being symbolically identical with it," speaks in order to help us understand our place among the living on earth. Death is thus emotionally disruptive to sentient beings among whom are human beings who pray to Mwari as a way of facing up to whatever forces contradict the divine purpose of creation when people die (Aschwanden 1989, 48). In short, Masowe Apostles are Shona-speaking Christians who fill themselves with emotions about Mwari, since European missionaries found "Mwari the most suitable term to use for God (Elohim)" (Daneel 1970a, 36). Mwari is now perceived as that hidden mystery whose breath made life possible on earth at creation and functions like the Holy Spirit when Masowe Apostles go to the wilderness to express their longing for spiritual fulfilment.

It is suggested that experiences of displacement, originating from a colonial economy forcing Africans to migrate to cities as cheap labor, explain the ritual behavior from which we can learn about the Masowe Apostolic way of turning the margins of the city into a vibrant landscape to which the Wilderness Apostles have gone to pray since the origins of the church during the 1930s. The city of Harare, like many other cities of Africa in this era of what Jenkins (2011) has called "the next Christendom," is filled with sites of struggle located in its margins, where African Christians either eke out their living by growing food crops or successfully turn the same margins of cityscapes into liminal places for reaching out to God in prayer for the poor and sick. Viewed as the source of life on earth and an ecological deity with holistic healing powers among the Shona in southern and central Africa, Mwari gives meaning to the ritual behavior of the Masowe Apostles. In fact, the ritual behavior summarized below tells us a lot about the emotions whose expressions amount to affective trajectories of faith in Mwari. Not only are Masowe Apostles a century-old church in which personal experiences of displacement give meaning to the work of the Holy Spirit; the prayer ceremonies have also incorporated a protracted history of Zimbabwe's political conflicts and economic depressions since the 1930s. This was followed by more human suffering as the neocolonial period of white supremacist rule (1964–1979), and the postcolonial context of more political violence (1980 onward), added to the spiritual needs for the poor and sick in independent Zimbabwe. Briefly, the trajectories of faith examined here are the result of social problems such as poverty, violence, the spread of diseases, unemployment, and other misfortunes which cause human suffering and death. The opportunity to do some fieldwork on Masowe Apostolic theological language for transforming the margins of the urban landscape into the setting for rituals, with a focus on Mwari's Voice, led to this paper. Not only is it common to find Masowe Apostles walking outdoors to the margins of the city landscape in places like Harare, but anyone who takes the trouble to attend their prayer meetings will find them expressing themselves in a variety of ways suited for discussion in this attempt to address the relation of religion, and African modernity, with the social theory about the "affective turn" outlined in the introduction to this book (See also Ticineto and Halley 2007). One observes people who share experiences of suffering, shed tears of sorrow, sing to stop preachers from talking, touch each other on the shoulder as a sign of empathy during prayers for healing, or are mindful of Mwari's association with the elements of nature that support life on earth. All the emotions created by experiences of suffering and death in Zimbabwean society led to this paper on the affective trajectories of faith among the Masowe Apostles encountered during fieldwork on the outskirts of the city of Harare between 1996 and 1999.

As shown below, certain symbolic actions and the religious language that go with the choice to pray on the margins of the urban landscape have been used to formulate prayers to a God whose main attributes are his "Voice" and healing power. By attracting believers to the margins of the city in different parts of Harare, where the gospel language of the poor and sick has been used to give expression to the idea of total dependence on the same God who led the people of Israel through the wilderness, Masowe Apostles further our understanding of Christianity among the poor anywhere in sub-Saharan Africa today. When it comes to the affective dimensions of Masowe spirituality, the locations for prayer on the margins of the landscape correspond to struggles to survive in a society whose political history is filled with talk about an ancestral legacy of Africans having rights to possess fertile land. Barren land on the margins of the city is now a way of using the exposure to the elements of nature to control anger, fear, and sadness associated with marginality in society and based on the belief that the healing power of the Holy Spirit is all around the sacred sites for prayer. This is important in terms of affect because the term *masowe* corresponds to observable patterns of uniform behavior meant to control emotions of anger, fear, and sadness starting with turning up for prayer dressed in white robes and walking in a calm manner associated with entering a liminal space or sacred wilderness.

While the material examined here is based on research limited to the margins of the cityscapes of Harare between 1996 and 2000, it is important to recognize the history of the Masowe Apostles. Masowe Apostles are known to have been dealing with the frustrations of social upheavals by praying in the urban wildernesses of Harare, Gweru, and Bulawayo in Zimbabwe, and in many other African cities to which Masowe Apostles have migrated since the origins of the church during the Great Depression of the 1930s. According to Dillon-Malone (1978, 14–15), the Great Depression marked a difficult era in colonial Zimbabwe and neighboring countries. Not only did political conflict which led to World War I (1914–1918) and to the Great Depression (1929–1941) in Europe upset the global market, but the Depression caused social upheaval throughout the colonial world.

The appearance of local prophets like Johane Masowe (1914–1978) does not merely coincide with the rise of religious innovation in indigenous societies experiencing conquest around the world; there are thousands of examples from Africa alone (Barrett 1968). Today, Gandanzara (the Land of Hunger) is more than the name of the village where the founder of the Masowe Apostles was born; it is now a place of pilgrimage distinguished by the site of the prophet's burial on a rock (Dillon-Malone 1978, 15). Gandanzara is expressive of the emotion out of which arose Johane Masowe's longing to transform Africans into converts to Christianity in search of spiritual ways of controlling angst through prayers for healing.

Besides the side effects of colonial conquest, economic depressions, political conflicts, the poverty created by the sudden introduction of Western technologies, industrialization, urbanization, and what Timothy Burke calls "the commodification of society in modern Zimbabwe" (1996, 10–15) explain the popularity of Masowe prayer gatherings. Furthermore, sporadic droughts during the 1930s economic depression caused so much anxiety that many youths ran away from rural areas to cities like Harare. Hence the majority of Masowe Apostles in suburban Harare, where large numbers of Shona men hoped to find jobs as domestic servants or factory workers or from where they would travel further to provide cheap labor for European-owned mines, railway lines, and newly built manufacturing industries for all sorts of western material goods for developing trading relations with European countries and introducing white-controlled capitalism to Africans (Schmidt 1992, 42; Jeater 1993, 35ff; McCulloch 2000, *passim*; Elizabeth Schmidt 1992, 42). With so much of the job market built for turning African men into cheap labor as required by European colonial architects of industrial Zimbabwe, it is no wonder men lead while women outnumber them among as the most vulnerable members of the patriarchal world (Schmidt 1992, 42; plus observations from fieldwork done in Harare by Mukonyora during 1997). The human cost of building cities and industries run by men aside, the experiences of displacement articulated during ritual activities are so Christian in character that they can be seen as originating from a critique of the oppression which European missionaries associated with advancing God's plans for a universal redemption.

I am suggesting that not much has changed to eradicate the emotions that were once blamed on British imperialism and a global patriarchal Christianity. A recent BBC news report on Zimbabwe reads:

> Once the breadbasket of the region, since 2000 Zimbabwe has struggled to feed its own people due to severe droughts and the effects of a land re-

form program which saw the seizure of white-owned farms redistributed to landless black Zimbabweans which led to sharp falls in production. . . . Cash-strapped and impoverished, Zimbabwe's economy faces severe challenges. Unemployment and poverty are endemic and political strife and repression commonplace. Many Zimbabweans have left the country in search of work in South Africa. (BBC News 2016)

Many other citizens who have stayed in Zimbabwe are not unlike the Masowe Apostles when it comes to finding ways of turning experiences of displacement into an African interpretation of the personal God of Christian orthodoxy as Mwari in Shona religious language. Just before I wrote the conclusion to this chapter, a Pentecostal preacher of His Generation Church was in the news for using a national flag to mobilize a nation whose independence is characterized by making the country and its cityscapes places to fight against corruption, economic mismanagement, and unemployment in Zimbabwe (*Zimbabwe Daily*, October 16, 2016). By wearing the national flag around his neck and using the language of suffering and hope for salvation for the people of Zimbabwe in a city church, Reverend Mawarire is a good example of a religious leader using the symbolic speech of the colorful flag to communicate the general experiences of displacement and hope for salvation. In other words, this study of affective trajectories of faith among Masowe Apostles can be applied to other theological concepts regarding that which creates the mood for prayer in a society where most African Christians experience the problems of life in urban Zimbabwe (J. Burke and Enders 2016).

THE URBAN WILDERNESS OF HARARE
AS A "THREATENING SPACE"

Briefly, the background setting for this chapter is a Zimbabwean society built on memories of violence so that "shedding blood" acts as a reminder of the civil rights of the poor. Historians, politicians, and ethnographers interested in studies of Zimbabwe (cf. Alexander, McGregor, and Ranger 2000, 19) generally recognize the disruptive effects of violence caused by one problem or another since the British South Africa Company conquered the territory by fighting off indigenous people who opposed the establishment of the British colony of Southern Rhodesia in 1890. The First Chimurenga, meaning the first uprising against colonialism, which took place between 1893 and 1896, left behind strong emotions such as grief, anger, and especially the longing for Mwari to correct the injustice of huge tracts of land being seized from Zimbabweans to create a modern capitalist and urban colonial society. The fact that a minority population of white people interested in building cities from which to collect material wealth and conduct international trade viewed the biblical God as the transcendent masculine God of dominion behind the conquest of the land coincided with many abuses of power, including uses of education, to make the subjugation of Africans as Christian men whose subordinate roles in society came with missionaries failing to recognize the central place of women as mothers, farmers, and hunter gatherers. Hence, right from the beginning of the conquest of Zimbabwe, says McGregor, "marginalized minorities invoked a relation to the landscape in their claim to resources. Ideas about relationships with the landscape are thus more than statements of idealized cultural norms of the past: they are ways of creating meaning at a personal and family level, often in contexts of dispossession and hardship" (2003, 105). The fact that the majority members of the Masowe Apostles are women makes sense vis-à-vis the much-needed African critique of missionary Christianity as colonial politics.

During the Great Depression of the 1930s, when Masowe Apostles first appeared on the outskirts of Harare, the experiences of displacement caused by colonial conquest reminded people of Mwari's Voice the First Chimurenga, high levels of unemployment, and a severe drought (Dillon-Malone 1978, 14). Today, the national flag of Zimbabwe uses the symbolic color red to highlight the shedding of blood in a guerrilla war (1964–1979) and related human suffering as the price for freedom (Mukonyora 2012, 139). The Second Chimurenga, or "struggle for liberation," which took place between 1965 and 1980, made poverty more acute and Masowe Apostles even more popular and transnational (Mukonyora 2006, 67–68). As Britain imposed economic sanctions and encouraged other European countries to follow its lead, the white regime led by Prime Minister Ian Douglas Smith (1919–2007) agreed to the first democratic elections held in Zimbabwe in 1980. Masowe Apostles gained popularity because they had established rituals through which Zimbabweans could express their emotions as part of prayer to a God who comes to the aid of Africans whose ritual behavior corresponds to the mood of different believers. Masowe Apostles traveled from city to city with their founder and leader, Johane Masowe (John of the Wilderness), leaving behind amorphous communities of believers that mirrored the continued spread of Masowe Apostles throughout the Second Chimurenga (Mukonyora 2006, 65–66).

These social upheavals of the Chimurenga wars not only caused more and more Zimbabweans to migrate to urban areas but also worsened the suffering among the poor in cities like Harare. Even the name *Chimurenga* is a reminder of the psychological effects of the displacement experienced by national heroes (i.e., individuals prepared to leave home to fight and kill if necessary). The image of the wilderness as the setting for prayer has continued to function as a reminder of the psychological turmoil that becomes blunted through uniform symbolic actions at prayer meetings that would go on for an average of five to six hours at every weekend prayer gathering of barefoot, white-robed Christians (Mukonyora in Harare, 1996–1999).

Mainly because I decided to become a participant observer intent on finding out the emotional appeal of the image of the sacred wilderness, this chapter focuses on a period associated with the threat of the Third Chimurenga, an economic war caused by the failure of politicians to keep promises made to the masses about stopping war and reducing poverty. As Kanji (1995, 36–37) found, the 1991–1995 Economic Adjustment Program produced more poverty and strife than wealth. When it comes to attempting to theologize with the emotions of Africans whose experiences of modern life are riddled with the continual problems of the urban poor, it is safe to say that the emotions that characterize the religious aspirations of Masowe Apostles are rooted exactly in these experiences of displacement and urban marginalization. As Terrence Musanga found in his study of the Mugabe regime's attempts to use violence to cleanse the city of Harare of its poor:

> The boundaries between "safe" and "threatening" spaces are constantly transgressed by Zimbabwean urban dwellers in their day to day struggles for survival in a harsh and unrelenting economic and political climate. This political and economic environment has resulted in most Zimbabweans being insecure as testified by heightened intra-urban mobility. Furthermore, the insecurity and intra-urban mobility are exemplified by the creation of unstable identities premised on fear, anxiety, and restlessness as characteristics of affect that characterize the lives of most urban dwellers. (2015, 102–103)

This is interesting to relate to the Masowe Apostles because their name can be said to describe the religious response to anxieties caused by political conflicts since the colonial era. Consequently, between 1996 and 2000, I regularly visited the margins of suburbs north of the city of Harare where the University of Zimbabwe is located and I lived. Besides Lake Chimombe, a popular location for baptisms, I saw barren land onto which workers from nearby factories added random piles of trash. Wandering in the urban wilderness thus acquired a special meaning for me as the theologian experimenting with the anthropology of Christianity for the first time. This urban wilderness was easy for me to access on a bicycle; it consisted of at least five acres of a meadow surrounded by main roads across Avondale, toward Mount Pleasant, Marlborough, and Borrowdale—the expensive suburban homes built for Europeans to occupy, with Africans serving them as domestic servants since the colonial era. The more this inquiry involved my own wandering across the urban wilderness north of the city of Harare, the more convinced I was of the suggestion being made in this book that there are affective trajectories of the Christian faith in Africa. In this case study, deep-seated emotions were triggered by experiences of displacement originating from racial hierarchical uses of the power to dominate Africans whose own concept of God explained the ritual behavior of Masowe Apostles.

As hinted at earlier, the general idea of an ecological deity is much like a sentient being whose "Voice" and healing power are coterminous with his presences among victims of oppression, poverty, sickness, and other misfortunes. The Christians I met in the urban wilderness of Harare respected each other as believers whom the Holy Spirit inspired through prayer. As one female Masowe apostle put it: "God speaks to us here . . . God loves all his children equally, and talks to us in our hearts. . . . The Bible is an ancient source of knowledge about the same God who continues to speak directly to his children today." She then looked toward the meadow as birds flew across the sky above. This emotional God-talk and numerous other expressions of people sensing God in their hearts or consciences explain the topic of this chapter insofar as its aim is to examine the expression of ritualized ways of allowing believers to express their grief, anger, and fears about being human in Masowe religious language. In short, rather like dressing in uniform, making a point of talking about being equal before God during healing ceremonies produced peace and harmony as well as gave everyone present a shared hope for salvation (Werbner 1985, 267–268).

My first personal encounter with a Masowe Apostle in Harare took place in early February 1996. A woman in her late twenties was walking across a meadow all by herself, upset because her husband had died of AIDS, leaving her self-employed as an urban vegetable farmer who sold her crops by the side of the road. Madzimai Sarah not only had a way of using the margins of the cityscapes to address an acute problem of poverty by growing vegetables but also was a member of a community of Masowe Apostles who met for prayer on the same meadow. The regular visits to the prayer site that followed my first meeting with Madzimai Sarah showed just how deep-seated the emotions were that led her to the belief that God spoke to people in the wilderness and could heal the poor and sick (Mukonyora 2012, 136–159). According to Engelke (2007, 109–136), the gift of prophecy and healing power act together as a hermeneutical tool through which "a live and direct language" of God is formed. What is more, Engelke argues that power importantly mediates healing and transcendental experiences. By contrast, I will emphasize that my interlocutors, most of them unknown to official leaders, emphasized God's personal voice and direct experiences of the power of the Holy Spirit.

In the late 1990s, it was possible to find poor people who planted food crops on the outskirts of the city going to pray without any interest in being noticed as official members of the church. It is fair to characterize the Third Chimurenga as a time when the poor wandered between communities, if it was possible to find soul mates at prayer meetings. Wherever there is a city and opportunities for cheap labor, wandering in the wilderness is a common way of practicing Christianity among Masowe Apostles (Mukonyora 2006, 59–80). As it happens, the margins of Harare are also a good example of a city filled with "high-density suburbs," meaning homes that are so crowded by people who are poor that the longing for places to go to and share one's emotions became connected to believing in God as the one who responds to humanity by speaking through the Izwi, or Holy Spirit.

As Hammar, McGregor, and Landau observed, "Since early 2000, political violence and dramatic economic contraction have displaced people within and beyond Zimbabwe's borders on an extraordinary scale. The politicized state intrusions into Zimbabwean rural and urban economies, the dramatic disintegration of public services, rampant hyperinflation, destruction and redistribution of assets (planned and unplanned) have all had more than simply local effects" (2010, 263–264). In the following section, I describe how I found my way into exploring the emotional experiences of Masowe in the urban wilderness of Harare since the Third Chimurenga.

THEORY AND METHOD

Somewhat struck by the fact that I was about to finish a doctoral dissertation, titled "The Complementarity of Male and Female Imagery in Theological Language: A Study of the Valentinian and Masowe Theological Systems" (Mukonyora 1999), without meeting Masowe Apostles for myself, I decided to do precisely that. By acting on my limited knowledge of the

FIGURE 2.1 Children of the wilderness church. Photo reprinted by permission of the National Archives of Zimbabwe.

anthropology and sociology of religion, where one must employ empirical methods of research, it became clear that my first book was not going to be about gender imagery in theological language. By the time I finished my first year as a lecturer in the history of Western theology at the University of Zimbabwe in 1996, I was used to seeing men, women, and children dressed in white robes walking past my house into the meadow across the road to pray; I also learned from watching the quiet mood associated with walking toward the sacred sites for prayer. "We are going to the masowe [wilderness]," said one of the young mothers, making sure I did not distract her by holding hands with a little boy of five or six years. Such direct encounters opened my eyes to fieldwork before I came across Ninian Smart's book *The Phenomenon of Religion* (1978), an exploration of empirical ways of studying religion with what can be observed of religion, rather than its claims of truth as primary sources of knowledge.

For the next three years I spent half of my weekends in the National

Archives of Zimbabwe in Harare, looking at reports on Masowe Apostles produced by white settlers, most of them concerned by the political ramifications of the practice of Christianity outdoors instead of in church buildings, speaking in Shona to relate independent ideas about God without the supervision or guidance of European missionaries. It made sense to combine my fieldwork with a more detailed focus on the human conditions in which Masowe Apostles had emerged in the first place. When not looking at archival documents produced by colonial administrators and European missionaries worried about Africans who were turning away from their established churches during the 1930s, I wandered through the city, looking for Masowe Apostles who were going about the business of praying outdoors.

All sorts of open-air places on the margins of cityscapes were filled with reminders of the displacement and marginalization of Zimbabweans from their ancestral land, which turned out to be known as the masowe, meaning a sacred wilderness as far as Masowe Apostles were concerned. The attention paid to the general problem of human suffering and healing in *Wandering a Gendered Wilderness* (Mukonyora 2007, xi–xix) thus began with both a scholarly attempt to face analytical challenges to do with the history of Masowe theology through the study of textual data, and participant observation at prayer meetings held by either members of the same family or coworkers and good friends interested in each other's well-being, rather than the power of the official leaders of prayer groups.

Tempting though it was to ignore the origins of the Masowe Apostles and start describing the obvious place of emotions in their ritual behavior and related theological language, it seemed wrong to overlook the pivotal figure, the prophet Johane Masowe. This prophet is the author of the oral tradition of Christianity that attracts its African audience to dramatize knowledge about God under discussion. Against the background of difficult human conditions caused by oppression, the founder of the Masowe Apostles Church applied to his personal experiences of suffering in the British colonial world of the 1930s what he had learned from popular stories used by missionaries to draw attention to God as a loving supreme being who liberated the people of Israel in the Exodus, and through Jesus offered salvation to the victims of Greco-Roman colonial conquest. What Johane Masowe learned from European missionaries he adapted to a modern world in which his experiences of British colonialism caused enough sadness, fear, and anger to lead to the dramatization of a lived understanding of ritualized attempts of controlling angst (Ticineto and Halley 2007, 1–33).

Briefly, this response to the invitation to write on Masowe Apostles in a book focused on "affective trajectories" that draws attention to a world of affects and emotions would have been extremely difficult to follow through without having had the previous opportunity to do fieldwork in parts of the city of Harare frequented by men, women, and children whose sole purpose for going to the masowe was to worship God, or Mwari in Shona, their mother tongue, in the practice of an oral tradition of Christianity.

First, the Shona language that is used to communicate ideas about the biblical God in the practice of Christianity is analyzed against the background of metaphorical speech about Mwari as a supreme being with powerful feelings and emotions to do with his intimate relationship with the living in a world filled with sadness and "no place to go." As Schmidt put it, "Unequal exchange between African commodity producers and industrialized countries is a legacy of the colonial era that has contributed to the deep impoverishment of African populations" (2013, 9). Second, toward the end of this chapter, I will attempt to explain the "affective turn," not so much in descriptions of it but in relation to the ritual behavior used to reduce sadness, fear, and anger to things caused by Satan. I will do so by describing three examples of ritual behavior that I observed during fieldwork on the margins of the cityscapes of Harare. The case studies summarized here are important not only because this book is concerned with "affective trajectories" but also because the examined cases draw attention to the goals of faith against the background of a dread of Satan. Venturing into the wilderness to investigate religion made it necessary to treat empirical methods of inquiry as part and parcel of the study of Christianity in Africa. Writing about Christianity as it is practiced alone presents an interesting challenge for anyone trying to make sense of traditional Christian ideas about God, Christ, and the Holy Spirit from a Western theological perspective. Let us begin by considering God-Mwari and the Voice that is said to create certain emotions, which will help us to understand Masowe Apostles.

MWARI AND THE HOLY SPIRIT OF THE CITYSCAPES

According to Daneel (1970a, 23), the high god Mwari of the Shona was a territorial spirit of the ruling lineage of the Shona people, the Rozvi, when the British seized the country of Zimbabwe. The violent means of conquest triggered an immediate emotional response to the seizing of African ancestral land, followed by the building of a new landscape. Since Shona people believed that Mwari spoke directly to the living not only in the thunder and the wind but as a voice heard in places "approached by the living with sacrifice and supplication" (Ranger 1967, 22), it is easy to see why the margins of the city became significant among Masowe Apostles. Ranger states that the Shona people had reacted to European domination by invoking Mwari as a territorial spirit in whose name the Shona and Ndebele planned a revolt in Southern Rhodesia in 1896–1897 (17–18). Whether one has in mind the Shona concept of God as creator, with the power to control human beings, or the view of him as the Mother, the source of planetary life (Aschwanden 1989, 26–31), these basic facts about Mwari and the living can be said to explain some of the emotions and feelings about the biblical God whose voice Masowe Apostles associate with the promise of salvation for *vanhu vatema* (black people) or Africans.

The Christian God is thus viewed by Masowe Apostles as Mwari, a supreme being revealed through sentient beings, among whom are human beings who respond to messages of divine love by worshipping God and taking the time to listen to Izwi, meaning the Voice of God or the Holy Spirit. Key to the development of a theology of liberation in which the special Voice of God heard in the wilderness touches the human heart is rather like the Paraclete (Greek: παράκλητος; Latin: Paracletus). The latter is an advocate or helper, which is just another way of describing the emotional function of the Holy Spirit, who is equated with the Voice of God in Masowe teaching. God is capable of speaking to the human conscience in a way that helps believers develop not only an emotional capacity for love and a concern for virtue but also the courage to face *kufa*, the Shona term for all kinds of human suffering and death, which fits in with the social upheavals mentioned earlier and explains the emotional response of Mwari, which is arguably an affective trajectory of hope in salvation.

The defeat of negative emotions of hate, anguish, and the fear of kufa (death) furthers our understanding of the places chosen to worship God on the margins of the landscape where reminders of the social causes of kufa are easy to relate to in terms of their historic roots in colonialism (Werbner 1985, 251–252). It is time to end this discussion aimed at highlighting the religious root causes of the development of a theology that brings together the image of a biblical Elohim and Shona traditional ideas of God as the source of life with a Voice to be heard, and a presence to be felt on earth. Mwari's Voice, or Izwi, seems to be directed at the conscience, so that one's emotions become part and parcel of God-Talk among Masowe Apostles.

As Aschwanden observed, Mwari is more than an ecological deity who responds to human emotions: the almighty has a female dimension that is the same as Mother Earth, shaped like a fertile Womb of Earth. This image is used to further our understanding of the observable fact about the biological origins of life and need for humans to procreate, nurture life, and promote good on earth (Aschwanden 1989, 11–45).

As mentioned previously, Masowe Apostles worship close to the elements of nature, which is a way of invoking the healing power of the ecological deity Mwari. The apostles are thus often seen dressed in white robes to draw attention to the masowe (wilderness). Revelation 6:11 reads, "Then they were each given a white robe and told to rest a little longer, until the number of their fellow servants and their brothers should be complete, who were to be killed" (English Standard Version). So, anyone looking for Masowe Apostles will find them situated in places they call masowe (wilderness). By dressing in white robes, praying barefoot, and sitting, standing, and kneeling on dirt and facing east to listen to Mwari's Voice, they turn their surroundings for prayer into a threshold from which to expect divine intervention, a way of consoling affective trajectories blamed on sin behind which is Satan.

NAMING AFFECTIVE TRAJECTORIES

In the Shona background culture of the Masowe Apostles, names may be used to describe either deep satisfaction or anguish. For example, the name *Tafadzwa* suggests someone's feeling of joy. *Rutendo* expresses gratitude. *Tapera*, on the other hand, means someone is afraid of being destroyed, while *Muchazviona* suggests a deep longing for revenge (Mukonyora 2007, 77–89). As a young man, the prophet Johane was among the thousands of Zimbabwean youths who ran away from the difficult human conditions created by colonial conquest. His experiences of displacement, sickness, and fear of death are thus foundational to the establishment of his legacy of a Christian faith practiced on the margins of society. Johane Masowe traveled from Gandanzara (the Land of Hunger) to different parts of urban Zimbabwe, where he hoped to find jobs during the Great Depression of the 1930s, from Reshape to Harare, Norton, and Bulawayo and across the border to Gaborone, Johannesburg, Durban, Lusaka, and Ndola, where in 1978 he died of a cardiovascular disease (Dillon-Malone 1978, 15). Fears of kufa in a colonial society that was creating permanent victims of oppression were central to the founder's theology of liberation centered as much on naming as on ritual behavior and dramatizing wandering in the wilderness (Mukonyora 1998, 191–192).

Johane Masowe not only suffered from acute headaches, which reminded him of death as that silence to be broken only by the Voice of Mwari, but also was beaten up by the police for preaching with neither a license nor permission to preach outdoors (Mukonyora 1998, 191–207). Moreover, as the term *kufa* covers every negative emotion possible, the emotional attachment to Christ and God the Father will not go away anytime soon. What we have today are "disparate trajectories of identity politics in postcolonial transformations" of colonialism (Werbner 1985, 22). These transformations, says Schmidt, "include wars of terror" (2013, 18).

By going outdoors, Johane Masowe may have been driven by his anguish. He also dramatized a few powerful religious stories about God's Voice and developed a lasting source of knowledge about the consequences of colonialism and responses to it based on sharing expressions of total dependence on God and the work of Christ represented by the Holy Spirit. In this way, Masowe Apostles have a way of turning experiences of marginality, whether psychological, economic, gender-relational, or political, into the establishment of a mood and a motivation of ritual action.

The liberation theology under discussion is thus distinguished by the self-empowerment of the believer, whose experiences become embodied in ritual actions of the hope for salvation among people who are encouraged to feel things and express their emotions. According to Nengomasha, one of his immediate followers, Johane Masowe not only addressed the personal problems of life in a colonial society but also turned the acuteness of his suffering into a hermeneutical tool for attracting fellow Africans to the margins of the cityscapes (National Archives of Zimbabwe, Harare File AOH/4). Thus, we have a perfect example of African Christians who draw our attention to an experiential path to understanding God in the contemporary history of Africa, which starts with naming the affective trajectories of Johane Masowe's charisma. Emotions shaped by ritual experience and articulated by symbolic language therefore become a source of empowerment for those who live at the margins of society. The next section illustrates how symbolic language articulates emotions of marginality, which concern both the economic conditions people in Harare live in, and experiences of social exclusion and isolation in the anonymity of the city with no one to care for them.

The *Standard Shona Dictionary* defines the root word *sowe* as a derivative of the Bantu word *sasa*, meaning "uninhabited fringes." The word *sasa* could be used to describe any uninhabited fringes, barren land, swamps, and/or forests, especially those filled with the most common indigenous trees, called *msasa*. In the book *The Sacred and the Profane*, Mircea Eliade says that the human quest for transcendence leads people to create sacred spaces away from the humdrum of daily life (1959, 25). Eliade also says that "the threshold is the limit, the boundary, the frontier that distinguishes and opposes two worlds so that one world is profane and the other sacred . . . within the sacred precincts the profane world is transcended" (25).

This is interesting because the Masowe Apostles identify their frontier for the Voice of Mwari in places that do not always look like a wilderness removed from the humdrum of life in the city. I carried out my fieldwork next to a golf course just off Second Street north of downtown Harare, behind a popular suburban shopping center with a movie theater and a fancy coffeehouse called the Italian Bakery in Avondale. Most of the time the threshold for prayer is near the highway to avoid the need for too much walking. At the same time, these are real thresholds insofar as there is a limit on uninhabited fringes (sasas) with which to explain their shifting definitions in the context of the Masowe theology of liberation.

Nonetheless, the terms *sasa* and *sowe* still describe uninhabited places where it is possible to find Masowe Apostles (by the river, at the edge of fields, among bushes near the well, up or down the hill), some of them ancestral and/or territorial spirits. In fact, the word *masowe* has a modern meaning behind the writing of this chapter, referring to liminal spaces called *masowe*, most of them found at the margins of the cityscapes of Africa. Under the circumstances, it makes sense to conclude that there are many trajectories of the Holy Spirit insofar as our knowledge of them comes from meeting Masowe Apostles on their own terms, in places almost as diverse as the feeling and emotions that attract people to worship Mwari in the open air (Mukonyora 2007). My own favorite image is just behind a garage, a space that the city council had transformed into an open-air market by the end of 1998. Perhaps the power that Mwari must commune with believers is rather like the rays of the sun, capable of touching any believer who reaches out to God by going out to pray, if people agree.

In the context of the rise of a Masowe Apostles liberation theology, emotions that correspond with the hope for salvation are needed to adapt the self to conversion as what enables one to counteract the feelings of displacement with those of belonging to a sacred realm where justice, peace, and love are expected to prevail (Barrett 1968, 156). The dynamic interplay between reality and imagination becomes obvious in Masowe Apostles' spiritual language, for instance, in how they associate God with the image of people who go out to pray in the wilderness (Werbner 1985). As far as Madzimai (Mamma) Anna and her family and close friends, described later, were concerned, God-Mwari exists and becomes known through echoes of the Izwi, the human conscience, and should therefore be known emotionally first. For anyone *ari kufa* (suffering or dying) of hunger or disease (which in this context includes HIV/AIDS), the appropriate spiritual help the believer can hope for is existential. Hence, the role of deep emotions was central from the start in the development of Masowe theology. By dressing for the sacred wilderness in white robes, removing shoes in places, agreeing to sit for prayers on dirt and facing either east or west, almost as if the universe is one big dictionary of symbols of the divine, Masowe Apostles create room for each other to express the hope that negative experiences of reality will end because of the sacrificial suffering of Christ, with the margins of the sacred wilderness partially left to the imagination.

Mwari is expected to send the Holy Spirit as a voice that individuals can hear when they sit on the ground and face east to listen. The sense of touch is invoked by the laying on of hands during healing ceremonies so that the elements of nature such as the sun, dirt, and wind become part and parcel of the setting in which emotions about God are expressed. All this fits in with past ways of portraying Mwari as a deity concerned with life on earth. Like the rays of the sun, Mwari touches the hearts and minds of humans who seek him in the masowe, or urban wilderness. Although the author of the *Standard Shona Dictionary* (1984), the Catholic priest Father Hannan, is correct to mention "prayer and fasting," there is more to be said about ritual behavior and theological language from the fringes of cityscapes. There is a strong connection between places and the subjectively felt power of rituals and words that fosters a sense of belonging and of connectedness between God, health, and participants of the prayer.

Briefly, the term *masowe* does more than describe a variety of things, starting with the environment used for prayers for healing: it is also on the fringes of cityscapes, masowe, where one finds the Africans who call each other Masowe Apostles. The conclusion that they are Christians has a lot to do with patterns of ritual behavior that are tied to belief in God as the creator as he who gives hope to people living with death, among other misfortunes. In short, God as the omnipotent, omniscient, omnipresent deity over all of creation has been translated into an African concept of God as Mwari, the ecological deity who is appropriate to worship in places that are in many ways direct reminders of evil as that which destroys life on earth.

It is fair to end this discussion by pointing out that Masowe Apostles gained popularity because the term *masowe*, or wilderness, has a variable meaning. It not only denotes being in physical space in the wild but also is associated with a sense of being touched by God's word; it is a promise of healing, belonging, and wholeness that is instilled through rituals endorsing the earth. Rather like the name Johane Masowe, this term points to a religious idiom related to the name of the founder, his church, the margins of the cityscapes, and most of all human emotions that need expression in societies riddled with problems of kufa. Masowe Apostles are biblical theologians in their own right insofar as the Shona language used for prayer corresponds to problems of displacement caused by social changes paralleled with the concerted effort to overcome them. As Werbner (1985) puts it, a certain mixing of images takes place so that the masowe become a people of the wilderness looking for a promised land like those in the Bible, only their "argument of images" of the wilderness is also very African.

Emotions are thus key to this study's characterizations of affective trajectories (see the introduction to this volume), which are ways of making the urban wilderness into a symbolic speech whose aura of factuality corresponds to anger, grief, and other painful emotions that the Holy Spirit, or Voice of Mwari, addresses at prayer. Prayer comes up many times in this chapter because it is the formal way of mapping the perceived predicaments and contradictions having to do with life on earth. Put in terms of the Shona language about the all-powerful Mwari, the source of life is the Father of all sentient beings. It matters that his voice is heard in response to everything said about the affective trajectories and corresponding emotions that characterize life in the sacred wilderness.

THE QUEST FOR DIVINE LOVE, PEACE, AND HARMONY:
A COMMUNITY ON THE MARGINS OF SOCIETY

In this section, it is important to share something more about the special effort made to employ phenomenology in the study of Christianity, and at least demonstrate some of the emotions evoked by dressing in white robes and going out to pray. It did not make sense to pry into the Apostles' personal affairs, so in July 1997 I shifted my focus to a sowe three miles away, to a small field behind Avondale Shopping Center. There I met a group of sixteen white-robed Christians who opened my eyes to the importance of developing good relationships between men, women, and children sharing the same space, wearing similar white robes with shoes carefully arranged to mark the boundary of the threshold for prayer, and developing a discourse about God, love, mutual respect among the believers, and shared hopes for healing.

Once I arrived dressed in a light blue dress to make sure I was not mistaken for a member of the church, I too removed my shoes and sat next to a woman elder, who introduced me to her daughter and three of her grandchildren playing in the meadow before the prayers for healing began. During prayers, the children sat next to their mothers, as everyone was now concerned about the direct efficacy of prayer. I spent every other Saturday afternoon observing up to eight women with their four children between the ages of four and six years. One of the women brought her sick husband and let him sit next to the only men present—three men already known to the young preacher who was in his midtwenties. If not part of the same extended family, this group of Masowe Apostles were close friends employed in the same job market as domestic workers. Whatever other difficult emotions influenced them, the most striking factors here were the loving relationships that the Voice of Mwari made apparent. Even the sick husband looked peaceful as he listened to a sermon about Mwari having love for all his children, young and old being guaranteed an equal status according to the Voice. In fact, the reason for insisting on men sitting separately from women and children resonated with the Shona custom, where it was and still is considered normal for people to sit in this gendered fashion in huts as the special place where the family unites to eat, entertain, and educate one another.

The women and their children were often seen walking down Arundel School Road, always deep in conversation about God, his revelation, and the true nature of the gifts of the Holy Spirit. On one occasion, a mother of two became upset about a wandering preacher who was trying out his skills and failing miserably to show humility before God when addressing fellow believers. "He knows nothing about the Holy Spirit," she complained, "because there is no love in his voice. This means there is no God in his heart. He should go." Speaking in Shona, she expressed an opinion held by women members of the wilderness church. The Holy Spirit, women often insist, is a blessing or gift from God and must not be treated as the reason to abuse power in the church: "One knows the work of the Holy Spirit because its 'power' comes with a generosity of heart, kindness, love, and humility before God."

Madzibaba (brother) Petros, who was the subject of the discussion, was said to lack certain virtues, yet he pretended to have the power to see into the minds of believers. I could not tell quite what Petros had pretended to see that my informer found so unsettling. It was only clear that Petros's behavior had provoked this discourse on the meaning of Christianity. Two of the six women went on to accuse Madzibaba Petros of being obsessed with the power to control others in the name of the Holy Spirit. They did not accuse their leader of being possessed by evil spirits, as one would expect of talk about Satan in popular culture. It was only that the way in which Madzibaba Petros delivered the news about Mweya Mutsvene (the Holy Spirit in the Shona Bible) made him sound too sure of himself. The following week, Madzibaba Petros was gone, most likely back to a neighboring group of Masowe Apostles where he had no chance to exercise authority as a preacher. Harare is filled with large groups of Masowe Apostles who prefer to concentrate the power of the Voice of Mwari on one person who claims to know the proper *mirao*, or the norms of faith.

The fifth time I decided to follow the groups of women walking past my neighborhood in Mount Pleasant to the Avondale Shopping Center almost a mile down a small path meandering across a dry meadow, I realized that the women had an intimate knowledge of each other's problems and cared for each other enough to share food and protect one another's children. The most striking part of this behavior when it comes to the subject of emotions of peace and harmony was the ritual meaning given to the affective trajectory of walking to the sacred wilderness. It was almost as if this was a time to educate each other about the horizontal relationships that follow from understanding Mwari as the origin of the Izwi, and Christ as a human symbol remembered because of his compassionate sacrifice made from love for the poor and sick. I did not have to insult my new friends by asking them about the mystery of the doctrine of the Trinity. Their language about Mwari went hand in hand with ritual activities that included pointing to nature as evidence of the existence of an omnipotent, omniscient, and omnipresent God of love and source of life on earth. Elaborate God-Talk about the Trinity would have been impossible to express in Shona.

HEADING AND THE SACREDNESS OF SPACE

The second case study aims at highlighting the significance of all that effort made to explain Shona terms that tell us something about Masowe theology. It also illustrates the importance of the landscape as a site of affective trajectories, and of how Masowe Apostles come to usurp the outskirts of the city as space for healing bodies and minds through the Voice of God giving rise to a diversity of emotions. I focus on one of the large groups of Masowe Apostles, the Johane Masowe Apostles Church, to remind us of the normative role of the emotions of the founder, whose personal journey was discussed earlier. It was impossible to walk to this sowe, located all the way across the city on the outskirts of a much less affluent neighborhood, the African township of Marimba. Besides attracting thousands of Masowe Apostles who take the trouble to tell stories of the founder figure's personal experience of izwi raMwari, the "Voice of God," it was much more exciting to start by looking at the surroundings.

After taking a bus to the nearest stop in Mufakose Township, I walked across a railway to a piece of land surrounded by a few masa trees left by people who had cut down some of the original trees to supplement their incomes by growing food crops like corn, sweet potatoes, and pumpkins. Left to create a small woodland were enough msasa trees to provide shade for a crowd of nearly two hundred men, women, and children, who came dressed in the same white uniform as other Masowe Apostles and used their shoes to signify the liminal. It was early one afternoon during the month of August 1998 when I arrived as a participant observer, once more interested only in learning as much as possible about the believers' moods and motivations for calling upon the Voice of God.

The traditional connection between words like *sasa* with *sowe* came to mind when I glanced at factory furnaces releasing smoke at one side of the sacred wilderness, and heard the sudden noise made by a passing goods train on the other side. I had an emotional reaction to sitting down with so much noise and black smoke fifty yards away from a sacred wilderness but then remembered that I was, in fact, traversing the fringes of the cityscapes, as was appropriate for prayer as far as these Johane Masowe Apostles were concerned. They brought under one roof numerous small groups of believers with strong bonds enforced by either working together or having family ties. The area of Marimba is also perceived as a sacred wilderness remembered as the place visited by Johane Masowe while he was fasting for forty days.

This religious experience is mentioned here, first, because the knowledge that Jesus also went to the urban wilderness of the city of Jerusalem to pray makes the sacred wilderness attractive to Christians of a certain type, by which I mean Masowe Apostles who practice fasting as a way of clearing the body and mind of negative emotions associated with sin.

On another deeply emotional level, wandering into this crowded sowe in August 1998, I found myself dealing with a community led by preachers using a location for prayer to build upon the memory of the suffering and death of the founder figure, Johane Masowe. For Johane Masowe is reported to have been on Marimba Hill when he fasted and then, feeling acute pain, lay unconscious, "as if dead," when he heard God's Voice. God said, "Do you know why you have been ill so long? You have been ill because of sins which you have committed against me on earth since the day you were born." After this, the founder was anointed John the Baptist, recovered from his near-death experience, and began to roam the outskirts of the city of Harare, looking for places to preach and heal the sick (Dillon-Malone 1978, 144). The decision to say something about the founder of the Masowe Apostles serves its own purpose when it comes to groups of Masowe Apostles whose high regard for the founder has led to the extraordinary annual ritual attended by thousands of his followers. The Johane Masowe Apostles, some from as far away as Nairobi, Kenya, visit the rock on which Johane was buried in Gandanzara to perform rituals that can trigger strong emotions about death, as well as hope for the return of Christ to the wilderness (Mukonyora 2006, 66).

Again, central to this trajectory of faith is the Paraclete supplicating for the vanquished as the most sought-after affective trajectory of the Masowe Apostles. In this instance, the sowe visitors have a high regard for their "John the Baptist" in surroundings as grim as the land between the factories releasing toxic dust and a bad smell, the railway, the weeds, the crops, and the msasa trees nearby, which, taken together, form a typical African township built during the colonial period. With the township now bursting at the seams with people who would rather suffer as members of the growing urban Shona society than a rural one, it was hard to compare the emotions experienced in Marimba with those of the Masowe Apostles who worked as domestic servants for some of the richest members of Zimbabwean society in the suburbs to the north of the city of Harare. Spending hours praying in the Marimba township, I could relate to the Masowe theology of liberation, not so much because I felt good about the defeat of the forces of evil through

Mwari's Voice but because I was surrounded by too many reminders of human suffering brought about by urbanization, individualism, poverty, overcrowding, and the spread of diseases such as HIV/AIDS. The harsh reality of kufa became the overwhelming emotion with which to reflect on the threshold of prayer among Masowe Apostles, depending on where they go.

CONCLUSION

This chapter has employed an anthropological method of inquiry to study both small groups of Masowe Apostles and big crowds. Worshipping on the fringes of different parts of the landscape surrounding Harare and other cities found in Zimbabwe and across its borders in Botswana, South Africa, Zambia, Malawi, and all the way to Nairobi, Kenya, are communities waiting for scholars to examine them with the same questions as those raised by the scholars who have contributed to this book (see the introduction to this volume; Mukonyora 2006, 59–80). Millions of Africa's poor are finding spiritual fulfillment in dressing in white robes and going to pray in the urban wilderness because of what Werbner (1985) identifies as postcolonial encounters with social changes that continue to transform identities, rather than reduce the problems of life on the margins of the global village.

In the limited space available, I hope I have successfully shown how the urban wilderness acts as both a space of affective trajectories and a symbolic universe from which emerges a way of turning ritual behavior into an emotional language concerned with reducing the damaging effects of the difficult human conditions of injustice, sickness, and general misfortunes that also give a meaning and purpose to the God of the wilderness. Earlier, Madzimai Sarah was described as wandering the outskirts of Harare feeling the loss of her husband, a victim of the HIV/AIDS pandemic. She is a good example of a Masowe Apostle living with the hope that God's love can be felt, just as his healing Voice can be heard during prayer. I realized it was not the preachers alone who established an official platform to express their emotions, sometimes by yelling at women about sex and witchcraft as deadly sins. Throughout this inquiry, Masowe Apostles identified each other as emotional beings who needed to talk to one another about the challenges facing them in their day-to-day lives, and, by laying on hands at healing ceremonies, stimulating each other with proclamations of faith, singing and acting as equals. Preaching, as well as singing and moments for silent prayer, were all ways of communing with God-Mwari using a combination of Shona words, biblical imagery, and symbolic actions. All these

FIGURE 2.2 Revelation 3:8. "Wear white garments so that you may clothe yourself, and that the shame of your nakedness will not be revealed." Photo reprinted by permission of the National Archives of Zimbabwe.

are central to this chapter, where theology faces a rather special analytical challenge rooted in social anthropology.

Finally, as this chapter has explored the term "affect" as associated with either religious emotions relating to experiences of displacement, or positive ones linked to ritual behavior and reaching out to God on the margins of the urban landscape, it is fair to end on a positive note. For a theologian interested in the critical analysis of modern and postmodern inquiries about God in urban Africa, it has been possible to reflect on a unique African Christian way of handling human suffering in the city of Harare in Zimbabwe. Some readers might wonder why social history and anthropology are as important as the main theological idea of a God whose Voice has a healing effect on the believer in Masowe theology. In this global society, which is increasingly being disturbed by social upheavals, the destruction of the environment, and human suffering, it seems important to recognize the need for more case studies where knowledge of God corresponds to problems specific to the believers concerned. In this case, being asked to talk about affective trajectories is a welcome challenge, reminding me of a way of understanding God corresponding to the deep emotions and feelings of displacement. As shown here, theologians can learn a great deal from other disciplines, especially when it comes to Christianity in the global South (Jenkins 2011, 73–100). As Jenkins has noted, Christianity is at its most vibrant in countries found in sub-Sahara Africa, like Zimbabwe.

3 THE SITES OF DIVINE ENCOUNTER AFFECTIVE RELIGIOUS SPACES AND SENSATIONAL PRACTICES IN CHRIST EMBASSY AND NASFAT IN THE CITY OF ABUJA

MURTALA IBRAHIM

> Being in the church environment, I don't feel like going home. I feel that the church environment is my real home. If your eye is open to spiritual things, you will not want to go home. You will want to stay in the church because the Bible says the church is the pillar of truth. So you will want to protect and guard yourself because outside the church is darkness and church is the light. Church is the center of my religious life, it is where I pray and meet my God.

This remark was made by one of my Pentecostal interlocutors in Abuja, a thirty-three-year-old male civil servant who has been a member of Christ Embassy, a Pentecostal church, since 2007.[1] The experiences he reported were not exclusive to Pentecostals in the city, however, but were shared by my Muslim interlocutors too. The sensation of feeling attached to their respective places of worship was commonly expressed by both Christian and Muslim men and women in Abuja. As suggested by the church member's statement, this sensation is tied to the fact that places of worship are sites where people sense an emotional connection with the divine. Thus, a comparative-analytical perspective is required to understand how members of different religious groups experience (and shape) the city of Abuja by developing an affective attachment to particular religious places and practices.

Abuja is experiencing a rapid expansion of religious structures, which are spreading throughout the city, some with exquisite designs that resemble modern theater buildings rather than places of worship. The building of new places of worship in the city is being spearheaded by Pentecostals (Marshall 2009), Islamic reformists (Loimeier 1997), and piety movements. This chapter argues that these places of worship are affective structures insofar as they constitute settings of sensational religious practices and orient their members within the wider social, economic, and emotional context of the city. In an attempt to understand how sensational practices produce affective spaces, I adopt the praxeological perspective propounded by Andreas Reckwitz, which offers a framework for analyzing emotions and affects and simultaneously pays attention to artifacts and material space. Reckwitz argues that "every complex social practice—as far as it is always spatialising and necessarily contains perceptive-affective relations—implies a form of affective space. In modern societies, this spatialising often results in built, architectural spaces that are made for and correspond with specific practices" (2012, 254).

Since affect and emotion are central analytical concepts in this chapter, I have adopted the definitions of these terms proposed by Brian Massumi and Eric Shouse. Massumi describes affect as "prepersonal intensity corresponding to the passage from one experiential state of the body to another and implying an augmentation or diminution in that body's capacity to act" (1987, xvi). In his reading of Massumi, Shouse (2005, 1) states that an affect is a nonconscious experience of intensity, a moment of unformed and unstructured potential. Affect cannot be fully realized in language because it is always prior to and/or outside of consciousness. According to Shouse, "Emotion is the projection/display of a feeling. In another sense emotion is an expression of an internal state and other times it is contrived in order to fulfill social expectations" (1). In the introduction to this book, the volume editors refer to a distinction between affect and emotion in the literature, which defines "'affect' as a form of preconscious experience that establishes a largely unstructured and embodied relationship between individuals and the social and material world, on the one hand, and 'emotion' as the culturally and socially mediated articulation of this experience, on the other." This chapter suggests that sensational religious practices in Christ Embassy and NASFAT (the designation NASFAT is the acronym of the Arabic phrase *Nasrul-Lahi-Fathi*, which translates as "Allah's help is triumphant") orchestrate bodily experiences of affect, which members recognized as a "divine touch" or the "presence of God." This bodily experience of divine presence is always followed by the outpouring of emotion and the cognitive interpretation of the experience within the framework of the respective religious tradition.

This chapter studies sensational prayer practices such as prayers of adoration and glossolalia, and *zikr* (repetitive invocation of God's name) in Christ Embassy and NASFAT settings that generate a palpable experience of the divine presence. It can be argued that the affects generated in sensational religious practices leave traces on places of worship and transform them into affective spaces. The chapter will also examine religious spaces as sites of affective religious participation that involve fellowship activities with a strong sense of communal bonding. The affective religious structures in the city reinforce the dreamlike atmosphere of the Abuja cityscape that enchants the imagination of the city's inhabitants.

DOING RESEARCH ON CHRISTIAN AND MUSLIM "AFFECTIVE SPACES" IN ABUJA

Regarding my own positionality, I hail from the central Nigerian city of Jos, from ethnic Hausa Muslim parents with roots in the northern city of Kano. Most of the members of NASFAT (see Adetona 2002) are Yoruba Muslims from southern Nigeria, who, in their perceptions and practices of Islam, differ from their northern Muslim counterparts. Hausa and Yoruba Muslims accuse each other of syncretism and a lack of authenticity in their Islamic practices. Most members of Christ Embassy in turn regard all Hausa people as conservative Muslims. As a result, many interlocutors expressed surprise that a Muslim man was doing research among Christians. As a result of this ethnic-cum-religious difference, I was perceived as a stranger in both Christ Embassy and NASFAT and also felt as such.

Christ Embassy, which is also called "Believers' Loveworld," is one of the most active and influential of the Pentecostal churches in Nigeria that are growing rapidly in the country's urban centers. The famous charismatic pastor Chris Oyakhilome founded the congregation in 1981 as a campus fellowship at the University of Benin, Benin City. Akukwe (2012, 1) reports that Christ Embassy has a regular membership of more than three million in Nigeria alone and more than ten million people who belong to other denominations, but who regard Pastor Chris as their "alternative pastor." In Nigeria, many people refer to Christ Embassy as Oyakhilome's church.

Ukah writes about the founders of newer Pentecostal churches, including

Pastor Chris, as a "bank of grace, repository of charismata, and a special bridge between his followers and God. He controls both charisma and cash; his word is law" (2007, 15). For this reason, one cannot do research on any branch of Christ Embassy without referring to Pastor Chris. NASFAT started as a prayer group in Lagos in 1995, but it quickly transformed itself into a powerful religious organization with numerous spiritual and social programs. NASFAT is the main Islamic group to have introduced Sunday worship services that are very similar to Pentecostal services (Soares 2009).

Both Christ Embassy and NASFAT are influential religious movements in Abuja, with large memberships and numerous places of worship. According to Soares (2009), NASFAT's founders launched an Islamic organization that has become dynamic, influential, and perhaps one of the largest in contemporary Nigeria. NASFAT is nonsectarian and nonpolitical, but over time the movement has focused on questions of piety and ethics and has become deeply engrossed in social and economic activities. In this chapter, I will first discuss the idea of Abuja as a city of dreams that has been shaped by, among other things, the growing presence of a large number of affective spaces belonging to diverse religious groups. I will then examine sensational prayers in Christ Embassy and NASFAT that trigger affective and emotional states and experiences through their respective practices and spatial structures. Furthermore, the chapter will explore the communal participation and small fellowships that engender a sense of conviviality and belonging among both groups.

ABUJA AS THE CITY OF DREAMS

Abuja, the Federal Capital Territory, is the capital of Nigeria and is located in the center of the country. It is a planned city, built mainly in the 1980s, and officially became Nigeria's capital in 1991. At the time of the 2006 census, the city of Abuja had a population of 776,298, making it one of the ten most populous cities in Nigeria. The unofficial metropolitan area of Abuja has a population of well over 3 million and is the fourth-largest urban area in Nigeria (Demographia 2015). Abuja is a microcosm of Nigeria in the sense that ethnoreligiously diverse groups coexist in the city and that both Christianity and Islam are highly visible in the cityscape. Since the middle of the 1990s, Abuja has grown exponentially, with new buildings rising and gradually changing the landscape into a megalopolis. Construction cranes have become part of the structures of the city. The roads have been widened, and in some places ten lanes have been constructed to accommodate the ever-growing amounts of traffic. Several flyover bridges have been built to ameliorate the traffic congestion.

The passing luxury cars further adorn the streets that are lined with new structures of steel and glass. The buildings of government ministries and other institutions pervade the city center. Some of the buildings in the city are intended to showcase the prestige and power of the state. One such building, which houses the Ministry of Defense, was designed in the form of a gigantic naval ship. It is in this vein that Bekker and Therborn write, "The nation-state projects its power through the urban landscape and spatial layout of the capital city. This power is manifested in the capital's architecture, in its public monuments and the names of its streets and public spaces" (2012, 1). According to Adebanwi, in many countries of the world, "capital cities are supposed to make statements. They often represent the best face of their countries, in both symbolic and concrete terms" (2012, 2). This is precisely the case with Abuja, where the presence of the state manifests itself in the spatial configuration of the city.

Residents of and visitors to Abuja are often stunned by the radically new city plan, with its aesthetically designed architecture. This experience invokes dreamlike, phantasmagoric imageries of the city that induce specific affective sensations. According to Pile, Walter Benjamin uses the term "phantasmagoria to suggest that many surface appearances of the city gave it a dream-like or ghost-like quality" (2005, 20). Pile further affirms that "the feel of the big city was different and this was visible in its street life. Cities were different, moreover, because they were constantly throwing people into contact with new experiences, new situations and new people" (17). One of my Christian interlocutors, who worked with a satellite dish installation company in the city, expressed his view as follows:

> I have lived in Abuja for seven years now, but still I am not able to shake off the powerful appeal I feel toward the aesthetic landscape of the city. The city still shouts back at me. There is a strong appealing force the city has, which I would call Abujaness. This can be likened to a beautiful, seductive lady who uses makeup with expensive cosmetics and charming beauty to seduce people. If you are rich and powerful you can date this lady. If you are poor, you can only dream of having her. (interview, March 2, 2014)

This statement mirrors the imagination of many Nigerians for whom Abuja is only a pleasant and glittering dream: the city is "real" only for the rich and powerful. The statement also highlights an extreme form of spatial exclusion and alienation that defines the city of Abuja. Rabindra Kanungo suggests that "an individual in a state of separation from an object was assumed to experience a certain affect toward the object" (1982, 10). The affect, according to Kanungo, usually involves hostility, aversion, and despair. Those with low incomes, among both government employees and the self-employed, are pushed to the settlements far outside the city and forced to suffer a grueling daily commute into the city due to the exasperating traffic jams. This daily ritual into and out of the city, which gives people a taste of something they cannot possess, generates both desire and anger among the excluded lower classes. One interlocutor stated: "Every time I travel to Abuja, my impression is that I am in a movie. Finding myself in the midst of strange buildings and vehicles, and even some white people passing by, I feel lost in this nonreal movie-like scenery" (interview, March 27, 2014). Another interlocutor said: "Having grown up in a small impoverished city in Plateau State, I felt disoriented in Abuja. The city looks out of place to me, it is not authentic; it is too artificial to me. Even the lifestyle of the people is artificial" (interview, March 25, 2014).

By dissociating Abuja from authenticity and realness, or likening it to a movie scenery, it has come to be labeled a city of dreams, its unique structures prompting wishful thinking and enthralling imagination. As a city built from scratch and still in the process of development, Abuja constantly mesmerizes its inhabitants with new structures and new spatial layouts, hence evoking desires and aspiration. Abuja is an expression of dreams of the future initiated as part of the modernization project conceived by the nation's ruling elites. To many people, living in Abuja implies stepping into a dream of the future that is difficult to realize for the country's population as a whole.

This imaginary of Abuja as a dream city is captured, enhanced, and disseminated by the northern home video movie industry. The centers of the northern film industry are Kano and, on a smaller scale, also Jos and Kaduna. But because these centers lack modern and fanciful infrastructures that abound in Abuja, most film producers begin to shoot their movies in Abuja even though they are mostly based in Kano. The obvious reason to shoot in Abuja and focus on the imposing structures of the city, such as the flyover bridges, multistory glass and steel buildings, elegant sitting rooms, and exquisite gardens, is to entice the imagination and taste of the audience for the modern lifestyle and its refined material culture.

This is precisely what Birgit Meyer (2015) describes in her book on the imaginary of the city in the Ghanaian movie industry. According to Meyer,

Ghanaian filmmakers focus on the most beautiful sides of Accra and block the messy and dilapidated areas of the city. Meyer argues, "These movies may best be regarded as both mirrors of and windows onto a popular imaginary of urban modernity, with its particular material culture, lifestyle, and notions of personhood and belonging" (2015, 84). Similar to Ghanaian movies, northern Nigerian films mediate the city of Abuja and expand its popular imaginary into a modern, neoliberal utopian city of dreams. As Meyer notes, the films become mirrors and windows through which people access the vision of the city as it is reconfigured and represented on the screen through editing, selected shots, and other techniques of film craft.

AFFECTIVE RELIGIOUS SPACES

Diverse religious places of worship have been incorporated into Abuja's dreamlike architecture and spatial layout to create an "affective cityscape." Among the great religious buildings are the Central Mosque and the National Christian Centre, whose impressive structures dominate the center of the city and attract the attention of passersby. Another important mosque in the city is the Fouad Lababidi Mosque in Wuse Zone 4, built by a Lebanese businessman, who handed it over to the Wuse Muslim Community Association in 2003. Another colorful mosque is the Al-Habibiyyah Mosque, which is located at Wuse II IBB Way.

The major Pentecostal churches in Abuja established branches in different parts of the city, including its most expensive areas. The Mountain of Fire and Miracles Abuja headquarters is a massive, conspicuous two-story rectangular structure located in a business district along Jabi Road. The ash-colored marbles that cover the building make it sparkle in the sunlight. This building, like most of the other Pentecostal churches in the city, such as Lord Chosen, Dunamis, and Redeem, breaks with traditional church architecture and experiments with varieties of modern design.

Many religious organizations nowadays are engaged in building megastructures in Abuja and its surroundings. Some Pentecostal churches and Muslim organizations have established enormous religious campuses along the Masaka-Abuja highway. Living Faith has acquired huge areas of land in Masaka near the highway, where it has built a gigantic church, a university, and a massive estate called Goshen City. Passersby are greeted by a large billboard on which is written "Welcome to Goshen City." The Redeemed Christian Church of God has bought another large stretch of land close to

FIGURE 3.1 National Christian Centre in Abuja. Photo by Murtala Ibrahim.

that of Living Faith, where hundreds of thousands of people gather during the church's annual Holy Ghost Congress.

The Ahmadiyya Muslim Society has followed suit by building an enormous mosque on the same highway. As these massive places of worship emerge, this area is gradually being transformed into what Janson and Akinleye (2014) call a "spiritual superhighway" in their description of a similar situation along the Lagos-Ibadan expressway, which was also transformed into a gigantic religious site. This appears to be a new trend of recently established megachurches and mosques having to go outside the city to build huge structures that can accommodate the crowds that attend their mass religious services (see Dilger 2014 for an analysis of a similar phenomenon in urban Tanzania).

Christ Embassy is one of the dominant churches within the Pentecostal spectrum that exists in the city of Abuja. Instead of building one enormous

FIGURE 3.2 National Mosque in Abuja. Photo by Murtala Ibrahim.

church that can accommodate tens of thousands, as in the case of its head-quarters in Lagos, Christ Embassy built numerous churches in different parts of the capital city. The central church, which serves as the church's regional headquarters, is located at Durumi, Area One. It is a huge, impressive structure designed like a modern secular building, able to accommodate up to five thousand people in my estimate. The stage is designed and decorated with small geometric objects like cylindrical forms, pyramids, and polygons coupled with colorful flower arrangements. The stage's main color is blue, combined with other colors, such as gold and white. The entire stage is illuminated by different colors of light.

NASFAT branches in the Federal Capital Territory are located in Karu, Nyanya, Dutsen Alhaji, Kubwa, Gwagwalada, and Utako. The Utako mosque is NASFAT's zonal headquarters in Abuja and is located in the city center. The building is decorated with white marble inside and out. Numerous rows of white pillars inside the mosque enhance its aesthetic appeal. The mosque consists of three floors, with a gross floor area of 4,272 square meters and a seating capacity for about five thousand worshippers. The ground floor was designed to accommodate the male congregation; the second floor is reserved for women, while the top floor is the conference hall, which can accommodate fifteen hundred people.

As places of worship and retreat, religious buildings offer a spiritual experience to the wider community, being a place where the clamor of urban life can melt away in a space designed to be used collectively and individually for an encounter with the divine. Nevertheless, many of the religious buildings in the city of Abuja serve simultaneously as public spaces for the overall life of the community. Religious buildings in Abuja highlight the multiple ways in which people connect with and gather in public, ultimately showing how communities collectively share experiences and emotions. One of my Christian interlocutors put this as follows:

> I feel God is there. I feel God's presence that makes my mind to see anything. Whenever I visit my church, I open my heart to receive spiritual blessing from God because I feel his presence there and anything can happen. I also feel there is nothing impossible especially when people are in the presence of God. (interview, January 1, 2014)

Another interlocutor, who is a member of NASFAT, stated:

> I regard the mosque as the house of God. In Islam it is more meritorious to pray in the mosque than at home. Even though God is everywhere, his presence is more accessible in the mosque than other places. Therefore, the mosque is a sacred ground that is permeated with God's presence. Mosques give me a sense of peace and security. Even when I travel to strange and unfamiliar places, when I enter the mosque I feel secure. I feel I am in a safer hand because I feel closer to God than at any place. (interview, January 17, 2014)

These two quotations highlight the affective perceptions people have toward places of worship. Praxeological approaches do not see space as the sole producer of affect. Reckwitz argues that "affects only form when a space is practically appropriated by its users, which always activates these users' implicit cultural schemes and routines" (2012, 255). People certainly create routine in places of worship in Abuja. Most Pentecostal churches, including Christ Embassy, hold services three times week. Some members go to the church almost every day. NASFAT and groups such as Al-Habibiyya hold special services on Fridays and Sunday apart from daily prayers. Another "trigger" of emotional practices is the particular arrangement of human bodies in places of worship:

> The presence and arrangement of human bodies within particular settings form another significant aspect of affective space: the number of bodies, their being gathered or separate, their being distant from or close to each other. . . . These complex arrangements of space suggest and engender, via their sensual qualities, specific forms of affectivity relating to them, between intimidation and coziness, between conviviality and the sublime. (Reckwitz 2012, 254)

In NASFAT the congregation is required to wear white robes, and often a small cap. The leaders emphasize that white is the official dress code for the service. Thousands of worshippers sit close to each other, chanting and praying in synchronized ways. In addition, the members of the choir wear special uniforms, designed with dramatic color combinations. As Scheer notes, "Other people's bodies are implicated in practice because viewing them induces feeling. These effects are stored in the habitus, which provides socially anchored responses to others" (2012, 211). The arrangement of bodies in uniform dress, engaged in embodied religious performances, generates affective relations among the participants. In both Christ Embassy and NASFAT these practices are recorded with video cameras. In the large churches of Christ Embassy, the service is projected onto a big white screen on top of the stage. Projecting larger-than-life, live images of the stage onto the screens and amplifying the sound with public address systems reinforce the emotional impact of the religious performance.

PRAYERS OF ADORATION:
THE PERFORMANCE OF SACRED EMOTIONS

Prayers and songs of worship play a central role in the services of Christ Embassy and most other Christian churches in the city. The songs are led by the respective church's choir group playing their own musical instruments. Any member of the church who feels he or she has a talent for music and wants to join the choir is welcome to do so. Christ Embassy has about eighty types of songs of worship, and most long-term members know all the songs by heart.

Services in Christ Embassy on Sundays and Wednesdays start with adoration prayer songs that last for about thirty minutes. During the singing, people stand up, raise their hands, and sing with strong displays of affectivity and devotion. Many close their eyes and perform their feelings with their entire bodies. Some songs are accompanied by soft affective music, others by disco music, with people dancing and jubilating in the church. The songs contain praises to God and Jesus and emphasize emotions of love and devotion and the importance of surrendering to them. The lyrics to the song "Awesome God," for instance, are as follows:

> Holy are you, Lord
> All creation call you God
> Worthy is Your name
> We worship Your Majesty
> Awesome God, how great thou art
> You are God, mighty are Your miracles
> We stand in awe of Your holy name
> Lord we bow and worship You

In my interviews with several members of Christ Embassy, most asserted that the songs of worship were the cornerstone of their spirituality, keeping them close to God and sustaining their faith. When they were singing, they felt what the lyrics of the songs said, and this invoked the presence of the Holy Spirit in their bodies. The songs reminded them of the sacrifice Jesus Christ made for humankind and of how fortunate they were to be saved from eternal death by Christ's atonement. One of my interlocutors related: "Whenever we engage in singing the worship songs, I feel the presence of the Holy Spirit. The experience always comes with strong sensation all over my body. The moment I realize that the Holy Spirit is with me, I feel happy because I have assurance that I am a saved soul" (interview, January 11, 2014). This description reveals how affect is felt in the body and eventually broadcast as emotion and "framed discursively" (Bialecki 2015, 97). The discursive framing of emotion in the experience of my interlocutor translates it into the language of salvation (cf. Lutz and Abu-Lughod 1990).

At the NASFAT Sunday services, the group's melodious recitations of the prayer book are the most important prayers of adoration. The 132-page book, which was written by NASFAT chief missioner Alhaji Akingbode, contains prayer verses from the Qur'an, prayers taught by the prophet Muhammad, the ninety-nine sacred names of Allah, and different kinds of *salat*, which are praises and prayers to the Prophet. The book contains Arabic text along with English and Yoruba translations. The most important aspect of Sunday worship is the recitation of the prayer book, which is led by the imam and takes about one hour to finish. The following passage is found in the NASFAT prayer book:

Oh! Lord of heaven and earth, the Lord that provides for those in heaven and earth, the Lord we worship both in heaven and earth. Let us be steadfast in Islam. We cherish the prophets who are protected from all distress. The distress experienced by those who have not come into contact with Islam. We are conscious of living unholy life for fear of not meeting up with the teachings of the Prophet of Islam Muhammad (PBUH). If one does not follow the tenets of Islam, then he has no meaningful life. (54)

The recitation of the prayer book plays a paramount role in the devotional lives of NASFAT's members. They recite it with vigor and intensity, and I noticed that some members knew the entire book by heart. There is an outpouring of devotion during the recitation, and on one occasion during the youth camp the tempo of the recitation was so intense that two young women fainted and had to be taken out of the mosque. Afterward, I asked one of the youth leaders what had happened to the young women, and he said: "It was called *jazabu*, it was the spirit of the zikr or invocation of God that descended on them. Sometimes it happened to me during the recitation; I feel a strange cold permeate my body." This is another example in which affect generated by practices is recognized as a manifestation of the divine. This practice can be seen in the words of Marilyn Gottschall's "sacred sound performance" (2004, 2) because the prayers and the Qur'anic verses are seen as sacred words that have the capacity to transform the internal and external lives of the performer.

Prayers of adoration express affection and praise in the form of melodious recitation in NASFAT, on the one hand, and songs and music in Christ Embassy, on the other. The melody and music enhance the affective and emotional touch of the prayers. Poetic invocation and glorification of God rendered in melody and music with emotional undertones create the sense of a divine presence. It is apparent that music (in Christ Embassy) and melody (in NASFAT) help generate affect during worship. Shouse argues that "music provides perhaps the clearest example of how the intensity of the impingement of sensations on the body can mean more to people than meaning itself" (2005, 1). Many members of the two groups told me about strong emotional experiences they had had during group worship. One of my interlocutors from Christ Embassy said the following about so-called worship songs:

My spirit leaps up, I don't know where I am, and I will just be singing and chanting. This singing in the group raises my spirit high. When you sing a worship song, you know, you feel well satisfied inside knowing that the presence of God has been invoked. Worship songs are ways of saying, "God, do it because we cannot," or "God hear, take all the glory, take the entire honor because you deserve it." Or "God, I thank you because I cannot keep quiet because you have done so much to me. I am calling to give you all the thanks." (interview, March 22, 2014)

One of the members of NASFAT reported the following experiences with the prayer recitations:

> Whenever we start the recitation of the NASFAT prayer book, I feel joy in my life. When we invoke the name of Allah and praise him, I feel his presence all around me. This practice increases fear of God in my heart and keeps me in God's remembrance constantly in my life. Recitation of the prayer also increases love and respect to the messenger of Allah, the prophet Muhammad. (interview, March 28, 2014)

The articulation of devotion, invocation, veneration, and benediction to God through melodious recitation and worship songs can thus be viewed as an emotional practice. Scheer described the concept of emotional practice as follows:

> Access to emotion-as-practice—the bodily act of experience and expression—in historical sources or ethnographic work is achieved through and in connection with other doings and sayings on which emotion-as-practice is dependent and intertwined, such as speaking, gesturing, remembering, manipulating objects, and perceiving sounds, smells and spaces. (2012, 209)

"Doings and sayings" in Christ Embassy and NASFAT include the performance of worship at services, the recitations of the prayer book (NASFAT), and the singing of worship songs (Christ Embassy). These prayers use emotive words to describe God, including the terms "mighty," "glory," "majesty," and "awesome." Many of my interlocutors told me that they "feel" these emotive words and the powerful lyrics of the prayer songs in their bodies when they perform them. They affirmed that they had these experiences as a result of addressing God in a poetic language with strong words coupled with the emotional melody. They feel the power and glory of God as they recite or sing the prayer. The affective states generated in the practices of adoration prayers are reinforced by the presence of and immersion in the group. When observing prayers of adoration in Christ Embassy and NASFAT, it is apparent that emotions are shared between individuals. Thus, during the service some people display intense emotions to the extent of falling to the ground. This display of hyperemotion becomes contagious and affects other members.

Apart from the Sunday service, NASFAT holds *tahajjud* prayers, or night vigils, during the night of every first and third Friday of the month for purposes of sustaining spiritual rejuvenation. Night vigil prayers start around ten o'clock and continue until dawn. The prayers consist of long performances of *nawafil*, or supererogatory ritual prayer, and varieties of melodious recitation led by the chief imam and his assistants. Another significant spiritual practice in NASFAT is LailatulQadr. According to the teachings of NASFAT, and of Islam in general, LailatulQadr is the night of majesty—a special night on which God "pours out" his blessing, mercy, and forgiveness. It occurs on any day during the last ten days of Ramadan, but it is most likely to take place on the twenty-seventh day of the month. These sensational practices have a notable affinity with the emotionally charged modes of worship in Pentecostalism, which are based on the bodily experience of the Holy Spirit. Meyer describes the place of experience of the Holy Spirit among Pentecostal congregations as follows:

> The all-pervasive presence of the Holy Spirit goes along with the valuation of the body as a vessel for divine power. The Holy Spirit is an experiential presence that invokes feelings. One of the most salient features of Pentecostal/ charismatic churches is their sensational appeal; they often operate via music and powerful oratory, through which born-again Christians are enabled to sense the presence of the Holy Spirit with and in their bodies, wherever they are, and to act on such feelings. (2010, 742)

This kind of sensational bodily experience of the divine presence is very appealing to urban dwellers and plays a vital role in the success of Pentecostalism. During my fieldwork I asked a woman who had moved from her Roman Catholic church to a Pentecostal church why she made this spiritual move. Her response was that "Catholic modes of worship are too stale and formal, but Pentecostal worship is more attracting because it provides immediate experience of divine presence." There is no doubt that this experiential dimension also plays an important role in the remarkable spread of NASFAT in the Nigerian urban environment.

In both Christ Embassy and NASFAT, religious leaders play significant roles in the orchestration of emotion during religious services (see also the chapter by Cazarin and Burchardt in this volume). Pastors of Christ Embassy regularly use suggestions during sensational religious performances with words such as "something is happening here" or "God is present here, therefore increase the tempo of your prayer." They also employ other techniques such as dramatic bodily gestures to express emotion to elicit the same in their congregations. In NASFAT, the imam who leads the recitation of the prayer book elicits certain emotional states by standing up and repeating a particular phrase from the book and moving his hand up and down. The congregants follow suit by standing up, raising their voices, and repeating the prayer phrase with excitement and enthusiasm.

GLOSSOLALIA AND ZIKR:
THE PERFORMANCE OF AESTHETIC SPEECH

Glossolalia is one of the most important and sensational religious performances among Pentecostals in the city of Abuja. In the evenings, between 5:00 and 8:00 PM, the sounds of glossolalia emanate from many of the Pentecostal churches that dominate the cityscape. Glossolalia, also called speaking in tongues, is a religious practice characterized by the fluid utterances of speech-like syllables that do not have any readily understandable meaning, believed to be a divine language unknown to the speaker (Martin 1995). Glossolalia occurs most often as an ecstatic utterance in religious groups, which provokes trancelike experiences during their usual rituals (Koić 2005, 1). Samarin (1972, 82) argues that glossolalia consists of syllables made up of consonants and vowels taken from the speaker's native language or a foreign language known to him, with much repetition, alliteration, and rhyme. However, the syllable stream does not form words, and glossolalia is distinct from other types of language in the sense that it lacks coherence between its segment units and concepts, and also does not communicate meaning.

Pentecostal Christians view glossolalia as a spiritual gift or an unknown language granted by the Holy Spirit to born-again Christians (Dale 1995). In every congregational service in Christ Embassy, there is a special session for speaking in tongues. On many occasions when someone is called onstage to lead the prayers, he or she prays in tongues, and when the pastor's preaching becomes very intense, this person begins to speak in tongues. While other Protestants view glossolalia as a spiritual gift that is given to a select few, Christ Embassy sees it as the natural right of every born-again believer.

The performance of glossolalia involves the prediscursive expression of affective experience. This is because both glossolalic expression and the affect it generates occur "prior to explicit language categorization" (Knudsen and Stage 2014, 19). Glossolalia itself remains at a prediscursive state because it is a sound form that lacks the communicative or intelligible meaning of ordinary language. Weiss writes that "glossolalia is a language where the relation between sound and meaning breaks down; it is the realm of pure sound, the manifestation of language in the realm of its pure materiality" (1989, 118). Members of Christ Embassy believe that the sound of glossolalia is evidence of the presence of the Holy Spirit in the human body. One of my interlocutors remarked, "When I am in tongues, it is my highest being in connection with God. I am talking, but I do not know what I am saying. My body at that time has been taken over by the Holy Spirit. When I finish I feel spiritually reinvigorated" (interview, March 24, 2014). The bodily sensation generated by the performance of glossolalia corresponds to Massumi's (1987, xvi) description of affect as "prepersonal intensity," since the experience is subjected fully to the influence or possession of the Holy Spirit.

Zikr is an Islamic practice of repeating the names of God. In Islam, God has ninety-nine names that can be invoked to facilitate prayer. Each name describes different attributes of God. Zikr can be performed melodiously in a group or privately by individuals in the form of chanting. In NASFAT, both group and individual chanting is accepted and performed. The NAS-FAT prayer book contains different names of Allah that are melodiously chanted during worship services. On some occasions, when the imam was leading the melodious recitation of the NASFAT prayer book and he came to the point where one of the names of Allah was mentioned, he would turn it into zikr and chant it with the congregation melodiously for several minutes before he moved on. For instance, the congregation would keep on repeating the name of Allah melodiously: "AllahAllahAllahAllahAllahAllah."

The chanting usually became highly emotional and was mirrored in bodily gestures. One of my interlocutors stated that "calling the sacred names of Allah [purifies] the heart from spiritual disease and also increases *taqwa*, which is fear of Allah. Moreover, repeating the names of Allah moves one close to him" (interview, March 13, 2014). This statement indicates that zikr is associated with the fear of God and the desire to move closer to him. This probably is the reason that group invocations of the name of God generate affect that is interpreted as religious experience in NASFAT.

Glossolalia and zikr resonate with each other in the sense that they are both forms of aesthetic sacred speech. Zikr, like glossolalia, does not contain a language structure that communicates meaning. Members of NASFAT believe that the spiritual significance of zikr is encapsulated in the sound of the attributes of God. Zikr is not a prayer that demands the satisfaction of needs from God, but rather the sound that is embedded with spiritual potencies to invoke the presence of God. Zikr is an instrument for generating divine presence that is usually experienced as affect in the body. Most of the members of NASFAT with whom I interacted told me that they felt happiness, joy, and a sense of accomplishment when they experienced the presence of God. These experiences corroborated the assertions of the editors of this volume, who in the introduction explain that affect denotes an "intensification of bodily states that makes individuals act or relate to their surroundings in particular ways," which—in the case of my two field sites—correspond to the bodily experiences during the practices of glossolalia and zikr. Emotion in turn is seen by the volume editors as translating affective "experience into the domains of language, cognition, and other modes of representation," which correlate with the interpretation of affective experiences of glossolalia and zikr as highly accomplished experiences of divine presence. These religious performances (prayers of adoration, glossolalia, and zikr) are embodied practices because they heavily engage the human senses and bodily movement. Csordas (1994a) sees embodiment as perceptual experience and as a mode of presence and engagement in the world. Religious performances of Christ Embassy and NASFAT incorporate the three elements of embodiment mentioned by Csordas—perceptual experience, mode of presence, and engagement with the world. Affect is also an embodied experience, as it occurs on the human body. The embodied nature of prayers of adoration in Christ Embassy and NASFAT also makes them spatial practices, since embodiment involves presence and engagement in space.

AFFECTIVE RELIGIOUS PARTICIPATION
AND BELONGING IN THE NEW CITY

The city of Abuja differs from other major urban centers in Nigeria in the sense that it was built recently and has loose social ties and expensive residential properties. As a result, many people decide to leave their families in their hometowns when taking up employment in the city. In the course of my fieldwork, I noticed high religious participation and affective community bonding among all the religious groups I interacted with, including the members of Christ Embassy and NASFAT. Religious involvement and the sense of communal bonding are stronger in Abuja than what I observed, for instance, in Jos, Lagos, Kogi, and other cities that I have visited in recent years.

For example, among all the branches in the country, it is the Abuja branch that adopted a Pentecostal practice of dividing its members into smaller units for fellowship and extrareligious activities. Consequently, it can be argued that there is a link between active religious participation and the need for a sense of belonging in the city of Abuja. Many people claimed to have found personal fulfillment through bonding with their religious brethren and active participation in religious activities. This fulfillment counterbalances their disrupted sense of identity, engendered by the severing of their ties with their immediate family and places of origin. Abubakar Musa, who left his family in his hometown in Gombe State due to the high cost of living in Abuja, stated the following:

> I participate in most religious activities in the mosque, including giving lectures and teaching. I also work in close collaboration with the Abuja Association of Friday Mosques Imams and Islamic organizations in the city. I regard my fellow Muslims in the city as part of my family, and I derive joy and fulfillment in engaging with them in different ways of rendering service to Islam. Apart from delivering lectures on Islam, I also teach working-class women the basic tenets of the Islamic religion. (interview, February 22, 2014)

Many of my interlocutors asserted that religious participation helped them adjust to a new and rapidly changing environment. Lim and Putnam (2010, 914) argue that religious people experience satisfaction in their lives from regularly attending religious services and building social networks within their congregations. However, the effect of within-congregation friendship is contingent on the presence of a strong religious identity. On the issue of belonging and identity, the Social Research Issue Center Report adds that "the notion of belonging, or social identity, is a central aspect of how we define who we are. We consider ourselves to be individuals, but it is our membership in particular groups that is most important in constructing a sense of identity" (2007, 4). Similarly, some scholars recognize that people's sense of identity is attached to a sense of place. Inglis and Donnelly write: "as well as being a social label and cultural indicator . . . , place is also often about a sense of bonding and belonging. It is about feeling at home with others, that they are similar, that there are shared understandings, dispositions and ways of being in the world—what Bourdieu referred to as habitus" (2011, 133).

The sense of belonging to a particular geographic place is an integral part of identity formation. Identification with a place was an important marker of belonging for my interlocutors. When this strong sense of belonging to a place is disturbed by relocation to another place such as Abuja, religious places of worship and communities of believers provide their members with a second home and second family. To many of my interlocutors, the new communal sense of belonging and bonding has forged affective notions of emplacement in the city. As confirmed by my interlocutors' extensive engagement in communal religious practices, such involvement creates and reinforces the sense of belonging to religious communities and a sense of emplacement in their new environment. People receive counseling from their religious leaders and financial assistance from their small group within the church or mosque. Religious places of worship are the centers of these activities and thus become sites of affective religious participation and convivial fellowship.

CONCLUSION

This chapter has argued that affective and emotional experiences generated by sensational religious practices transform places of worship into affective spaces, as well as sites of the human-divine encounter. These sites are growing rapidly and becoming intertwined with the fabric of the Federal Capital as the Pentecostal Christian and Islamic renewal movements expand throughout the city. It is arguable that affective religious structures have added another layer onto the dreamlike Abuja landscape, which has become entangled with the lures and enchantments of an "aspiring city." Some places of worship, such as the National Mosque and the National Christian Centre, are iconic structures that are designed to make an impression on those who see them. Therefore, aesthetic design and sensational religious practices have combined to turn religious spaces in the city into affective infrastructures. This is because Abuja serves as the national and regional headquarters of many religious organizations.

This chapter also suggests that religious places of worship are centers of activities and participation that are inextricably connected with people's sense of identity and belonging. Through a range of affective practices, believers develop a strong connection to their religious spaces to the extent that the latter become an inherent part of their social identity. After services of worship, many people stay behind in both churches and mosques and engage in casual conversation that can be described as convivial relationships. Places of worship are not neutral spaces even to people of other faiths. Both Muslims and Christians make emotional comments on each other's places of worship that range from disapproval and disrespect to, sometimes, admiration. During interreligious riots in some parts of the country, people have attacked and violated the sanctity of other people's or congregations' places of worship in order to inflict emotional injury on the owners of the space.

As places of divine encounter, religious spaces provide a sense of hope and security to those who are affected by a precarious urban existence. In one of the Sunday services I attended in NASFAT, the imam said that the only solution to what is happening in Nigeria—the insecurity, insurgency, and violent crime—is to establish fellowship with Allah through regular attendance at services of worship in the mosque. Pentecostals also believe that they can overcome the challenges of urban life, particularly poverty and sickness, through sensational prayers in their churches. Therefore, sensational congregational prayers are instruments with which one engages with the challenges of urban life, as well as producers of affect and emotion that shape religious spaces and urban landscapes in more general terms.

Finally, it can be argued that places of worship in the enchanted Abuja landscape become affective spaces through sensational embodied religious performances, which can therefore be understood as spatial practices. In the introduction to this volume, the editors emphasize that "affect and emotion are always embodied in the relationships between individuals and their wider social and material environments." The phenomena of affect, embodied/spatial practices, and aesthetically designed buildings combine to create an affective, dreamlike cityscape.

NOTE

1. This chapter is extracted from the data I collected in Abuja for my PhD thesis, entitled "Sensational Piety: Practices of Religious Mediation in Christ Embassy and NASFAT" (submitted to and defended at Utrecht University in 2017). Using ethnographic methodology, I spent eleven months between October 2013 and September 2014 in the city of Abuja. During this period, I participated in and observed several sessions of religious services of Christ Embassy, NASFAT, and other religious groups. I have interviewed about thirty people from both religious groups, including leaders, young people, and women.

4 RELIGIOUS SOPHISTICATION IN AFRICAN PENTECOSTALISM AN URBAN SPIRIT?

RIJK VAN DIJK

In this chapter, I would like to start by drawing attention to a specific quality of urban life, including in Africa, which we can term "religious sophistication."[1] By suggesting this term, and developing it from an earlier publication (see van Dijk 2015b, 5), I am interested in bringing together a number of insights on the development of urban life and sentiment that have become relevant in understanding especially the manner in which Pentecostalism can be seen to offer a particular infrastructure of emotional life in an urban context. I am defining "sentiment" in contradiction to "emotion" by following Appadurai (1990) in the manner in which he speaks of a "community of sentiment," that is, taking sentiment as a communal expression that at the same time operates as a signifier in the social imaginary of the community and its identity. In contrast to short-lived and personalized emotions, we can delineate the collective-affective dispositions of sentiments by emphasizing the way these are publicly shared and acknowledged in a community, and extend over a longer period of time (see also Throop 2012).

I suggest defining the term "religious sophistication" in anthropological fashion as primarily a sentiment that shows how religion and (scientific) knowledge are brought together in people's desires for religious self-understandings. I am diverting from the manner in which Chiswick (2008,

31), in her historical study of Judaism in America, has used the term "religious sophistication" as meaning the level of skill in executing religious customs and rituals.[2] In turning the exploration of religious sophistication into a question of an anthropological exploration of sentiment, I am also diverting from Schmidt (2018), who defined "religious-political sophistication" as the level of knowledge among religious people and groups of political issues as informed by church-based teachings—an analysis that as such is marked by a modernist interpretation of a divide between religion and the state and its politics.

Whereas there has been a long and protracted debate, including in anthropology, on modernity's meeting of religion and science as being one of the markers of a "secular age" (see Taylor 2007; Meyer 2012b; Burchardt, Wohlrab-Sahr, and Wegert 2013), by coining the term "religious sophistication," I am interested in exploring the contextual and local self-understandings of, in this case, Pentecostal believers' perceptions of an embrace of scientific knowledge—that is, how a trajectory of sentiment can be discerned in the manner in which religion navigates an increasingly personal as well as collective relationship with specific elements of scientific knowledge. The exploration of religious sophistication is thus not inspired by a discussion of how a "secular age" has emerged in which a scientific study of religion has been made possible, including in anthropology, by the way in which the discipline "was founded by freeing itself from the confines of religious authority" (Lambek 2012, 1). By employing the term "religious sophistication," the object of study becomes a different one in seeking to understand the believers' increasing interest in reaching out to a kind of epistemological sophistication in which (scientific) knowledge can be perceived as relevant to faith and conviction. This is therefore not proposing a further discussion on an "evolutionary" perception of thinking whereby people in religion move from the primitive, the magical, and the prescientific into more rationalistic and scientific orientations; instead, this chapter is inspired by a search for an understanding of a trajectory of appreciation. In other words, what I aim to table for discussion by this contribution is the question of how to understand religious sophistication as a reflection of shifts in the religious appreciation for, and sentiments about, scientific knowledge. This sophistication therefore represents a particular, cultural, and processual pathway of religion engaging various domains of knowledge.

In line with a Kantian understanding of the significance of the rational and cognitive capacities of humankind in producing moral, aesthetic, and spiritual certainties, religion may pursue forms of knowing that are not exclusively based on revelation, something for which Kant ([1793] 2003) employed the term *Vernunftreligion*. The question is the following: In present-day Pentecostalism in Africa, can we discern a sentiment for the pursuit of the inclusion of knowledge, an inclusion that is being marked, experienced, and perhaps even celebrated as a form of sophistication? Is this a sentiment that becomes akin to Kant's Vernunftreligion, whereby this expression of epistemological sophistication in religious thought and practice indeed becomes a particular "form of life" (see Salazar 2015)?

The relationship between a religious formation such as Pentecostalism and notions relating to epistemological sophistication can only be properly understood if we define what we mean by epistemological sophistication as compared with other forms of sophistication. Whereas Litvak (1997, 12) claims that the comprehensive historical and anthropological study of sophistication remains to be written, I would argue differently and claim that first and foremost the study of sophistication, with its connotations and sentiments of refinement and socioeconomic distinction, has been well developed in the African context too. First of all, the rise of forms of socioeconomic sophistication in African urban contexts has been demonstrated in the anthropological literature interested in exploring particular models of fascination for distinction in terms of social stratification (cf. Bourdieu 2010; for a more global appreciation of the same, see Illouz 1997). Studies such as those of Friedman (1994) on the urban flaneur in the (post)colonial history of the Congo, Newell (2012) on the urban *bluffeur* in Ivory Coast more recently, and Spronk (2009, 2014) on the rise of an urban middle-class youth culture in Kenya all point to the importance of this specific urban sentiment that can be called "sophistication."

Here again, sophistication appears to represent a particular and predominantly urban-based trajectory of sentiment—a trajectory that stretches across time and space in how different modalities of these affective relations with style, beauty, and performance occur. The empirical evidence, therefore, of an intimate intertwinement between urbanity and these forms of sophistication is overwhelming and something for which the African context does not represent a particular exception. There is not only a local history of these specifically urban-based sentiments of sophistication and distinction as expressed through clothing, style, attire, beauty, the body, and forms of consumerism; a specific attention has also been drawn to its global and transnational connections, as Susan Ossman (2002) has demonstrated in her famous book *Three Faces of Beauty: Casablanca, Paris, Cairo*. In other words, all these authors appear to argue that the urban creates and harbors the specific conditions and parameters under which this sentiment of socioeconomic sophistication can emerge and is placed on a trajectory of ever-greater exposure and exuberance since the urban space provides for profitable access to (global) markets, consumer goods, and the circulation of images of style, fashion, and beauty. These make possible a high-velocity turnover of the rise and (dis)appearance, the waxing and waning, of forms of distinction that allow for an unceasing production of yet new styles of sophistication. All of this, these authors seem to agree, is usually hardly available in rural areas, which makes these forms of sophistication an urban phenomenon par excellence.

Yet, in this chapter I aim to argue and demonstrate that this understanding of sophistication in the socioeconomic terms of distinction is important but is at the same time not enough in light of a rounded view of the significance of sophistication as an urban sentiment. Nor would I want to define this interest in glamour and refinement as a form of sophistication in the meaning of "deception." While there is some interest in how sophistication may potentially mean and include trickery, dishonesty, and faking (see Goodwin 2011, 49), I suggest expanding this understanding of sophistication to see it also as a sentiment that expresses a desire for and interest in knowledge and the expansion of understanding. This is another form of sophistication—an epistemological one—for which religious forms such as the Pentecostal groups in Africa are generating an increasing interest. By religious sophistication, I propose a concept that aims to indicate a form of religious inspiration and revelation that becomes increasingly inclusive of, and interested in, domains of knowledge that relate to education, science, skills, and expertise. In a sense, the two "modalities" of sophistication—that is, the one produced by socioeconomic developments in African urbanities, as distinct from a modality of epistemological sophistication—should not be seen as mutually exclusive. Instead, it can very well be argued that these modalities of sophistication work greatly in tandem, especially in the context in which I will explore urban Pentecostalism in Africa (see also van Dijk 2015b, 5).

Many authors, including myself, have indeed placed the rise and attraction of urban Pentecostalism in the context of the emerging middle classes, changing lifestyles, and changing aspirations and appetites, including increasing orientations toward consumerism (see, e.g., van Dijk 2010, 2015b; D. Freeman 2012; Haynes 2012, 2014). In this sense, Pentecostalism as a religious discourse and practice can be interpreted as embracing and co-producing sophistication in its socioeconomic understanding by pointing to how this faith encourages middle-class and elite styles, professes prosperity, proclaims God's abundance and (material) success for the confirmed believer, and creates notions of distinction in these particular ways as well, much as these distinctions include and espouse inequalities (the point of the Pentecostal embrace of inequality is well developed by Haynes [2012, 2014]). Yet this is not the sole modality of sophistication the faith appears to foster; in the following sections I will draw attention to the manner in which Pentecostalism appears to foster a form of religiously inspired sophistication in which the inclusion and propagation of certain forms of knowledge, understanding, skills, and competences become part of the distinctiveness of the faith as a whole. Sophistication here means and implies a specific relation to other bodies of knowledge and their placement in and inclusion of religious thought and practice. Like the other modality of sophistication, this epistemological sophistication is also marked by desires, emotions, and appetites in the way people may eagerly pursue forms of knowledge, strive to incorporate this in religious thought and practice, and aim to create distinctions with others on the basis of what they have learned. Again it is important to emphasize the urban circumstance of this modality of sophistication: it is urban because of its required access to knowledge, understanding, and skills, which are often not readily at hand in rural areas and which require the active involvement of educated and well-positioned classes. It also requires the specific functioning of (religious) authority, the media, and access to globally circulating domains of knowledge, skills, and their connectivities (for such debates, see, e.g., Marginson, Murphy, and Peters 2010; Asamoah-Gyadu 2010; de Bruijn and van Dijk 2012). However, in further exploring religious sophistication as informing and relating to Pentecostal spirituality, the next section will suggest viewing this form of sophistication as being a particular sentiment as well—a sentiment about the relation of religious convictions to forms of knowledge that can be termed a sentiment of "amplification."

UNDERSTANDING AMPLIFICATION

I need this term to pinpoint a particular aspect of urbanity that seems to be of great significance in understanding the present-day modalities of the combination of religion and sentiment in African urban areas. By using the term "amplification," our attention can be drawn to the manner in which urban contexts often appear to make things stronger, to amplify their presence, to make things stand out, and to create particular visibilities and audibilities. The urban seems to produce the need to put things in sharper relief and to employ the specific competences, techniques, and objects that make this possible. This sense of the need for amplification as an urban phenomenon of religion and sentiment certainly plays a role as a particular driving force of change, the question being: How and why do religious groups engage with the techniques, skills, and competences to make their urban presence clearly recognizable? In other words, amplification as an answer to the "how to?" question of urban presence that reflects this desire for sophistication that I am introducing. Let me give a few examples so as to attune our thought to this particular feature of amplification in urban religious contexts:

1. In terms of audible amplification that is often crucially developed in urban religious life, one obvious example is the use of modern public address systems. Modern forms of Christianity, Pentecostalism in particular, began introducing this form of amplification in urban African contexts. Amplification here almost became a euphemism for the touching of hearts and souls that went on in massive public Pentecostal rallies organized in cities' open-air sites, sport stadiums, cinemas, markets, and so on. I have been witness to the early years of this coming of loud Pentecostal presences to the urban spaces of Blantyre, Malawi, for example, where the amplification of religious thought and practice was considered a strikingly new phenomenon in the late 1980s and early 1990s (see van Dijk 2001a). In Ghana, I reported how this form of amplification led to direct and violent conflicts with other religious groups in Accra's metropolitan area, causing the Ghanaian government to start applying "environmental protection laws" so as to control decibel levels in an attempt to restore public calm and order (van Dijk 2001a; de Witte 2008). The Task Force on Nuisance Control was deployed to drive around the city to dispatch officials armed with decibel meters, who would enter the premises of many of the large Pentecostal churches to check their noise levels (de Witte 2008, 697). If found to be in violation of these protection laws, the church could be warned and forced to reduce its levels of amplification. Yet beyond the environmental control, the push that this amplification and its public reaction gave to further religious developments was the opening of a public domain for the profiling of what came to be known as "neotraditional" groups that, in the pursuit of their forms of ancestral veneration, now ordered moments of public

quiet and servitude as a way of countering the influence of Pentecostalism and a way of producing a new postcolonial agenda of worship and religious life (de Witte 2011; Meyer 2010).

2. A second example can be found in relation to the same forms of Pentecostalism, where, as various authors, especially Krause (2014), have been demonstrating, an explicit effort is made to pray to God for the amplification of the workings of biomedicine; that is, prayers are directed to heavenly forces to encourage them to amplify the medical treatments that people are receiving so that these will work even better, or longer, or more efficaciously. This is a kind of amplification of healing power that does not regard biomedicine as being antithetical to God's provenance but instead perceives of it as being a product of the same benevolence for which the power of the Holy Spirit can be called upon to do miracles (Krause 2014, 239, 242). This form of the amplification of (biomedical) healing, as Krause has recorded it, must be perceived as different from a more problematic relationship between religious healing (such as that of Pentecostal healers) and the rise of biomedicine in local African societies in other contexts. It is well known, for example, that in the context of AIDS, Pentecostal churches initially held the view that God's wonder-working power would be able to cure the incurable disease, and proclaimed on other occasions that true and confirmed believers should put their fate exclusively in the hands of God (Dilger 2007; Burchardt 2014). Yet a change came, including in the context of the rollout of antiretroviral therapies, in which the discourse became more inclusive of biomedicine as involving practices that could be amplified through supernatural means (see van Dijk et al. 2014). This also meant an amplification of the role and position of Pentecostal leaders such as the well-known Dr. Dag Heward-Mills, who trained as a medical doctor and is the leader of the megachurch Lighthouse Chapel International, whose headquarters is located near the Korle-Bu Central Hospital in Accra. He became an international "inspirational" figure fostering "understanding" in many social programs of behavioral change, a form of intellectualism that, according to his writings, must be strengthened, fostered, and pampered, instead of being just reliant on an exclusive focus on spectacular healing miracles.[3]

3. Yet, at the same time, the third obvious example of amplification is precisely the rise of mediatized and sensationalized miracle healings that draw spectacular media coverage in glossy magazines and televi-

sion broadcasts regarding what is happening onstage. The effect here is not simply increased blurring of the distinction between religion and entertainment that seems to draw the attention of ever-increasing public domains, as if they were derivative of these emerging publics (see Meyer 2004b); they actually *produce* publics at a highly expansive rate (Meyer 2010; Asamoah-Gyadu 2010; de Witte 2012; Fumanti 2013). It is not simply, as mentioned in example 1, that modern techniques allow these religious groups to expand and amplify their messages in and in relation to a public domain; they have been able to expand and amplify the significance of the public domain as such on their own account, and forcefully so. Infrastructure, networks, and connections have been vital for this, much as the city is usually capable of offering at least a measure of such services; yet many of these groups have indeed been able to produce, construct, and expand such networks, connections, and facilities themselves (Pype 2012). This merger of religion and entertainment has amplified infrastructure, which in its turn has increased the presence of the spectacle and the miracle in the urban milieu. Both Meyer (2010) and Promey (2014) have called this the rise of "sensational religion," a motif for which Promey and her coauthors have indicated wide-ranging historical and cultural-comparative analyses of the interlinking of city (archi-)texture and sensory cultures; that is, in many cases the built environment of the city is conducive to this rise of sensationalism as well.[4]

Taken together, these examples of the manner in which there is an urban spirit of amplification at work require further analysis of the forces that may drive this specific city-based process and of how religiosity, urbanity, and sentiment coalesce. Why would the urban be the prototypical domain of such diverse processes of amplification as the examples just mentioned appear to demonstrate, rather than rural areas? In brief, my answer is that these processes of the amplification of religious sentiments in an urban milieu relate to a longer process in and through which sophistication is crucially located in the "survival" and expansion of religion in the African city. While ongoing massive expansion and massive rural-to-urban migration have turned many African cities into sites of the "bare life" of survival (see Comaroff 2007 on notions of bare life in Africa as developed in the context of HIV/AIDS in particular), this reality of urban survival does not apply only to the *body personal* but also to the *body social*.[5]

An extensive literature has discussed the significance of urban survival in the context of religious innovation. Initially basically Marxist in orientation, this literature hypothesized a functioning of new urban religious forms, such as the so-called Zion independent and other prophetic healing churches, as providing not only a homecoming for the rural-to-urban migrant in particular but also a "body of power and a spirit of resistance," as the well-known title of Jean Comaroff's (1985) monograph captures it. Hence, religious innovation, which some of these interpretations qualify as being forms of "superstructural reconstruction" (see van Binsbergen 1981), perceived urban and capitalist structures as requiring a spirited, inspirational response. Superstructural, because these innovations did not do much to change or improve the (infra-)structure of the city, its inequalities, poverty, and misery, as many of the materialist conditions remained the same, despite this wave of new African Christianities. Reconstruction, because of the manner in which the urban was perceived as a place of "destruction," a consequence of perceiving the rural as the site of primordial and pristine forms of religion, ritual, and symbolism. As I have argued elsewhere (van Dijk 2007, 2009), scores of anthropologists have thus continued to interpret urban religious innovation as particularly addressing and redressing uprootedness, alienation, and strangerhood in the rapidly expanding cities by representing a notion of these religious movements as being islands of safety and relative comfort, mostly in a more spiritual and (social-)psychological meaning of the term.

This interpretation of urban religious sentiment died a silent death, basically because new generations of urbanites no longer could perceive of the rural as their "cosmological home," thus suggesting that urbanity is a particular and estranging deviation of this. However, we may run the risk of overlooking a particular history of sophistication—that is, of the "how to?" question of urban presence and relevance—that this development of urban prophetic and spirit-healing churches may have been representing. While much of this was continued in the later development of the Pentecostal and Charismatic movements, here we already find the ways in which sophistication became important also as a form of institutional survival, instead of just being about personal well-being. Hundreds of these churches emerged in the rapidly expanding cities in the period roughly between 1920 and 1970 (as is well recorded in groundbreaking studies from that of Bengt Sundkler [1961] on southern African prophetic movements onward; for an overview of such schisms, see Barrett 1968; Manyoni 1977). Competition became fierce, fission and fusion markers of institutional developments, and a new sense of a religious market developed by and through which all sorts of competences came to be required to be able to face challenges. The pursuit of sophistication here is the rise of a sentiment emphasizing the importance of knowing *how to* run an institution, to inspire a body social as an institution, and to place it on an upward trajectory of social mobility. We can call this a spirit of sophistication as an emerging code of conduct in the way Weber interpreted the Protestant ethic as a conflation, a coalescence, of notions of rationalization (of labor, of the market, of the state, of the public domain) *and* a source of inspiration (from God, the Holy Spirit, the ancestors, and so forth) that perceives success, progress, and expansion as a fulfillment of destiny, purpose, and permanence.

Why permanence as a major focus of rationalities in the service of God's purpose in knowing how to run an institution? In this emergence of urban religiosity, the waxing and waning of churches as an institution became the ultimate litmus test of God's providence in conquering the urban space. Churches sprang up in great numbers but always ran the risk of disappearing again as easily as they had emerged. Urbanity amplified the sense of impermanence. While these syncretic churches commonly conflated elements of the world religion of Christianity with locally rooted historical traditions of healing and of worshipping specific ancestors and other deities, nothing in this bipolar orientation and foundation seemed to guarantee the permanence of their existence in the urban domain. Competition was and is stiff, resources are few, keeping up with modern developments tricky and difficult to maintain, while relationships between the rank and file on the basis of mutualities and reciprocities often appear unsustainable. The sophistication required in terms of knowing how to build an institution like a church that could survive meant, above all, tackling the problem of how to create permanence. Cabrita (2014) has recently demonstrated the significance of textuality in creating a permanent public appeal in leadership, in resources, and in being able to stand up to fierce competition in a rapidly expanding religious market (see also Asamoah-Gyadu 2010). In Kirsch's study (2008a, 2008b) of institutional bureaucracy and documentation in these churches, this sophistication in creating permanence and continuity through such techniques as record keeping, minute taking, board meetings, and devotional prayers that would appeal to the presence of the Holy Spirit in minutes, church records, and all sorts of church-related certificates (birth, marriage) speaks strongly to this code of conduct.

Another telling example of how this institutional sophistication appeared to operate can be found in Birgit Meyer's (1998b) and my own work (van Dijk 1997) on the so-called Pentecostal prayer camps that often emerged in the vicinity of large urban areas in Ghana. In their older forms, these prayer camps, often located in areas in a sense "halfway" between the rural and the urban, provided places where people were able to stay for a time to receive prayers, medicinal baths, and concoctions so as to alleviate important problems and issues in their lives. While initially representative of the syncretic movements that combine Christianity with local historical traditions and conceptions of healing, through their inclusion in Pentecostalism, a particular form of sophistication set in. Both Meyer (1998b, 193) and I (van Dijk 1997, 145) reported how crucial questionnaires and records became in the entry of people into these camps in their pursuit of (spiritual) healing. These forms of documentation consisted, for example, of lists of questions pertaining to the many possible and potentially harmful (religious and ritual) practices that the person may have been subjected to in the past and for which an unbonding of the past through deliverance would have to take place. The questionnaires and entry records thus produced a technique of disclosure of the past in an attempt to portray the camp as a place of opening up a new future informed by detailed and recorded knowledge of oneself, one's past, and one's current predicament, especially relating to the idea that a close and competent inspection and diagnosis may lead to an effective (spiritual) intervention. Not only did these camps become extremely popular, with thousands of people streaming to them on a regular basis, but the appeal of this level of sophistication amplified their significance enormously, as it represented a form of social engineering on a spiritual basis through which attendants were able to refashion their lives. In my view, the continuing popularity of these prayer camps until today (see Daswani 2015, 119) needs to be approached from the perspective not only of the attraction of healing, inspiration, and revelation, but also of sophistication in the manner in which these forms of detailed inspection have come to play a significant role through the use of questionnaires and counseling.

The point is that, in light of a spirit of sophistication (i.e., in knowing how to handle institution-building by creating new levels of competence), seeing the responsive, reactive, if not passive stance of these forms of religiosity as a "superstructural reconstruction" proved insufficient. The rise in great numbers later of Charismatic or Pentecostal-style churches demonstrated that a "home away from home" type of analysis of this emergence (see, e.g., Adogame 1998) would simply be irrelevant; instead, a further trajectory of this spirit of sophistication seemed to become important.

THE SOPHISTICATION OF DISCERNMENT
BETWEEN SPIRIT AND SENTIMENT

This spirit of sophistication, meaning a code of conduct emphasizing that a drawing in of other bodies of knowledge, competence, and experience is desired to conquer the urban space and create permanence, became the hallmark of the new Charismatic-cum-Pentecostal churches. Whereas the enormous rise of these churches in many cities in sub-Saharan Africa has been qualified as the rise of the urban miracle and the urban spectacle (see Ukah 2018), their orientation toward publicly performed healing miracles, booming economics, and miraculous success and wealth must not be read as a counter to, or as an interruption of, the history of the spirit of sophistication. Over time even these miracles, counterintuitively perhaps, became increasingly sophisticated in how they began involving institution-building and the drawing in of other bodies of knowledge, competence, and experience, other than "just" biblical revelation and inspiration. Institutional survival means knowing not only how to establish and build a church but also how to expand it and to create new institutional "additions."

While many examples can be given of this process, it might be illuminating to draw here particularly on the insights that the work of members of the Research Network on Religion and AIDS in Africa have been producing, which is contained in numerous publications.[6] Some of these studies pointed out that, in the early phase of the crisis, a number of Pentecostal churches adopted a problematic-ideological position in which, on the one hand, they were pointing to AIDS as a punishment that God meted out to "sinners," and on the other hand, contested biomedical science by claiming miraculous healing for a disease for which there was no panacea (Gusman 2009; Parsitau 2009). Over time, however, the network soon began noticing the emergence of sophistication as a process in these Pentecostal positions, as internal debates were reported to occur surrounding issues of the acceptance of biomedical interpretations of and interventions in the disease (see especially Dilger 2007) or the acceptance of the idea of having biomedical tests to prove the efficacy of any form of healing, including spiritual ones (Dilger 2012). This sophistication also involved a range of issues, such as the Pentecostals becoming exposed to and associating themselves with humanitarian organizations of care, support, and prevention, to expertise about how to relate to external and international donors, NGOs, and FBOs, to organizing programs aimed at behavioral change, responsibilization, and a changing understanding of and discourse about the body, sexuality, and relationships.

Much of the engagement with biomedical knowledge and practice on the part of religious bodies in Africa, including the Pentecostals, has been researched, highlighting in particular how this involvement of religion with the care, treatment, and prevention of HIV has resulted in the opening up of new socioreligious spaces. Perhaps the strongest location where this kind of sophistication happened in which biomedical knowledge and understanding came to be placed centrally in religious practices was and is counseling (Burchardt 2009; Moyer, Burchardt, and van Dijk 2013; Nguyen 2009; van Dijk 2013). Here the notion that biomedical knowledge could be enlisted to amplify religious-moral principles and interventions concerning private lives and intimacies was developed in depth. This biomedical knowledge not only pertained to notions about the body, sexuality, and thus safe-sex practices, treatment adherence, abstinence, and mother-to-child transmission, it also involved the knowledge of the psychological, states of mind, stress, anxiety, and personality characteristics. As I have also demonstrated (van Dijk 2013), counseling practices in Pentecostal churches in Botswana easily and eagerly engaged with psychological textbook knowledge about, for instance, personality traits, and they were quick to design extensive questionnaires and other materials meant to analyze and render open for discussion, inspection, and intervention particular personal characteristics of the counselees. These exercises involved psychological methods as a means to lay bare and reveal the strengths and weaknesses of the counselees' personalities for use in such matters as premarital counseling, abstinence-pledging, AIDS-testing counseling, and marital enrichment counseling. Nguyen (2009) describes this as being part of a whole set of confessional technologies. These exercises of disclosure fit extremely well into a much wider "theocratic" praxis of how to open one's inner personal drives and emotions through such practices as testimonies, revelations, prophecies, and confessions.

Much of this religious-cum-medical program of disclosure, as highlighted by counseling, deliverance, and a new lexicon of sexuality and intimacy, involves a play on sentiments, as exemplified in personal sentiments of affection and desire, or in moral sentiments concerning the permissible, acceptable, and desirable and their negation. However, much of this does not involve spirituality. For effective marital or testing counseling, strictly speaking no ecstasy or "infilling" by the Holy Spirit is required, no display of the presence of heavenly inspiration through speaking in tongues, prayer-healing, or prophesying are required as a precondition for assuming the efficacy of the practice. This is not to say that this Spirit has no role to play at all, especially in the Pentecostal domains of the practice, in addressing, strengthening, or highlighting such sentiments of marital affection or moral sensitivities concerning private lives. In these Pentecostal contexts the one—Spirit—is often interpreted as amplifying the other—sentiment (see also Krause 2014). Yet by perceiving this direction of amplification as a format, a template is emerging in and through which a sophisticated distinction between spirit and sentiment increasingly has to be made. Not every sentiment is required to be spiritualized, and not every spirit-manifestation requires a particular sentimentalized rendering.

A good example of how this sophistication in creating a further analytical separation between spirit and sentiment seems to be at work for ordinary Pentecostal members in Botswana can be found in the practice of *botsetsi*. Botsetsi is the moment of postpartum seclusion whereby the young mother becomes separated from her male partner and other close kin while staying together with her newborn baby for an average period of around three months. As I have noted while doing fieldwork in Botswana, in most cases she will take up residence in her mother's compound, either, if the space or size of the compound permits, in a separate hut or small house, otherwise in a separate room in her mother's house. Her mother's proximity and availability means that she and the baby will receive a lot of care, good food, and much that is needed in terms of clothes, hygiene, and even medicines, while the elderly mother also functions as a kind of "trainer" for the transmission of know-how and skills in the postnatal period. This know-how and related skillful practices involve things such as the massaging of the body of the young mother and the baby (for instance, in the case of stomach ache), but also a whole range of more or less spiritualized do's and don'ts—spiritualized since some of these practices, taboos, and concerns involve and relate to the protection of especially the newborn baby, as the infant is considered especially vulnerable to such sentiments as jealousy, envy, and witchcraft. Of particular concern is what is known as the ritual temperature (see Jakobson-Widding 1989) and its difference between the "coldness" of the baby and those who are sexually active, itself known by the expression of having "hot feet." The heat of the sexually active can reflect badly on the health of the baby, which is why the male partner cannot "stay" together with the young mother while she and the child are in botsetsi, and also why the young mother cannot engage in sexual relations while she is nursing in this context. As I have indicated in an earlier publication (see van Dijk 2010), in state-driven global health-related programs designed to curtail what are known as multiple concurrent partnerships (MCPs), the botsetsi practice is particularly marked as a "problematic" time for the male partners, since, in being deprived of sexual access to their partners, the men are assumed to engage in other relations for the duration of this period of seclusion (van Dijk 2010, 286). The elderly mother of the young mother can indeed be very strict in maintaining this temperature-based protection and seclusion of her daughter and her grandchild, as I have experienced myself (in that I was considered to have "hot feet" too). Some of the male partners with whom I was in contact were indeed highly anxious not to come near the house or the compound, kept a safe distance, and did not set foot in the room where the mother and the baby were residing.

How do Pentecostals generally deal with this practice? A few of my interlocutors went through the process of childbirth and were themselves young mothers subject to the botsetsi prohibitions, but were members of a Pentecostal church as well. Yet, while being Pentecostal and being acutely aware of the way Pentecostal teachings usually perceive of cultural traditions from a particularly critical vantage point, often calling for a "break with the past" (Meyer 1998b) and a moral rejection of these traditions, without exception the young Pentecostal women were keen to maintain this tradition. Take Mrs. X., a well-educated person and living in the capital, who went back to stay with her mother after giving birth to her firstborn. She and her new husband are both members of (different) Pentecostal churches and consider themselves to be active and confirmed believers, yet very much wanted the botsetsi, despite potentially opening themselves up to exposure to practices that could easily be considered "demonic" in nature or significance from the perspective of a Pentecostal morality. Interestingly, the expansion of a Pentecostal domain by including the institution of botsetsi and making it fit their urban lifestyle (basically by reducing the length of the period of seclusion so as to make it congruent with the woman's maternity leave from work) was based on their analytical separation of spirit and sentiment; botsetsi could be classified as emphasizing and amplifying a particular sentiment, while making sure that, in terms of its spirituality, the "non-Christian" elements were rejected. For example, in this case the young husband was allowed to visit the house, to see the baby, and to enjoy these moments intensely, because both parents felt and were convinced that the possible effects of him having the wrong kind of ritual temperature no longer applied and could in any case be contained. The sentiment that the institution makes it pleasant for the young mother to be pampered, to receive a lot of care, and to become beautiful again can easily be integrated into the wider Pentecostal emphasis on middle-class lifestyles, class, glamour, status, and success. Hence, the discernment that is part of this sophistication is to understand and to know how—even as ordinary members of a Pentecostal church—a particular cultural institution can be fashioned so as to adopt it in a particular lifestyle and religious conviction in which giving birth and taking care of a baby are sentimentalized.

A final example of how a spirit of sophistication may work to discern the separating of spirit and sentiment, thus helping the institutional expansion of Pentecostalism, can be found in the newest addition to the International Central Gospel Church in Accra. As I have argued elsewhere (see van Dijk 2015b), here the well-known leader Mensa Otabil has opened the first Pentecostal gym, which he calls the "Body Temple," in an attempt to combine religious doctrine with the shaping of the body. A newspaper report described the opening of the gym:

> The International Central Gospel Church (ICGC) has officially opened an Ultra-Modern Gym and Sports Facility at Christ Temple on Sunday, 1st September 2013 at Abossey Okai, Accra.
>
> The facility, named "Body Temple," is expected to encourage the habit of regular exercise among church members and the community at large. The choice of name was informed by 1 Corinthians 6:19 which states that our bodies are the temple of the Holy Spirit. "Body Temple" is fully equipped with cardio equipment which includes treadmills, upper body resistance, pull down equipment, weight benches with weights, dumbbells, indoor recumbent bikes, Smith machine, leg extension and several other gym and sports equipment. ICGC is committed to promoting the health and physical well-being of its congregations and members as well as their spiritual well-being.
>
> After the prayer of dedication, members who visited the facility expressed their gratitude to the General Overseer, Pastor Mensa Otabil, for the well-equipped facility and promised to exercise regularly and to cultivate a healthy lifestyle.[7]

In light of our discussion of the rise and development of a spirit of sophistication, there are many aspects here of, on the one hand, a sentiment concerning healthy lifestyles and the need to draw in the knowledge and techniques to achieve this, and, on the other hand, the spiritual embrace and moral justification of the interest and inspiration to do so. The religious appeal to biomedical notions of the healthy body, to the need for bodily exercise and physical well-being of the person *and* the community, is seen as being logically and fully complemented by the same on a spiritual level. The sophistication of the one amplifies the workings of the other: the institutional "addition" of the church by building this new institution and by drawing in new forms of (body) knowledge appears to generate this promise of the continuing relevance of the faith to the everyday lives of its urban followers. The sentiment of having healthy bodies appears to amplify the relevance and significance of the faith, while the spirit in Pentecostalism of demonstrating the benevolence of heavenly forces in one's success, status, prestige, and health amplifies the pursuit of this sentiment.

CONCLUSION: A VERNUNFTRELIGION?

By way of conclusion, I would like to suggest to not simply interpret this notion of the rising dominance as a sentiment of sophistication but instead as a spirited pursuit of sophistication from the perspective of a "rationalization" of religion that Max Weber saw in Enlightenment Protestantism—that is, perceiving the rise and expansion of rationalities (as in labor, production, law, bureaucracies) as also "affecting" the modalities of the faith in forms of disenchanted Calvinism.[8] While there is a host of literature that seems to argue that the "disenchantment thesis" does not hold much water in explaining situations such as those in Africa, where religion is not waning but waxing (see Meyer 2012b for a decisive counter-Weberian interpretation), and where religious growth can particularly be explained by its fascination with fighting "the powers of darkness," there is another dynamic at play in positioning the emergence of the spirit of sophistication, as I have indicated in this chapter. Here we need not only scholars such as Weber on the Protestant ethic and its modes of disenchantment and rationalization, or later thinkers such as Taylor on the rise of the Western secular, but especially also Kant ([1793] 2003) on the significance of what he termed *Vernunftreligion*. Vernunftreligion is a useful concept for demonstrating the rise of a religious double, a mirror, in which the capacities of reason and rational reflection become integrated into the experience of religion. For Kant, revealed religion is fundamentally different from *Natur-religion*, that is, the extent to which either an external source must be recognized that reveals religious truths to the people through particular mediums such as the Bible, or alternatively a situation in which there is an internal knowing and relating to the workings of the supernatural without other mediation. This is the creation of an internal logic in religion so as to render it viable and recognizable to the individual things that would otherwise remain foreign, inexplicable, contradictory, "magical," or even senseless. Vernunftreligion allows for a sense of reason to inhabit the experience of the unreasonable and the unthinkable—in Christian religion the logics of resurrection, salvation, destiny, and provenance. One could even go so far as to say that, for Kant, "knowing" can itself be worshipped. If we maintain this line of thought in considering the relationship between science and religion, one might say that Vernunftreligion thus allows for a process of the insertion, incorporation, and inclusion of disciplines of knowledge in religious thought and practice. God's hand, so to speak, is then seen to operate through these disciplines, which by themselves are not bound to acknowledge the "invisible hand." Medical science, psychology, pedagogics, economics, and so forth expand religious logic; they do not destroy it. As Paul Ricoeur (1967, 349) has noted, instead of the individual being placed in a direct and unmediated existence with and from God, it allows for a deeper appreciation of the wonders and the miracles that scientists can begin to see by an increasingly closer introspection of man and nature. In other words, already in Kant's thinking, "knowing" can amplify religion and can strengthen religious convictions, representations, and practices, since it fosters a particular sentiment about the religious significance of *Vernunft*. Hence, while the spirit of sophistication seems to lead believers to distinguish sharply between spirit and sentiment (whereby the one can amplify the other and the other way round, as I demonstrated in the cases of botsetsi, counseling, etc.), the pursuit of the spirit of sophistication is a sentiment in and of itself. The pursuit of Vernunftreligion can be made a sentiment, which, as this chapter has attempted to demonstrate, has especially become part of the repertoire of urban Pentecostals in Africa in recent decades—an unfinished history of the rise of this spirit so far.

NOTES

1. A draft version of this chapter was presented as a keynote address at the conference "Spirit and Sentiment: Affective Trajectories of Religious Being in Urban Africa," Berlin, May 28–30, 2015. I am grateful to the conveners of and participants in this conference, as well as to the editors of this collection, for their comments on earlier versions of this chapter.

2. For an archaeological perception of religious sophistication, see R. Z. Cortazar, "Scholar: Cave Paintings Show Religious Sophistication," *Harvard Gazette*, April 26, 2007.

3. On the one hand, he published a booklet entitled *Amplify Your Ministry with*

Miracles and Manifestations of the Holy Spirit in 1999, yet one of his many and later booklets published in 2015 is entitled *A Good General: Science of Leadership*, featuring, for example, a paragraph (no. 57) entitled "Fight with Technology." This Pentecostal leader is in no way unique in publishing tracts and booklets of this nature; see also publications by Mensa Otabil such as *Mastering Your Life* (2006) or *Four Laws of Productivity* (2002).

4. This point is clearly linked to the current interests in the postmodern turn in urban geography for religion and the "scalar perspective" in understanding differences of scale in urban-based interactions within and across nation states (see, e.g., Glick Schiller and Çağlar 2011).

5. The analytical distinction between the body personal, the body social, and the body political was introduced to medical anthropology by Nancy Scheper-Hughes and Margaret Lock in an article in *Medical Anthropology Quarterly* (1987) and later developed by Scheper-Hughes (1994) in work on AIDS and the social body.

6. Worth mentioning here in light of this article's argument (yet without being exhaustive) are, e.g., Prince, Denis, and van Dijk 2009; Dilger, Burchardt, and van Dijk 2010; and Beckmann, Gusman, and Shroff 2014.

7. Christian Guide Newspaper Friday, September 20, 2013, https://issuu.com /christianguide/docs/final_ist_issue_12 (last accessed June 20, 2019).

8. For a counterargument, see Mohr's *Enchanted Calvinism* (2013).

PART II EMOTIONS ON THE MOVE

5 AFFECTIVE ROUTES OF HEALING NAVIGATING PATHS OF RECOVERY IN URBAN AND RURAL WEST AFRICA

ISABELLE L LANGE

Te-nɔ-kpɔn-Mawǔ-tɔ ɔ àfɔ nɔ kú ì ǎ.
—Fon proverb

À celui qui attend Dieu, les jambes ne fléchissent pas. | Whoever confides in God will never lose hope. // Patience in God has no limit.

I am perched on a wooden stool next to Dominique, a Togolese woman in her early twenties, in her pastor's compound on the outskirts of Lomé on a muggy weekend afternoon. She is telling me how, a year after a painful, debilitating tumor began swiftly growing out of her mouth, she finally found her way to surgery to remove it:

> I stayed at my parents' house in August, fasting, when a voice told me to get up and leave the house. . . . Three days later I received confirmation of this voice when my sister arrived and told me that she had also had a revelation that I should leave the house at the end of the month. So I listened, and in September, I basically left my house and moved to my sister's place. We traveled to Accra [from Lomé] and had blood tests and other analyses done. I stayed there until the end-of-year festivities, when the doctors told me to come back in the new year. They scheduled my surgery for January 20, but I didn't know how I was going to pay for it—we had already depleted our

funds with the travel and blood tests. After I got back home, my pains started coming back, and my sister went to look for a pastor in the neighborhood to pray with me. During the time we prayed together, the pastor told me that a boat had arrived in Benin and he had a friend who was on board. Bizarrely, it was this twentieth of January—the day of the operation in Accra—that I was also on the boat. Before, I had also had a vision of me on the beach, and healing coming to me over water. Because when I prayed, I asked for God's healing, but I didn't know it would happen like this.

Dominique traveled from Lomé to Cotonou in neighboring Benin and showed up unannounced at the ship—an American humanitarian "mercy ship" that offered medical services along the West African coast—without passing through the crew's traditional surgery preselection routine, usually scheduled months in advance. After she first made contact with the ship, she stayed in hectic Cotonou to await the results of her blood tests, and upon being given the all clear to proceed with surgery, she walked up the gangway and moved on board.

In this short account of how the Mercy Ships organization came into her life, Dominique explained how she navigated her way along paths taken and not taken, made decisions fueled by hearing voices and God's interference or by apparent chance, and how things eventually worked out against the odds. She gave credit to God for bringing her to the ship, but it took a year for this help to arrive, by which point she was in tremendous pain and had difficulty breathing and eating as a result of the tumor in her mouth, as well as financial problems from no longer being able to work. Other patients who sought out the ship recounted similar plotlines. Mercy Ships' patients sometimes framed their journeys to the ship by giving indefinite reasons why they were drawn there or were accepted for surgery: gut instincts, a sixth sense, the influence of God. These narratives also extended to their movements away from the ship, back into their regular lives, back to the cities and villages they inhabited. As Dominique's story demonstrates, the navigation of patients' illnesses and recovery between surgeries, back in their communities, was infused with affective elements: the social and private, inarticulable yet expressed, grounded in their physical experiences and simultaneously present in the spirit.

This chapter draws on fieldwork with patients on the *Anastasis*, a Christian hospital ship run by the international faith-based organization Mercy Ships that docked in Cotonou, Benin, and then, two years later, nine hours overland down the coast in Tema, Ghana.[1]

Framed by extensive health-seeking experiences over the course of five years, I focus on the time between these two outreaches, when patients who needed multiple operations had completed one step in the process and were waiting for the second. Their period of waiting and limbo was determined by their body's healing time between procedures, the ship's movements in and out of the local ports, and their inability to find other affordable expert health care in the interim. To get through this period of diminished health and finances, patients navigated their networks for medical care and economic, spiritual, and social support through movements between groups, resources, and locations.

The interplay between the ship and urban and village networks proved to be a vital part of creating a path to healing, and this chapter looks at how these highly heterogeneous networks were used together to maximize opportunities. Urban networks proved especially valuable not only in terms of finances and information but also as points of rest, expansion, and continuity. The arguments here draw on conceptual work on "social navigation" (Vigh 2009), looking at how actors build on the health care they received on the ship and deal with the remaining uncertainty and difficult health outcomes by weaving their way between city and village lives to shape identities, nourish their emotional being, and stay afloat. As outlined by the editors of this volume in the introduction, I show how emotion and intellect draw together and are central to the decision making that shapes individuals' affective pathways. In this chapter, after a brief reflection on this literature and some contextual background to my field sites, I describe the experiences of a few of the patients to show how their movements between localities contributed to the creation of their networks of health and healing.

"ON SE DEFEND":
MAKING ONE'S WAY IN AN UNCERTAIN WORLD

In polite company in Benin, when one meets a stranger or an acquaintance one hasn't seen for some time, it is routine to rattle off a series of questions: "How are you? And madame/monsieur at home? How is the family? And the children? And the house? How is your health? And business/work/the crops/the market?" In these scenarios, generally the responses are an almost automatic "Bien, très bien, bien, merci, ça va, oui, aussi, merci," as the questions are run through. However, when meeting a friend or an individual who is part of one's routine daily life in Cotonou and southern Benin, at certain times the response to "Comment ça va? Comment allez vous?" will be a slow "É. . . . On se defend."[2] Literally, this means "[I, or one] defends oneself. . . . I'm on the defense," a noncommittal answer that avoids going into the details of what forces are at work in a person's life that need defending from, but that also draws the conversational partner into a complicit understanding that life is hard, life can be tough, the balls are up in the air, but one is managing as best one can. A clear, understated "I'm in it. Things are not good, but I am keeping up the fight" highlights the active need for protection against the onslaught that life offers. It invokes an air of passive action toward life's challenges that one cannot control while at the same time showing a quiet strength in the face of dealing with them.

Another expression that implies a sense of managing and muddling through employs the verb *se debrouiller*, a term that Henrik Vigh (2009), in his efforts to theorize the concept of social navigation, evokes from the Portuguese language when working with his material from Guinea-Bissau. There, his informants used the term *dubria* or *dubriagem* to sum up what they had to do to survive: a sort of weaving, swaying, maneuvering, and shadowboxing through life. Vigh's work on social navigation builds on ideas from Susan Reynolds Whyte, particularly her ethnography *Questioning Misfortune: The Pragmatics of Uncertainty in Eastern Uganda* (1997), in which her informants engage in "extrospection"—looking to outside occurrences rather than only within themselves for explanations, and for whom religious faith is not a crutch to cling to when things go wrong but part of a process of experimentation with various strategies in an attempt to make things go better. As her work illuminates, uncertainty is unavoidable in human affairs, but the work of humans is to hedge against it, organize it through the advantages of social experience, and modify its profound ambiguity with deliberate agency.

This idea of employing "social experience" to better combat the indeterminate plots in life resonates when one looks more deeply at meaning-making and notions of living well. Michael Jackson explores one dimension of the struggle to make one's way in a world that offers challenges and deprivation when he writes in his ethnography *Life within Limits: Well-Being in a World of Want*: "For Kuranko, it is how one bears the burden of life that matters, how one endures the situation in which one finds oneself thrown. Well-being is therefore less a reflection on whether or not one has realized one's hopes than a matter of learning how to live within limits" (2011, 61). He explains that the people he has been working with in Sierra Leone over a period of thirty years negotiate and renegotiate the parameters of their explanations and desires. Expectations are modified and adapted to given situations, reframed in order to help lives make sense, instead of lives and their outcomes being used to explain situations.

Health and illness are at the intersection of many frames of human life, making the search and care for well-being vital arenas for the exploration of the patterns that form in the spaces penetrated by these experiences. In recent years, many theorists have turned their attention to exploring the "affective" nature of the social world. This work, carried out in the social sciences and cultural studies, considers affect as linking the personal, spiritual, social, and material worlds. Affect can be seen as "felt bodily intensity that is: different from emotion and language; pre-social, but not asocial; material—or somehow pertaining to matter; dynamic and energetic; rife with possibilities to produce 'new' and 'emergent' phenomena" (McGrail, Davie-Kessler, and Guffin 2013). Instead of the focus on emotion, which is considered to be more individualistic, affect looks at how forms of behavior, responses, and emotions are shaped and influenced by the social context. This social context is then interpreted liberally, and the interactions between the material, interpersonal, and spiritual worlds are included in it, thus emphasizing the roles that place and space play in creating the affect of experiences. Affect, in this respect, is "the unconscious experience of intensity" (Shouse 2005).

Shifting between spaces means that affective routes are generated not just in the different places but through the act of traveling between them. As many scholars examining the world through the lens of affect point out, this is not a new concept, but it creates a meeting point between the body, the social, the individual psyche, and the collective (Blackman 2012). It helps frame the paths of the actors in this chapter, as, I argue, they are making decisions in the interests of their wellness not solely on the basis of intellectual deliberations, nor because of reactive emotions, but based on a physical understanding of their experiences that is permeated by their connection to the social and spiritual realms in which they dwell. Through this affective process, their trajectories become "structured and intelligible" (see the introduction to this volume), responsive, rational, and considered.

Coming back to Vigh, he elaborates on how identities are created through social navigation, as he finds it a useful concept to work with when trying to understand ways of surviving in uncertain circumstances. In his definition, agency, while still critical and active in individuals, takes a backseat, while the external forces at play that define living situations for those who do not have as much control over their surroundings as they would like take a more central role. In this sense, agency is a reaction to the movement and fluidity of the daily and exceptional forces that shape a person's life. He describes *dubrigem* as "equally directed towards both the near and the distant future as the practice of moving along an envisioned, yet frail and tentative, trajectory in an unstable environment" (Vigh 2009, 424). Key to his analysis is the word *navigare*, literally "navigate," designating "the practice of moving within a moving environment."

This resonates with the lives of my informants after their encounters on the ship. While they re-create themselves in fluid, unpredictable settings, the struggle for their lives continues, even though some aspects of their lives are resolved. Maintaining and reorienting faith were shown to be crucial parts of the process of organizing one's life after the dramatic encounters on board the hospital ship. Notably, this "weaving" involved capitalizing on the opportunities offered by different geographic spaces, cities and villages in particular, but also the wider, nonterritorialized space of potentialities (i.e., the ship) out of which one might be healed: resources, emotional content, and nourishing possibilities shifted as they approached different spaces for what they could provide. As movement generates an affective route, the imprints of each of these different destinations comes along with the traveler. A city is a "locus for the composition of social processes" (Simone 2010, 5), dense and convoluted with an impact that extends beyond the reach of its borders. The porosity of the city and its capacity to be shaped through experience set the scene for a negotiation between actor and everything the place brings to light. After some brief comments on the contextual backdrop to this research, I begin by sharing some of Francine's illness narrative, which had already generated different affective spaces from the time she fell ill and sought care.

A CHRISTIAN HOSPITAL SHIP IN BENIN

The *Anastasis* was a hospital ship run by Mercy Ships, a nondenominational American Christian organization with its headquarters in Texas and offices in sixteen countries worldwide. Of the ethos of this faith-based organization, its founder writes: "Mercy Ships seeks to become the face of love in action, bringing hope and healing to the world's poor, with ships serving every continent of the world in the 21st century" (Stephens 2005). Under the umbrella of "hope and healing" fall other aims of Mercy Ships, which include allowing ill people to have "normal" lives again through medical intervention. Mercy Ships offers medical care to patients of any religion, and although it carries out some specific evangelical activities with a clear goal of converting people, its overarching aim is to spread the word of God through the volunteers' good deeds without conversion being an overt objective.

Before each outreach, Mercy Ships staff negotiate an invitation from the local national government to carry out the organization's work. They routinely choose to serve in postconflict areas, where health services have been compromised. Benin's recent past has been peaceful, but despite a political reform that began in 1990, its economic situation had not led to significant improvements in social or medical infrastructure by the time of my fieldwork. As a result, the country's health indicators showed a population at risk of serious episodes of poor health, with financial limitations on care-seeking. For example, in 2000, many Beninese suffered health problems related to malnutrition (29 percent of children had low weight for their age), and the under-five mortality rate was 146 per 1,000.[3] Benin trains more doctors who are working abroad than at home. In 1996, there was approximately 1 doctor per 17,000 people (USAID); by 2016 that figure rose to 1.5 per 10,000 (comparatively, the United Kingdom was at 28 per 10,000 and Germany at 42 per 10,000 in 2016) (World Health Organization 2016). Like many sub-Saharan African nations whose health care systems declined in the 1980s and 1990s (Ilife 1998; Dilger, Kane, and Langwick 2012), Benin relies on foreign aid and nongovernmental organizations (NGOs) to provide health care services and health education. Mercy Ships is one of these NGOs, and those patients who cannot afford out-of-pocket payments for complicated or catastrophic health episodes are its main target community.

The 522-foot *Anastasis* was the world's largest nongovernmental hospital ship during her time in service. Acquired by Mercy Ships as the first of a fleet in 1978, the ship held three fully equipped operating rooms, a laboratory, and an X-ray unit and had a fifteen-hundred-ton cargo capacity. Up to four hundred volunteers could be housed on board during outreach. In need of continuous major repairs, the *Anastasis* was retired and replaced by the *Africa Mercy* in 2008.

The *Anastasis* was like a small city, with her own rules and regulations that governed ship life. She was practically self-sufficient while at sea and gave the impression that she could be while in port as well. During outreaches, the ship was filled nearly to capacity, providing a home to a complete range of medical staff (nurses, anaesthetists, surgeons, dentists, dental assistants, etc.) in addition to the staff who ensured the smooth running of the ship (welders, engineers, etc.), community development staff (educators, administrators), and support staff (schoolteachers, cooks, cleaners). In addition, patients lived on board, staying in the ward for periods varying from one day to three months.

The physical barriers to the space the *Anastasis* claimed are evident: a floating vessel separate from land, capable of sailing away; its white, bright mass visible on the horizon of the sea and sky from points in town; the wide buffer area between the ship (the private) and the city (the public) in the form of a port; and security guards' power over access, meant to determine whether someone has a sanctioned reason to come on board, whether one *belongs* to the mission. Traditionally, a cordon sanitaire, acting as a quarantine zone, encircles an area perceived to be dangerous to prevent any harmful contagion from leaving it. In the case of the *Anastasis*, one could view the ship as creating a protective enclosure around its people and beliefs, a "safe" zone erected as a shield to keep any threats away from it.

This space links up a third dimension in the distance between the city and village on land: a parallel world conjured up by the inequalities that history has brought to a country, and an attempt at resolution brought about through the incarnation of a modern twist in the form of a hospital ship. It draws people to its hulking body for purposes of health care and healing, for opportunity and change, creating another point on the route toward (hopefully) being healthy again. Lived interpretations in this new space on the ship open up new worlds for the experiences of their illnesses. "Space," Alice Street writes, in her study of a hospital in Papua New Guinea, "is a particularly important vehicle for and transmitter of affect" (2012, 46). The dynamics produced by the day-to-day psychological and material environment can determine people's behavior and choices. The movement between places and spaces—and the interactions with people, distances, and environments that this entails—is a powerful force that is amplified through the act of not simply tapping into a single sphere but instead drawing on the variety of constellations that feed and motivate a person's actions.

Usually the ship offered a "protected space" to patients. In addition to the technically advanced health care delivered by experts using shiny modern equipment otherwise rarely found in the area, it created a controlled zone in which to recover and heal. Bedsheets were provided and freshly washed; air-conditioning cooled the humid tropical air; nurses smiled and spent time with each patient; mealtimes served up tasty local fare; and, importantly, procedures and medication were offered for free without any hint of the need for bribes or under-the-table payments for preferential treatment. These were all cited by patients as being drastic departures from their experiences in the government facilities they could afford on land. In addition, their access to friends and family was considerably altered: while visitors were allowed, they needed to have invitation cards to be permitted on board, and often the distance of the ship from home meant that few could make the journey regularly. As such, in this controlled space, contemplation and healing turned inward, removed from the typical obligations and instead being played out in this capsule connected to land by a floating gangway.

What follows are stories of navigation between ship, village, and urban life, guided by an affective understanding of how the physical and social bodies meet urban and rural spaces along paths of healing.

A QUICKLY MOVING ILLNESS AND A SLOW RETREAT

Francine recounted to me in greater detail the history of her illness and how she came to the ship after we had known each other for about a year. She had received care from Mercy Ships in Lomé about three years previously and had been on board the ship in Cotonou two years later for follow-up surgery. She told me and Dzifa, another former Mercy Ships patient who interpreted for me, most of the following story one afternoon at her father's compound in Lomé. Francine's, Dominique's, and Dzifa's tumors were benign and not cancerous; they were caused by overactive tooth enamel that did not stop growing, though Dzifa's did not grow as large as Dominique's before it was operated on. For a patient with access to skilled care, a dentist would have removed the tissue before it ever showed, but left unchecked the tumors can grow quickly, weigh a few pounds, and eventually cut off passage for food and air, causing their victims to suffocate, choke, or starve to death.

Francine grew up in her birth village in Ghana but came to Lomé at a young age to stay with her older brother. By the age of eight, she was already serving as a housemaid for a family in Lomé, a job she carried out for four years until she started to work as an independent vendor in the heart of the city.

Her illness started *petitement* when she was fifteen or sixteen years old. One morning, as she was brushing her teeth, she saw a small growth along her gumline. A week later, it was still growing and had affected all her teeth along the lower right side. Two weeks later, she alerted her mother about what was happening. People around her suggested it was a hemorrhoid, so she picked up medication for hemorrhoids at the pharmacy. This seemed to help for a time, but then the swelling came back. Within a year, it had taken over her whole mouth, with the growth disfiguring her face as it pushed out of her jaw. Eventually, she could no longer eat or drink on her own and had to tilt back her head to open the passage so that someone could pour fluids into her mouth.

Before it got to this point, Francine went to the hospital in Lomé, but the doctors there could not help her, saying they did not know what the disease was. She was becoming discouraged, as none of the treatments she tried worked. Some people told her to put her faith in God; some people whispered that she had been infected with the disease by sleeping with men, saying she was "loose." All the talk and rumors got to her. "When I left the house in Lomé, I was ashamed because people would ask me so many questions when they saw me. So, I usually stayed in the village, far away from people who would talk to me. If I did go out, I'd cover myself in a shawl so that people wouldn't speak to me and ask me about my face."

During her time in her village, Francine tried at first to blend back into old family structures. She had attended the Assembly of God church when she lived in Lomé, but she went to a Pentecostal church in the village, as that was the only denomination present. What was important to her was that she was attending church, no matter which denomination, though she eventually gave this up and opted for private prayer.

Her sister took her to Korle Bu, the teaching hospital in Accra, where she was again told in consultations that the doctors did not know what the disease was. However, one of the doctors took her aside and told her that he could heal her at his private clinic for an outrageous sum. She did not have the money but together with her sister made an agreement with the doctor to pay in installments, and she proceeded to meet him, with each consultation costing 20,000 cedis (about five euros). Finally a day for the procedure was agreed, but when they showed up for the appointment, the doctor told them that he had not been able to borrow the "machine d'operation" from his friend because he was away. Francine told me, "Basically, after all that, we understood that the doctor was conning us. I was so disappointed by this story that I couldn't eat for a time. I suffered." To pay for the advances to the doctor and multiple five-hour journeys by collective taxi to Accra from her village for herself and her sister, she had taken money from acquaintances who had pity on her, she said, as well as from her parents, who had been saving money in every way they could. She felt humiliated by having nothing to show for all the energy she had put into finding a solution and for the efforts of her network.

Still, they kept searching for a cure. Francine's aunt in her birth village was a powerful healer, but no one in her inner circle thought that Francine was cursed, so the aunt could not help other than by offering strengthening herbs and financial support. Francine recalled, "We went everywhere. We went 'chez les traditionnels,' but in vain. My dad took me to a *vodunsi* [Vodun priest], but even after taking his herbal concoctions I wasn't healed. I couldn't disobey my parents, and so I followed them wherever they took me. Eventually I left everything to God because I was tired and I wanted to die because I was ready to die."

Francine reflected constantly about her life and illness from the early stages of the tumor because she felt that it did not fit into her life story and that she had to figure out a solution: she and her family did not have any money to be sick, especially not with a disease that no one knew anything about. She worried about being a hopeless case and a financial drain on the family, and wondered if she should kill herself. She prayed and had faith in God but felt very restricted in what she could do and no longer felt at ease with herself.

The pain wore her out as well. Sometimes it was not so bad, but there were times when it was agonizing, and she did not have access to any painkillers. At times, if she had them, she took tranquilizers to get through the interminable awfulness of her situation. For a period she withdrew and stayed on her own near the village, away from the family compound, because she was so fed up with her situation. Because the disease had struck only her mouth, she was able to take care of herself. During this time, she would typically wake up, perform her domestic chores, and go back to bed again. She said her isolation was self-imposed, that no one shunned her, forcing her to live on her own. Only her father and sister came to visit her from time to time, bringing her food and supplies, in addition to a priest from a nearby village who helped her pray on Sundays. She was bored but said there was nothing else she could do.

Francine's father came one day to tell her that a boat that healed the sick had arrived and was taking patients at Kégué (the stadium in Lomé). Four days later she returned to Togo, collected her father, and headed to the stadium for the medical screening. Five days after the screening, she received the results of her blood tests confirming she could be operated on, and three days later she was on the ship—the eve of her surgery. Remembering her first night on the ship, she said: "I felt good because they welcomed me onto the ship well, but I also had to reflect a bit. I was scared. I went to wash myself, and once back in bed for the night, I told myself: if it happens that I die here, or not, I can only thank my God."

Within two weeks of hearing about the ship, her situation changed drastically. It had been two years and seven months since she discovered the abscess in her mouth, the first year of which she had spent in Lomé, and the remainder in the village.

Throughout the course of her illness, Francine moved between places as they sustained her. The city was where she fell ill, and where she could no longer support herself. The village did not serve as enough of a retreat at some point and could not heal her socially or physically, so she secluded herself even further to take care of herself. The city had also disappointed her and taken her money, thanks to the dishonest doctors and the burdensome costs of repeatedly traveling there. Still, the information for her healing came from the city, when her father brought her the news of the ship. Her connections kept her afloat and offered her another chance. With Alexandre, whose story I turn to next, we see an enactment of the reverse—the city served as an aspirational place and a place for him to rest and to bask in anonymity. In the city, Alexandre augmented his network of spiritual and economic support. In any case, no matter what they got out of their respective city or village spaces, it was his and Francine's intuitively being drawn between these multiple spaces for healing and recovery that created the "arc of the affective journey" (H. Solomon 2011) within their healing. The following section describes how Alexandre tapped into what he needed, dealing with his compromised situation by creating a tapestry of resources defined by his suspended presence between the village and Cotonou.

RESITUATION: THE CITY AS PROMISE

When I arrived back in Benin after six months away, Alexandre was living in his birth village located a ninety-minute drive out of Cotonou. Before I left, he had undergone two operations in Ghana and Benin for cancer on his face, a disease that had progressively spread across his face and, eventually, his neck, since he was sixteen years old. Now, another sixteen years and numerous treatments later, he had finally received surgical care from Mercy Ships, which had cut out the cancer and patched together a new face with skin taken from his legs, arms, and even his scalp to mimic a sort of beard around his chin. Whereas before he had removed himself from social activities that involved eating, now he said he felt comfortable doing this in public. The difference between a face half consumed by a deep, open, necrotizing flesh wound and this patchwork of both smooth and bearded skin was striking, both visually and physically.

Other Mercy Ships patients were also doing well after surgery. The physical transformations enabled previous lives to be resumed and new trajectories to be followed. Better health permitted a reengagement with social activities previously rendered difficult or impossible. However, the overwhelming majority of Mercy Ships patients did not have the resources to seek health care elsewhere, meaning they also had limited budgets on which to draw when embarking on their postsurgery lives.

Some patients whose operations were successful experienced their reintegration as an ongoing struggle that involved continuous action, maneuvering and strategizing, even with restored health. But there was also the struggle that involved maneuvering and strategizing at a much slower tempo, with a lot of waiting and "dead time." The slow, heavy ambience of dead time permeated people's days and shaded these periods of uncertainty with a sense of stagnation and permanence, even as their health conditions continued to develop. Francine experienced this, as did Alexandre. To sit out the waiting period after his second surgery, upon his return from Ghana in July, Alexandre moved back into his aunt's house in the bustling suburbs of Cotonou.

This home had been Alexandre's urban base many times over the years. He first moved to Cotonou to attempt to study, which ended after one semester due to his cancer, but after years of staying in the village as his illness progressed, after surgery he was continuously drawn back to Cotonou to rest and relax—in a reverse form of migration to most people's ideas of where it is best to relax—and in order to have access to options for medical care. Alexandre did return to his village a few times in this period, but usually these were day trips, and his mobility was further compromised by a lack of funds to make the trip. By living this way, he was better able to control who he was surrounded by and also to fight against being isolated socially. While he did not have a job during this time, he found various other ways to hold his own.

De Boeck writes about the contradictions inherent in living in the city that those who do so have to cope with: "Urban living is ceaselessly rhythmed by its excesses and scarcities; its dispersals and immobilisations; its homogeneity and heterogeneity; its total boundlessness and the totalitarian nature of its endless restrictions; its frequent moments of violent effervescence and the boredom of endless waiting that also characterise urban life" (2015, 51). He writes of the city (in his case, especially Kinshasa) as an onslaught of risk and uncertainty, its landscape punctuated by an aggression that its inhabitants must weather and respond to, without resting. Alexandre had to deal with the precarious aspects of the city—the probing attention to his unusual appearance; the dust and pollution that collected in his wounds; the commotion and crowds involved in transportation, taxing for his weakened state. But he chose this city for what it also afforded him: further resources of spiritual and financial support, space from gossiping neighbors and an identity he had carried for years, and a reminder of the pathway that he had once planned on for himself. Staying in Cotonou was performed as something of an aspirational move on Alexandre's part, surrounding himself with his counterparts on a trajectory he had once imagined for himself. In the city he was forced to be surrounded by the bustle and be aware of the passage of time, as others moved forward without him. "A city does not exist 'in itself,' it is produced," writes Martinez (2014, 649), and here we see that beyond choosing a city, Alexandre produced a city that served him. Through learned navigation, he dealt with the contradictions and uncertainties the urban scenario presented him.

SUMMONING SUPPORT

I had the sense that, in addition to wanting to be away from the usual place in which he lived—a small town without much privacy and no escape from the public's continuous tracking of his health status—Alexandre wanted to be in an area where he could choose the people he spent time with and the people who supported him. He was fortunate in that he had another place to live and could exercise more control over the people playing a role—of spectator or otherwise—in his life. In the city, when he had the energy he visited other relatives and a couple times a week went to a cybercafé, where he would write to nurses he had befriended during his stay on the ship. Twice a week he went to two churches, once on Sundays to the evangelical family church in town near the Étoile Rouge, and on Wednesday mornings to another evangelical church in Zogbo for a five- to six-hour session especially for the sick and those who supported them.

This service took place in a rough, low cement construction set on a sandy street surrounded by similar buildings—when there was no service in session, it would not be obvious that the building was actually a house of worship until one stepped inside it. Other than that, it was the usual scenery of Cotonou—a concrete shell, open, gasping for any breath that could pass through on a typical hot, humid Sunday morning. The ground floor was wide open, with pews that would pack in three or four hundred people. However, the Wednesday sessions were held in a dark, crumbling room beneath the pulpit that became increasingly cramped and steamy as the worship continued, unless the rains managed to keep some attendees away. The services were dominated by pastor-led prayer and the testimonies of the believers. Speakers would stand and tell their story of pain, confusion, and disappointment, and, depending on what stage of illness they were at, the subsequent resolution to their problems that had come from the power of prayer in these sessions. The themes were generally about witchcraft and family troubles, with a particular emphasis on reproduction and giving birth. The testimonies were followed by a period of intense prayer that involved a pastor calling for blessings, forgiveness, and strength, after which the room would break into private prayer.

On some days, Alexandre also gave testimony at this service, focusing on Mercy Ships and all the friends who had encouraged him during this period. He described what he had felt moved to testify:

> I speak about God and my illness, and about how God helped and saved me from my sickness. I tell them about how on the ship, every morning and evening, the crew came to pray with me in their maternal language: in English, French, Chinese, Fongbe. I had visitors and friends come by. My life on the ship helped me so much, and thanks to this experience my life changed. Before the ship, I didn't pray for others, but now I pray for others and I pray for myself, because in praying for others, God helps you more.

He also thanked the church members for supporting him and felt that their prayers made him stronger, enabling him to resist temptation and encourage his faith regarding his illness. God had come through again. Everyone present then prayed together that he might be healed soon and that he be blessed.

This sort of activity in the church conveys one way in which ritual is enacted in order to create a sense of community and hope. The collective anticipation of fulfillment and the recounting of instances of fulfillment by members of the group are as important, if not more so, as the fulfillment itself. This is the creation of a congregation (Lange 2016), a unified body with a sick person at the center, instead of a sick person being outcast, as is so often highlighted in other literature and in other examples of the stigmatization of people with facial disfigurement (Knudson-Cooper 1981; Ablon 2002). It is an enactment of faith that embraces the sick person instead of casting him or her out, forming some of the ties that bind people together.

Turning to these services and opportunities is a way of watching out for oneself and creating a community where there otherwise might not be one. A unifying characteristic among the ship's patients that I followed was that they actively sought out faith and its ritual enactment to reconstruct their worlds. The other people in their lives who were a part of these networks may have come and gone, but the networks and options remained, the search for them becoming an integral part of daily life. Many patients had the opportunity to extend their search beyond one place; often, original homes were limiting and disappointing in this regard, and urban centers offered another chance. Those who had the ability to keep moving tried to expand their networks, negotiating other outlets beyond their home communities.

BOUNDARIES AND SEPARATION:
MOVEMENT BETWEEN RURAL AND URBAN

Not only did the affective experiences and characteristics of the cities and villages play an influential role in patients' navigation of their networks, but the distances between them were also used to their advantage, as well as being a way to create borders and boundaries. Keeping space between locations allowed for the re-creation of personal stories of illness and healing. For example, the Abidé family, whom I met during the *Anastasis* medical screening, had a little girl who had an operation on the ship for a cleft lip when she was almost one year old. Her parents waited until after her surgery had been completed before taking her home to her mother's village, only a two-and-a-half-hour drive from the city. Many months and hurdles passed before the girl was considered "OK" enough (or, acceptable) to be taken home to meet the family, whereas her two older brothers had both made the trip within the first weeks after their births. Healing this illness was seen as a stepping-stone on the path to "right" the wrong, and the first real homecoming was saved for after her face had been "fixed."

Dzifa, who was mentioned earlier, provides another example of using distance to moderate one's story. As a student in Lomé in his early twenties who had been operated on for a large obstructive facial tumor, Dzifa did everything he could to avoid going back home to his village four hours away during his illness and kept this up for a period of six years. Initially, I thought his intention was to return only after he could show he had been healed. In fact, he wanted to manage his image, returning when he was healed *and* when he could show he had made it in the city with his university studies (which proved to be nearly impossible with the preset success quotas at the university favoring those with connections). The village came laden with expectations, but could be managed and controlled by cordoning it off, away from one's life.

These are examples of the rural home, often seen as a refuge and place of support and nourishment, having a sort of repelling effect on some patients, when they had the autonomy to navigate their courses of healing as they wished. At times the porosity of the village—its characters, curiosity, and embrace—created difficulties for these individuals (as also explored by Jackson [2011] and Stoller [2014]), and they sought out the compartmentalization, the bunkerization (De Boeck 2007) of the city, with its bustle, boundaries, and edges. Jackson (2011) writes about "the village" being pregnant with expectations of those who have left, awaiting what they achieved outside it that they can bring back home. In turn, those who leave carefully negotiate their relations with the village, as they seek to sustain their emotional and practical lives outside it. This situates their action in terms of not only surviving their lives in the city but also holding a thread to their previous lives. Alexandre, for example, managed his relationships with those in the village back home, using his access to a space to stay in the city as a way of dealing better with the ultimate home base the village provided him. Navigating the distance between places was one way of keeping ownership of one's uncertain trajectories.

Nevertheless, as De Boeck writes, "To deal with the city is to deal with hazard" (2013, 545). This was the case for Francine, who, unable to support herself in the city, retreated still farther from her village by secluding herself more remotely to be on her own. My informants sought to live their illnesses beyond solely the nurturing aspects of their nearest and dearest; they sought communities and spaces for sustenance farther afield when they had agency in their choices.

CLOSINGS

In this chapter, I have analyzed the affective landscape that is established in the healing journeys of West African patients that transect both their rural and urban networks, as well as the space of potentialities that is established by Mercy Ships. In a context of scarce resources, these patients' affective journeys include the quest for well-being, as well as their search for identification, belonging, and (re)orientation.

Through these individuals' navigation of their trajectories, we observe their strategic behavior and awareness of what they need as they deal with the uncertainties surrounding their health. Already they had an episode with the ship, an answer to their calls for help for healing. They then were thrust out of the safe space on board and needed to resituate themselves as they dealt with the difficult, indeterminate steps that followed. As such, this chapter has looked at the different possibilities that city and village homes afford people who are in treatment or recovery from reconstructive surgery, and sometimes in compromised positions of choice and autonomy due to their health, to live out their networks of social and spiritual support. Alexandre, in his search for healing, enacted a "reverse migration" to the typical trajectory of city dwellers moving from the hectic, polluted center to the outskirts or back to the village for peace. He was better able to rest by moving into the anonymity of the city, giving himself the capacity to choose his social network, including the special weekly evangelical Christian mass where he could recreate himself from his identity in the village. Francine moved back and forth between her secluded spot, her maternal village, and Lomé to cope and to receive the care she needed as she dealt with the "dead time" that came with waiting for healing, waiting to be able to work, waiting for a future.

For both of them, the city represented a counterpoint to their rural homes: anonymizing pools, a "thickening of fields" (Simone 2004), spaces pulsing with unknowns to be organized more or less effectively into resources, friendships, networks, and—hopefully—healing. They tapped into the nexus of affect, emotion, and intellect when they turned to the city to shake up their situations, to, in essence, generate the paths they then could embark on navigating. This even allowed them to reproduce stability, a fabrication of exterior flux to counter the boredom, the worry, the pain, and the erosion that could dominate from within.

Harris Solomon (2011) has explored the contribution of affect to medical tourism—a health-seeking modus generally infused with more choices and options than my informants experienced in their quest for surgical care. Nevertheless, he considers that the "sentiments instantiated through medical tourism exemplify [a] pull and push of subjects: across geographic borders, through healthcare's apparent dead-ends of solemn resignation and promising, unexpected detours, and into relations with caregivers far from home" (H. Solomon 2011, 107). Through similar themes enacted in very different settings, he sees the action and movement involved in health-seeking and recovery as being part of what defines the experience for his informants.

For my informants, for whom Mercy Ships was often their only hope, and without which their trajectories fumbled through quotidian challenges, their affective journeys were permeated by any limitations they confronted. One way of approaching their stories is to think about the kinds of crises they navigated emotionally and how their emotional intelligence led them in one direction rather than another. What is interesting about affect is the suggestion that emotion is as important as intellect in decision making: "Affect refers to those registers of experience which cannot be easily seen and which might variously be described as non-cognitive, trans-subjective, non-conscious, non-representational, incorporeal and immaterial" (Blackman 2012, 4), and as Francine, Alexandre, and the others navigated their paths, we see choices that might appear counterintuitive. It is about more than personal emotion—it is about the powerful confluence of emotion, experiences, opportunities, influences, power, space, and trajectories that lead to affect. Religion, quest, healing, uncertainty, and illness are all part of that. Affect is about movement, and it is not stable. In this sense, the very act of navigating and choosing between such drastically different spaces, while embodying the uncertainty, doubt, and compromised health that their illnesses entailed, amplified the affective experience they inhabited. Through their pathways, they came to hold a sophisticated knowledge (see the chapter by van Dijk in this volume) of their journeys by linking the many inputs they allowed onto their course—biomedicine, religious faith and healing, social collectivity, solitude—to shape and reconcile their experiences.

Here between the contexts of the city and the ship, these moves were a method of maintaining, reorienting, and affirming their healing trajectory; the moves informed their paths as they negotiated expectations of personal worth and value, productivity, contribution, and responsibility and how they impacted their lives. The contrast between the settings and the repeated movement between them intensify and create new attachments and affective networks as my informants inhabited liminal spaces between illness and wellness. They were dodging, weaving, shadowboxing their way through their situations. *Dubria. On se defend.*

NOTES

1. I carried out fieldwork for this chapter between 2004 and 2009 in Benin, Togo, Ghana, and Sierra Leone as part of doctoral research exploring Mercy Ships as a site of transformation for both the crew and the patients who come to the ship for health care reasons. I continued informal fieldwork until 2016 in Benin with some of the individuals written about here.

2. This is not a translation of a typical Fongbe response, the predominant language around Cotonou and common in the south of Benin.

3. Estimates developed by the UN Inter-agency Group for Child Mortality Estimation (UNICEF, WHO, World Bank, UN DESA Population Division) published by child-mortality.org and accessed at http://data.worldbank.org/indicator/SH.DYN .MORT?page=2 (accessed April 12, 2014). Since 2000, according to UNICEF statistics, these indicators have improved in Benin, at a similar rate to that of its neighbors.

6 THE CLEANSING TOUCH

SPIRITS, ATMOSPHERES, AND AT*TOUCH*MENT IN A "JAPANESE" SPIRITUAL MOVEMENT IN KINSHASA

PETER LAMBERTZ

Early on a Saturday morning in 2012, the square next to Rond-point Victoire, in the heart of Kinshasa's Matonge neighborhood, is clothed in an exceptionally thick cloud of brownish dust. As I approach one of the city's most intensely frequented crossroads, where many Kinois (Kinshasa's inhabitants) change their taxi or minibus connection throughout the day and evening, I perceive a circle of about twenty people equipped with brooms, sweeping their way centrifugally out from the Monument des Artistes at the center of the square.[1]

The thick fog that covers the square is caused by the followers of Église Messianique Mondiale (EMM), which is carrying out its monthly public cleansing campaign, called *nettoyage publique*. Ignorant passersby, but also Messianiques (EMM's followers) themselves, identify this task intuitively as *salongo*, a concept that sticks in people's memories from former Zairian times, when President Mobutu Sese Seko aimed to encourage a national work ethic through collective public cleaning work.[2]

Two men are digging their fingers into the earth to remove patches of grass at the edge of the square. As one Messianique, Ntumba, explained to me, "We believe that by changing the living conditions of our ancestors, we can also change the living condition of our living brothers and sisters."[3]

Jacques, one of EMM's ministers, put it this way: "The more we are in an unhealthy environment, the more power evil spirits have over us. But if the surroundings are clean it will be difficult for them to influence us."[4] It is striking how ardent, enthusiastic, and visibly concentrated these Messianiques are about this ritualized cleaning work, which, as I would later find out, is aimed at the tactile transmission of a positive "sentiment" to ancestral spirits attached to urban space. Farther down the road, a number of women have teamed up and made shovels out of cardboard with which they are lifting quantities of rubbish into a container. Workers in the town hall of Kalamu, one of Kinshasa's municipalities, had brought it along, happy about the unusual offer from the followers of this *église* (church) to take over their job. This is not just some cleaning as a performance laid on for others but real corporeal engagement with the smelly rubbish, which is touched and carried with the bare hands.

A third group has moved on to sweeping the courtyard and wiping clean the building of the town hall of Kalamu. At around 11:00 AM, a total of about seventy Messianiques have gathered here to complete this day's salongo session by cleaning the town hall itself. Eventually, three of EMM's superiors are granted the privilege of entering and wiping clean the mayor's office. Before they return to EMM's church compound to conclude the cleaning campaign with Japanese mantra chanting, they place little ikebana flower arrangements in the clerks' offices to embellish, purge, and aesthetically seal the spiritual labor of the day.

A "JAPANESE" SPIRITUAL MOVEMENT IN KINSHASA

Église Messianique Mondiale is the locally used name of the Japanese new religion Sekai Kyûseikyô (Church of World Messianity), which was founded in 1935 in the context of rapid urbanization and industrialization in Japan. Followers refer to its founder, Mokichi Okada (1882–1955), as Meishu Sama (Japanese for Master of Light). In the 1950s, EMM spread to Thailand, Sri Lanka, Europe, the United States, and also Brazil, where, along with Seicho-no-Ie and Soka Gakkai International, it became one of the country's major Japanese religious movements, which, since the 1990s, has attracted mainly former Catholics from the middle class. In Brazil, along with the Pentecostal revolution of the 1990s and alternative spiritualities such as Candomblé, Umbanda, and Kardecism, Japanese new religions also increasingly became a mainstream option (Carpenter 2004), offering their followers a highly personalized focus on individual problems, which, like Pente-

FIGURE 6.1 Messianiques during salongo at Rond-point Victoire. In the background, billboards advertise Joseph Kabila's "Cinq Chantiers" program for the restoration of public infrastructure, to which Messianiques implicitly contribute. Photo by Peter Lambertz.

costalism, contrasted with the focus on wider social issues that the Catholic Church had prioritized under its "liberation theology" (Matsuoka 2007, 53).

In the rapidly growing urban centers of Africa, "spiritual movements," as they are locally often called today, ever since they were first "imported" by Africans in the 1970s, have been the privileged harbors of elite circles, who used them to cultivate a mystique of power based on the idea of the secret manipulation of occult forces (Cohen 1981; Lambertz 2018).[5] However, along with the wave of democratization of the 1990s, which led many African states to liberalize the spheres of the media and of religion, a tendency toward the democratization of access to and interest in "spiritual movements" can also be observed. In Kinshasa, for instance, where former class divides had been disrupted by the overthrow of Mobutu and the subsequent Congo Wars (1997–2004), the followers of spiritual movements today include an increasing number of noneducated yet curious urban youngsters, who seek to complement their chiefly Christian religious trajectories with spiritual technologies from other parts of the world. Though numerically speaking spiritual movements, which Pentecostal Christians continue to condemn as "occult sciences," remain minorities, they are thus undeniably part and parcel of the religious landscape of contemporary urban Africa. In Angola, where EMM first arrived from Brazil in 1991, it acquired a followership of about thirty-seven thousand.[6] In the Democratic Republic of Congo, the official figure is currently around twenty-five hundred, which, however, excludes an important number of unsteady seekers roaming around Kinshasa's spiritual supermarket. Among the spiritual movements that are currently present in Kinshasa are Soka Gakkai International, Eckankar, the Brahma Kumaris Spiritual University, the Grail Movement, the Association of the Supreme Master Ching Hai, the Rosicrucian Order, and Sukyô Mahikari.[7]

Though trying to follow the organizational model of the uncountable églises that continue to mushroom in the city, EMM, by advocating reconciliation with rather than a break with the African past, differs from most trends within African Pentecostalism (Meyer 1998b; Kalu 2008).[8] Considering itself a "superreligion," EMM is explicitly syncretic and has incorporated practices from Shintô, Buddhist, and Christian/Catholic repertoires (the symbol of the cross, the Lord's Prayer), as well as from Congo's more long-standing religious tradition: Messianiques take pride in the practice of "ancestor worship," which, although of Japanese inspiration, provides a powerful means to re-/produce "African" heritage in a seemingly modern form.[9] There are important differences in etiology, too: suffering is not caused by the devil as an external agent but is the result of one's own and one's ancestors' sins. Taken together, these sins, as well as one's virtues, determine one's karma, which corresponds to the level of fortune or well-being and accords well with the logic of the Central African fortune-misfortune complex (De Craemer, Fox, and Vansina 1976). By ascribing any form of suffering the beneficial function of personal and, by implication, collective, purification, suffering is seen as a beneficial struggle that purges humanity and the world of collective sins and blockages.

This positive purpose of suffering indicates that, with the increasing religious pluralism of Africa's urban centers, a pluralism of theodicies is also emerging that serves to explain the world and its hardships and that translates into different aesthetic and affective modes of experiencing and acting in the city. EMM is a good example: through a healing ritual called Johrei (Japanese for "purification of the soul"), which is done in silence by two persons sitting motionless who mutually transmit invisible healing "light" to each other, an aesthetic difference—as perceived by others and by the practicing self—is tuned into the bodies of practitioners so as to embody a spiritual presence within the sensational overdrive of the city of Kinshasa (cf. Lambertz 2018). Like other spiritual movements, EMM's aesthetic repertoire is based on a politics of sensory distribution,[10] which focuses on silence and the maintenance of inner peace. This contrasts with the aesthetics of sensory intensity that is well known from Pentecostal deliverance rituals. Yet, despite these differences, EMM's success, like that of Pentecostalism, is also due to its ability to encourage a sense of (in)dividual personhood that is particular to city life and the numerous challenges it entails (Pype 2011). Through both intellectual and ritual practices, urbanites are guided to "come to terms" with the material and intellectual challenges of life in the city.[11]

By looking at EMM's emphasis on the role of sentiments and the work of assigning the city's problems of rubbish, accidents, and other uncanny events a particular place and meaning, this chapter deals with one such attempt to come to terms. All these problems take place in spaces that inspire feelings of uncertainty, fear, discomfort, or unease, such as crossroads, markets, transport hubs, or other sites of passage where accidents are frequent and police agents abound. This makes the coming to terms above all a challenge on the affective level, which EMM explicitly addresses through its multifaceted practices of *nettoyage*. Originating in Japan, practices of nettoyage (such as salongo) offer a way to deal actively with vengeful spirits that seem to concentrate in and threaten particular places of city life.

By following EMM's practices of nettoyage, two things, which I will lay out in this chapter, become apparent. First, EMM deploys its own reflexive theory of sentiment and affective behavior as a core theoretical grid to explain the concentration of mishaps at certain places in the city, as well as the vicissitudes of city life. Second, practices of nettoyage have implications for a sentiment of belonging, which I suggest is grasped by the concept of "at*touch*ment." After elucidating these two respective arguments in the following section, the chapter moves on to the field of Kinshasa and EMM's cleansing activities here and then closes with a conclusion.

EMM teaches that the origins of evil in the world are essentially to be sought in the individual self, which henceforth ought to seek purification in order to be freed from sin and what is seen, in Kinshasa, as spiritual blockage. The quest for salvation ought to start in one's own inside, by cultivating a "sentiment" of love (Lingala: *bolingo*, French: *amour*) and gratitude (Li. *botondi*, Fr. *gratitude*) vis-à-vis one's ancestors and God. Messianiques use the concept of "sentiment" in both French and Lingala to designate an intimate emotional disposition, an inclination or attitude that may best be captured by the concept of "mood." It can be generated, trained, and cultivated so as to last and endure, very much like an "individual's conscious anticipation of an event and [which also justifies] the appearance of a corresponding [i.e., emotional] response" (Reihling 2014, 31; see also the introduction to this volume). Next to this level of lasting sentiments, I use the concept of "affect" to indicate the ways in which Kinois intuitively and spontaneously perceive and respond to particular places in their city. I agree, however, with Reckwitz that affects can never be precultural, that is, that they are "always embedded in practices which are, in turn, embedded in tacit schemes of interpretation. . . . They are bodily reactions and they are enabled/restricted by interpretative schemes at the same time" (2012, 251).[12] EMM offers precisely such a scheme of interpretation that enables its followers to engage affectively with the places that surround them in order to challenge and replace locally dominant schemes of interpretation.

Messianiques put forward a framework that places the two levels of lasting sentiment and intuitive short-term affect into articulation with each other. The founder Meishu Sama had devised a theory according to which houses and individual persons have their own respective "spiritual atmosphere." In Kinshasa, where urban spaces are also said to have such a spiritual atmosphere, this is explained by Messianiques as the sum of sentiments held by the ancestral spirits that are attached to these places and bodies.[13] The person who encounters such a place or body will be intuitively touched, enveloped, or affected by the respective atmosphere, and his or her mood will change accordingly. In the longer run a mutual tuning takes place, harmonizing the sentimental constitutions of both the surrounding atmosphere and the encountering human agent. In other words, the intuitive affective short-term reactions we have vis-à-vis places and people are interpreted as manifestations of the respective spiritual atmosphere these places radiate, that is, of the moods and sentiments of the spirits that inhabit them.

In the academic literature linked to the affective turn in the social sciences (see the introduction to this volume), spirits have so far rarely been considered to be constitutive parts of affective relations. Yet, as I wish to argue in this chapter, there is an impressive degree of comparability between EMM's theory of sentiments and affects linked to spaces and bodies, on the one hand, and the theoretical debate about affect and emotion in anthropology and the social sciences, on the other.[14] A most striking parallelism can be seen in the recent rehabilitation of affect and space as constitutive of social practices. As has been powerfully suggested by Andreas Reckwitz (2012), spatial and affective dimensions have long been excluded from social analysis, especially with regard to their mutual interdependence. Though Messianiques' teachings are less in the tradition of Spinoza and Deleuze, it is fair to say that their engagement with affects and the sentimental production of space appears to respond to Reckwitz's claim for the integration of affects and space into the study of social practice. But there are more homologies: in her piece on "affective economies," Ahmed (2004) ascribes to emotions an autonomous ontology, quite comparable to that of spirits in Kinshasa. She writes, "In such affective economies emotions *do things*, and they align individuals with communities—or bodily space with social space—through the very intensity of their attachments" (2004, 119). Could this not be read as an explanatory comment on EMM's "spiritual atmosphere"? Moreover, both these theorical strands of affect postulate a spectrum of affective/spiritual intensities (rather than a set of preclassified basic emotions) comparable to that put forward by Deleuze and Guattari (1994) and Massumi (2002). Messianiques' theory suggests a scale of emotional gradations between the ideal-typical spiritual states of "heaven" (peace, joy) and "hell" (fear, anger, vengeance), which opens up a spectrum of intensities rather than a classification of postulated emotions. One's respective position between the two determines how one generally feels, that is, one's current emotional/sentimental situation (and, by implication, one's level of physical, social, and economic mis-/fortune).

The transformation of the atmospheres of bodies and places by way of nettoyage has an obvious consequence: places, and through their association with ancestral spirits also the memory attached to them, are kinetically redeemed and appropriated. This process of moral transformation, of both bodies and urban places, can be seen, I argue, as an affective politics of sensory at*touch*ment through which the city and its space are viscerally appropriated and brought about. The concept of at*touch*ment points beyond a dichotomization of purely symbolic/meaning-based and material/sensory ways of connecting with space. It allows us to come closer to emic understandings of space and affects, which locally are not structured according to the body/matter-versus-mind/meaning divide, but rather conflate this doubtful dichotomization.[15]

EMM's politics of sensory at*touch*ment contrasts with Pentecostalism's emphasis on breaking with the past and demonizing ancestral forces (Meyer 1998b; De Boeck 2004, 102–113; Marshall 2009, 123), which is supported by the conception of the Holy Spirit as a categorically evanescent agent who cannot be bound or territorially fixed but encourages territorial detachment, mobility, and the quest for ever more insatiable salvation (Kirsch 2008b, 137–144; Robbins 2006).

TOUCHING THE CITY:
SPIRITUAL INTENSITIES IN THE URBAN SPACE

Mary Douglas's (1966) argument that dirt is "matter out of place" and that conceptions of purity must, therefore, constantly be stabilized by (ritual) cultural practice may account for the fact that there are various traditions of ritualized cleanliness throughout the world. EMM's teaching that spiritual danger resides in the urban environment is not an intervention from Japan but has a long-standing local history in Central Africa as well. In Kinshasa, just like in Congo's rural areas, the sandy soils within private compounds are routinely swept on a daily basis, usually in the early morning hours. During fieldwork in a village among the baYombe in Lower Congo in 2006, I learned that sweeping was remembered as being done formerly to remove unwanted spirits of the night. Morning sweeping draws neat and orderly lines in the soil, generating a pattern of order and alignment, and visualizing accomplishment and control. Yet, the ritual importance Messianiques attach to their cleaning efforts resonates strongly with the Japanese Zen Buddhist tradition. As Ian Reader explains with regard to Japan, "It is hard to avoid the overt, potentially obsessive, concern with ordering the personal and spatial environment in Japan," where "communal cleaning activities may occur in the day-to-day flow of life" (1995, 239). This focus on public cleanliness originates in Zen Buddhism, which, by virtue of ritual purity, involves "some form of cleaning of the temple grounds and environment, such as sweeping the tatami floors of the halls of worship, meticulously dusting the Buddhist altars, washing out the toilets and scrubbing and polishing the wooden corridors, cleaning up the graveyard and sweeping up leaves" (231).[16]

TOUCHING HOUSES, SOIL, AND PEOPLE

Among Messianiques in Kinshasa, *nettoyage* is a key word. It refers to the overall paradigm of cleaning, cleansing, cleanliness, and purification, which EMM's multiple messianic efforts of flower arranging, Johrei healing, the chanting of Japanese mantra prayers, and the ritual cleaning of private and public urban spaces are all about. The entire movement can indeed be seen as a transnationally organized cleansing campaign. Driven, as it claims, by the messianic project to create paradise on earth, it is actively involved with constituting little models of cleanliness around the world. EMM sees itself as the chosen minority whose exemplary efforts radiate from the inside out.

In Kinshasa, a first space that is systematically subjected to cleanliness is the sacred space of the different Johrei centers. Every morning at a given time (usually at eight o'clock), a missionary sweeps the respective site with a broom and cleans it. He or she also wipes the altar and the photograph of the founder, Meishu Sama, and occasionally freshens up or replaces the ikebana flower arrangement that decorates the *autel* (Fr. *altar*). During the daytime, when Johrei is dispensed here, at least one person regularly sweeps the hall with a broom and makes sure that the unused plastic chairs are put back on the stack next to the entrance. Especially in EMM's more modest and at times still somewhat improvised prayer sites, the attention given to cleaning and cleanliness surprises one and points to the ritualized nature of its Japanese Zen Buddhist origin.

Nettoyage is also carried out during home visits to individual practitioners. Soon after a new follower has started frequenting one of EMM's branches to receive Johrei and decides to give the remaining ritual repertoire a try, a small group of Messianiques pays a visit to his or her homestead equipped with brooms, cleaning products, and the sentimental fervor that accompanies the cleaning campaign. Mostly these cleansing actions are intended to fight a particular problem the practitioner is encountering in his or her life. On one occasion I participated in the nettoyage of the house of Maman Florence, who, "thanks to EMM," was recovering from the dreadful *mbasu* disease, a spiritually caused disease that transforms entire limbs into swollen ulceric lesions, and which, in her case, had deformed the left side of her head and face.[17] EMM's twenty-seven-year-old missionary Barbara explained to me that the disease was an ancestral punishment for the "sexual disorder" Florence had caused by "making a man from another of EMM's branches commit adultery with her." The housecleaning thus had the explicit purpose of spiritual cleansing with a view to uplifting the spiritual atmosphere, that is, Florence's ancestors' sentiments, and thus enhancing her recovery.

All the walls, ceilings, and floors of the different rooms were first swept with brooms, then the floors were washed with water and liquid soap, before flowers were put in place and arranged. The team of eight Messianiques physically attacked the house and its "dirt." In particular, old items that had lost their utility were thrown out, such as a broken television set, empty cardboard boxes, old rags, and worn-out clothes from a dusty corner of a shelf. Most of these were burned as a matter of purification. After this cleaning, a good thirty minutes of collective chanting of EMM's key mantra prayers was repeated in each of the rooms of the house. Finally flowers were arranged, and the little community spent thirty minutes transmitting Johrei in silence to each other in the living room of the house.

Ritual housecleaning for spiritual purposes has obvious precedents in Central Africa. The missionary ethnographer William F. P. Burton (1961, 124) describes a thoroughly ritualized housecleaning session among the Luba, where a "medicine man" visits a home to remove an upset ancestral spirit. In the reported case, the husband of the family had upset his mother's spirit, who was now blocking his wife's fertility. The medicine man swept the house with the help of what Burton called a "magical broom" made from the nerves of the oil palm, with which he collected dust and dirt from the house, which were ritually burned by the woman of the house and later disposed of as ashes at a nearby crossroads to prevent other spirits from coming back.[18]

The flowers and decorative leaves placed in Florence's house had been brought from EMM's own little flower garden. In Messianiques' understanding, flowers can store and remediate sentiments. In a weekly teaching session, minister Jacques explained to his listeners how the sentimental work of flowers can heal people from bad temper:

> If you arrange flowers, you transmit your sentiment to them. They must not be prepared in anger. You can fight with somebody, you swear at people, and you then will arrange flowers. You will see, the flowers that you arrange like this, which usually last up to a week, will die already after two or three days. Why? You didn't put the right sentiment into the flower. When you prepare

the flower, speak like this to God: "all those who enter my house, may the flower illuminate them, give them joy in my home." This is the sentiment with which you should arrange your flowers. And if it fades, don't leave it there. Remove it the next day. If you have a turbulent child at home, a stubborn child, a younger brother or a stubborn kin with bad behavior, when you make the flower call him or her and ask: How do you like this flower? He or she will say: Ah! It is beautiful! It is really beautiful.[19]

In line with the teaching about the spiritual atmosphere, the flower uplifts not only the temper of a child but also that of houses. The conviction that some rented houses may have been built with "dirty money," that is, with money that the owner has earned by resorting to the help of *magie* by sacrificing family members, is a theme often heard in Kinshasa. The vengeful spirits of the sacrificed victims are known to attach themselves to the respective house that was built with the money they had been sacrificed for. But rarely is the link made between such a haunted house and its cleanliness. It is here that EMM offers an alternative interpretative scheme. The "bad vibrations" of a house could easily be improved by cleaning the house, by placing flowers in it and by cultivating a sentiment of gratitude toward the unhappy spirits that inhabit it. It should be noted that this stress on spirits as part of a place's affective relations appears to be a local version of the spiritual atmosphere theme.

The underlying logic is that, like Johrei, nettoyage, and the chanting of prayers, properly arranged flowers can also actively improve the spiritual atmosphere of a place or a person. As mentioned earlier, the teaching says that the atmosphere of houses and persons can be intuitively sensed. This remarkably resembles the German philosopher Gernot Böhme's aesthetic theory, presented in his book *Athmosphäre: Essays zu einer neuen Ästhetik* (2013). Before perception may occur, Böhme contends, our human senses are tuned, and in a way positioned, by what he calls atmospheres.[20] In Kinshasa this seems a well-known lived reality, beyond the vicinities of Messianiques. The difference lies in the fact that, instead of drawing in concepts equivalent to "perception," such as *Befinden*, *Sinnlichkeit*, or *Ästhetik*, as Böhme does, the language used here is one of active spirits.

Messianiques explained to me that the spiritual atmosphere that results from the spirits living in a house, for instance, permeates the people who live in it. The stress lies on the mutual attunement of the spirit's and the inhabitant's sentimental constitution. Messianique missionary Barbara formulated it like this: "Everything you utter from your thoughts stays in the atmosphere,"[21] stressing that this includes thoughts, speech, and feelings, which, if negative, can have blocking effects on others living in the house.

Also, agricultural work (Li. *bilanga*) in one's home garden and in the church's field garden, close to the Mangengenge mountain on the outskirts of Kinshasa, is a central task within the catalog of EMM's ritual precepts. The choice of the field site near this mountain reflects the importance of older local spiritual geographies. For several centuries, at least, the rock has been a local holy site, which Catholic missionaries appropriated by turning its ascent into a crosswalk and a pilgrimage site.

Like flower arranging, the activity of bilanga depends on the "sentiments" of love and gratitude toward the soil one is to touch. Soil (Li. *mabele*) is understood as the abode where ancestral spirits dwell. While practicing bilanga, every follower is encouraged to develop these sentiments within oneself.

While some, usually younger, practitioners carry out the work—as I observed it, and as can easily be imagined—as a community exercise with laughter and fun, others deliberately separate themselves from the group so as to continue laboring on their own, their afflictions pushing them to try to mobilize an amount of sentiment so as to seemingly force their gratitude and love onto their ancestors. On one occasion a man repeatedly murmured for more than twenty minutes the sentence *Nazo sala musala oyo pona bakoko ya mboka na biso oyo* (I am doing this work for the ancestors of our country), which reflects how serious the prescription of zealous gardening with sentiment is taken by some so as to encourage the hoped-for beneficial pragmatic outcomes of the act.

Just like Johrei, which can be seen as a matter of "getting in touch without contact," the practice of organic agriculture is also essentially understood as spiritually reaching out to and literally "touching" one's ancestors, with both hands and sentiments. The aim is to earn their favor and protection for one's own upcoming activities. Jacques, who is in charge of some of EMM's regular teaching sessions, phrased it thus: "By touching the earth, by growing crops over here, we are touching our ancestors in the spiritual world."[22]

TOUCHING URBAN PUBLIC SPACE

Certain streets and public areas are cleaned by Kinshasa's inhabitants during the public salongo hours prescribed by the state on Saturday mornings. These are places used on a daily basis, by market women or merchants who run a business or a *malewa* street restaurant. Many corners and crossroads, however, which cannot be clearly ascribed to the supervision of a particular user, remain untouched by these cleaning efforts, inviting Kinois to use other strategies to conquer them. It is to these *bisika ya pamba* (places good for nothing) that De Boeck's (2004, 256) main argument of the city as an invisible architecture of words powerfully applies: what cannot be made, conjured, or controlled with hands, cement, or bricks is done with the building blocks of words and the demiurgic power of imagination. On the one hand, spiritual theories such as that advanced by EMM can be seen as such an invisible architecture of space appropriation. On the other hand, this works through systematic mockery and the cementing effect of laughter, as the well-known Kinois joke about Kin-la-poubelle masterfully shows.[23] In a way, Kinshasa's rubbish is the city's own laughter, a dirty smile indeed, driven by anger and despondency. As an expression of "fake," or pretend, alienation, it creates sufficient distance and detachment from the root causes of the problem to conjure up a protective shield of indifference, which is vital for self-respect to survive. The seriousness of religious ritual and the mockery of the city's abysses go hand in hand, the one offering at*touch*ment, the other de*touch*ment as a solution.

EMM's practice of nettoyage, on the other hand, is also done to touch those ancestors that affect the lives of Kinshasa's urbanites collectively. Given the connection between mishap, fear (i.e., danger), and the presence of unhappy ancestral spirits, the places chosen for cleaning campaigns are those neighborhoods, crossroads, or markets that Kinois deem spiritually dangerous, where insecurity thrives and urban life feels threatening.[24] In this sense, just like the choice of Mangengenge as the site for installing EMM's nature farming site, salongo responds directly to Kinshasa's urban spiritual geography as it grows in the affective imagination of its inhabitants.

One category of such places are crossroads, which are not only the sites of repeated, often fatal accidents, but also the spatial road hubs that cause Kinshasa's intimidating traffic jams. Contact between ordinary people and police officers is most intense here. Apparent insufficiencies in terms of road size, lane capacity, potholes, and so forth are a very convenient infrastructural potential here not only for police agents in search of a "tip," but also for ambulant vendors, pickpockets, street children, and others.[25] In such places, salongo also has a clear proselytizing aim. Given that active proselytizing is against the ideal posited by the founder, Meishu Sama, EMM uses its salongo sessions to attract public attention, to get in touch with people and garner publicity.

Repeated salongo sessions have been organized and carried out by EMM at the crossroads of Rond-point Ngaba, where the important transport axis from Lower Congo reaches the city. Another crossroad is Pascal on Avenue Lumumba, which links Kinshasa to the airport and with Congo's interior. Rond-point Victoire, mentioned in the vignette at the beginning of the chapter, in addition to its central location as an everyday hub in the pulsating heart of Matonge, also stands for the commemoration of Congo's artists, which is important for EMM given the explicit Japanese teachings on the importance of beauty for human development.

Salongo has also been carried out on the market of Simbazikita next to Kinshasa's Ndolo domestic airport, where, on January 8, 1996, an airplane crashed into the market crowds and killed 237 people. The event is popularly remembered as *l'accident du marché Type K*, while press reports refer to *la catastrophe de Kinshasa*.[26] Meishu Sama's teachings on the consequences of unnatural deaths such as accidents, suicides, or murders directly correspond to interpretations that have been documented in Central Africa, as well as in other parts of Africa.[27] EMM's teachers preach that the spirits of people who died in unfortunate circumstances such as accidents or suicides must be looking to avenge their unhappy fate by wandering close to the place of their physical demise, where they seek to possess other living beings so as to continue partaking in a material existence. The spiritual necessity of cleansing the market of Simbazikita so as to console the resentful spirits of the victims is obvious.

Another market frequently targeted by EMM is the central Zando market: some people sweep market stalls, collect rubbish, or burn waste, while others distribute little flowers. Zando is less of a hot spot for accidents, but the density of people, the ongoing haggling and negotiating, and the more general intensity of hustle and bustle suggest an atmosphere of insecurity that causes many to avoid the place. All these places to which EMM devotes its cleansing attention are locations Kinois generally prefer to avoid, indicating the negative affective relationship they generally have with them.

Another crossroads is Point Chaud (Place of Heat) in the neighborhood of Kingabwa, where EMM did salongo twice in 2013. When, on another evening, I wanted to sit down there for a beer with my friend André so as to observe the hustle and bustle, André soon got up again, insisting, "This is not a good place, I don't like it here. Can we go somewhere else?" When I asked him what was up, he said, "I don't know, there are places which I feel are not good to hang around at," adding later, though, that he had noticed the "cachot" (prison cell) of the nearby police office.[28]

There are also iconic places for Congo's national past, which EMM cleans so as to touch the collective ancestors of the Congolese nation. One such place is an abandoned space between Avenue Huileries and the Stade des Martyrs (de la Pentecôte) (formerly Stade Kamanyola). Its new name was given to it at the time of Laurent-Désiré Kabila's rule to commemorate the four "martyrs" of Congolese independence, whom Mobutu had killed in June 1966 in an effort to display and consolidate his authoritarian rule. "It's the third time we go there," explained Minister Jacques, who continued:

> It is to posit a model of beauty. And it is where the martyrs died. It will surely influence them and the authorities. Apparently there were also some that were hung from the Kasa-Vubu bridge (not far from there), some who had been into politics, whose lives were ended there. By touching these places, one can always influence and touch the sentiment of all these persons, who are now in the spiritual world, and who maybe even find themselves in hell. But we at EMM think that through the work we do we are able to save all these spirits, little by little, and make them rise back to heaven.[29]

Driven by the aim to offer a sentimental touch to former political actors who, like the martyrs, died in unhappy circumstances, Messianiques also offer their tidying touch to the city's cemeteries. The cemetery of Kitambo has already been taken on, just like a cemetery of Teke chiefs in the neighborhood of Nsele, but a priority now is the cemetery of Gombe, where many formerly illustrious personalities (politicians, musicians, etc.) are buried. Mr. Jacques explained to me:

> Imagine the state in which these prime ministers, these heads of state are. They have been assassinated, they have feelings of resentment against us. Imagine our president, Mzee (Laurent-Désiré Kabila), what does he think, over there, where he is? I have worked hard and, eventually, they have removed me. All this, the sentiments of these people, it affects our politics. . . . These politicians, in the spirit world, at which [spiritual] level are they? You see? So, we communicate our sentiments.[30]

Mr. Ntumba provided a similar explanation by invoking Joseph Kasa-Vubu, whom Mobutu drove out of power in 1965:

> NTUMBA: The ancestors, also those of this nation, are always at work. They are active where they are, in the spiritual world. But they have quit power

full of resentment [Fr. *ressentiments*]. . . . When Kasa-Vubu went . . . , voilà, he died with this resentment. There is a tie between us humans . . . , and he was a head of state, so he had a tie with all Congolese. . . . So his resentment has been reaching all Congolese people. . . .

PETER: And what about Mobutu? Should one therefore commemorate him?

NTUMBA: Not only commemorate. . . . Better would even be: repentance . . . , offerings . . . , but he (Kabila) did not do any of this so far.

That the commemoration of defunct political actors carries a political charge and can easily become a bone of contention is well known. The yearly debates in Japan about the official commemoration of World War II heroes at the Yasukuni shrine are but one example. The absence of former president Mobutu from any depiction in Kinshasa's public space is another. Though until twenty years ago the entire Zairian nation was incited to extensively wear printed cloths (Li. *liputa*, Fr. *pagne*) with Mobutu's head on them, it is impossible today to find a single one of them in public. Even if today a growing nostalgia for Mobutu and his empowering nationalist rhethoric is gaining ground,[31] after his overthrow by the current president's father, Laurent-Désiré Kabila, in 1997, the nation was at odds with one of the most disastrous political economic leaderships ever. It was unclear whether it would ever be possible to mourn for Mobutu's Zaire (cf. White 2005), especially in the context of Laurent-Désiré Kabila's efforts to turn the victory of his rebellion into a triumph of order and discipline over the years of political decadence. As is clear from the debate about the repatriation of Mobutu's body from Morocco to his Congolese home turf,[32] the memories of Mobutu and his legacy are far from having lost their political thrust. The logic of paternalism that Mobutu as the *père de la nation* (the nation's father) so strikingly incarnated adds to the complexity (Schatzberg 2001), especially when we take into account the cultural logic of elders who deserve respect and veneration, no matter whether alive or dead (Kopytoff 1971).

Ntumba's call to offer gratitude, even repentance and offerings, to Mobutu's spirit could thus be read as a political maneuver to criticize those who have succeeded him and attempted to force him into public oblivion. Yet, here it is less about political opinion. As Ntumba explained to me in another conversation, before anything else democracy is a matter of embodied will and "sentiment" vis-à-vis the past. If what happened in the past were categorically acknowledged, regardless of the moral quality of former leaders, the politics of victor's justice and nepotism in the present could be overcome.

FIGURE 6.2 Cleaning session at the Nsele cemetery, Kinshasa.
Photo by Peter Lambertz.

The aim is not to judge who was good or bad, but rather to integrate the past and its actors into the sentimental consciousness of the present. EMM thus promotes a politics of memory and, through its tactile cleaning service, also of temporal at*touch*ment, which aims at positing and inscribing the present into its own respective historical *Gewordensein*, its have-become trajectory. This can be seen as a criticism not of contemporary politics but of the widespread culture of presentism and timelessness, the never-ending present in which so many Kinois are continuously locked up.

CONCLUSION

Kinshasa, Africa's second-largest city, with an estimated population of twelve million, presents significant challenges to its inhabitants, which they attempt to come to terms with in a variety of ways. Religious movements partake in this endeavor, as both local and transnational actors. Although of Japanese inspiration, EMM inscribes itself well in the history of local religious experimentation well known from the Ngunzist tradition of Kongo prophetism (MacGaffey 1983). The city, with its numerous challenges, fosters and encourages this experimental quest for symbolic, material, but also sentimental stabilization.

More than mere intellectual and bodily gymnastics, EMM's salongo and bilanga cleaning activities in both the private and public spheres have a tuning effect on their practitioners' attitudes to the urban territories in which they live. In contrast to many Pentecostal churches, EMM thus promotes an affective politics of territorial at*touch*ment. By sensorially engaging ties with the sensational form (Meyer 2010) of rubbish, EMM's practice of salongo aims to generate an umbilical bond with one's neighborhood and the wider public territory of the city and the nation, including its very history and past. The accompanying messianic optimism about the civic abilities and real possibilities of Kinois and Congolese at large is decisively antiutopian in Messianiques' self-understanding, which goes against the self-mocking logic of the Kin-la-poubelle joke. EMM's ardent laborers, men and women, old and young alike, see their clean(s)ing efforts as a powerful voice against persistent Afro- and Congo-pessimism, which is so widespread among Kinois at large, even if, as we have seen with the Kin-la-poubelle joke, this pessimism can also be a technique for safeguarding one's self-respect.

Next to the level of symbolic meaning production, religious (and also "spiritual") movements tune their followers' sentimental lives: how surroundings are transformed, how cities and their aural, visual, and tactile architectures are shaped by religious actors, as well as the ways in which religious movements affect popular perceptions of this very material space by modulating their followers' sensitivities and interpretative schemes. Reckwitz concludes his article on "affective spaces" by stressing that "changes in emotion discourses and changes in artefact-space constellations are thus obviously able to impact in complementary or opposing ways on the emergence of new affective attitudes and atmospheres, of new affective cultures" (2012, 256). EMM exemplifies well how religious movements can also become protagonists in the generation of such new affective cultures. Because of their frequent cleansing activities, Messianiques start feeling their city differently, as well as themselves living in it. This important sentimental aspect of space-making has been overlooked for too long.

The way people do or do not move across their city because of perceived spiritual (in)securities, how they feel vis-à-vis the house in which they live and the next-door crossroads, have obvious implications related to power, in terms of both social formation through shared sentiments and aesthetic sensitivities (Meyer 2009) and the ethics of civic engagement and citizenship.

EMM, a new religious movement from Japan, is very active on the level of the senses, and it also explicitly theorizes this dimension. Drawing on theories ranging from the Japanese folk, Shinto, and Buddhist traditions, but also from American New Thought spiritualism, its teachings resonate well with more long-standing conceptions in Central Africa. While the original teaching of the spiritual atmosphere mentions only homes, individual persons, and EMM's Johrei centers, Messianiques in Kinshasa have reengineered the theory to include places in the city's urban public space, which is home, among others, to Congo's national ancestors who are in dire need of sentimental uplifting. The oblivion of affects and space in social theory is thus also being responded to by theories deployed in the global South. EMM's "Japanese" ritual cleansing work and the theoretical framework that accompanies it qualify in exemplary fashion as a "theory from the South" (Comaroff and Comaroff 2012).

NOTES

1. The monument is a pyramid-shaped homage to Congo's deceased artists.
2. Salongo, the weekly public cleaning service, was introduced in Zaire as a civic obligation by former president Mobutu. Still today, early Saturday mornings before ten o'clock are reserved for public cleaning, and shopkeepers are often fined if they are caught selling during these hours. For the concept of salongo, see White 2005, 178–179; Pype 2009, 103.
3. Interview, Mr. Ntumba, Mbinza, November 26, 2010.
4. Interview, Mr. Jacques, Mokali, July 10, 2010.
5. Except for Brahma Kumaris, all spiritual movements present in Kinshasa today were introduced by Congolese individuals. They should not be seen as resulting from external missionary endeavors. Sekai Kyûseikyô has locally undergone four different schisms, which were all orchestrated by Congolese individuals. Beyond this sociological component, movements like EMM actively re-/produce older patterns known from religious movements in Central Africa. This is particularly visible in the sphere of healing (see Lambertz 2018). This important element of local agency explains the geographic attribute "Japanese" in the title of the chapter.
6. Figures according to Sekai Kyûseikyô Izunome's website www.izunome.jp/en /border/africa/ (accessed August 10, 2016).
7. For earlier work on spiritual movements in Africa, see Hackett 1989; Wuaku 2013; Louveau 2012.
8. Kinshasa has a long-standing history of healing churches, ranging from the African Independent Churches that originate in the Lower Congo's prophetic *ngunza*

tradition (cf. Devisch 1996) to a massive proliferation of Pentecostal Charismatic Churches since the early 1990s when Mobutu liberalized the religious sphere (cf. De Boeck 2004; Pype 2012).

9. For similarities with Hindus in West Africa, see Wuaku 2013.

10. The expression follows Rancière 2004.

11. For spiritual and moral geographies in Kinshasa, see also De Boeck 2004; Pype 2012; Gondola 2012.

12. This is reminiscent of the Lingala verb *koyoka*, which conflates the abstract dimensions of meaning-based "understanding" and the materiality of touch and sensual perception as in "sensing" or "feeling." It can mean "to understand," "to hear," or "to listen," but also "to feel" and "to perceive," as one can feel the wind, and thus serves to "unsettle the hierarchical organization of these binaries and the privilege typically accorded to one side of them" (see the introduction to this volume). Reckwitz thus does not draw a strict line between the terms "emotion" and "affect," though he prefers "affect" because it "is reminiscent of 'to affect' and 'to be affected' and thus of dynamic and interactive dimensions that the term 'emotion' lacks" (2012, 250).

13. The original teaching reads, "Every home, every individual has a spiritual atmosphere. There are homes which are warm and friendly. Others impart a sense of discomfort, loneliness, even coldness. The atmosphere of each home reflects the attitude of the people who live within it. In one place love and understanding prevail, but in the other home, self-centredness and lack of consideration prevail. There are individuals in whose presence we feel warmth, while others make us feel uncomfortable and ill at ease. It is their mental spiritual qualities which produce this effect on us. Johrei centers are governed by the same principle. Some expand rapidly, others do not. The depth of understanding and the love radiated by the leaders and workers greatly influence the growth of each center. People are attracted to it, and the center grows naturally. Location and size have a certain influence, it is true, but its effectiveness is through spiritual communication rather than by the method of presentation. The all-important factor is the genuine love radiating from the persons in charge" (Okada [1984] 1999, 59).

14. It should be noted that a large section of the followers of EMM and other spiritual movements identify themselves as "seekers," which is understood according to the French *chercheur* as equivalent to the scientific understanding of "researcher."

15. The German term *spüren* comes close to *koyoka* (see note 12). In German it points to the dimension of prophetic or investigative intuition and knowledge, which in Central Africa, however, would be expressed as "seeing" (Li. *komona*).

16. An ideology of public cleaning service has also developed in India as part of religious nationalism, orienting the service toward the benefit of the (national) community rather than that of the private self. Service work (Hindi: *seva*) took on institutionalized forms most prominently in the Ramakrishna movement of Swami Vivekananda (1863–1902), as well as in Baden Powell's Boy Scout movement (cf. Watts 2005), Sikhism, and the Sathya Sai Baba movement, which has also brought it to East Africa (Srinivas 2008, 142–145).

17. In biomedical terms, Buruli ulcer disease is caused by mycobacteria from the same family as those that cause tuberculosis and leprosy. The symptoms are ulcerated lesions of sometimes frightening dimensions and aspect.

18. For Burton and his work, see Maxwell 2008. For similarities in rural Hausaland, see Last 2011.

19. Teaching session by Mr. Jacques, Mokali, June 22, 2011.

20. He writes: "Das primäre Thema von Sinnlichkeit sind nicht die Dinge, die man wahrnimmt, sondern das, was man empfindet: die Atmosphären. Wenn ich in einen Raum hineintrete, dann werde ich in irgendeiner Weise durch diesen Raum gestimmt. Seine Atmosphäre ist für mein Befinden entscheidend. Erst wenn ich sozusagen in der Atmosphäre bin, werde ich auch diesen oder jenen Gegenstand identifizieren und wahrnehmen" (Böhme 2013, 15).

21. Interview, Barbara, Ngaba, Kinshasa, June 2011.

22. Interview, Mr. Jacques, Mangengenge, June 2013.

23. The city's very soil has made it a classic object of laughter and self-ridicule in the local popular culture of postcolonial mockery. From the early 1960s onward, Kinshasa had become known across the continent and beyond as Kin-la-belle, the archetypal place of cleanliness and order. Taking up this theme, over the years the Kinois themselves started commenting on the critical situation of their city's public space by turning Kin-la-belle into Kin-la-poubelle (Kinshasa the rubbish bin). The simultaneity of identification with and alienation from the urban territory revealed in this joke holds some potential for analogy with the logic of laughter: laughter simultaneously reveals and conceals, suggests but withholds, may be inclusive yet exclusive at the same time (Bergson [1900] 1959).

24. It should not be forgotten that the Pentecostal fixation on the devil and his army of demons entails a spatialized imagination of spiritual warfare being carried out in the city (e.g., Kalu 2008, 218–219; Pype 2012, 27–62).

25. For the anthropology of infrastructure, inclusive of its reverse side, see De Boeck and Baloji 2016, 107–112.

26. See, for instance, Andreas Spaeth, "Chaos am Himmel über Afrika," *Die Zeit*, January 26, 1996; or "Catastrophe de Kinshasa," Wikipédia, http://fr.wikipedia.org /wiki/Catastrophe_de_Kinshasa (accessed July 3, 2013).

27. Okada 1999 [1984]. See also Klaege 2009; MacGaffey 1986, 109.

28. On a poster inside the police major's office, the anniversary of "Poste de Point Chaud" is officially celebrated. The crossroads has come to carry the name Point Chaud "officially" as a result of being the hot spot of aggressive anti-Kuluna (street gang) measures by an especially tough police major. Neighbors remember that suspected evildoers who had been caught were exposed in the sun, handcuffed, and bound up here, visibly suffering in this "point of heat."

29. Interview, Mr. Jacques, Mokali, July 10, 2010. The fact that this spot is a sort of no place without an identity may not be without significance, as it is usually here that the abandoned spirits of the recently dead are supposed to dwell. MacGaffey reminds us that this notion is in fact not of Japanese origin: when it comes to witches, for instance, they are supposed to "become 'ghosts,' not 'ancestors,' and are condemned to

anonymous wanderings in the trackless and infertile grasslands that lie between the forests and the cultivated valleys" (1986, 73).

30. Interview, Mr. Jacques, Mokali, October 7, 2010.

31. In 2017 this incited one of Mobutu's sons to officially (re)open the former state-party Mouvement Populaire de la Révolution, reinitiating the wearing of a *pagne* cloth with Mobutu's head on it.

32. A comparable debate has been unfolding about the repatriation of defunct opposition leader Étienne Tshisekedi's remains.

7 LEARNING HOW TO FEEL
EMOTIONAL REPERTOIRES OF NIGERIAN AND CONGOLESE PENTECOSTAL PASTORS IN THE DIASPORA

RAFAEL CAZARIN AND MARIAN BURCHARDT

Nigerian-born Pastor Emmet is the founder of a Pentecostal church in Johannesburg where we attended services in 2014.[1] The church was the largest and the most structured church of the four migrant-initiated congregations we visited in the city, but according to its leader it has not always been like that. In a long talk about his religious and migrant journeys, Emmet explained to us his dreams, prophecies, and migratory struggles and the miracles that had helped to shape his personal journey, as well as how he became the founder of a transnational ministry with branches in Nigeria and Kenya. After witnessing him hosting church services and Bible schools, hearing his prayers on a radio show, and watching his web-based video messages, it became evident that this pastor's subjectivity and practices conveyed more than biblical knowledge. In one of our encounters, Emmet told us that as an engineering student he began to attend prayer groups and fellowships organized by friends from his university. Through these experiences he gradually became knowledgeable about the Bible as much as he started to feel the "miracle of faith." In one conversation he explained to us why faith needed to go beyond biblical knowledge:

By knowing that the Bible is God's word I wanted to study the Bible. I wanted to know what God is saying and what am I supposed to do in different life situations. The more I studied the Bible, the more I realized that a lot of people don't know what I know. A lot of people are not enjoying the joy that I have. And I also found powerful that what God commissioned us to do is to spread and to teach all nations these truths as we are finding out. The more I studied the Bible, the more I discovered how gracious God is, how loving God is, and how we need to tell the world about that. Anyone who doesn't believe in Lord Jesus Christ cannot enjoy life, cannot enjoy forgiveness of sins, and cannot enjoy peace.

Grace, love, joy, compassion, and peace: for Emmet, subjective emotions were not abstract ideals but states of mind and body to be achieved through the learning of parables, prayers, and verses. For him, someone who had been raised as a devout Anglican, being a believer implied that he had lived a process built upon a religious journey in which he had to actively engage with. As he narrated the ups and downs, doubts, and eventual choices in his quest for knowledge, and the final acceptance of his calling to become a pastor, it became clear that Emmet's trajectory was marked by the crafting of a repertoire of emotions. However, these emotions were not uncontrollable forces. Between curses and blessings, his account of the personal transformations he had achieved through the Holy Spirit showed that his emotions were based on spiritual knowledge. His experiential transformations were thus marked by a specific emotional balance, while certain moods and feelings also encouraged him to transform other people's lives as well.

Importantly, Emmet's story resonates with the narratives of other migrant pastors in Johannesburg, as well as with those of Nigerian and Congolese church leaders in the northern Spanish city of Bilbao, which was the second site of our field research. Given that social conditions, economic opportunities, and religious contexts in Johannesburg and Bilbao are enormously different, the similarities in Pentecostals' emotional repertoires in these two urban contexts are striking. In both settings, emotional repertoires included skilled ways of relating emotions such as anger and sadness to the specific social and moral ills believers faced because of their status as migrants, and of relating positive emotions such as joy and love to individuals' acquisition of spiritual knowledge and their cultivating such knowledge through religious practice. In particular, these similarities raise questions about the ways in which notions of desirable and legitimate emotions travel and circulate through the global public sphere of transnational Pentecostalism. For this reason, this chapter is conceived as a transnational comparison of Pentecostal emotional engagements with the challenges of urban life in the diaspora in two geographically distant migrant hubs.

Clearly, these resonances between pastors' narratives are not only outcomes of their positions as migrants and shared transnational imaginaries: they were also produced by emotional forms of connectivity and belonging. Feelings and sentiments are the symbolic bridges between "spaces for the establishment of kinship and social networks while extending the emotive religious experience initiated by Pentecostal churches in the homeland" (Akyeampong 2000a, 209). In other words, emotional and cognitive experiences seem to travel with African Pentecostals in the diaspora while being shaped by a transnational emotional regime that leads people to "live loss and hope as defining tension[s]" (Clifford 1997, 312).

MEDIATING PENTECOSTAL EMOTIONS

Because Pentecostalism is a religious tradition in which subjective experiences of the divine are fundamental, emotions are a key category for understanding Pentecostal beliefs, practices, and forms of belonging. Thus far, sociologists and anthropologists have tackled these emotional dynamics by focusing on two issues: first, the ways in which Pentecostal practices engage the human body and rely on particular kinds of embodiment of religious experiences (Csordas 2002); and second, the ways in which emotions are linked to and mediated by not only encounters with spiritual forces but also religious materialities and the creation and deployment of particular sensorial registers and capacities through which believers are able to engage with material objects and environments (Meyer 2008).

The first of these two strands was animated by observations of how conversions to Pentecostalism involved emotional transformations that are enacted in conversion rituals. In these rituals, as well as in subsequent everyday conduct, the status of being "saved" and having become a born-again Christian acquired particular kinds of embodiments. Anthropologists who have contributed to the second strand of research have focused on how Pentecostals used sound and song—in ways that testify to what van Dijk (in this volume) calls "amplification"—to spawn emotional states that are variously seen as either expressive of or instrumental in achieving deliverance and salvation (Oosterbaan 2009; Meyer 2011; V. Brennan 2010). Both kinds of inquiries were animated by the urge to understand the sources and effects of the often ecstatic forms of worship that are characteristic of Pentecostal practice across the globe. Pentecostals often celebrate the glory of God in ways that appear extraordinarily exuberant and energetic, excessive and transgressive, and engage in prayers at maximum intensity. In her study of prayer in Nigerian Pentecostalism, Butticci cites a well-known church founder with the following words:

> Spiritual violence is needed. You must have violent anxiety. You must burst forth with holy anger, violent determination and faith. You must possess holy fury, fierceness and madness. No soul that ever cried violently to God has been disappointed. There are prayers you must say and actions you must take so that fellow human beings look at you and say you are a mad person. If you want to survive in this crazy world, you need a crazy faith! (2013, 244–245)

Similar to Butticci, and following on the heels of this pastor's emotional injunctions, many studies describe spontaneous outbursts of religious energy that occur in the context of Sunday services, small prayer groups, or large prayer camps (Ukah 2014). In these situations, people's access to salvation is usually concomitant with their access to the kind of emotions through which they recognize the power of the Holy Spirit and into which religious experiences are folded.

Conversely, in this chapter we suggest a third perspective by focusing on how emotions are taught, inculcated, cultivated, and learned. In other words, we are less interested in the immediacy of emotional experience than in the ways in which emotions are indeed mediated through particular rules on how one ought to feel. Thus, we begin with the premise that, whenever people are enjoined to observe certain "feeling rules" (Hochschild 1979), the cognitive and the moral are inextricably entangled. In doing so, we take up other scholars' insights into how African Pentecostals have developed new forms of training and counseling that involve new therapeutic styles and practices of introspection and intellectualization (van Dijk 2013, Moyer, Burchardt, and van Dijk 2013; Burchardt 2009).

In what follows, we explore the emotional repertoires evoked by Pentecostal leaders as expressions of a particular transnational regime of emotions, feelings, and sentiments. We understand *emotional regimes* as persisting over time and transcending individuals, "shaping what they can feel, how they can feel it, the way they can express their feelings, and hence the forms of social relationship and courses of action that are open to them" (Riis and Woodhead 2010, 12). *Emotional repertoires*, by contrast, are variable outcomes of the ways in which Pentecostals take up and engage with emotional regimes. Whereas emotional regimes suggest power and authority over believers, emotional repertoires emphasize agency and creative adaptation and performance. Drawing on these repertoires, pastors are able to listen to, feel, and express divine messages and lead individuals to develop their own lives in the same way. Similar to how the authors of the introduction to this volume describe the workings of moral sentiment, emotional repertoires circumscribe pastors' abilities to shape affective dispositions that underlie ephemeral affective states.

In order to understand such processes of becoming that are individually apprehended and socially recognizable while being bodily and emotionally pervasive, we further draw on Luhrmann's (2004) notion of metakinesis. By this she means the process of how body-mind states are "subjectively and idiosyncratically experienced" by worshippers in their intimate relationship with the divine (Luhrmann 2004, 520). As Luhrmann explains, such states are "lexically identified, and indeed the process of learning to have these experiences cannot be neatly disentangled from the process of learning the words to describe them" (520). She suggests an analytical triad in the process of learning the "cognitive/linguistic knowledge" that pervades believers' personal experiences with God: the lexicon, syntax, and conversion narratives. Such learning processes interact, merge, and rearrange the way in which worshippers interpret reality while inculcating a "new" framework for narrating emotional dispositions. In other words, they are part of an emotional intelligence and of the ongoing learning and maintenance of an emotional repertoire (M. Rosaldo 1980).

Framing biographies as "unstable and heterogeneous processes" (Blanes 2011, 93) that reveal hegemonic understandings, constructions, and regimes of justifications (Burchardt 2010b, 6), we analyze pastors' narratives in two distinct ways: first, we explore their definitions of knowledge; second, we view emotions as mediations of that knowledge. The contribution is based on ethnographic fieldwork carried out between 2012 and 2015. During this period, we attended the services of six African Pentecostal churches in south-north (Bilbao) and south-south (Johannesburg) migratory contexts.

While drawing on a broader set of life stories, we focus on the stories of two church leaders in each of the settings. These pastors preach in the same church but do not share family bonds. In this way, we intend to privilege their understandings of emotions and emotional experiences in relation to their respective congregations and religious journeys. In the Spanish context, we focus on Pastors Edward and Ingrid, who since 2006 have been preachers to a congregation in Bilbao. In South Africa, we emphasize the experiences of Emmet and Hector, born-again fellows and missionary partners who cofounded a branch of their Nigerian-based denomination in Johannesburg in 2009.

BECOMING A PASTOR IN THE BASQUE DIASPORA

In the first half of the twentieth century, the Basque Country (Autonomous Community of the Basque Country [CAPV]) became one of the main economic hubs of southern Europe, attracting mainly migrants from Portugal and other regions of Spain (Galdos Urrutia 1981). Decades later, during the country's economic boom of the early twenty-first century this autonomous community also benefited from the almost six million migrants who arrived in Spain (Escribano and Suárez 2006, 444). In the following years, mainly through internal migration in Spain, the three largest Basque cities (Bilbao, San Sebastian, and Vitoria) became alternative destinations for those migrants who initially arrived in major urban centers such as Madrid, Barcelona, or Valencia (Olabuénaga and Blanco 2009). International migrants mainly originating from Africa and Latin America have helped to increase the size of the foreign population in the Basque Country from 15,130 in 1998 to 151,894 in 2013.[2] According to the 2014 *Ikuspegi Bulletin on Migration*, the proportion of immigrants reached 7.7 percent of Bilbao's municipality population. Of those, 8.2 percent are from sub-Saharan Africa. At the regional level of the Basque Country, the percentage of migrants stands at 6.5, with 8.7 percent of them coming from sub-Saharan countries.[3] Most of them are Catholic Christians and Muslims, with only a small percentage belonging to Pentecostalism. Thus, African Pentecostals are an ethnic but also a religious minority. In 2015, 12.6 percent of the registered churches were classified as evangelical Christian.[4]

Similar to other Spanish cityscapes, Bilbao's urban space continues to be dominated by the "Catholic tradition." The growing number of Pentecostal churches, as well as mosques, Baha'i, and spaces for other religious minorities, is a relatively recent phenomenon, although evidence of Christian minorities such as Jehovah's Witnesses and Adventists dates back to the 1960s (Vieytez 2010). Starting informal or formal places of worship, religious minorities have been mostly circumscribed to Bilbao, the city with the largest metropolitan area and urban population in the CAPV. Pentecostal churches and mosques have a similar spatial distribution throughout the city, being concentrated in the neighborhoods of San Francisco, Zabala, and Bilbao La Vieja, the areas with the highest percentages of nonnationals.[5]

San Francisco is popularly known for its ethnic shops, ranging from Halal butcheries and Moroccan restaurants to African hairdressers, as well as supermarkets that specialize in Latin American products. The area also has a reputation for crime and the presence of sex workers and drug dealers in the streets. At the same time, numerous church posters placed in the streets of San Francisco call worshippers for "miraculous services," night prayers, and special celebrations. On one of these posters we identified Pastor Edward and Pastor Ingrid's church, an old, spacious warehouse in San Francisco's neighboring area of Errekaldeberri. With a less infamous reputation, Zabala and Bilbao la Vieja are undergoing gentrification that has brought artists and other professionals from the creative industry to the area. The proximity to San Francisco turns these areas into a fertile ground for religious and cultural activities that attract migrants and nationals from other Basque provinces as well. In particular, the semiperipheral urban location of these neighbourhoods provides churchgoers easy access to Bilbao's major transport hubs such as the bus, metro, and train stations that connect the city with its metropolitan area.

During our fieldwork, churchgoers and pastors also informed us about a number of Pentecostal churches in other major Basque cities such as Vitoria, San Sebastian, and Barakaldo. In some cases, these churches were related through interdenominational networks operating within the Basque region, configuring a vibrant matrix of relationships among leading pastors and worshippers. Many pastors we interviewed who travel to preach in these cities emphasized the importance of these religious networks. At the same time, they also create a constant movement of worshippers throughout the network, for instance, through invitations by church leaders in Bilbao to visit services from their fellows in Vitoria or San Sebastian.

Currently, African churches are managed and attended by those migrants who are relatively established in the country—having lived there from five to fifteen years—often accompanied by family members. This is, for instance, the case with our informants Ingrid and Edward. Often referred to as the prophetess of the church, Ingrid was born in Benin City, southern Nigeria, to a family of mixed Baptist and traditional religious backgrounds. In 1997, at the age of seventeen, she migrated to the Italian city of Turin, encouraged by some relatives who were already living there. After a couple of years she moved with a friend to Valencia because of the better prospects for naturalization in Spain at that time. In 2005, she moved to Bilbao and founded a congregation together with her husband the following year. One year after establishing the church, she met Pastor Edward, who assisted her husband in preaching and in running the church.

Edward was born in the Democratic Republic of Congo and told us about his early conversion to Christianity at the age of seven and his baptism in 1981. His migratory journey started when he first left Congo for Kenya, followed by work experiences in Namibia. Pastor Edward moved to Spain in 2004, and the following year he joined Ingrid and her husband in the church, which was primarily attended by Nigerian migrants. Besides church life, both pastors dedicated time to their partners and children. Although Edward held a degree in business, his qualifications were not recognized in Spain, and he made a living from various unstable and informal activities such as organizing events for African migrants. Ingrid was finishing her degree in nursing and divided her time mostly between studying, preaching, and the household.

During our research, the families of these two pastors often shared personal celebrations and leisure activities and built friendly relationships outside the church. Their close religious and personal relationships certainly contributed to weaving a common understanding of emotions at the church. They also had a shared understanding of the most important problems and difficulties for African migrants in Bilbao: prostitution, alcohol and illegal drug abuse, and homosexuality, but also skepticism, divorce, mistrust, and domestic violence. Importantly, they also agreed on what they saw as the main source of these problems: a lack of knowledge. For Pastor Edward, migrants had a low spiritual level, since they were driven by the ambition to achieve financial success. They would just "use" the church for meeting friends, networking, and socializing. Furthermore, Edward described Spanish society in which African Pentecostals lived as "broken" and dangerous, emphasizing how his evangelizing mission offered dignity and a sense of value to African sex workers who attended the church. He recalled how African women were still falling into prostitution when he first arrived in Bilbao, whereas after years of hard work the lives of African women in the church environment had changed. Several times he mentioned the importance of having the "knowledge of sin" and "spiritual knowledge," "understanding the word of God," and "getting to know the message." Edward's following explanation of the knowledge of sin illustrates what we call "the pragmatics of emotional knowledge." In other words, the pastor used biblical knowledge as practical know-how that helped to address specific emotional states caused in worshippers by sinful, "dark," and negative experiences, and forged a particular understanding of undesirable moods, emotions, and feelings:

> Many people, they don't know what sin is all about, they don't know that if I do this, I sin. So when you don't know that this is a sin, you can't come to repentance. He can't say God to forgive him because he sinned because he doesn't take it as a sin. He has to understand that even this act is a sin in front of God. So we (pastors from the church) started demonstrating what sin is so people would understand that maybe some acts are not good. Secondly, we came to speak about how sin can be manifested. After knowing that this is sin, it needs to be acted upon and to be manifested. And this starts from the mind. Then from the mind brings the desires. Then the desire opens the door for the temptation to come; after the temptation then the sin will be manifested.

Edward emphasized the importance of "attacking" body and mind with "knowledge" of the word in order to be delivered from sin (an idea he and other pastors often quoted from John 8:32: "You shall know the truth, and the truth shall set you free"). The importance of looking at such pragmatics is apparent not only in pastors' discourses to their followers but also in the way they framed their own journeys as born-again Christians. As is clear from Edward's crusade against the sins of the mind, the pastors we worked with had a stock of emotional knowledge (Schütz 1970) that they deemed crucial for African Pentecostals in the diaspora. As a resource to be accessed by individuals, this stock was individually and collectively articulated among born-again Christians. As we will show, while this articulation similarly punctuates pastors' biographies and religious lives in Bilbao as in Johannesburg, the local reworking of transnational Pentecostalism's emotional regime entails some nuances.

AUTHORIZING AND NEGOTIATING EMOTIONAL REGIMES

Emotional socialization is a dynamic process involving the agency of individuals and their interaction with the surrounding reality (Denzin 1984). It may range from a single moment and a series of events to a group of people or a particular institution. In this way, emotions operate as part of the way we experience situations through a reflexive and cooperative relationship with the world (Holmes 2010). For born-again Christians, their emotional resocialization pervades a series of activities and events such as deliverance,

Sunday services, counseling, fellowships, and Bible schools. These religious interactions helped to synchronize repertoires generally, evoking experiences of the supernatural (dreams, visions, miracles) and building up one's agency (breaking with "the profane world," reformulating one's relationships and lifestyles, etc.). However, the actual conversion was sometimes narrated as a singular event that constituted a turning point in the biographies of born-again Christians. Alternatively, the discovery of a preacher's own spiritual gifts was defined as a process or a chain of events requiring several confirmations. In fact, the development of spiritual gifts is precisely what differentiates a "simple church-goer" from those who will later acquire leading roles (see Cazarin and Cossa 2017; Cazarin and Griera 2018). From her first religious experiences to the development of spiritual gifts, Ingrid narrated to us a journey marked by a series of discoveries that "tuned her senses." She said she had always felt a gift inside her that was not developed or brought out until she started to read the word of God.

RAFAEL: And you started working as a prophetess more here in Bilbao, or did you start in Benin City?

INGRID: Well, I would say here, because right from when I was a kid I had this gift in me, but I wasn't in the word. When I say "I wasn't in the word," I said I'm an "unbeliever," but that gift was there, and I swore that when I was not in the word I was not going to get married with a man of God because there is a big responsibility: "I want to go to discotheque, I want to go to party, I want to be free." But when the offer came, when a man of God came across, I never said, "Let me think about it, I'm going to give the answer tomorrow," instantly . . . and sometimes I see it and I say, "How come I agreed so weakly and so cheap? I don't know." Something acted. I believe, since that gift was there, I was seeing God's divine connection to make that gift to begin to come out of me. I saw it like this, so it is! Also if you have a gift and you don't know how to reach that gift, the gift will go. It's like a footballer—if you lose the ball and the stamina you lose . . . you need to nourish it, you need to feed it, to cherish it. I need to be closer to God, I need to read the word of God, I need to . . . by times you get closer to God, he opens your eyes to see things, and you can be able to pass it to the people.

As mentioned in the previous section, the pragmatics surrounding this and other tools permeates the life of a born-again Christian in several ways, and pastors seem to unpack such logic as frameworks for agency that are particularly relevant in migratory milieus. Feelings and emotional states only made sense when combined with the acquired knowledge, the latter being the fuel that kept the learning process alive. In this way, Ingrid gradually came to sense reality in a different way, an experience that helped her, for instance, assist other women who, according to her, were controlled by men who sometimes wanted to break marriages and as a result were turned into sexual slaves. For the pastor, this happened more often in this migratory context not only because African women in Bilbao were economically deprived but also because they forgot their spiritual roots and were surrounded by spiritually weak relationships. Ingrid learned to "designate" threats of the devil, possessions, and imminent evils just like her husband, whom she mentioned as a reference for these matters due to his studies in demonology. According to the church leader, every Christian should know the spirit of "designation" from the Bible as a tool that protects and equips a born-again Christian to fight the battle against evil.

Pastor Edward also illustrated the emotional outcome of mastering biblical know-how in the sense of receiving a spiritual mission as a godly conviction. This was evidenced by the fact that in the previous year he had initiated his own ministry in parallel to his formal position as a resident pastor at Ingrid's church. With no financial stability, the unemployed church leader moved forward with his project convinced by what he interpreted as confirmation from God:

> If I don't have a conviction, although I can feel things, I wouldn't do so. So the element the Lord put in my spirit and the conviction comes to confirm. This one God has spoken to me, it was in me, I was sleeping with it, and I was working out with it, so it took time because I was first of all asking myself [if] I needed time. I was praying to God, then I said, "God is [it] really you speaking to me? Convince me!" When the conviction is there, I move without asking any question. We came to this place completely without anything. But in a short time God brought people, and I began to buy this, buy the guitar, buy that; so what we have here, it just came in a very short period. It was like God put it in me, and I just moved. So speaking in the way God speaks with me, he speaks in my spirit, he confirms with a conviction.

As an experienced missionary, Edward showed no reticence when it came to narrating his experiences on feeling the messages coming from God, as well as mastering their usage. Where many African migrants would see scarce alternatives in mobilizing resources, social and material capital, for Edward, his spiritual understanding of the context became a source of resilience. Such a quest frames the reinforcement of one's authority over these choices, as well as inspiring self-confidence and control in contexts of un-certainty. What can often be seen as an imminent failure, a risk that would discourage other migrants (nonbelievers) in a similar situation, is "twisted" by Edward into an emotional tone dominated by bravery, resistance, and heroic qualities of sorts.

Moreover, following a divine calling also appears to come through the sensitizing of one's conscience, a growing awareness of the needs of other people, of their problems and difficulties. In this way, by increasing one's scriptural knowledge and developing one's spiritual gifts, one is also able to identify a "dysfunctional" regime of experiences and to adjust oneself (and others) to a more "functional" alternative. As metaphorically addressed in a Pentecostal hymn, through the learning and living of God's words, one is able to navigate turbulent waters to reach the tranquillity of divine shores. In sum, the knowledge these leaders acquired is what seemed to regulate the "ups and downs" of their own migratory circumstances. Ole Riis and Linda Woodhead (2010) expressed a similar idea when pointing out that religion can be an effective framework for emotional adjustment. They explain that "by offering to order emotional lives not just differently, but in accordance with a truer, more foundational, more satisfying pattern, religion proposes a new structuring of relationships and with it an emotional restructuring" (Riis and Woodhead 2010, 70). This double restructuring is evident, for in-stance, in the accounts of both pastors regarding trust and stability when analyzing the maintenance of affective relationships in Bilbao. In Ingrid's case, fears were often related to female concerns and the various ordeals of conjugal life (divorce, infidelity, domestic conflicts) or a lack of respect by children toward their parents, and behavior that is believed to derive from the spiritual ignorance of a secular society. To make sure that her lessons will reach women, Ingrid used the Sunday services, knowing that "on Sun-days, automatically they [the women] will be here with the kids, so I'm able to capture them and pass those teachings to them on how to take care of the children, take care of their husbands."

In turn, Edward constantly highlighted the importance of the spiritual knowledge he had learned in deliverance when overcoming failures in his life and avoiding "falling." He interpreted "falling" as a curse from which one must be freed and delivered:

It was through the deliverance that I understood the Lord Jesus more, the word of God more, and the knowledge of the word of God. I understand something when the Lord teaches me something that it's happening in my life, for example, when I am struggling to abandon a life of sin which I can't leave, I keep falling there, and falling on the same situation. Whenever I read the word of God, I understand that with the love of Jesus, with the death of Jesus, we are free. So having this knowledge on me took me directly into the process of deliverance. I began to apply this word of God. I said, "No I can't be victim of sin, to be falling, falling, falling all the time when the Bible is telling me that through the Lord Jesus I am already free."

In sum, the transformative process of "walking in the spirit" does not automatically lead to believers abandoning what they now see as evil behavior that they feel they acquired by emulating forms of behavior that are dominant in the wider society. There is, rather, an acceptance that the born-again believer is an individual "under construction," although she or he is now clearly immersed in a course that requires discipline and obedience to be followed and where the goal is to feel godlike and free. Thus, this approach affirms that pastors acknowledge and rework the vicissitudes experienced by migrants throughout the processes of conversion and migration under the same premise: that of regaining control over one's "surroundings" through the emotional self-regulation of the utopian/dystopian tensions that are often found in diasporic cultures (Beckford 2011).

BECOMING AN EMOTIONAL TEACHER IN JOHANNESBURG

While Nigerian or Congolese communities are not particularly prominent in the Basque Country or Spain,[6] their presence among migrants is much more notable in South Africa, especially in its richest province, Gauteng. Together with Zimbabweans, they make up the top three nationalities among documented African foreigners in the country (Statistics South Africa 2013). Although there are no adequate data on the religious affiliations of international migrants, the number of Christians among them is estimated to be 1.3 million (Pew Forum on Religion and Public Life 2012).[7]

The Gauteng Province is one of the main economic hubs of the African continent and the center of South Africa's mining industries, trade, and transport networks. Immigration to this region is mostly motivated by economic opportunities and the search for upward mobility. In 2007, 5.6 percent (578,387) of the province's population was foreign-born (Landau and Gindrey 2008). Within Johannesburg, the percentage climbed to 7.9 (Landau and Gindrey 2008), with most migrants concentrated in a few neighborhoods such as Yeoville, Randburg, and Rosettenville. These so-called migrant neighborhoods benefit from relatively easy access to transport, banking, goods, and other facilities that are often lacking in the more peripheral townships.

However, despite the successive emergence of a dense network of migrant socialities in these neighborhoods, none of the pastors we interviewed was comfortable with the idea of leading "exclusively" migrant congregations. Emmet illustrated this perception by explaining, "We try to accommodate everybody, make it cross-cultural, and keep it in a language that everybody can understand." However, he also often showed a fair level of national pride when comparing the faith of Nigerians with that of South Africans, for instance, when it comes to supporting religious leaders with tithes and other material benevolences. Despite the fact that some of the differences in religious style are related to national or ethnic cultures—for example, in Kimbanguism, the Aladura churches, or the Church of Pentecost—a Pan-African vision remains strongly alive in the current discourse of Pentecostals in Johannesburg, as throughout the diaspora (Anderson 2001).[8]

Emmet remembered his first religious experiences as coming from his Anglican parents when he was around eleven years old. During his years at university, he became a born-again Christian. Before establishing his own congregation in Port Harcourt, he preached in several ministries in Nigeria, went on missions to Kenya, and visited churches in the United Kingdom. The initiation of the South African branch of his church also involved a coreligionist from Port Harcourt, Pastor Hector, who is now his assistant pastor. Hector, who grew up in Port Harcourt, attended the Orthodox Church through the influence of his parents. He mentioned having known the Holy Spirit at a young age, from the time he was about nine years old. Later on, after graduating from secondary school, Hector had his born-again experience. Thus, this church leader would bring to bear on his ministry in Johannesburg accumulated experiences as a preacher in different parts of Nigeria, Benin, and Niger, as well as his own religious mobility, not having been born into but having sought and found the true faith.

In Emmet and Hector's church, we were particularly impressed by the Bible school program that offered education in multiple areas of everyday life: finances, emotions, relationships, professional skills, and so on. These lessons involved concepts such as "logics of the soul," "charismatic leadership," and "conflict resolution." Significantly, both pastors described these lessons as teachings in spiritual knowledge. From their point of view, a strong passion for spiritual teaching and an understanding of each and every activity in terms of spiritual growth was indispensable to becoming a pastor. As Hector stated:

> When I graduated from secondary school to go to university, I realized "Oh! There is something that I was missing," and the ladies all of a sudden kept asking me, "Do you have emotions at all?" And I was like, "Yes, I do." I found real love, a relationship with the Holy Spirit, and I changed my entire life. I would go to school and I would find myself, right after the bell had rung, just wanting to be in my room to engage with God. It was real—this is not a story—I found God, and it was the happiest thing that ever happened to me. I started to find purpose, I started to see a lot of things about family, about career, how to treat people, and then I just, like, keep praying and things would bring to my mind, reviewing my life.

In parallel to what Pastor Edward in Bilbao expressed as the necessary "conviction" in performing any religious calling, Hector emphasized the discovery of a passion for religious matters as a leitmotif. In our interviews, Hector remarked how his process of transformation, of "walking in the spirit," implied a review of certain relationships and a change of environment as an adjustment to the current situation. Moreover, he was also affected in terms of his own understanding of the new affective bonds to be established by attributing a religious meaning to emotions such as happiness, love, and hope. These relationships, bonds, and emotions seemed to be reshaped by the mirroring of one's interaction with the divine (Ellison and Levin 1998).

Furthermore, Hector reaffirmed the repertoire of Pentecostal leaders in the struggle over whether to accept or reject one's spiritual calling, an aspect that was also echoed by his superior, Pastor Emmet. Besides Hector's remarks on the importance of a deep understanding of the Bible, both preachers also legitimated their calling through experiencing unusual feelings and emotional states that they felt were difficult to explain or, from our conceptual perspective, that belonged to a different emotional repertoire, one that was often regarded as "more real," righteous, and truthful than the previous (secular) one. Furthermore, Hector described a clear change in his affective relationships, one that ascribed a different meaning to love. All this came to such a point that, after he was born again at university, some of his friends questioned his religiosity and the "new ways" to feel expressed by him: "The ladies all of a sudden kept asking me 'Do you have emotions at all?' And I said, 'Yes, I do!' I found real love, a relation with the Holy Spirit, and I changed my entire life." Hector's and Emmet's accounts of their transformations slightly altered the role of emotions or feelings as consequences of scriptural knowledge, as remarked in the narratives of Pastors Ingrid and Edward. Instead, they focused on the importance of emotional stimuli in seeking scriptural understanding. This "twist" seemed to favor their notion of knowledge in two ways: (1) as inherent in a particularly positive emotional regime when legitimating their calling or the development of spiritual gifts; and (2) as an input into self-regulating negative experiences lived by worshippers that were dissonant with their positive emotional regime.

TEACHING HOW TO FEEL

In 2014, we were invited as guests to the church's Bible school and, as such, received printed and online material that was used in the courses. The materials were separated into chapters and organized into various levels of understanding for beginners, intermediate students, and advanced students. The course, which lasted for five months, promised to bring spiritual knowledge to attendees who wanted either to acquire greater religious empowerment through knowledge or to take the course as part of their education for eventual future leadership. Following the pastors' advice, we took the classes called "Holy Spirit" and "Spirit, Soul and Body." The former was based on a brochure titled "The Holy Spirit, His Symbols, His Names and His Personalities"; likewise, the latter was based on a brochure titled "Anatomy to the Total Man, Identification of the Human Spirit, Functions of the Human Spirit" (figure 7.1).

Apart from the brochures provided by the organizers, we were encouraged to explore the online lessons uploaded onto the church's website. Only those who attended the course after being properly registered in the Bible school had access to the videos. Introductory tutorials were available through streaming as teasers for people to develop an initial interest in the course. In one of the classes we attended, Emmet was also being recorded so that a video could be uploaded later, as was usual in many other instances. By reading the brochure, we worked through a series of guidelines using bullet points and biblical verses, which had been put together in short paragraphs mostly written by Emmet, as well as paragraphs on several aspects of human beings, from physiology to psychosocial behavior. In particular, a series of fragments attracted our attention because of how they indicated which emotions and senses were inscribed in the spirit and soul of a Christian and how they offered insights for their interpretation:

IN HIS PRESENCE

Bible
School

Spirit, Soul & Body

Anatomy to the total man. Identification of the human
spirit. Functions of the human Spirit.

IN HIS PRESENCE

Bible
School

Holy Spirit

The Holy Spirit, His Symbols, His names and His
Personality

FIGURE 7.1 Brochures for a Bible school in Johannesburg, 2014.
From the personal archive of Rafael Cazarin.

The word of God can control your emotions only when your mind is renewed by the word. The response of the emotion of man is controlled by the predominant content of the mind. If your mind is not full of god's word then when things happen, negative emotions could be stirred up in you because there is no word in you to control the reaction or response of your emotions. . . . The sense organs of the body depend on the soul of man to appropriately interpret what is going on in the body. The organs of the body do not process information, rather the soul does the informational processing.

Similar to the Pentecostal counseling settings van Dijk (2013) studied in Botswana, the information provided was organized in the format of a manual. In contrast to the usual flamboyant preaching of Pentecostal pastors, the words and expressions were "cold," with little space for nonbiblical anecdotes. In order to justify the importance of educating and cultivating the spirit, the text attributed to the soul all sorts of emotional and cognitive aspects. Ideas were presented as statements in a series of logical reasonings led by syllogisms and relatively superficial assumptions, which the preachers reworked during the courses. In class, our teachers, Emmet and Hector, illustrated the material with personal stories of their migration journeys, described the daily vicissitudes of those who lived in Johannesburg, and framed the moral challenges of modern life.

In the Bible school, the teaching of emotional knowledge and religious understandings of the senses was meant to safeguard the believer's relationships with the self and with others by reinforcing positive emotions. In this context, the pastor performed and simultaneously embodied the skills of teachers, parents, therapists, or doctors assuming the archetypal role of the spiritual guide. Sometimes, the pastor asked us questions about personal issues to illustrate the utility of the gifts of the spirit in solving our problems. After quickly acknowledging that we spoke different "languages"—in other words, that we lacked spiritual knowledge—Hector saw the opportunity to "learn our language" and to teach us the word of God by focusing on the emotions that he was able to identify in this moment. In his view, we expressed different kinds of insecurity, anguish, and fear, but he told us that these could be "cured" by the word of God. Emmet made a similar effort to interpret the presence of a female colleague of ours emotionally and to generate some kind of empathy. Several times he alluded to "feminine" emotions or feelings, and after asking my colleague about her perspectives on affective relationships, he recommended his "school of marriage" as an avenue for learning how to feel:

We do it in a seminar style, where we take a series and sequences of teachings and try to define what religion should be, what love really is. We try to differentiate love from infatuation, we deal with conflict resolution, we also try to teach on the values and commitment of relationships, sex and relationship, God's idea of what a relationship is, and then we also teach on how to choose a life partner, what do you look for, what are the values. We also teach on magnetism, laws of attraction, and how do you actually evaluate your attraction factors, because sometimes you think you are attracted and then realize that it only lasts for two weeks or six months, so we try to show the core things that should be the foundation of real love.

Afterward, Emmet emphasized that the aim of the school was to provide "practical" knowledge, arguing that many churches failed in this regard. His definitions of affectivity were drawn from the emotional regime that his colleague Hector typically called the "righteous" and the "real" one. Both pastors were particularly concerned to teach emotions in such a way that they permeated affective relationships and certain forms of behavior in areas such as sex, friendship, or marriage (Bochow and van Dijk 2012; Burchardt 2015). Moreover, these and other themes were often aligned with biblical passages and addressed in terms of an African Christian morality that should guide worshippers in navigating social life. Brian Massumi and Joel McKim (2009, 3) explain affect as a comprehensively interactive set of elements existing in time and as a matrix of variation involving emotions, objects, identity, and subjectivity, with unpredictable outcomes generated from the dynamic interaction of these elements. In many ways, Emmet's and Hector's efforts in teaching how to feel were about giving shape to affectivity and gaining control over its unpredictable directions and intensities. In this way, they also resonate with the ways in which Pentecostalism's emotional repertoires allowed Congolese immigrants in Uganda's capital city of Kampala to manage trauma as Alessandro Gusman describes in this volume.

CONCLUSION

In this chapter, we have explored how Pentecostal pastors in Nigerian and Congolese diaspora communities in Bilbao and Johannesburg are developing and deploying emotional repertoires as a means of shaping the religious subjectivities and spiritual lives of their followers. We wish to highlight three aspects that are central to this process.

First, Pentecostal emotional repertoires are chiefly outcomes of the ways in which diaspora pastors draw on and rework globally circulating Pentecostal concepts of emotions. These concepts and repertoires include definitions of good and bad emotions and make up the Pentecostal emotional regime. They also involve ideas about the sources of these emotions and describe adequate emotional responses to the challenges migrants face in their daily lives in urban environments that are understood as potentially dangerous.

Second, as a bundle of interpretations, prescripts, and proscriptions, Pentecostalism's emotional regime is held together ideationally through shared theologies, and materially through manuals for emotion schools, teaching, and counseling. These manuals assemble global audiences of followers, while pastors interpret and "translate" them according to the local circumstances of urban life. While the actual experience of an emotion often ties believers to the immediacy of their bodily presence, the strong focus the pastors we worked with placed on teaching and learning suggests to their followers an idea of emotions as cultivated states of mind-body that come about through personal efforts to acquire spiritual knowledge. As we have shown, pastors never tired of tracing all kinds of emotional states to the level of spiritual knowledge, that is, knowledge about how to engage scriptures and connect to the divine. If Luhrmann's concept of *metakinesis* meant that learning to have an experience may be inseparable from learning the word to describe it, we suggest that, for diaspora pastors, having certain emotions is not neatly separable from spiritual knowledge as a condition of the self from which they emerge. In other words, if Pentecostals codify emotions in manuals and books and enact these codes in processes of teaching and learning emotions in counseling and religious encounters of all kinds, then the idea of emotional repertoires implies that knowledge and emotions are "comobilized" and reflexively coconstitute religious experiences.

Third, we emphasize that reflexivity is central to understanding processes of teaching and learning emotions and that, in order to uncover the work of reflexivity, biographical approaches are particularly useful. Pentecostal pastors did not engage in their teaching from an impersonal abstract perspective but always drew on their own experiences. Teaching Pentecostal emotions is thus always a matter of "leading by example" and of conveying to followers a sense of how to gain control over one's life by casting off the shackles of spiritual poverty and backwardness. More generally, we find that the focus on rational learning is intimately tied to the notion that, in order to be successful in life, one must become the master of, and remain in control of, seemingly uncontrollable circumstances and developments, something that all pastors understood to be particularly important for migrants living far away from home. The significance of Pentecostal practices of teaching emotions for urban life "away from home" thus lies in the fact that they enable pastors and followers to navigate and manage unfamiliar worlds of urban heterogeneity.

This also implies that the distinction between emotional regime and emotional repertoire that was introduced at the beginning of the chapter may be generally useful for the study of emotions, but that it is *conceptually* linked specifically to diaspora Pentecostalism. Repertoires are always about using a designated set of skills acquired elsewhere to handle newly emerging situations. Similarly, emotional repertoires are always about creatively adapting to the new lives migrants have to craft for themselves in host societies while drawing on a defined set of rules and tools. If Pentecostalism is, as Robbins (2004) has famously argued, the deterritorialized religion par excellence, relying as it does on the ready portability of the Holy Spirit, then its transnational emotional regime—its injunctions on how to feel—is fundamentally an unending series of pragmatic reworkings, retoolings, and refashionings geared toward the sculpting of an ideal believer, which is limited through the repertoire created in the urban context.

NOTES

1. This chapter is the outcome of collaborative research. Most of the field research on which the chapter is based was carried out by Rafael Cazarin. Marian Burchardt has also done research in Johannesburg, but his contribution to the chapter is based on more general reflections on the agency of pastors in South African Pentecostalism and theoretical considerations. For reasons of clarity, we use the collective "we" throughout.

2. Report from Ikuspegi—Observatório Vasco de Inmigración, Población Africana en la CAPV, "Población extranjera en la CAPV, 1998–2014," www.ikuspegi.eus/documentos /powerpoints/2014/capv2014provCAS.pdf.

3. Report from Ikuspegi—Observatório Vasco de Inmigración, "Población Africana en la CAPV," no. 51, November 2013, www.ikuspegi.eus/documentos/panoramicas /es/panoramica51casOK2.pdf.

4. Report from Observatorio del Pluralismo Religioso en España, "Explotación de Datos, Directorio de Lugares de Culto, December 2015," www.observatorioreligion.es /upload/16/40/Explotacion_Directorio_Diciembre_2015.pdf.

5. Report from Ayuntamiento de Bilbao, "Observatorio de la Inmigración en Bilbao," 2017, www.bilbao.eus/cs/Satellite?cid=3000062046&language=es&pageid =3000062046&pagename=Bilbaonet%2FPage%2FBIO_contenidoFinal (accessed February 14, 2018).

6. Nigerian nationals configure 2 percent and Congolese nationals 1.6 percent among all registered migrants in the CAPV. In Spain, both groups together make up less than 1 percent of documented migrants (Ikuspegi Observatório Vasco de Inmigración, "Población Africana en la CAPV," no. 51, November 2013).

7. Pew Forum on Religion & Public Life, "Faith on the Move: The Religious Affiliation of International Migrants," Washington, DC, March 2012, www.pewforum .org/wp-content/uploads/sites/7/2012/03/Faithonthemove.pdf (accessed February 14, 2018).

8. After significant events took place in the early 1900s, the movement's growth stagnated until the 1950s, when the South African evangelist Nicolas Benghu promoted the "Back-to-God" revivals in the region (Kalu 2008). By recalling notions of social change and racial equality, Benghu promoted an early version of pan-Africanism embedded within a Pentecostal worldview (Kalu 2008, 58).

PART III
EMBODIMENT, SUBJECTIVITY, AND BELONGING

8 "THOSE WHO PRAY TOGETHER" RELIGIOUS PRACTICE, AFFECT, AND DISSENT AMONG MUSLIMS IN ASANTE (GHANA)

BENEDIKT PONTZEN

In 2011, the people of Kokote Zongo conducted their *'id* prayers in an open venue in the middle of town.[1] This was done, as Malam Hamid put it, "to show the town that we are here, that we are many, and that we are one."[2] Through their collective religious practice in the open, the people of the *zongo* claimed a space in the city and (re)presented themselves as a community within it. In the local Asante context, zongos are wards of immigrants from the northern regions. While these immigrants have quite heterogeneous origins, they share a common ground and values in their religion. Islam is thus fundamental to their "home-making" (Adogame 1998; Eade 2012) and a central value that leads them in their everyday lives. Moreover, it distinguishes these wards from their predominantly Christian surroundings (Pellow 1985; Pontzen 2014; Schildkrout 1978; Verlet 2005). Thus, Islam, the religion of the people of the zongo, partakes in the making of their wards and informs their relations to their surrounding cities, while the people of the zongo enact, engage with, and thereby (re)make their religion in their community. In the zongos as much as elsewhere, African cityscapes, religions, and the affects and emotions that these engender are intertwined with and co-shape each other (see the introduction to this volume).

For the people of the zongo, the 'id prayers mark the major Islamic festivities—the feast of sacrifice and the end of Ramadan—and provide them with their main communal events. As my interlocutors often stated, their collective religious practices are central not only to their being Muslims but also to the continuous (re)formation of their Muslim community. They conduct their congregational prayers during these festivities and on a daily basis in the form of the *salat*, the common Islamic prayer. These prayers provide them with a shared sense of belonging and an affective ground for their community. The conduct of the salat is thus informed by and feeds into the affective regime that this religion values and establishes. As suggested by the editors, "religious ideas and practices offer affective regimes that regulate the hermeneutics of the self" (see the introduction to this volume). Religious ideas and practices engender specific affects and emotions, and they propel affective trajectories by which the people of the zongo integrate into their Muslim community and relate to their surrounding cities. Meanwhile, these affective trajectories are open to people's various engagements and experiences. They are thus as much informing their lives and biographies as they are lived and co-shaped by them.

In this chapter, I describe and discuss how the people of the zongo become and are Muslims by virtue of the Islamic practices and experiences in which their Muslim "selves-" emerge. They encode these and render them meaningful in their Islamic discourses and understandings. This process is grounded in and takes off from the affective states that are brought forth by their religious practices. Furthermore, a shared sense of belonging to the *umma* (Arabic: the Muslim community) emerges in these practices and their surrounding discourses. Nonetheless, this is anything but straightforward. How the people of the zongo experience their religious practices and how they render them meaningful differ: affects do not have a unidirectional impact on those who are caught up in them. The Muslim community of the zongos is marked by religious disagreements, and the Islamic affective regime encountered in these wards encompasses a considerable religious diversity and ongoing debates that remain irreducible to a single understanding. These ambiguities are fully acknowledged, debated, and lived by the people of the zongo themselves; in the following, I convey a sense of their divergent affective experiences and the states they evoke.

How are we to get a sense of this Islamic affective regime and the diversity that it encompasses? In what follows, I dwell on the religious practice of the salat that is central not only to the self-perceptions of the people of the zongo but also to perceptions of them by the Asante: "Ɔmɔfrɛ Nyame"

(Asante Twi: "They call out to God") is a common reference to the people of the zongo by their members.[3] And the people of the zongo refer to themselves as "those who pray together." As my interlocutors frequently exhorted: "Yɛn nyinaa yɛ salat, yɛn nyinaa yɛ nkramo" (Asante Twi: "We all do the salat, therefore we are all Muslims"). Accordingly, I focus on this daily religious practice and on the intensities, affective states, thoughts, and emotions that it entails to convey a tentative sense of the Islamic affective regime in these wards, along with its different impacts on their residents, and of how these inform the very processes whereby my interlocutors become and are Muslims.

Therefore, I first delineate my theoretical framework, dwelling on the notion of affect and how it relates to the formation of subjects. Thereafter, I move on to a short description of the context and history of the zongos, introducing them as Muslim wards in Asante and depicting Kokote Zongo, the site of my fieldwork, in more detail. Against this background, I turn to the practice of the salat and to a discussion of the affective states and experiences that my interlocutors related to it. As I argue, the salat brings forth an affective state in which an incipient Muslim "self-" emerges. This "self-" becomes a Muslim subject that is rendered meaningful and emotionally apprehended in its religious discourse. I describe this process as becoming and being Muslim by virtue of one's religious practices. Yet, this is anything but straightforward. As I discuss in the last section of the chapter, the people of the zongo pertain to different Islamic groups and use their religious practices to (re-)create their religious differences. This feeds into an ongoing discourse through which they engage with their religion, relate to each other as Muslims, and agree on or contest their various understandings and implementations of their religion.[4]

FROM AFFECT TO EMOTION, FROM "SELF-" TO SUBJECT

Their Islamic practices and rituals bring forth certain affects and emotions that the people of the zongo render meaningful in their religiously informed discourses. Yet, while they express and qualify their emotions and feelings in these discourses, the affects of their religious practices have an impact on them before their discursive renderings.[5] While emotions receive "[their] meaning and force from [their] location and performance in the public realm of discourse" (Abu-Lughod and Lutz 1990, 7; cf. Lutz and White 1986), affect is a prediscursive *something* that happens. It catches one up and affects one, but this concern is prediscursive, not yet signified or qualified (Massumi 2002, 25–28; Stewart 2007, 2). Affect involves one and one's ways of relating to the world (Massumi 2002, 27–28; Thrift 2004), and one experiences and qualifies this concern as responses to the world and as the emotional states one finds oneself in (Massumi 2002, 28). Affects actually prompt one's emotional discourses, which can nonetheless not grasp them in their embodied and *unqualified* impacts on the senses (28). This major problem in dealing with affects has been pointed out by Brian Massumi: we lack the vocabulary with which to address them (27).

Deriving from the Latin *afficere*—"to do to" (OED 2014)[6]—affect designates a change in one's subjective state and experience that influences the content of one's thoughts and imagination (Regenbogen and Meyer 2013). Affects take place in embodied relations with the world: "They're things that happen [and] catch people up in something that feels like *something*" (Stewart 2007, 2, emphasis in original). This is yet unqualified, but not without consequences—in these intensities, an incipient subjectivity, what Massumi calls a "self-," emerges (2002, 14).[7] One's subjectivity is thus bound up with and emerges in the affective intensities it experiences and by which it relates to the world in the form of embodied dispositions. In distinction to a Foucauldian self (cf. Hirschkind 2006; Mahmood [2005] 2012), this "self-" is "not a substantive but rather a relation" (Massumi 2002, 14). Simultaneously, one qualifies these intensities and relations to the world as one's thoughts and feelings and thereby renders them meaningful. As Kathleen Stewart has argued, "[The] significance [of ordinary affects] lies in the thoughts and feelings they make possible" (2007, 3). Affects thus resonate in and interfere with one's thoughts and emotions (T. Brennan 2004; Massumi 2002, 25). The latter fix these intensities, turning their unqualified and affective *something* into a qualified and emotive *this feeling* (Bialecki 2015, 97; Massumi 2002, 27–28). On this level of comprehension language and discourse set in, experience comes to be signified, and affect is turned into emotion (Abu-Lughod and Lutz 1990; Lutz and White 1986; Massumi 2002, 27).

This poses some methodological challenges for descriptive and analytic dealings with affect. How are we to access the affective dimension of the lives of our interlocutors when we are always already on the level of language and discourse in our conversations and writings? Stewart persuasively suggests that we try "to slow down the quick jump to representational thinking and evaluative critique long enough to find ways of approaching the complex and uncertain objects that fascinate because they literally hit us or exert a pull on us . . . by performing some of the intensity and texture that makes them habitable and animate" (2007, 4). In the field and in reading, we should hence hone our senses to the affective intensities that impact us and our interlocutors (Bialecki 2015, 106–107).

Another methodological challenge remains. As embodied and personal experiences, affects and their intensities are bound up with a "self-" that discursively takes the first person as its narrative point of view.[8] The focalization is internal: that is, the narrator says only what the subject knows (Genette [1972] 1980, 189). But here, as in other ethnographic texts, the author cannot treat the "I"/"we" of his*her interlocutors as his narrative voice.[9] My affects and experiences as a non-Muslim and as an outsider are not theirs, nor did I immediately partake in theirs. Accordingly, I rely on my interlocutors' personal accounts, which I reproduce to capture some of the intensities generated by the Islamic affective regime in the zongos, as well as lending them some density and texture through ethnographic descriptions. In doing so, I attempt to delineate the lived experiences of my interlocutors in their waxing and waning intensities. This is not to be confused with an empathy in shared universal emotions (Lutz and White 1986, 414–416). My descriptions and retellings of the affective experiences and emotions of my interlocutors do not make them available in their immediate intensities, but they could convey a sense—or perhaps a feel—of the affective impacts of their prayers on the people of the zongo and on their community.

KOKOTE ZONGO: A MUSLIM WARD IN ASANTE

Kokote Zongo lies on the western outskirts of Offinso, a small Asante town. It is home to the majority of the town's Muslims. About fifty-five hundred of the town's sixty thousand residents live in this ward (Pontzen 2014, chap. 3). In relation to the majoritarian and hegemonic Asante, who make up 75 percent of the regional population and who are predominantly Christians (UNDP, Ghana 2007), the people of the zongo are a religious and ethnic minority in the local setting. Virtually all of them are immigrants from the northern West African subregion who have settled down in Kokote Zongo in the last three generations. They came with the trading caravans that have crossed West Africa since at least the eighteenth century (Abaka 2005; Arhin 1979; Lovejoy 1980; Pontzen 2014; Schildkrout 1970) and moved into Asante during colonial rule, when they were no longer kept in check by Asante authorities. Hence the name of these wards: *zongo* means "trading post" in Hausa (Pellow 2002; Schildkrout 1978). Up until this day, zongos have remained "alien" to their surroundings, and their inhabitants find themselves as strangers (Asante Twi: ɔhɔhoɔ) in the local setting (Fortes

1975). They are not integrated into Asante society, as their interactions with the Asante are mainly limited to the economic sphere of the local markets, and intermarriages and mutual participation in each other's lives are rather exceptional.

However, when it comes to ethnic belonging, the people of Kokote Zongo are also strangers to each other. They identify as members of nineteen ethnic groups and speak more than twenty-five languages in their daily interactions (Pontzen 2014, chap. 3). The cultural and linguistic differences between the peoples of this ward are vast. Additionally, their original economic solidarity, which was founded on the long-distance trade with the Sahel, has largely collapsed along with the decline in this commerce in the late twentieth century. Thus, their shared religion provides these otherwise quite heterogeneous people with a common ground and shared values which allow them to conjointly make a home. As Muslims, they relate to each other, partake in each other's lives, and intermarry. As Muslims, they also integrate into the translocal umma that encompasses their wards, their regions of origin, and the transglobal community of Muslims. This lends them a sense of belonging (cf. Burchardt and Becci 2013, 12–17) that differs from the locally rooted one of the Asante. In terms of origin or point of reference, their sense of belonging is somewhat diffuse and relates to an *elsewhere*, outside their immediate surroundings. Zongos are thus not only distinct parts of town; they form a distinct, albeit quite heterogeneous community, as their inhabitants are more involved with other zongos and their places of origin than with their neighboring Asante.

However, in the zongos as elsewhere, Islam is anything but monolithic, being matter to and of a "discursive tradition" (Asad 1986) by which the people of the zongo relate to or contest each other's religious imaginaries, conceptualizations, and practices. Up to the 1970s, the Tijaniyya Sufi group (Abun-Nasr 1965; Seesemann 2011; Triaud and Robinson 2000) was the regionally hegemonic Islamic faction. Since then, they have come under open challenge from the Sunna (Dumbe 2013; Kobo 2009; Pontzen 2014, chap. 2), a Salafi-/Wahhabi-oriented group of reformers, who refuse to follow them in their Sufi tenets or practices and do not recognize them as religious authorities. Hence, they refuse to pray behind them—the most basic form this recognition takes in the zongos. As the two groups are struggling for religious hegemony in these wards, the allegedly simple act of praying is thus always already caught up in this struggle. But let me first address the shared understandings of the salat before I turn to its status as a marker of distinction.

It was during his ascent to the heavens that the Prophet received the salat from Allah, who has "created the *jinn* and mankind for nothing but to worship Me," as stated in the Qur'an (51:56).[10] The salat is not a given object but a religious practice that is largely fixed by the *sunna* (Arabic: the tradition of the deeds and sayings of the Prophet) in form and content (Holmes Katz 2013; Pontzen 2014, chap. 4). It is to be offered five times a day and requires a state of ritual purity that is established through ablutions and the declaration of one's intent. In this state, the males gather in the mosques to go collectively through the prescribed ritual cycle of bodily postures—standing, bowing, prostration, and kneeling—along with the respective recitations in Arabic. Afterward, they disperse into the zongo again, greeting each other with "Allah ƙarba!" (Hausa: "May Allah receive it!")

As a divine revelation and ordainment, the salat is of central importance and of high value to Muslims across the globe (Bowen 1989, 1993, 2012, chap. 3; Debevec 2012; Henkel 2005; Mahmood 2001, [2005] 2012; Parkin and Headley 2000; Simon 2009). In the zongos, the Islamic prayer is not solely a religious practice—it provides the people of these wards with a cornerstone for the formation of their community. As Aminata, one of Kokote Zongo's leading Muslim women, stated, the salat is the very foundation of Islam and of one's being a Muslim.[11] Or, as the people of Kokote Zongo frequently put it: "Yεn nyinaa yε salat, yεn nyinaa yε nkramo" (Asante Twi: "We all do the salat, therefore we are all Muslims"). Mr. Tariq, the headmaster of an Islamic school, explained this as follows: "Islam means you submit yourself fully to God. It is like you own yourself, but you do not own yourself." According to him, the sense and "the beauty" of the salat are that one submits oneself unconditionally in one's full being to God. In doing so, one acknowledges, (re-)creates, senses, and experiences one's submission to and dependence on Him.[12] In this affective state, one becomes and is a Muslim in one's corporeality. In the act of prayer, "theology is made flesh, or word," as John Bowen has noted (2012, 52).

This resonates with the focus on embodiment in the "materialist turn" (Meyer and Houtman 2012; Vásquez 2011) in religious studies, which pays greater attention to the corporeal aspects of religions (Asad 2014; Csordas 1990; Meyer 2012a) and the "sensational forms" (Meyer 2009, 2013) through which people relate to the divine (Orsi 2005, 2012) than a strictly discursive or textual approach. I follow this turn, as well as Saba Mahmood in her understanding of the (praying) body and its behavioral forms "as a signifying medium [and] as a tool for becoming a certain kind of person and attaining certain kinds of states" (2001, 837). In the following, I convey some insights into this process, relying on the personal accounts of my interlocutors in a juxtapositional manner. In doing so, I do not render the salat as it is, but I shed light on some of its central aspects to convey a tentative understanding of the senses the practitioners make of and with it.

RELATING TO THE DIVINE

The salat consists in a pregiven cycle of postures, gestures, and recitations by which the praying person enacts and experiences one's submission to God in its embodiment and affects. Malam Hamid, one of Kokote Zongo's Islamic scholars, referred to the three bodily postures of the salat as follows: the *qiyam* (Arabic: standing) in the beginning is a standing before God, and by raising the hands to the earlobes, one surrenders to Him; in the *ruku'* (Arabic: bowing posture), one makes oneself small before God; and in the *sujud* (Arabic: prostration), one is reminded that one is nothing before Him.[13] The same point was made by Sheikh Nazeer, a preacher from Kumase, who described the prostration as "bringing the seven postures of which one is proud and with which one is and acts in the world under God." The feet on which one stands, the knees with which one walks, the hands with which one acts, and the head with which one thinks and talks—one can do nothing with these during the sujud, as they are all under Him, and this is how we humans find ourselves in this world: "We are all under Him."[14]

Both Malam Hamid and Sheikh Nazeer are Sunna *malams* (Asante Twi: Islamic scholars), and they largely agree in their prosaic renderings of the affects of the salat, but for Abdul Malik, a Tijaniyya from Kumase, such prosaic descriptions only touch the surface of the Islamic prayer. For him, the salat has a "deep" meaning that is only accessible to the spiritually imbued who have reached a "deeper" understanding of Allah and one's submission to Him. In the salat, one becomes one with God. As Abdul Malik claimed, this is a strictly experiential state that makes itself *felt* to those who are open to it, but it cannot be conveyed through language.[15] For Abdul Malik, the affective state he experiences during prayer amounts to a co-presence with or dissolution in the divine. This is unacceptable for Malam Hamid and Sheikh Nazeer, who reject this idea of a unification with the divine. Hence, the affective states of one's submission to God that are engendered by the act of prayer are experienced and qualified not only in different but also in contrasting ways by my interlocutors. As stated by the editors of this volume, these disparate perceptions and renderings of the salat show "that the biographically rooted embodiment of affecting and being affected is rarely restricted to the individual's situation alone but is always a critical articulation of larger . . . configurations" (see the introduction to this volume). Here, my interlocutors' perceptions and renderings are co-shaped by the different Islamic factions they belong to.

Yet, in the salat one does not simply bring oneself under God; one relates to Him in a specific way. This was made clear to me by Hamidou, an "ordinary believer" from Kokote Zongo: "At the time when I leave the mosque, I go with God. God has entered my heart, and I verily bear Him in my mind."[16] He is thus not only submitted but rather committed to Him, and this state is experienced and acquired by him enacting the Islamic tradition in prayer. This was rendered meaningful in our conversations, and my other interlocutors frequently stressed as well that the salat does *something* to them and to how they feel: it entails their intense awareness of their commitment to Allah and His religion. Prayer is conducted with and affects one's entire being—the *honam* (Asante Twi: self-flesh).[17]

ENACTING AND EMBODYING ONE'S RELIGION

As Malam Hamid stated, "The salat stems from the Prophet" and is not to be altered.[18] It is "rigidly imitative of the Prophet's own tongue and style" (Headley 2000b, 205), and any change in it would come tantamount to an act of *bid'a* (Arabic: illegitimate innovation in the religion of Islam). Accordingly, the praying person reproduces the salat in its original form but does not author it. Marcel Mauss's observation about prayer in general thus holds especially for the salat, namely, that "it is through the phrases of the ritual that one composes one's interior discourse. Accordingly, the individual merely appropriates a language he has in no sense made to his personal feelings" (1968, 379).[19] In its gestures and recitations, the salat surpasses the praying person, who engages with, is affected by, and embodies a whole tradition, the sunna, in its practice (cf. de Certeau 1987, 40; Heiler [1919] 1923, 105; Henkel 2005, 489; Holmes Katz 2013).

This is not to be understood as the symbolization of an external tradition. According to Malam Fusseini, another Islamic scholar from Kokote Zongo, the salat is something one does with one's entire *adwene* (Asante Twi: mind) and *honam* (Asante Twi: literally "self-flesh," body and self).[20]

It requires, involves, and affects one's entire being: "In prayer, the faithful person acts and thinks. And action and thought are closely united" (Mauss 1968, 358).[21] This begins with the ritual ablutions and proclamation of one's intent to pray by which body and mind are attuned to the prayer. Thus, one enters a state of physical and spiritual purity which enfolds one's entire being. "Your whole being is in the salat," remarked Malam Ali, one of Kokote Zongo's Sunna malams. "When I raise my hands for the first *takbir* during qiyam, this means that I remove the world from my mind. The lowering of the gaze and the folding of the hands on my chest means that I enfold myself in prayer, and when I bow and prostrate myself, I bring myself under God, I submit myself to Him."[22] This was also noted by Abdul Malik, who said that prayer gives him peace and "lifts him from the confusions of the world."[23] According to my interlocutors, prayer affects them in their entire being: they are not only involved in but shaped by their prayers. One becomes and is a Muslim by devoting oneself to God and His religion. The salat is hence "a signifying medium [and] a tool for becoming," or, as Michael Lambek remarked of religious rituals in general: "Ritual definitely links the *is* and the *ought* . . . in such a way that the former is to be judged in terms of the latter instead of the reverse. Moreover, participants are subject to ritual acts, in part constituted by them" (2000a, 314–315, emphasis in original).

The salat requires and brings forth certain virtues and thereby coconstitutes the praying subject. As such, it is a highly virtuous practice (cf. MacIntyre [1981] 2007, 190–191), as stated in the Qur'an (29:45). Hamidou commented on this as follows: "Prayer belongs to me, it is part of me; without prayer, I cannot live. Without prayers you live an empty life."[24] In our conversations, the people of Kokote Zongo related several virtues to the salat: patience, forgiveness, zeal, peace, and humility. I would like to comment on two of these here. In the zongos, humility not only is considered a virtue in regard to religious practice but also has a high social-cultural value. The people of the zongo value humility, and their relationships are marked by mutual respect, which finds its realization in a humble demeanor. In their interactions, they avoid confrontational behavior, lower their gaze, and elevate the other, thereby expressing their mutual "respect." This not only holds for social-cultural minors or inferiors, as the zongo's authorities are expected to act humbly as well. Another realization of humility is one's readiness to forgive, and this is also consolidated in the salat. Hamidou stated: "For the salat you repent in your heart and you seek forgiveness from God, and if you seek forgiveness from Him, you have to forgive your fellows, too."[25] By establishing peace among the participants, the salat thus contributes to the maintenance of the zongo's community.

THE SALAT AND THE FORMATION
OF THE RELIGIOUS COMMUNITY

As argued by Émile Durkheim, religious rituals are central to the formation of a "moral community" ([1912] 2007, 48, 93). However, while my interlocutors stressed the central value of their conjoint religious practice for their mutual identification as Muslims and for the establishment of their community, no one ever suggested the emergence of a "collective consciousness" from this, nor did I encounter a "synthesis of particular consciousnesses" (595) among them. As Malam Abdeen stated, the salat brings forth a physical and spiritual unity before God and helps to strengthen the affective ties of solidarity and of belonging among Kokote Zongo's Muslims, who "pray as one,"[26] but neither with one body, nor with one consciousness. According to my interlocutors, praying together deepens their faith, and their common faith imbues their relations with a quality that is at once morally binding and a comfort to them (cf. Farneth, Gross, and Youatt 2009; Heiler [1919] 1923, 431; Henkel 2005, 500; Lambek 2000b, 86).

The resulting community not only encompasses those who actually pray together. The salat is "for the whole world," as Malam Fusseini noted, and enfolds its practitioners in the transglobal umma (cf. Lambek 2000b, 69; Parkin 2000, 16).[27] The praying individuals orient themselves toward the Kaaba (Arabic: the black cube in Mecca) and recite their prayers in Arabic as a "supraethnic" or "universal" language (Gellner 1981, 24; Henkel 2005, 495). For the otherwise quite heterogeneous people of the zongo, this provides a common ground that affects them, that they can all claim alike, and that encompasses their ethnic and linguistic diversity. Mosques are not ethnically marked, nor is the conduct of the prayer, and Arabic is its most important medium. The salat provides them with a supraethnic orientation and the means to integrate into a shared community, or, as my interlocutors frequently put it: "We all do the salat, therefore we are all one." But this does not go uncontested, as the salat is also a central space for the (re-)creation of the religious differences that run through their community. Let me now come back to the 'id prayer from the beginning of the chapter to address this point.

FIGURE 8.1 Women gathered for prayer at the Mawlid in Prang.
Photo by Benedikt Pontzen.

THE SALAT CONTESTED: RELIGIOUS DISSENT IN PRACTICE

On August 30 and 31, 2011, two *'id al-fitr*, the communal Islamic prayer
conducted at the end of Ramadan, took place in Kokote Zongo. As in previous years, the people of Kokote Zongo parted ways to conduct the same
Islamic ritual in different venues. Though they are all Muslims, some refused to conduct this major prayer behind the Tijaniyya imam of the town.
The Sunna and their adherents went to another venue, assembling twelve
hundred people on their prayer ground, all of whom had similar misgivings
about praying behind a Tijaniyya. In the other venue, roughly thirty-five
hundred people followed the Tijaniyya imam in prayer. In form and content, the two prayers did not differ, but the people of the zongo disagreed
on who had the authority to lead them in their religious practice.

The 'id prayers are not the only ones carried out in different venues. As
with their daily prayers, the people of the zongo were divided by convic-

tion into separate prayer spaces, re-creating, in a ritual sense, their religious differences.[28] Until the mid-1990s, there was only one central mosque in Kokote Zongo where the people convened for the Friday prayer. Then, the Sunna built their own Friday mosque on the opposing hillside, and the people of Kokote Zongo no longer congregated as one.

The salat not only is central to the formation of Muslim communities across the globe but also frequently contested between and within them (Bowen 1993, 296–314; Lambek 1990, 30–33; Launay [1992] 2004, chap. 5). As its form and content are largely pregiven by the sunna, its apparently minor details, such as the audible against the silent utterance of the *basmala* (Bowen 1993, 306–309) or the positioning of one's hands (Holmes Katz 2013, 27–28; Launay [1992] 2004, 123; Loimeier 2014, 23–24), can become markers of distinction and matter to ardent debates. In the zongos, the central dispute revolves around the question of whom one is willing to pray behind and thereby acknowledges as one's religious authority (cf. Headley 2000a, 235; Holmes Katz 2013, chap. 4; Larkin and Meyer 2006, 305; Pontzen 2014, chap. 4; Topan 2000, 102).

Since the 1970s, the previously hegemonic Tijaniyya have faced open challenges from the Sunna, who criticize their Sufi tenets and practices. To the reformers, these are tantamount to bid'a, and they refuse to acknowledge those who promote them as properly observant Muslims, still less as religious authorities. In Kokote Zongo, they refused to pray behind them and established their own prayer grounds in front of the house of their leading malam, about a hundred yards away from the central mosque. As in other zongos, this was not taken well by the Tijaniyya and their adherents, who perceived this separation as an open affront. In turn, they rebuked the Sunna for promoting *fitna* (Arabic: schism) in the community, criticized their malams as parvenu imposters, and prompted their adherents not to follow them. This resulted in a tense atmosphere that flared into open violence in 1997 when the Sunna mosque was destroyed by their opponents. The state and traditional authorities had to restore social peace and order. Since then, tensions have "come down," and the atmosphere is less tense and prone to violence. Nowadays, the controversies between these Islamic groups are mainly carried out in discourse, and the sermons held at the Friday prayers are central to this, as the malams criticize each other's tenets and practices or reply to the criticisms of others in their preaching. The audiences carry their arguments into their conversations, thereby perpetuating these controversies and debating their religion, which results in an ongoing "give-and-take."

The act of praying has also been dragged into these controversies. Praying behind a specific malam is conceived and read as expressing one's personal alignment with his tenets and with the criticisms he might voice toward others. In recent decades, the Sunna have gained ground, and as they are competing with the Tijaniyya for religious hegemony, prayers are commonly perceived and discussed as a kind of public display of one's personal allegiance in these contestations. The struggle for religious hegemony between these two groups thus reverberates in the religious practices and bodies of their adherents. This engenders specific affects and emotions: people feel anxious or nervous about praying behind the "wrong" malam, while they feel blessings flowing through the "right" one,[29] and they feel offended or relieved when those close to them pray with them or refuse to do so. These feelings were expressed in open consultations with the malams after sermons in the mosques or in more intimate settings in the zongos' homes. Furthermore, the people of Kokote Zongo felt insecure about the validity of their prayers due to these ongoing conflicts. They were affected by the struggle between the Tijaniyya and the Sunna in their very senses and in their practical relating to the divine. This lends their conflicts their intensity and perils: they feel as if they are about *something*.

CONCLUSION

Islam provides the people of the zongo with a common ground to integrate into a Muslim community. The religious differences that currently run through their community threaten it and resonate in the Islamic affective regime one encounters within it. The religious conflict between the Tijaniyya and the Sunna makes itself felt to the people of the zongo in their basic religious practices and thus affects their interrelations and interactions, as they feel *somehow* anxious about acknowledging the others as "proper" Muslims. Nonetheless, they recognize each other as Muslims and also integrate into one Muslim community by means of their very debates in which these conflicts and the emotional responses to them are brought to the fore.

This community is (re)actualized and experienced in its shared religious practices. As Birgit Meyer has argued, "In order to become experienced as real, imagined communities need to materialize in the concrete lived environment and be felt in the bones" (2009, 5). This is accomplished through the "sensational forms" (13) that these communities perpetuate. The salat provides such a "sensational form" for the people of the zongo. Its common practice comes with intensities and affective states that are at once experienced and shared by the members of the congregation. The people of the zongo embody their community in their religious practice. They and their community become and are Muslim in the affective trajectories engendered by the practical realization of their religion. On this level, their self-reference holds: "We all do the salat, therefore we are all Muslims."

However, how these affective states are rendered meaningful and emotional, how an incipient Muslim "self-" becomes a Muslim subject, and how one's religion is qualified are anything but unanimously agreed upon. How my interlocutors rendered the affects of prayer into qualified feelings or emotions varied, remained open to their individual engagements with their religion, and resounded with the controversies between the Tijaniyya and the Sunna. The subjective qualifications of the salat are thus reached in an open but neither ungrounded nor decontextualized process that starts in people's embodied and affective relations to the world (Massumi 2002, 14) and to the divine (Orsi 2005).

The relations between the salat as a phenomenon *an sich*, the affective states it brings forth, and their qualifications by those who pray are thus anything but straightforward. It can be employed by the people of the zongo to relate to Allah, His religion, and each other, or to align themselves with the one praying in front or with one of the zongos' Islamic groups. And though quite rigidly fixed in form and content by the *sunna*, the salat is open to a variety of individual engagements and experiences that are informed by and inform the actual context of these wards (cf. Simon 2009; Starrett 1995). Accordingly, I have complicated the notion of the salat by investigating the senses the praying persons make of and with it. This should not be confused either with the theological and perhaps unanswerable question of what Islam *is* or with the associated question of who is a good Muslim. With Veena Das, we should remind ourselves that "even God waits till judgement [*sic*] day to make such a pronouncement" (1984, 298). It is not incumbent upon us to make determinations on this, but rather to listen to and to report the responses as provided and lived by our interlocutors and, perhaps, to get a sense of what is at stake for them in this.

NOTES

1. I carried out fieldwork in Kokote Zongo and other zongos in 2011, 2012, and 2013. Kokote Zongo lies in the Asante town of Offinso, one hour's drive north from Kumase, the regional capital. My main methods were participant observation and informal conversations with Asante Twi as the main research language. I supplemented the

data gathered thereby with more formal interviews and some archival research. The informal and personal ways in which I conducted research were barred to me in approaching women in these places. Therefore, my research and data have a markedly male bias.

The research formed part of my PhD thesis, titled "Islam in the Zongo" (Pontzen 2014), and was funded by the Berlin Graduate School Muslim Cultures and Societies. Writing this chapter, I was funded by the Dahlem Research School and the Bayreuth International Graduate School of African Studies. I wish to thank these institutions for their support. I also wish to thank Hansjörg Dilger, Astrid Bochow, Matthew Wilhelm-Solomon, and the anonymous reviewers. This chapter was initially presented at the conference "Spirit and Sentiment: Affective Trajectories of Religious Being in Urban Africa," Freie Universität Berlin, May 28–30, 2015.

2. Malam Hamid, Kokote Zongo, November 7, 2011.

I use pseudonyms to refer to my interlocutors. The people of the zongo speak numerous languages in their interactions, with Hausa and Asante Twi being the main lingua francas. Their religious vocabulary is mainly Arabic, and English terms or phrases are part of their active vocabulary as well. I mark such English terms by quotation marks, while I note the other languages in my translations in the text. The transcriptions have been simplified and leave out most diacritics.

3. This notwithstanding, the usual characterizations of the zongos and their inhabitants among the Asante were rather negative and derogatory.

4. This discourse is held within the zongos only. In the Asante parts of town, it is neither noticed nor of any importance. For the Asante, the people of the zongo are commonly "just Muslims."

5. As employed in this chapter, "feeling" refers to a subjective state or disposition that can but does not have to be rendered meaningful as an emotion. By "emotion," I refer to the culturally and socially mediated articulations that allow one to qualify one's feelings (see the introduction to this volume).

6. Note that the etymological root leaves both sides of the "to do to" unqualified; neither the what nor the whom is specified.

7. Massumi writes of this emerging "self-" with a hyphen to highlight its relational quality; a "self-" emerges only in relations.

8. Accordingly, the first-person narration is the prominent voice in the literature on affect.

9. The * is intended to open up a space for all genders and people who wish to find themselves beyond or not on an either/or side of allegedly binary genders.

10. As translated by Sheikh Nazeer, Kumase, July 17, 2012.

11. Aminata, Kokote Zongo, June 26, 2012.

12. Mr. Tariq, Kokote Zongo, June 6, 2012.

13. Malam Hamid, Kokote Zongo, July 25, 2012.

14. Sheikh Nazeer, Kumase, July 17, 2012.

15. Abdul Malik, Kumase, August 28, 2012.

16. Hamidou, Kokote Zongo, August 24, 2012: "Time no a, mefiri mosque, me ne Nyame nam. Onyankupon awura me akuma mu na mekae ne pa ara" (Asante Twi).

17. A similar notion is found in the German word *Leib*, the lived and living body as the very foundation of one's "being-in-the-world" and one's engaging with it in meaningful ways (Csordas 1990; Jackson 1983; Marzano 2007; Mauss [1934] 2004).

18. Malam Hamid, Kokote Zongo, July 25, 2012.

19. French original: "c'est avec les phrases du rituel que l'on compose son discours intérieur. L'individu ne fait donc qu'approprier à ses sentiments personnels un langage qu'il n'a point fait."

The Book of Common Prayer and the Lord's Prayer bear witness to the fact that this is by no means a specific trait of Islamic prayers only.

20. Malam Fusseini, Kokote Zongo, April 24, 2012.

21. "Dans la prière le fidèle agit et il pense. Et action et pensée sont unies etroitement."

22. Malam Ali, Kokote Zongo, June 27, 2012.

23. Abdul Malik, Kumase, July 24, 2012.

24. Hamidou, Kokote Zongo, August 24, 2012: "Prayer no a, ɛka me ho, ɛyɛ part of me, without mpaebɔ I cannot live. Without prayers, wolive empty life" (Asante Twi and English).

25. Hamidou, Kokote Zongo, August 24, 2012.

26. Malam Abdeen, Kokote Zongo, July 27, 2012. In the mosques, the males take care to touch each other by their little toes and shoulders to close the line through bodily contact; they also strive to pray in the same rhythm, led by the imam in front.

27. Malam Fusseini, Kokote Zongo, April 24, 2012.

28. Participant observation, Kokote Zongo, August 30 and 31, 2011.

29. Personal communications, Kokote Zongo and other zongos, 2011, 2012, 2013.

9 LONGING FOR CONNECTION CHRISTIAN EDUCATION AND EMERGING URBAN LIFESTYLES IN BOTSWANA

ASTRID BOCHOW

EDUCATED PROFESSIONALS' EMOTIONS IN A CONTEXT OF SOCIETAL CHANGE

A discussion with a group of sociology students at the University of Bots-wana in 2011 revealed the emotional weight that decisions about family and all related decisions have for the young generation of educated profession-als in Gaborone, Botswana's capital. I had given a lecture in a class on gen-der during one of my visits to Botswana, and a vibrant discussion unfolded afterward. I asked young educated people about their aspirations in life, and soon the discussion ventured into the topics of family planning, gen-der roles, and work. It took an unexpected emotional turn when one male student confessed, "In my church they teach me I am a man and therefore I am a provider. I have responsibilities! I want my wife to stay at home." His statement motivated one of the female students to speak. She became visibly emotional during her statement, with her tensed body posture, her husky voice, and tears in her eyes expressing desperation, pain, and anger. She told the group that her boyfriend wanted to marry her, but she was adamant that she did not want to. She believed that his plan was to entice her into the relationship, eventually having a child together, only to leave her after she had given in and accepted his proposal. "My church prohibits entering marriage early. We first have to make a living before we can have a family. I have been the child of a single mother and have suffered throughout my childhood. I knew my father; he had a family. He never acknowledged that I was his child and to see him there with this other family— I don't want to become like my mother! I don't want to marry early!" she exclaimed. The others in the group were visibly moved by her outburst, attempting to assuage her sorrow and anger and soothe her. One of the other young women suggested that her fellow student should try to forgive, and that she was now punishing her boyfriend for what her father had done to her. It was obvious that the speaker herself was surprised by her sudden outburst of emotions and allowed her fellow student to calm her down. The group discussion came to an end (field notes, March 3, 2011).

This group discussion was one of the many occasions on which I witnessed how urban educated youth in Gaborone expressed anxieties, fear, and experiences of pain related to marriage and family life. Remarkably, both students called upon the teachings of their respective Christian churches, which would allow them to break away from the suffering of their past by living marriage and parenthood in different ways than their parents. By doing so, they expressed not only their anxieties and their personal histories of pain but also their hopes for a different (and more positive) future. The students did not specify the denominations of their churches, but their anxieties and hopes regarding family life resembled many Pentecostal discourses on marriage and the family that I recorded throughout my fieldwork in Gaborone in 2009 and 2011. The incident shows that Pentecostal discourses on the family impress young educated people in Gaborone who exhibited ambitions to join the lifestyles of a newly emerging socioeconomic group of professionals with stable and considerable income residing in the capital city of Botswana, one of the few middle-income countries in sub-Saharan Africa.

The rise of these new socioeconomic groups demarcates one of the great changes Botswana has gone through in the past thirty years: On the one hand, these changes concern the introduction of new wealth starting in the 1980s with the processing of minerals. This led to the formation of new professional groups relating to a long-standing history of education and professionalism induced by Christian mission churches, of which the London Mission Society was the first, followed by the Anglican Church, Seventh Day Adventists, and the Roman Catholic Church in the twentieth century, originating from both African and European countries. Currently, half of Botswana's population is considered by international standards to be "middle class" and an estimated 29 percent are considered to be "stable" (nonfloating) (Mmegi 2015).[1]

The strict economic definition of "middle class" in the study cited here might be misleading with regard to the diversity of socioeconomic backgrounds, styles of consumption, and religious affiliations embodied by persons in this growing social collective (Ncube and Lufumpa 2014). However, many of these individuals have been shown to share a cosmopolitan outlook regarding family life, professional ethics, leisure time activities, and political orientation and thus can be regarded as part of what has been termed the "global middle classes" (Heiman, Freeman, and Liechty 2012). Writing about urban people with well-paying jobs, I prefer to use the more descriptive term "educated professionals." By this I mean people who hold a university degree and who are employed in accord with their qualifications in either the private or the public sector. Sometimes these employees are referred to as people with "white-collar jobs" (cf. Stephanie Newell 2002), a term that is not common in Gaborone. In Botswana the majority of these new groups of educated professionals reside in the cities, of which Gaborone is the largest, with an estimated 231,000 inhabitants in a country with slightly more than 2 million inhabitants.[2]

On the other hand, the lifestyles and worldviews of this growing number of urban educated professionals have been shaped significantly by the HIV pandemic. A wave of deaths caused by HIV/AIDS did more than have a lasting impact on the demographic composition of the society and its household structures (Ingstad 1994); local and transnational responses to HIV/AIDS also introduced new technologies and politics of relating to oneself and to others, as well as new forms of education intended to reform existing gender and sexual relations (cf. Heald 2006; van Dijk 2013). Finally, widespread experiences of HIV-related illness and death had strongly impacted the ethics of care and family relations in both rural and urban settings (Klaits 2010; Livingston 2003).

Taken together, these transformations brought about social mobility, for instance, with regard to the distribution of wealth and status and new professional opportunities, but also closures and ruptures, as, for instance, the lack of care due to HIV-related deaths. Because the majority of educated professionals reside in Gaborone, the capital is a place of intensification of social tensions and of emotions evolving in this situation (see the introduction to this volume). In this chapter, I will argue, following Sara Ahmed, that the family became an "object of emotions" saturated with many, partially conflicting emotions in the lives of members of the middle class in Botswana. By providing education and later counseling, Pentecostal churches, following the example of mission churches, have been instrumental in this historical process by training educated professionals into new models of marriage and family life and attaching these to economic and social success. I will explore this historical process in three sections. The first will show how Christian education first in schools and later in the framework of counseling by pastors introduced educated professionals to a passion for education and progress while also teaching them family planning, which became decisive for their economic performance. Second, I show that Christian education imagined the family as a space of social security and protection, which appealed to the anxieties of educated professionals in view of accelerating pressures introduced by growing expectations to join the conspicuous consumption associated with urban lifestyles since the 1980s. Finally, I argue that some Pentecostal churches in Gaborone encourage their members to cut off bonds of care with their relatives from the rural area who are in need, especially those children within the wider network of kin who have lost their parents. Taken together, I argue that Christian, and recently more particularly Pentecostal, ways of family life are both inclusive, as their teaching shows ways to join the urban middle classes, and exclusive, as they teach members how to cut off relations of care with the wider family.

THE CULTURAL POLITICS OF EMOTIONS
AND THE RECONFIGURATION OF SOCIAL FIELDS

As has been laid out in the introduction to this volume, emotions can be regarded as complex formations that comprise both cognitive elements and bodily sensations (Ahmed 2013, 5) and arise particularly in situations of cultural and social change (see Gluckman 1972). They are therefore a valuable methodological tool to research specific forms of social positioning of individuals or groups toward a certain social or cultural domain, and particularly in contexts of social transformation.

In her book *The Cultural Politics of Emotions*, Ahmed (2013) examines emotions as triggers of collective mobilizations and how these mobilizations delineate new objects of emotional concern. Her argument is thus well suited to understand the emergence of emotions in shifting social situations, as we find them in Botswana with regard to the emotions articulated by educated professionals about family life. As argued in the introduction to this volume, with reference to Ahmed's object-theory, emotions or affects are constitutive of the emergence of new social fields (cf. Ahmed 2013, 7): they shape social fields and are also shaped by the conflicts and tensions that arise in them, such as in the case of the earlier vignette where emotions constitute the object: the family. The ideal of the family evokes certain feelings and by doing so it changes what "family" represents. In other words, emotions directed toward the family come to encompass an entire social world and its objects.

The emotional object that I will examine here is how members of the middle class in Botswana talk and feel about the "family." In modern sociology, the transformation of family relations in Europe has been described as being marked by the *emotional intensification* of relationships between both spouses and their children, on the one hand, and the disentanglement between production and the household, on the other (Giddens 1992). In fact, studies on the so-called global middle classes show that such an ideal of the modern family has inspired many of the currently emerging middle classes worldwide to fashion and refashion their everyday life (C. Freeman 2012; Jones 2012; Katz 2012; Zhang 2012; Pauli 2010). These studies explore the contestations around gender roles and around the expectations of families and kin with regard to who people should marry, when they have children, and how they would live (Oppong 1981). In my contribution I am interested in showing the ambivalence of emotions attached to the ideal of the Pentecostal model of family that stresses premarital chastity and the unity of spouses.

Second, according to Ahmed, objects may encapsulate a long history of desires, anxieties, pleasures, or pains, which she attributes to historical processes of the production of social inequalities (Ahmed 2013, 11; see also the introduction to this volume). This history of inequality is enclosed in emotional objects so that some of them are saturated with their historical values. These emotions become what Ahmed calls "sticky" (17). An example of sticky emotions and sticky objects is the concern expressed in public imaginaries about migrants or refugees as intruding others from whom the community needs to be protected (Ahmed 2004, 134); this example reveals how discourses are constantly demarcating boundaries between nonfamiliar subjects or groups and belonging to (imagined) communities. Emotions therefore come to stand for histories of exclusion.

Ahmed's considerations about the configuration of social fields through emotions may become productive for understanding the emotions of educated professionals in Gaborone as these emerge in the context of a transforming society. However, the histories of educated professionals are histories not only of exclusion but also of social advancement and possible integration into new types of wealth flowing into the economy. In fact, these considerations coalesce strikingly with Biehl and Locke's reading of Deleuze and their "anthropology of becoming." These authors attribute great transformative power to desires over power and control and point out how people invent "fields of action and significance" (Biehl and Locke 2010, 317). Emotions therefore may be a driving force in the reconfiguration of social fields, in my case the urban middle classes in Gaborone.

Many authors describe the city as a space of marked poverty where experiences of exclusion forge emotions such as fear and anger (see the introduction to this volume); others describe postcolonial cities as places of emerging opportunities that concern both income opportunities and personal freedom and new privileges (Akyeampong 2000b; Little 1975; Bochow and van Dijk 2012). The urban space of Gaborone, however, can be seen as a space of intensification of *ambivalent* processes of emerging wealth, on the one hand, and the experience of loss and lack of support, on the other: all economically important bodies such as the Southern African Development Community, the headquarters of banks, and Debswana, the world's leading diamond producer by value, to name a few, are located here. In addition, five shopping malls have been built in the past fifteen years, which are the places where urban professionals spend their leisure time shopping, dining, and meeting friends. Driving through the city, one is also constantly reminded of the HIV/AIDS pandemic by large signs advertising prevention. In addition, visible signs of loss and suffering due to HIV/AIDS are long queues of cars on the roads leading to the cemeteries on Saturday, the funeral day.

As I will argue later, Christianity enhanced the openings of social fields of urban wealth in Botswana in many ways. By enabling education in mission schools, it opened new life paths alongside the teaching of new emotional models regarding the family. In the following I will show how Christian school education uniting voices of mixed denominations contributed to constituting the family as an object of desire and aspiration, but also anxiety and pain, throughout the twentieth and twenty-first centuries. In addition, Pentecostal counseling enabled educated professionals to navigate complex emotions of desire, anxiety, and fear that are attached to social mobility and the emergence of new wealth in the midst of the HIV pandemic.[3]

I visited Gaborone, Botswana's capital city, several times in the years 2009 and 2011. Many friends, colleagues, and interview partners became visibly moved during our conversations, interviews, and discussions on family life, HIV/AIDS, and reproductive medicine. The family was an overarching topic that popped up in many conversations even if these were not directed toward my research per se. People shared their pain, their loss, anger, desperation, and loneliness, but also their hopes, desires, inspirations, and aspirations. While interview partners were often imbued with emotions, I often was, too. I rarely interrupted their story line when it got emotional, for instance, a long narrative on an unhappy marriage that ended with a divorce. Other times, emotions were not necessarily expressed only by spoken words but sometimes also by things that remained unsaid, for instance, by a sudden change of mood or sentences that ended in silence. These affective moments drew me into my interlocutors' stories and narratives. In these cases when sadness seemed to cut the flow of words, I rarely insisted on asking further questions and often did not ask about certain kinds of "important information," such as when and how people had tested HIV-positive, whether they had communicated about their status, or even banal questions regarding their parents' professions. I also paused from taking notes because listening to my interlocutors' narratives and avoiding hurting them further with a misdirected word or glance required all my attention. (I took notes after the interview.) In that sense, emotions often took over the interview and structured the story lines I got to hear. Nevertheless, these moments of shared emotions drew me into my conversation partners' stories and explanations and gave me a sense that I "understood" their lives. In my writing I intend to recall and analyze these shared affective moments.

Church life importantly shapes the social life of many people in Gaborone, especially urban professionals. These people often live in single houses with gardens and rarely know or interact with their neighbors. They interact in extended and geographically widespread social networks, and church activities have become an important leisure time activity for them—next to shopping. Many of my friends and colleagues who were central for my research come from a Christian background of diverse denominations, many of them Catholics or Anglicans. These two churches belong to the missions that entered Botswana in the nineteenth century and are now attended by many of the educated professionals in Gaborone, especially the Catholic Church, which runs one of the top-performing secondary schools in the country. Others were committed members of a Pentecostal-Charismatic church or belonged to one of the many so-called African Independent Churches.

Pentecostal churches came to Botswana first in the 1980s and have attracted many of the educated professionals until today. Next to Pentecostal churches, African Independent Churches are strong in the southern African region. They were founded mostly during the first half of the twentieth century and were seen to embody resistance (Comaroff 1985). Currently, they differ considerably in their religious praxis as well as in discourses about the family and gender relations (for an example of the "masculine cult" of one African Independent Church, cf. Werbner 2011). In Botswana, mainline churches' and Pentecostal discourses and ethics featured heavily in educated professionals' views on the world and were part of general discourses on the family, intimacy, and personal suffering. In my ethnography I will therefore focus on these discourses and practices.

I interacted with people in many contexts, including different kinds of churches, two private hospitals in Gaborone, and the University of Botswana. When I met people to conduct formal interviews, I asked them to sign a consent form, assuring them I would maintain their anonymity, which many of them welcomed as a sign of a "good research practice." I spoke with educated urbanites from a wide range of professions, such as teachers, academics, pastors, and civil servants, as well as university students and educated people who were no longer (or had never been) employed. The sample thus reflects the heterogeneity of socioeconomic backgrounds prevalent among those urban educated professionals.

MAKING THE CHRISTIAN FAMILY:
TEACHING EMOTION AND THE FORMATION OF
NEW SOCIOECONOMIC GROUPS (1930–1965)

In this section I show how Christian education in colonial Botswana not only has established a new sense of professionalism with particular emotional attitudes toward work and careers but also has reconfigured educated professionals' emotional way of relating to marriage and family life. Formal education was brought to Botswana, by then Bechuanaland, by Christian missionaries settling there. It started with the foundation of Kudumane, the first training center for evangelists run by the London Missionary Society, in the 1840s and continued to be in the hands of missionaries throughout the nineteenth and twentieth centuries. From the very beginnings of their educational projects, missionaries placed a strong emphasis on religious teaching and evangelization and made an effort to reform the marriages and family life of local populations. A history book used in all four public secondary schools in Gaborone reports on struggles between local populations, especially chiefs, and missionaries over the content to be taught in schools. The topics of family, sexuality, and gender relations featured strongly in missionary teachings. In contrast, according to history schoolbooks, local populations aspired to learn English and subjects that were considered more "useful," such as technical skills (Tlou and Campbell 1984, 194–196).

Contestations over education continued throughout the colonial period. These concerned funding of schools and teachers, as well as struggles over the syllabus. From the beginning of the twentieth century, local governments (*dikgosi*; seTswana for "chiefs" or "elders") started to support missionary schools with donations. Throughout the nineteenth century, regional power struggles between missionaries of the Dutch Reformed Church and the London Missionary Society and local dikgosi influenced the development of single educational projects of a grand style, for instance, the Bakgatla National School in Mochudi founded in 1920. Secondary education, which was nonexistent until 1948, started with the building of the Moeng College in Mafekeng, today South Africa. The first secondary school founded by the British was the Gaborone Secondary School, which did not open until 1965, one year before independence. Those who wanted to acquire higher education had to go to South Africa or Lesotho (Tlou and Campbell 1984, 294–295).

As a result, by the time of independence, in 1966, there were only a few graduates in the country (Werbner 2004, 22–24). These early educated professionals exhibited strong ethics of obligation toward their communities, punctuality, and godliness. In addition, they married earlier and had children later in life than their peers. Take, for instance, Mma Musi, who was eighty-four years old when I interviewed her in September 2011.[4] As she continued school, Mma Musi's life became very different from the life of her siblings and neighborhood friends. She was the first one of seven siblings who continued school. Most of her mates went to South Africa for jobs as domestic workers or in the mines. Others became pregnant at an early age and stayed home. Earning money was attractive for those who went to South Africa after finishing primary education. They could afford to marry and build houses, and some of them invested in cattle. They felt that by working in South Africa, they had a quick and easy start at becoming an adult and a respected member of their society.

A similar situation applied to those who became pregnant early. An early childbirth proved their fertility, and women were proud of having shown their ability to have children. In addition, having a child gave them the status of female adulthood. The anthropologist Isaac Schapera, who undertook research among Tswana-speaking people at the beginning of the twentieth century, noticed a tendency for women to have children long before they married their children's father or someone else. The overall postponement of marriage in people's life courses was triggered by male labor migration but also by the increase of *lobola* (bride-price), which made it impossible for young men to marry early (Schapera 1933).

In contrast to her peers, Mma Musi recalled, she had a passion for education. She enjoyed going to school and loved books. "I always liked my books!" she stated. She also enjoyed going to Sunday church services and early morning prayers in school. In our interview she vividly remembered the Irish woman who taught her, mentioning that she adored her strictness, accuracy, and punctuality. This woman played a crucial role in Mma Musi's personal and professional development, recommending that Mma Musi continue with her schooling.

Mma Musi followed her teacher's advice and went to the teacher's training college in Lesotho. After completing college, she married her husband at the age of twenty and completed her training years as a teacher in Molepolole. During the first few years of their marriage, her husband worked as a teacher in Ramotswa while Mma Musi was in Molepolole until eventually both of them were transferred to Gaborone. Mma Musi did not dwell on the emotional weight of these three years in which they were separated; however, the couple's difficulties and their anxieties regarding when they would be able to start their life together were apparent through her sparse references to this period. Only when they stayed together in Gaborone did the couple have their first child, at which time Mma Musi was twenty-five years old. She did not talk about her family's reaction to the couple's family planning issues, but other couples among these early educated people who likewise postponed childbirth in the first years of their marriage narrated how they had to resist pressure from their families. One seventy-year-old teacher recalled her family saying, "You marry before you have children?! Are you crazy? How do you know that you can have children?" (interview, September 23, 2011). "We followed Christ. We believe that we should first marry and then have children," explained Mma Musi. In addition, it was important for the couple that both had finished their education so that they could rely on two incomes.

Passion for education and her admiration for strictness, punctuality, and professionalism continued to inspire Mma Musi, who became a teacher and later headmistress of a secondary school. Throughout our interview, she stressed her dedication to discipline and the quality of education. Mma Musi was one of those early educated professionals who were already working and in office at the time of Botswana's independence in 1966. They were well equipped to build the administration, as well as the educational and health systems of the young republic. Their skills and knowledge were greatly needed, as their number was limited. These early "white-collar workers" further came to witness and administer Botswana's economic boom in the 1980s caused by the processing of minerals. Many of these individuals came to occupy leading positions with a great deal of responsibility (Werbner 2004). They became statesmen and politicians but also university teachers, public figures, or headmasters, and managed to build a fairly well-functioning welfare state, often praised as the "African miracle" (Acemoglu, Johnson, and Robinson 2002).

Considering the narrative of Mma Musi's life, one recognizes that it was shaped by her passion for education and her admiration for her first teacher's strictness, as well as her teacher's sense of punctuality and godliness. These passions and virtues led Mma Musi to choose a career and life path that were unusual at the time. She presented her emotional decisions as mainly resisting temptations and desires for quick money and quick fulfillment of motherhood. On the emotional side, the account of her life appeared as almost coolheaded and planned. Later in life, her leading position brought not only responsibilities but also considerable wealth as compared with others in her community. Mma Musi's narrative is a good example of how educated professionals of her generation managed their emotions in order to obtain higher education and acquire a middle-class lifestyle. As mostly self-professed good Christians, these early professionals had lifestyles that centered on monogamous marriage with fewer children; their affluence and their cosmopolitan orientation, knowledge, and skills came to embody progress and prosperity in Botswana's blossoming economy since the 1980s.

FAMILY AND PAIN: CHRISTIAN ETHICS, PENTECOSTAL TEACHING, AND THE ANXIETIES OF THE EDUCATED URBANITES (FROM THE 1980S)

After independence, new professional groups emerged in Botswana primarily due to the increase in secondary and higher education.[5] Throughout the twentieth century, Christianity, and Pentecostalism in particular, continued to provide guidance and inspiration to the aspiring middle classes, especially beginning in the 1980s, when Botswana blossomed economically. From that time onward, highly trained personnel were needed not only to work in the mines but also to continuously expand governmental administration and services such as specialized medical services, health insurance, and education. Since the 1980s, the government of Botswana has invested in education and expanded both its educational system and its health care system, enabling free access to primary education and health care for all citizens. From that time, the building of the educational system took off: with the objective of enabling universal access to education, the government increased the number of primary schools in the country from 251 in 1966 to 654 in 1991 and the number of secondary schools from none in 1966 to 169 in 1991 (Weeks 1993, 51), thereby enhancing the social mobility of many people in Botswana through education.

Christian influence in education remained strong throughout the postcolonial period, as is apparent in a subject called today moral education. Before the educational reform in 1984, this subject was called Bible studies, highlighting the Christian legacy of Botswana's educational system. Moral education is one of the main subjects in primary and secondary education until today, with a syllabus determined by a committee of experts, most of whom are Christians from various denominations. One member of this committee was Professor Joseph Gaie, a theologian at the University of Botswana and a member of the Zion Christian Church, the most influential and in terms of membership the largest African Independent Church in Botswana. In a conversation Professor Gaie told me how the committee designed the actual syllabus for the subject moral education. Other individuals on the committee were members of the Dutch Reformed Church, the Catholic Church, the Lutheran Church, or a Pentecostal church. As a result of the work of this committee of mixed denominations, the syllabus does not exhibit a strong influence of one single denomination, although teaching materials may do so. Teaching ensures a *popularization* of Christian ideals and ethics, which means they are accessible for large parts of the population, namely, all those who go to school.[6]

The first units on moral education to be taught in secondary schools are dedicated to family matters, sexual ethics, and issues of gender equality. Alongside ethics of equality and chastity, the units promote the image of the family according to which marriage and childbirth within marriage appear as an emotionally secure space. For instance, textbooks in moral education for secondary schools discuss the consequences of teenage pregnancies

Key idea: Teenage pregnancies can ruin lives.

FIGURE 9.1. The consequences of teenage pregnancy. Source: Kgathi, Saganabeng, and Seretse (2006, 28).

not only as a probable interruption of educational careers, and a cause of desperation due to economic hardship but also as emotionally devastating. With this emphasis on chastity, such books show a similarity to Pentecostal teaching.[7] One book used in secondary schools in Botswana, published by Heinemann, points out the anger of parents and boyfriends when they learn of a pregnancy, often leading to a breakup on the part of the male partner, who leaves the teenage girl and the baby without financial support. For instance, under "effects of pregnancy on the girl," the authors list the following: "You would be expelled from school" and "Your family might not want anything to do with you. This may lead to resorting to prostitution in order to survive." They then stress, "Everything is ruined" (Kgathi, Saganabeng, and Seretse 2006, 27). Figure 9.1 depicts the threat of isolation teenage girls face when they become pregnant. It shows a young girl with a baby who needs to leave school, is pushed away by her family, and sits in front of an empty bowl looking for food. Later material in the book presents the family as the core social space of emotional and financial support. A break with the family means, therefore, complete "ruin," attaching high emotions to family life and its failures.

The passage indicates that living as a family with both parents under one roof and getting sponsored and supported by them not only privileges young people in their start to life, such as allowing them to receive better education, but also provides protection and emotional security. By producing this image, Christian education fosters the anxieties and insecurities of educated urbanites in the context of increasing monetarization of social relationships in the wake of Botswana's economic boom. Scholars have pointed out the enormous anxieties that were created by this rapid development of wealth in contemporary urban Botswana (Livingston 2009). They described the pressure that many of these urban professionals feel to meet the expectations of peers, families, and kin, for instance, by celebrating lavish weddings (van Dijk 2010), sending their children to private schools, building or buying their own houses, and driving a brand-new car. In their ways of dressing, living, and using their leisure time, they are inspired by glossy magazines edited in South Africa or the United States and often spend their holidays in Johannesburg, New York, or London.

In addition to these popularized Christian ethics taught in school, Pentecostal churches and teachings offer solutions for how to handle these insecurities and anxieties of the urban educated professionals and offer guidance and inspiration for these aspiring middle classes in how to reach their goals. Take, for instance, Steven, aged thirty-two, whom I met in a fast-food restaurant in Gaborone where we sat outside to enjoy a beverage. Steven presented himself as an ambitious and socially upward-oriented man who had been brought up in a rural area. He had enjoyed secondary education at a Christian-run secondary school and at the time I spoke with him was working as a sales manager for one of the few companies in Botswana. Christian teaching at school not only had provided him with knowledge and a valuable academic degree but also had inspired him in his future personal development. He was married with two children, and, being a member of the Baptist Church, he emphasized that he had wanted to have children only within marriage.

Before Steven met his wife, he told me, he had another girlfriend. "But I did not like how this one was behaving!" I could hear the anger in his voice when he shared his memories with me: "She sort of tried to press me into fatherhood. I did not like this. I had been the only son of a single mother. I didn't know my father. As a child I suffered from this feeling of having been neglected by my father. I had sworn that I would never do this to my own children. I wanted to be a good father to my children." As a consequence, he decided he wanted to have children only after he married. The teaching he received during childhood, and later the teaching and counseling of his church, introduced him to a new vision of life and inspired him for a future of social success and marital stability in Botswana's blossoming economy. Family planning and the timing of childbirth had been part of the plan. The teaching of his church provided the couple with technologies for modeling their emotional life in a way that fit the dream of the middle-class family. He told me that he and his wife had sat together and discussed how many children they would be able to raise. Considering their two incomes and their living expenses, they had decided that two children were enough. They also decided to have them within two years so that his wife would not need to stop working for a longer period. In our conversation, Steven was proud of the fact that he and his wife managed to have the two children born two years apart. "You invest in marriage; you invest and plan," he said. Their church, in this case the Baptist Church, provides them with counseling and knowledge on how to manage their household's finances as well as family planning, all designed to master the emotional and financial challenges of their marriage (interview, August 23, 2011). Steven's biographical narrative exemplifies the influence of Christian churches on members who hope to achieve the lifestyles of urban middle classes. Teaching family planning as a social technique to manage limited resources, Christian churches not only exert moral control over their members but also turn initial anxiety and pain into a motivation to change one's life.

PROTECTING THE HOME:
PENTECOSTALISM AND EXCLUSIVE PARENTHOOD

Over the course of the four years that I visited Botswana, I developed a cordial relationship with Dorothy (who was thirty-two years old when I first met her). She and her husband, Herbert, were Christians and emphasized partnership and equality in decision making, an approach that seemed to work well for them. For instance, they narrated how they took care of some of their dying relatives together and how they protected themselves against getting infected with HIV through their work as caregivers. Dorothy used to work as a teacher and was then enrolled in a PhD program at the University of Botswana. She was also a member of the International Pentecostal Church that I visited from time to time. When I talked to Dorothy in 2011, she was facing a difficult situation because her twin sister had died some months earlier, during my absence. The death of her sister not only made Dorothy sad but also had changed her personal situation. She told me that she was thinking about what to do with her sister's daughters: "I am especially concerned about the youngest daughter. She is still very young and misses her mother terribly." She would love to take the girl to her own house and raise her, and she would like to do this soon. "I resemble my twin sister and I believe it would help the girl to get over the death of her mother if she could live with me," she explained. However, her husband did not like the idea. Another niece of Dorothy's was already staying with them, and they also had three children of their own. Her husband thought there already were enough people in the house. "If Herbert says no, it's no!" said Dorothy.

I pointed out to Dorothy the specificity of this situation, and that a decision should be made in favor of a young girl who mourned her mother. I suggested Dorothy should seek the advice of her pastor because I knew that pastors were respected authorities who often mediated between spouses. In fact, she had already discussed this issue with her pastor. He supported her husband and reminded Dorothy: "In a marriage you discuss things. This home is for you and your husband. You should not allow your relatives' people to stay with you" (field notes, March 13, 2011). The pastor highlighted the primacy of the married couple over claims of relatives and kin. He therefore spoke to the Pentecostal paradigm according to which the home needs spiritual and material protection (Frahm-Arp 2012).

Many educated professionals face the problem of having to take care of orphans within their extended family. In her study on orphans and adoption in the wake of Botswana's HIV crisis, Bianca Dahl (2009, 2010) describes the ambivalent position of churches regarding adoption: on the one hand, churches defend adoption programs in the name of charity and compassion; on the other hand, she observed reservations vis-à-vis adoption among people within the church as they are common in Botswana. In fact, in my research on families many of my interlocutors had accepted children of their brothers or sisters into their households. However, the relationship between stepparents and their adopted or fostered children mostly remained a distant one, often evoking tensions and pain. Therefore, the ambivalent positions of pastors related to an overall rejection of allowing children into the family who were not "one's own."

Take, for instance, the story of Mirjam, a fifty-five-year-old woman who has remained childless. During the first years of their marriage, she and her husband had tried hard to conceive. The couple were both earning very good salaries, and they desperately wished for a child who could inherit their large property. Throughout their married life they had accepted children of some of their relatives into their household. One was the daughter of a late brother of Mirjam's husband; another was the son of her late sister. Both of these adults had died of HIV/AIDS. Over the years they developed a cordial relationship with these young people who lived in their house, with her late sister's son especially becoming close to them. Mirjam reported that they interacted freely and shared their meals. When this nephew enrolled at the university, they bought him his own apartment and bought his first car. Nevertheless, she would not expect him to take care of them in their old age. "It is only your own son that you would expect—he is his own," she tried to explain her situation without finishing the sentence.

The fact that the couple had shared their everyday life with their nephew, and despite their considerable and generous support even after he had left their house, they did not consider him obligated to take care of them in old age (field notes, March 12, 2010). A feeling of distance was conveyed throughout her narrative, and I sensed that the relationship was a friendly one based on mutual obligation; however, warmth and sympathy were lacking. Concluding from discussions on adoption and HIV orphans, I sensed that among urban educated professionals, parenthood is valued only for one's biological children. For instance, other conversation partners reported traumatic experiences when, in a quarrel, children detected that their foster parents were not their "real" (i.e., biological) parents. According to the conviction and experience of my interlocutors, lifelong care and support, offering someone a home, and enabling access to private education could not replace the strong bond that existed between biological parents and their children.

Churches supported local parental values. When I discussed the question of adoption and fosterage with Pastor Seithamo from the Apostolic Church Mission, he explained that the church advised its members not to adopt children from their late relatives. He spoke of these children as "being foreigners" and explained: "You never know what these foreigners bring to the house" (interview, March 24, 2009). In fact, one of my interlocutors reflected on this feeling of estrangement when she reported about tensions with one of her husband's nieces they had accepted into their household after the death of the girl's mother. "She is brought up in the village and even the way she communicates is different. At the beginning she was very shy," narrated Nadine, who had a good job in one of Botswana's ministries. "And I encouraged her to talk to us. Now, she talks a lot and I sometimes wish she would not talk that much. Also, my son is very jealous. He insisted that I should not spend as much money on her education as on his" (interview, October 8, 2010).

According to Pastor Seithamo, fostered children are seen as strangers. In his view, they bring tensions and jealousy into the house and embody death and loss. In his narrative he insinuated that these children could bring social malaise as well as spiritual threats. With a different habitus and communication style, they also might embody poverty and backwardness, as the situation with Nadine's niece illustrates. The clear position on excluding a late relative's children from the home appeals to the Pentecostal paradigm of the home as a social space in need of social and spiritual protection, which Dorothy's pastor had also supported. It helps (aspiring) middle-class individuals in Botswana to navigate their own desires to create a home and keep up with the rising costs of urban lifestyles, for instance, concerning education and the increasing demands on them to financially support children of relatives who have died, presumably from HIV/AIDS. Pastors support the ties between biological children and their parents but encourage urban households to cut ties with children in need from their late relatives in the countryside. This tendency could be observed in many situations among educated urbanites, who illustrate how parenthood is newly evaluated through Christian discourses and practices in the wake of HIV/AIDS. These discourses help educated professionals to draw and maintain clear lines between themselves and their own nuclear families and other relatives in need; Christian discourses on parenting become a source of exclusion in the context of social disruption brought forward by HIV/AIDS and its related deaths.

CONCLUSION: THE CULTURAL POLITICS OF EMOTIONS OF URBAN EDUCATED PROFESSIONALS

This chapter has shown how Christianity has contributed to the production of the family as an object of emotions alongside the history of wealth and education in Botswana. Through education, and in teachings and counseling in churches, "the family" became an object of many, sometimes contradictory, emotions related to desires, ambitions, and aspirations that Christian marriages of early educated professionals required: to relate to values of professionalism; controlling emotions; dedication to planning; and companion marriage. Family life came to be associated with promises of social, spiritual, and emotional security, along with being a source of anxiety when people saw their desires unfulfilled. By showing ways to overcome disappointment and pain and teaching people how to manage and control emotions, Christian teaching, and Pentecostal teaching in particular, enables educated professionals to reach their goal of having a stable family, being able to take care of their children, and attaining financial security. Christian churches thus work toward inclusion of those people with middle-class aspirations who feel otherwise excluded from middle-class lifestyles.

In addition, by providing clear tools and guidance on how to acquire an urban lifestyle, including a working marriage and a secure home, Pentecostal teaching supports members of the urban middle classes in Gaborone in drawing and maintaining lines between themselves and their relatives living under precarious conditions. This is most impressively shown in relation to the question of care for orphaned relatives and their integration into the households of urban professionals.

Pain, anxiety, desire, and hope enfold in the contexts of social transformations that are situated between opportunities for education and career advancement opening up in Botswana's blossoming economy and the rupture and closure brought about by demographic transformation related to the HIV pandemic and a wave of deaths caused by it. Here, Pentecostal teaching fulfills an ambivalent role: on the one hand, Christian education nourishes the anxieties of educated professionals by showing how failing families may cause failing life prospects and school dropout, leading to poverty and even prostitution. In Botswana's economic boom of the past thirty years, many people attained urban lifestyles marked by consumption and new modes of emotions tied to family life. By fashioning family as a source of emotional, financial, and spiritual protection as well as a source of love and personal fulfillment, Pentecostal teachings also introduce new forms of suffering and experiences of personal pain. By creating "the family" as an emotional object, Pentecostal churches fashion the emotional styles of members of the urban middle classes in Gaborone, with all the complexities that are involved in becoming a successful urban African in the twenty-first century.

My research was made possible by the support of the Fritz-Thyssen Foundation and the Max Planck Institute for Social Anthropology, Halle, and was conducted with the permission of the Ministry of Labour and Home Affairs, the Ministry of Health, the Gaborone Private Hospital (Dr. Music and Dr. Eaton), and the Bokamoso Private Hospital (Dr. Abebe). I thank all the institutions and people involved who have supported my research, both financially and intellectually. Pearl Sechele and Abigile and John Hamathi also assisted me greatly during my research. I especially thank John Hamathi for his inspiring words and his help in establishing connections with the right people; I also thank Sethunya Mosime, Godisan Mokoodi, and Treasa Galvin from the Department of Social Science, and Musa Dube and Francis Nkomasana from the Department of Theology and Religious Studies at the University of Botswana. Last but not least, I would like to thank Rijk van Dijk from the University of Leiden, who introduced me to these colleagues.

1. In the study cited here, the definition of "middle class" is a narrow one, focusing on spending power. People who can afford to spend twenty U.S. dollars a day are considered to be "nonfloating" middle classes; people who spend two dollars a day are considered to be "middle classes."

2. The population was recorded to be about 1.6 million in 2001 and had grown to roughly about 2 million in 2011 (Central Statistical Office 2001; Census Office 2011). There were, however, a number of problems related to counting the population. One concerns the possible exclusion of male household members who were absent at the time of recording due to labor migration. Another concerns the exclusion of migrants from other African countries, for instance, from Zimbabwe, who represent a considerable workforce in Botswana (Buthali 2003).

3. Christian discourses have been observed to play an important role in navigating the experience of both poverty and death in urban Botswana. In his monograph on male prophets of the Eloyi cult in Gaborone, Richard Werbner (2011) shows how Christianity enables urban men without a regular income to make a living and develop specific forms of male urban religiosity. Fred Klaits's (2010) monograph on a small church founded by a female prophet discusses the changed rituals and discourses of love and care in Christian practices of healing among Gaborone's poor inhabitants.

4. The following is taken from an interview I conducted with Mma Musi on September 14, 2011, when I visited her in her home.

5. This is quite unusual compared with other African countries where new wealth was generated by trading communities. Since the economic boom in the 1980s, these professional groups have been seen to form the "new emerging middle classes" (Ncube and Lufumpa 2014). Botswana's diamonds fed the large administrative and welfare apparatus of the country.

6. Compare with Niklas Luhmann (1986) for a similar point on the popularization of the model of romantic love in the twentieth century.

7. Note, however, that the emphasis on sexual discipline is not exclusive to Pentecostal teaching.

10 "HERE, HERE IS A PLACE WHERE I CAN CRY" RELIGION IN A CONTEXT OF DISPLACEMENT: CONGOLESE CHURCHES IN KAMPALA

ALESSANDRO GUSMAN

ENTERING PENTECOSTAL REFUGEES' LIFE-WORLDS

On a Sunday afternoon in November 2014, I was sitting in a small Congolese restaurant, relaxing and talking with Héritier and Eric, two young Congolese refugees in Kampala (Uganda); we used to have lunch there together on Sundays after the church service at Fepau, the congregation they belonged to, one of the dozens of Congolese churches in the Ugandan capital city. After almost four hours at church, we were all tired and hungry, so we ate the delicious fish with *fufu* and *sombe* almost in silence, interrupted only by some expressions of appreciation for the food we were eating. It was after finishing our lunch, while discussing the difficulties most refugees in Uganda find in the process of resettlement to a third country, that Eric said: "When you go to UNHCR and talk to them, they don't understand you. When someone who translates for you has his stomach full of food, he cannot translate correctly, because he cannot feel what I'm feeling while I'm talking."

I do not know if Eric's words were directed only to the personnel at the United Nations High Commissioner for Refugees (UNHCR) or to me as well; I never found a way to ask him about this (or maybe I just didn't want to know). However, in the days that followed, and after returning from the field, these few sentences often came to mind as a challenge to the possibility of my fully entering the "life-worlds" (Jackson 2012) of the Congolese refugees I had been working with. I kept on repeating to myself that I had done my best to approach their religious experience—the actual focus of my research—and to be as near as possible to my interlocutors, sharing long hours at church and outside in their everyday activities. True; and yet, as a white researcher from a middle-class background with no experience of forced displacement or tragic losses of the sort that most of the people I had been working with had experienced, was I really able to *feel* what Eric and the other Congolese refugees I met in Kampala were feeling while they were talking to me?

Although I have been working on religious experience in Uganda since 2005, focusing especially on young people's participation in the Pentecostal movement (Gusman 2013), I had never before experienced such a "margin of inadaptability" (Lanternari 1983) between my capacity to be empathic and the emotions and experiences Congolese refugees expressed, both in their words during interviews and informal conversations, and through their bodies during church services. As a nonpracticing Christian who grew up in a Catholic environment where the public expression of emotions in religious contexts was not even contemplated,[1] I had been challenged in my previous research by the problem of how to approach Pentecostals' beliefs and experiences of the baptism of the Holy Spirit, glossolalia, and possession by demons. The "problem of belief" is an age-old question in the anthropology of religion, concerning the limits of accessing tacit knowledge and the spiritual experience of believers from the "outsider's" perspective (Engelke 2002), so I felt in good company in acknowledging the gap between my own spiritual experience and that of the young Pentecostals in Kampala. But now this gap was doubled by the fact that the people I was working with were at one and the same time born-again *and* refugees, most of whom had a story of extreme suffering before their arrival in Kampala.

In spite of all my efforts to get closer to them, I felt I was unable even to imagine the level of suffering some of my Congolese friends were describing to me. How could I "analyze" their religious experience and the role of religion in their lives, given that most of them linked religion explicitly to concepts such as "solace" and "comfort"? My situation reminded me, at least in part, of Renato Rosaldo's (1993) confession that he was not able to understand the rage the Ilongot reported to him as the reason for hunting their enemies' heads until he experienced this same rage and deprivation when his wife, Michelle, died during fieldwork. I then started looking for a different approach to the religious experience of Congolese refugees in Kampala, following Eric's more or less involuntary suggestion not to write with a full stomach, while pretending at the same time to be able to fully understand this experience and the reasons that push refugees to find a "refuge" in Congolese Pentecostal churches in Kampala.

Phenomenological and existential anthropology, together with the concept of a "lived religion," contributed to building the framework for this chapter: to take seriously the religious experience that is so central to the refugees I talked with, to refrain temporarily from judgments and analytical insights (in phenomenological terms, making an *epoché*), and to give greater emphasis to my interlocutors' experience using their own words.[2] Taking this approach, in this chapter I will not try to "explain" Congolese refugees' religious experience but will rather focus on this same experience as it is "lived" (i.e., rooted in the contexts people are living in, and interpreted and narrated by the social actors themselves) and to show how Pentecostalism helps Congolese refugees to frame their emotional states in spiritual terms (see the introduction to this volume). Thus, the affective states of insecurity, fear, and hopelessness that mark refugees' everyday lives in Kampala are translated into a different realm of emotions in which faith in God and in his plans provides room for narratives of hope. If emotion is the capacity to discursively frame the affective experience (Bialecki 2015), then, in the cases I present in this chapter, religious meaning and language are central to the semanticization of the experiences that born-again refugees reported to me.

To this effect, the second half of the present contribution is designed as a sort of "documentary in words" in five scenes, each of them based on the story of one of the Congolese refugees I met in Kampala. Here, I take on the role of "director": I choose five of the persons I interviewed during my research, select some parts of our conversations, and edit the five scenes in the form of a documentary that describes their religious experience in a context of displacement as reflected in the stories the protagonists in the documentary told me in Kampala. My aim in doing so is to describe the representations of the five persons' spiritual experiences (as well as of other refugees who went through similar circumstances) through their own words, without analyzing their narratives in depth, but emphasizing religious meaning-making as it is lived (Knibbe and Versteeg 2008) in refugees' lives in Kampala.

Based on fieldwork I conducted in 2013 (July–October) and 2014 (November–December) on the role of religion in the lives of urban refugees in Kampala this chapter also discusses the hypothesis that Pentecostal churches become, in this context, a "refuge" in the refuge, a place where one can find comfort and a break from the non-sense of the past and, often, of everyday life in a displacement context. After introducing the situation of urban refugees in Kampala, I will focus on the presence of Congolese "refugee churches" in town, specifically in the neighborhood of Katwe.[3] I will then introduce the "documentary in words," describing through the actors' words the five scenes, corresponding to five significant moments in the spiritual and moral life of refugees: their arrival in Kampala; the first few months in town; the counseling session at church; deliverance and healing services on a Saturday; and the church service on a Sunday. Altogether, the five scenes aim to describe the spiritual experience of the Congolese refugees I met during my research in the Églises de Réveil in Kampala.[4]

AN EXISTENTIAL-PHENOMENOLOGICAL APPROACH
TO RELIGIOUS EXPERIENCE

Anthropology has undergone major transformations in the last three decades, since Marcus and Fischer (1986) declared there was a "crisis of representation" in the discipline and in the social sciences more broadly; the reflections that followed opened the way for new approaches especially aimed at focusing on the less objectified aspects of cultural reality. The reference to the philosophical thought of authors such as Edmund Husserl, Maurice Merleau-Ponty, and William James, among others, had a significant influence on the development of a wide range of phenomenological approaches in anthropology. Robert Desjarlais and Jason Throop (2011) identify four main phenomenological orientations in the discipline: hermeneutic, critical, existential, and cultural phenomenology. According to these authors, these approaches, while having different focuses, share some common points: the attention to life as it is lived, with its indeterminacies and ambiguities; the insistence on participation, with reference to William James's "radical empiricism" (Jackson 1996); the interest in intersubjective and embodied components in the interaction with the world; and a sort of anti-intellectualist attitude, recognizing that it is not possible to separate knowledge from the world in which people live and act.

Starting from these assumptions, and in search of a suitable approach to the "lived religion" of the born-again Congolese refugees in Kampala, I recognize that the "experience-near" approach (Wikan 1991) that other anthropologists have used to explore religious experience is not possible in my case, as it implies living events that make one close to the people one is working with. I cannot share my informants' experience in the way Jeanne Favret-Saada (1977) did by agreeing to become bewitched herself, or Paul Stoller

(Stoller and Olkes 1987) being initiated as a Songhay sorcerer. Aware of the limits as well as the potentialities of empathy in anthropology (see Hollan and Throop 2008), I follow the basic assumption of the anthropology of emotions that human beings are able to understand another's emotional state through the channels of empathic (usually nonverbal) communication (Lutz and White 1986).

I understand empathy here as a form of intersubjective emotional attunement that requires intentionality from all the actors involved (i.e., encountering one another in an effort to get close) and that it is not a constant state but rather manifests itself in specific moments, when emotional proximity permits an intersubjective alignment, despite the diversity and "opacity" (Crapanzano 2014) of other people's experiences. At the same time, I recognize that these moments of empathic connection—which can also be labeled a temporary "fusion of the horizons"—are elusive and carry with them the peril of "reducing the irreducibility of another's self-experience to the self-sameness of my own being" (Throop 2010, 777). I thus try to apply Veena Das's suggestion that our goal as ethnographers is "not some kind of ascent into the transcendent but a descent into everyday life" (2007, 15), and that this implies privileging the voices and views of our interlocutors.

The reference to the intersubjective dimension of the ethnographic endeavor is, of course, nothing new, being a part of the very definition of "participant observation"; yet, the specific focus on the intersubjective nature of ethnography has been described specifically in existential approaches (Jackson 1996, 1998). Going back to the original meaning of "intersubjectivity" in the philosophy of Edmund Husserl, it has to be conceived not just as actual shared understanding (knowing what others have in mind) but as a "possibility." As Alessandro Duranti puts it: "Intersubjectivity is thus an existential condition that can *lead* to a shared understanding—an important achievement in its own terms—rather than being itself such an understanding" (2010, 21, emphasis in original).

It is from the point of view I have just outlined that I will approach the religious experience of the five individuals who are the characters in the "documentary in words" that forms half of this chapter. This does not mean I am concerned here only with individual experience, but rather with the processes by which the specific moral experience of being born again simultaneously with being refugees in Kampala becomes possible. As the authors of the introduction to this volume point out, the way religious groups work to shape emotions and affect is not uniform; what they provide are "affective orientations and potentialities that are enacted and embodied along highly situated paths." The Congolese people I worked with, although each had a different trajectory and story, have all experienced the suspension of everyday life, the violence of forced displacement, and the need to rethink, spiritually and physically, their place in the world. In other words, they all went through those shifts in orientation to experience that Jarrett Zigon (2007) calls "moments of moral breakdown." If it is true that "affective trajectories" are modes of orientation that involve both memories and imaginations of the future, then it is my opinion that the Christian narrative of salvation, suffering, and redemption, which is particularly powerful in the Pentecostal discourse, helps Congolese refugees in Kampala to regenerate their moral worlds and re-create a sense of continuity in their experience.[5]

The Pentecostal focus is greatly on *dis*continuity, as is clear from the reference to the "break with the past" (Meyer 1998b) in many of these churches; this idea can help Congolese refugees make sense of their new situation, of the fact of not having the possibility to go back to the Democratic Republic of Congo (DRC) because their families have been killed and their houses burned. And yet, as Matthew Engelke (2010) has shown, languages of break and continuity are not mutually exclusive but can be complementary. The language of continuity, with its identification with biblical stories, especially the story of the forced migration of the people of Israel, can thus become an instrument with which to find continuity in a discontinuous experience, to find solace in the parallelism with the "elected people," and to rebuild a moral world based on the assumption of a future redemption (i.e., in refugees' experience, the possibility of being resettled in a Western country).

The idea that the success of Pentecostalism in Africa can be explained, at least in part, from the perspective of emotional and psychological solace has been criticized (Robbins 2009), and I have given it little consideration in my previous works; yet, the way Congolese refugees spoke to me about the church as a place of comfort and of moral regeneration led me to reconsider my previous position from a critical perspective and to think carefully about churches as sites for an expression of emotions that is often denied in refugees' everyday life.

THE CONTEXT: URBAN REFUGEES IN UGANDA

The DRC has been experiencing enormous waves of forced displacement for the last two decades, due to political repression and the continuous conflicts in the Kivu regions. An estimated population of around 850,000 Congolese currently lives abroad, the majority in other African countries. Uganda is by far the first country of refuge for people fleeing from the DRC, hosting almost 340,000 Congolese (data, June 2019).[6] Most of these refugees come from the Kivu region, on the border with Uganda. The backgrounds of Congolese refugees are heterogeneous: men fleeing alone from the DRC to escape persecution; women with children; children or young adults who have lost their families and reached Uganda alone or with other families who have "adopted" them. Data from the UNHCR show that the gender distribution is similar (49 percent men; 51 percent women) and that almost 56 percent of Congolese refugees are younger than eighteen.

According to the UNHCR, in April 2019 more than 1,200,000 refugees and asylum seekers were living in Uganda,[7] with an increasing number of them deciding to live in the urban setting of Kampala instead of in the camps. Among the 63,100 estimated by the UNHCR, around 30,000 are Congolese. These people usually arrive directly in the capital city, without passing through the camps, in search of security, a better livelihood, and access to services such as hospitals and schools for their children (Omata 2012).

While the literature on urban refugees in the global North is quite extensive, their presence in the towns of the South, especially in the fast-growing African urban slums, began to attract the interest of both international organizations and scholars only in recent years (Dryden-Peterson 2006). Yet, the number of refugees who choose to live in urban contexts is continuously growing, despite the fact that the majority of African countries' policies for refugees are oriented to keep the refugee population in the camps, with limited or no access to assistance for those who decide to live in urban areas; in some cases, living outside the camps is illegal (Fábos and Kibreab 2007).

In Uganda, refugees who live in urban areas do not receive any assistance from the local government or from the UNHCR; nevertheless, Ugandan legislation concerning refugees is considered a positive exception in the continent, as the Refugee Bill (passed in 2006 but applied only in 2009) recognizes refugees' right to live where they prefer, to move freely within the country, and to work (Kreibaum 2016). Before this law was passed, the presence of refugees in Uganda was ruled by the old Control of the Alien Refugee Act, which, since 1964, obliged refugees to live in the camps. However, despite improvements to the new law, the Refugee Bill was criticized because it is still largely insufficient to guarantee protection and assistance for those who live in the urban centers (Bernstein and Okello 2007).

In this situation, once they arrive in Kampala, Congolese refugees look for relatives or friends who already live in the city to receive initial assistance and to find a place to sleep. When they don't know anyone in town, as is frequently the case, they rely on the "protective networks" organized by religious organizations (Sommers 2001), which help them to settle in town and give them instructions on how to move and live in Kampala, including the process of obtaining refugee status. For those who arrive in Kampala from the DRC, the numerous Églises de Réveil in town are often the first place where they meet other Congolese and receive a welcome, food, and a form of counseling.

The weakness of the welfare services provided by the government and international organizations leaves room for alternative forms of assistance (and evangelization) from Congolese religious groups, which are numerous, especially in those areas where the number of refugees is higher. Congolese live in different parts of town, but mostly in Nsambya and Katwe, where I conducted my research and where there is the highest concentration of Congolese churches.

CONGOLESE "REFUGEE CHURCHES" IN KAMPALA

The role of religion in contexts of displacement, especially regarding urban refugees, has been little explored to date.[8] The few existing studies on this subject usually focus on the creation of churches and faith-based organizations as actors for assistance in social welfare in circumstances where national states and international organizations fail to provide help to urban refugees (Fiddian-Qasmiyeh 2011; Lauterbach 2014). While those topics are highly important, in this chapter I argue that the specific spiritual role of religious belonging in refugees' lives has been understressed and that there is a need to take it seriously. Religion does not enter in refugees' lives only as a resource in an emergency or as an instrument to establish social networks in the new setting; it also helps to make sense of a suffering that is often hardly understandable for those involved (Shoeb, Weinstein, and Halpern 2007; Adogame 1998).

An important aspect of the Congolese diaspora is the foundation of Églises de Réveil, which are linked to a mother church in the DRC or start a new congregation in the countries of arrival. Although churches of Congolese origin have been installed in Europe since the 1970s, a recent wave of Congolese churches has appeared in Europe, North America, and Africa, attracting the interest of anthropologists working in Canada (Mossière

2010), Belgium (Demart 2008), France (Mottier 2012), and Uganda (Lauterbach 2014). A significant case in this respect is the presence of recently founded Congolese "refugee churches" in Kampala. In November 2014, there were fifty-five Congolese churches registered under the association Communauté Chrétienne Congolaise en Ouganda in Kampala, and seventy in total in the country.[9] However, this figure depicts only a part of the scenario: according to the leader of the association, there are around 150 Églises de Réveil in Kampala alone.[10]

During my fieldwork, I mapped the presence of Congolese churches in the suburb of Katwe, a poor, rapidly expanding neighborhood with a significant component of Congolese refugees. I was able to locate fourteen churches in the area, considering only the congregations that have a fixed location, not those meeting in private houses (at least three or four on Sundays). All of these churches, with just one exception, arrived in Kampala or were locally founded after 2000. Their congregations usually are small, ranging from thirty or forty up to around three hundred members, and the size fluctuates, as members move quite frequently from one church to another, travel abroad, or move to a different neighborhood in Kampala and look for another church. Because of the composition of the congregations, these churches usually lack the means to build a permanent structure and are constructed of simple and perishable materials, such as wood and metal sheeting. The congregations of these "refugee churches" reflect the refugee population in Uganda, with a high number of children under the age of eighteen (around 30 percent of the total) and similar proportions of men and women, while the large majority of church officers are men. I conducted most of my research in three of these churches (All Saints' Church, Église de Jesus Christ, Fepau) and met those persons who became the characters in the five scenes of the "documentary in words" that constitutes the second part of this chapter. Their stories are not unique, but rather are representative of similar experiences other refugees told me; the aim of the following sections is to represent, through the voices of these five characters, the role of religion in the lives of Congolese refugees living in Kampala.

Scene 1. Arrival in Kampala:
Fear and Disorientation (Héritier)

Many Congolese describe their arrival in Kampala as disorienting: very few of them speak English before arriving in Uganda, and their efforts to communicate in Swahili are frustrated, as most Ugandans do not like Swahili or speak only a little. The taxi park, where the buses usually end their trip to Kampala, is a chaotic space, filled with hundreds of *matatu* (collective taxis) waiting to leave; most of the refugees I met reported that, after getting off the bus, they experienced a deep sense of solitude and dismay. Only a few of them had a contact in the form of a friend or relative. Some were taken to the police station, but in most cases people directed them to a church in order to find assistance and a place to sleep.

"Refugee churches" are often the first actor to give assistance (food, medicine, shelter) in the emergency of people just arriving from the DRC; this is not reserved for church members only but is given to anyone in need (Lauterbach 2014). Congolese Pentecostal churches are more efficient than other religious actors in providing this primary form of assistance; Stephen Kuteesa, the country representative of the Catholic Jesuit Refugee Service, admits:

> There are very many Congolese Pentecostal churches in this area and in Kampala. We have to partner with them: when you interview people you can even get none who would say, "When I came, I was hosted by a Catholic church." It is very rare, actually, if it is there. When they come, they will tell you "On arrival, I was received by friends who took me to a Congolese Pentecostal church" . . . so you realize that most of these people are already attached; you can't break this bond, because it is something that is already getting them together.[11]

The story of Héritier illustrates the reasons some of the Congolese refugees in Kampala converted to Pentecostalism after their arrival in Uganda.[12] At the time he fled from the DRC, in January 2011, Héritier was nineteen years old; he came alone, after escaping from the people who had attacked and killed most of his family. In 2014, Héritier had been living in Kampala for almost four years, except for six months when he went to a camp "because I was hungry and had no means to survive here in town. But life there was even harder, and after a few months I decided to come back to Kampala."[13] This is the story of Héritier's arrival in Kampala:

> When I arrived here in Kampala, I didn't know where to go; I just had a small bag with a few clothes in it; no documents, and only 30,000 Ugandan shillings [about 10 euros]; I was tired, lost. . . . I did not speak English, and I felt so weak and bad for what I had gone through. It was six in the morning when we arrived. I was a Muslim, at that time a serious Muslim. So I entered a mosque and stayed there all day long, without doing anything. During the prayer, I prayed; for the rest of the time I just stayed there, I felt so bad. After the evening prayer, when everyone was leaving, I hid myself for one hour behind a curtain, then when no one was around I lay down and slept until five in the morning, when I woke up for the first prayer. I hid my bag and went out; I was afraid of the police because I had no documents. I was hungry and felt extremely weak. I had not eaten anything for the previous two days. I feared to cross the road, so I sat down in a bar near there and asked for some tea and bread. While I was eating, a little boy of seven or eight years stood in front of me and said, "Maman, regarde, c'est Héritier." I turned my head and saw the woman, she was a friend of my family in Congo; they took me with them, and I lived with them for the next two years. I will never forget that first day here in Kampala, and the gift God sent me with that woman.[14]

This was the last occasion on which Héritier entered a mosque; he was disheartened because the imam did not help him, and he had to hide in order to spend the night in the mosque. The family who "adopted" him was Pentecostal, so he started going to the same church (Fepau), where at the time we met he was responsible for the sound mixer and the music arrangements. Héritier's adoption by the family he met on the first day is not at all an isolated case within the community of Congolese refugees in Kampala. On the one hand, refugees compete to get the little aid that international organizations offer and to obtain resettlement by every possible means, including bribing police officers and witchcraft. On the other hand, the other side of this Hobbesian "war of all against all" is a deep sense of solidarity that pushes people who live with a family (sometimes already eight to ten people) in a space of no more than twenty square meters to host a newcomer when he or she is alone and has nowhere to go.

Scene 2. The First Months in Kampala:
In Search of Oneself (Hortense)

Hortense is a tailor who arrived in Kampala from Bunya in 2002 with her three children. Her story shows the hardships single mothers face in conditions of exile, the difficulties people go through during the first months after their arrival in Kampala, and the different roles religious affiliation can play in such a situation. Praying is often referred to as one of the main means people use to recover from the violence experienced in the DRC and to find the strength to start a new life in Kampala, a context perceived not only as "strange" but often as hostile too.

Hortense interpreted the whole of her long stay in Kampala (she was resettled in Norway in December 2014) in light of God's plan for her and her children, stressing the importance of faith to survive in the new context at the beginning, and the role of the church in providing the networks that allowed her to begin her activity as a tailor and open a small shop in the suburb of Nsambya:

> The first place where we stayed here in Kampala was a Congolese church, near here, in Nsambya; we stayed there for three months; I was just trying to recover, doing nothing, I felt like I was no more able to work. After three months I decided that I had to do something; I asked a lady I had met in church to host my three children and started to live outside, on the streets. I did some small jobs to pay for food for my children, but I spent most of the time praying. I was praying, walking and praying; when I was tired I entered a church and slept for a while, then I woke up and started praying again. I left my children to that woman for three months. I felt I really needed to be free and pray; when I see such a desert, I multiply my prayers. Therefore, I was trying to look into myself and understand why nothing was going in the right direction, in my life. I asked God, "O God, why all this suffering? Why is this not going to an end?"

After three months living this way, Hortense started feeling better and able to work, but she had no means to start an activity; retrospectively, she attributed her opportunity in opening the shop to her faith and her prayers:

> It took three months, then I felt restored, and God helped me, connecting me with generous people at the church, who bought a sewing machine for me and gave me some money to pay the rent of the shop for the first three months. This is how I started my new life, and since then God has made

many things in my life, so I was able to send all my three children to school and keep them away from dangerous situations. Life here is hard for refugees, we need discipline; either you live in Christ or in the chaos, there is no other choice. Christ is the only one who never leaves you alone when you are in trouble.

This topic of the Manichaean struggle of chaos versus order (Satan vs. Christ) is a topos of the Pentecostal discourse about the "world-breaking" process (Robbins 2004) through which believers break with their past. In the case of the Congolese refugees, breaking with their lives in the DRC is frequently said to be a necessity: although some of them plan to go back to their home, most are aware that they will never live again in Congo because their relatives have been killed and their houses burned. Especially during the first months in Kampala, thoughts often go back to one's previous life. Hortense told me:

> When your heart is troubled, you are not able to do anything. You start comparing your actual life with the life in Congo; but here, we are in Kampala, you don't have your family and friends here. No one helps you except Christ; even if some people can help you, they will travel, or will not be able or willing to help you more, and will finally leave you alone with your problems. Only God will never leave you alone—my life is a testimony to this. That's why, when someone arrives from Congo, I always said: "You need to be patient and perseverant, and trust God"; because only God can heal you and give you a new life.[15]

The need to break with one's life in Congo is one of the reasons for the frequent recourse to deliverance in "refugee churches" in Kampala (Gusman 2016). Yet, chaos and dangers are not confined to the past: Hortense stressed that these dimensions are part of the present too. In her testimony, informed by the Pentecostal discourse about evil, suffering is the result of the activities of demons and witches in the physical world (Pype 2011). I will return to the theme of deliverance in the fourth scene.

Scene 3. Haunting of Spirits:
A Difficult Conversion (Roger)

Roger came alone to Kampala from Goma in April 2012. After two and a half years living in Kampala, he still felt "out of place"; one could see him walking in the streets near Katwe, hanging his head, with a bundle of clothes on his right arm. He went around trying to sell something, but he was not able to get accustomed to this kind of life. In the DRC he was the son of a *chef coutumier* (*mwami*, a traditional chief); his family had a nice house, big and well furnished. He could not accept the fact that someone was now living in his family's house, after killing his father and other relatives. Roger was able to run away, as his two brothers apparently did, but he had had no news of his family since he arrived in Kampala.

The story Roger told me is one of extreme violence (before arriving in Uganda, he was kidnapped by a group of rebels and kept in the forest as a slave for four months), witchcraft, and conversion to a religion in which he found some relief in counseling sessions. As Roger recounted:

> During the first eight months in Kampala I slept outside the police station in Old Kampala. I had no place where to go, and I was terrified that someone could come and look for me here to kill me. One day, it was February of last year, a pastor saw me there and talked to me. When I told him my story, he took me with him to his church, and I lived there for some months. I was traumatized, my head was not able to think clearly, and I had some problems with my stomach. The pastor and other people of the church came during the day and talked to me, they taught me the Word, and they counseled me. I even started singing in the choir.

This was the first time Roger was ever in a church; as part of the traditional, kinship-based system of power, his family had its own "familiar demons" (*mapepu*), as Roger called them. This made it particularly difficult to complete his conversion, as "demons are coming back to me, struggling to resist my will to be baptized in Christ." He frequently went to church for counseling on Thursday afternoons. He described how he felt an internal struggle between the Holy Spirit and his familiar demons and felt confused:

> When I'm in church and sing in the choir, I feel happy and I really want to be baptized; but when I'm in my room alone, I start thinking about my past and what happened to me, and the demons sometimes arrive. . . . They tell me they can help me take revenge against those who killed my family. I want to be a good Christian, you know, I want to be free of these things, but my thoughts are still confused; I don't feel free from my past yet.[16]

During counseling sessions, the pastor, after giving Roger advice on how to live and how to keep strong in his Christian life, prayed for him. Roger's body started shaking, until he fell down on the floor: his body and his mind had become an arena for spiritual warfare between good and evil.

Scene 4. Saturday at Church:
Deliverance and Healing Service (Célestine)

Collective deliverance is frequent in Congolese churches in Kampala. Some congregations organize sessions of deliverance during one of the weekly services, while others have a specific deliverance and healing session, usually on Saturdays. As Cazarin and Burchardt convincingly show in their chapter in this volume, deliverance sessions are part of a process of "emotional resocialization" through which believers' emotional repertoires are synchronized. Violence, wars in the DRC, and the difficulties refugees face in their lives in Kampala are explained in religious terms, as the result of the strong links people have with "traditional spirits"; believers are invited to bring their "fetishes" to church in order to burn and destroy them and break the covenant with the evil spirits (cf. Sasha Newell 2007). This iconoclastic attitude toward the tools of mediums and witches is part of the process of breaking with the past. Deliverance also has a prognostic component for Congolese refugees: the perspective of a future deliverance, often seen in terms of "traveling abroad" and achieving ultimate resettlement in a Western country, is central in the worldviews of Congolese refugees (Gusman 2018); in this way they are able to locate their suffering within God's plan and to make sense of the hardships they face in their daily lives by attributing them to the presence of demons that continue to follow them even after they have fled from the DRC (Demart 2008).

It was during one of these sessions that I saw Célestine crying out loud while lying on the floor of the All Saved Church; I had met her before, as she was a friend of Eric's. Outside the church, Célestine had appeared strong, a hardworking woman who went around selling small jewels or doing housework in exchange for small sums of money. Her husband had been killed in their house in Goma, but she had been able to escape with her three children and reach Kampala. I had an image of her as a very active woman, always smiling and welcoming people in her house, so it was strange, at first, to see her lying on the floor for more than half an hour.

The following is how I described the deliverance session in my field notes that same morning:

> After the fasting session, it's time for adoration; it starts as a series of joyful songs, but then soon turns into an incredibly powerful deliverance session, one of the most intense I have ever seen.

At first, only one pastor is delivering those who are showing the signs of possession (jumping or turning around, hurting other people). It's a real, physical fight between the demon and the pastor. It's around 1:00 PM (after four hours since we entered the church) when the atmosphere changes again; now the endless sound of the drums, the more and more disorganized songs and convulsed dances make more people show the signs of possession. There are now at a time four to five people shouting, jumping, rolling on the floor; the three pastors go around in the church, tired, covered with sweat, to keep on fighting with the many demons who are attacking the believers. The floor is covered with those who have already been delivered and now lie washed out, some of them crying. At the end, almost half of the participants have gone through deliverance; at 2:30 PM, with a last prayer, the service ends.

At the end of the service, I asked Célestine about her experience of that morning, and she responded as follows:

The service on Saturday morning is my space. I ask a friend to stay with my children and come here alone. I need this moment; the church is a space where I can sing to God, I can pray, pray, and pray, until I feel exhausted. I asked God to help me, to protect my children. It is also the place where I can express my emotions. During the week I work hard, every day. I go around, I walk for hours, my feet even hurt, but I know that I have to walk more if I want to sell my stuff and have the money to pay the rent, to buy some food. I don't have lunch, sometimes I just drink some water and go on working; I don't have money, and I don't have time to stop. I'm always worried, I fear that one day the landlord can kick us out of the house if I'm not able to find the money for it. When I go back home, in the evening, I'm so tired, sometimes the day was bad, I had not sold anything, but I have to smile and tell my children everything is OK, that life is good, and we have to be happy. But it's hard, it's hard to be here alone. . . During the week I have to keep on walking and smile to my children. I cannot cry; but here, here is a place where I can cry.[17]

The deliverance session, with its emotional effervescence, can thus be seen as lying beyond the "problem of belief"; as a space in which to express the emotions that are not allowed in everyday life, it provides a context in which suffering can become a dignified performance.

Scene 5. The Sunday Service: Staying Together (Fidèle)

Building a shared sense of "community" in diasporic contexts is a complex process, made even more difficult in the case of the DRC: Congolese people express the fear that the conflicts of their homeland may extend into transnational spaces among diasporic groups, thus preventing them from re-creating a sense of "home" and belonging in their exile (Russell 2011). In this situation, religious affiliation can become an instrument that transcends ethnic and national boundaries. This feeling of "being together" is central to the religious experience of Fidèle; in the DRC he was a member not of an Église de Réveil but of a classic Protestant denomination. When he arrived in Kampala in 2011, he had no place to stay, so someone referred him to Jésus Seul Sauveur, a Congolese Pentecostal church; he slept there for three weeks, then the pastor helped him to find a small room to rent. In the meantime, he had received the baptism of the Holy Spirit:

> Many among us lost our families in DRC or came alone to escape persecutions. We arrive here as individuals, but once we arrive in church, we already find a new family in which we can share our experience and find some help. We went through very bad experiences in Congo, so we have serious problems, internally. But when you enter a Congolese church and you hear other people speaking your own language, you already feel better. And from that moment you know that, if you are in need, someone will help you; if you fall sick someone will come and visit you at your place; you are no more alone.

To Fidèle, this was not so much a matter of material help but of spiritual relief; he did not see the church as a provider of services but as a "refuge" from the hardships of everyday life:

> I don't receive any material help from my church. This was only at the beginning, when I arrived and had nothing, no place to go. After some weeks or months, pastors tell you: "Now, you have to do with what you have." New people come, they have to help the newcomers; you see, means are limited here. So we don't come here looking for help from the pastor, but to stay together and pray to God. During the week, we are all busy struggling to find some money to buy food, we don't have time to stay together, to share thoughts and feelings. We don't try to obtain something from each other, because we don't have anything; when someone has no money to buy food, we collect 2,000 or 3,000 Ugandan shillings, that's all we can do. We come here to stay together and pray to our God.

Yet, there is another dimension to this discourse about "staying together," that is, the construction of the image of a morally self-righteous church member and of a community of people who are morally right. This construction is used to build a sense of "we-ness" and to negotiate their marginal position in relation to the wider Ugandan society (Brodwin 2003); the "break" not only with the past, but with the outside world, is an exercise in boundary-making (Daswani 2013):

> The people here, we are all together, we are never alone because we have all the same God, and God illuminates our lives. But outside, there are people who walk alone, in the darkness, they don't follow the light of God. It is very dangerous, in our situation, to stay far from God and alone; it is easy to take a bad way—you end up meandering, and you can easily become a bandit.[18]

CONCLUSION: UNDERSTANDING RELIGIOUS EXPERIENCE IN CONTEXTS OF DISPLACEMENT

The idea that fieldwork can lead to something different from the ethnographer's initial approach to the research topic is part of the rhetoric of "good ethnography"; instability and mutation are constitutive of the fieldwork experience, and "the worthiest of questions are not at all guaranteed to remain stable through the empirical course of their resolution" (Faubion 2009, 162). What Eric said during our Sunday lunch challenged me to think more carefully about my limits in understanding his (and other people's) experience of fleeing the DRC and of being a refugee and a born-again Christian in Kampala.

These considerations led me to shift my approach and adopt a less analytical one, in which empathy and intersubjectivity play a major part and which is not aimed at explaining the religious experience of the Congolese refugees I had worked with in Kampala, but rather at focusing on this experience as it is lived and represented in their own words. A significant number of Congolese refugees (around 30,000) live in the capital city, mainly in informal structures and in difficult living conditions; upon their arrival, many among them speak poor English or no English at all. In this situation, they describe the urban setting of Kampala as disorienting, hostile, uncomfortable, and dangerous. With limited assistance from international organizations, and unlikely to find a formal job, most of them turn for assistance to the numerous Congolese Pentecostal churches that have been founded in the city, especially in those poor neighborhoods like Katwe where Congolese refugees live. As I have shown with the five scenes of the documentary in words, in the Églises de Réveil they find both material help (as in the stories of Hortense, Roger, and Fidèle) and spiritual support; this led some of them (Héritier, Roger, and Fidèle) to convert to Pentecostalism after their arrival in Kampala.

These two aspects are significant to explore; yet, in this chapter I have focused especially on "refugee churches" as spaces for the expression of emotions and of ritual effervescence (Mossière 2007b; Jennings 2015). The religious discourse shifts everyday experience onto a different level, that of God's plan; in this narrative of suffering and redemption, the experience of suffering, marginality, and displacement becomes dignified (see also Brodwin 2003). In this way, it helps Congolese refugees to map the affective trajectories they experience through time onto emotional categories: for instance, fear derived from living in an environment perceived as hostile and dangerous is mitigated by hope that comes from the prediction that good things will happen (redemption). These "moral emotions," conveyed through religious ideas and practices, are also "moral judgments" that guide actions in everyday life (Parish 1994).

Part of this approach is the choice to organize the ethnography in this chapter as a "documentary in words" describing five scenes in the life-worlds of Congolese born-again refugees in Kampala through the voices and stories of five characters. With this documentary I have shown that religious experience in a context of displacement is marked by a significant component of discontinuity following the escape from the DRC. This situation can be described in terms of a "moral breakdown," one in which Pentecostalism, with its ritual effervescence and the stress on the communitarian aspect, can become a means to express emotions that are contained in everyday life and to create a feeling of "being together." Religious experience is thus a "refuge in the refuge" and a meaning-maker, for the references to suffering and redemption and to the break with the past help Congolese refugees re-create their moral worlds after the violence they have experienced, and escaped from, in the DRC.

1. The post-Conciliar Catholic Church leaves room for a certain degree of emotional expression, i.e., with more lively music; yet, here I am referring to a rural district in the northwest of Italy in the early 1980s, where the main innovation consisted of playing acoustic guitar instead of the organ during the Sunday "youth service."

2. "Lived religion" is a fluid and elusive concept, which has been applied especially to the American context (Hall 1997); I use it here as a tool to approach the religiosity of individuals and groups as rooted in their life-worlds (Streib, Dinter, and Söderblom 2008) and to acknowledge the work of social agents as narrators and interpreters of their own experiences and stories (Orsi 1985).

3. With the expression "refugee churches," I mean churches where the majority and sometimes almost the totality of the congregation is composed of refugees or asylum seekers. Katwe is one of the poorest and fastest-growing neighborhoods in Kampala. If in the 1960s it was still largely occupied by forests and swamps, it has been expanding for the last three decades, mainly through informal settlements.

4. The name Églises de Réveil (Awakening Churches) refers to a constellation of churches originating in Congo and in other French-speaking countries. These are Pentecostal-like churches, both independent or part of larger evangelical denominations, that call themselves Églises de Réveil, in opposition to "classic" evangelical denominations.

5. I do not mean here that this narrative of salvation and redemption is the only or even the main reason that Congolese refugees turn to "refugee churches" in Kampala; I recognize that the material help and support these churches provide, especially to newcomers from the DRC, are important aspects, especially in the absence of welfare from the Ugandan government and from international organizations (see the next section). In three of the five stories I present in this chapter (Hortense, Roger, and Fidèle), the role of these elements is evident. Yet, my aim here is to show that the specific spiritual role of religion in refugees' lives has been understressed and that there is a need to focus on this dimension, too.

6. UNHCR, Operational Portal, Refugee Situations, "DRC situation," http://data.unhcr.org/drc/regional.php (accessed June 5, 2019).

7. UNHCR, Uganda Comprehensive Refugee Response Portal, https://data2.unhcr.org/en/country/uga (accessed June 5, 2019).

8. Two issues of the *Journal of Refugee Studies*, whose topics, respectively, were "Religion and Spirituality in Forced Migration" (no. 2, 2002) and "Faith-Based Humanitarianism in Contexts of Forced Displacement" (no. 3, 2011), are an exception in this regard.

9. The Communauté Chrétienne Congolaise en Ouganda was established in Kampala in 2010.

10. Personal communication, December 2014.

11. Interview with author, August 23, 2013.

12. While some of the Pentecostal Congolese I met in Kampala had already been born again in their home country, a significant number of them converted after their

arrival in Uganda, usually coming from Catholic or "classic" Protestant churches. I was able to identify only two Congolese who converted from Islam.

13. Interviews with Congolese refugees have been translated from the French by the author.

14. Interview with author, December 12, 2014.

15. Interview with author, September 10, 2013.

16. Interview with author, December 9, 2014.

17. Interview with author, October 7, 2013.

18. Interview with author, December 18, 2014.

11 MEN OF LOVE? AFFECTIVE CONVERSIONS ON TOWNSHIP STREETS

HANS REIHLING

The drum set, electric guitars, and minister's desk with its white cross looked strangely out of place in the bland concrete parking lot in front of my host's brick-walled home in a township I call Dunefields, in the sandy Cape Flats of Cape Town, South Africa. Youngsters commonly passed this spot when going to a drug house just across the street. On this afternoon in February 2008, however, drug dealing had come to a standstill. Three shy young men were intermittently playing rock music with Christian themes. Then a minister's shrill and angry voice blasted through the speakers. The self-declared ex-gangster urged those assembled to seek refuge in the love of Jesus Christ and to abjure the evil forces of gangsterism and drugs. Although the event was directed toward all "lost souls," male gang members were explicitly asked to seek forgiveness for the crimes they had committed. Every month, Pentecostal churches held events like this one all over Dunefields. For a couple of hours they reclaimed the streets for the Lord. Some young men saw these parking-lot crusades as the only viable way out of crime and misuse of *tik*, the local name for methamphetamine, or Mandrax, the sedative methaqualone. They changed their lives after being "touched" by the Holy Spirit.

My ethnography focused on young men's vulnerability in some of the most impoverished neighborhoods in Cape Town (Reihling, forthcoming). In this context, the term "gang" could be elusive and refer to loose assemblies of youngsters exchanging stolen goods and drugs on street corners to large illicit enterprises. I became interested in how men engage with religious practices to pull out of the urban informal economy. Several of my research participants turned to Pentecostalism in the course of my fieldwork. Little is known about how men disassociate from gangs through involvement in religious communities that offer solidarity and care. In particular, the effects of Pentecostalism on men who were involved in gang membership and the informal economy of drugs have hardly been explored in urban Africa. Thus, I started to ask questions about what male gang members were doing to reform themselves as "born-again" Christians. Pentecostal churches aggressively tried to disengage them from gangs *on* the streets. This was exceptional, since no other organization or entity was invested in disengagement programs through outreach in one of South Africa's most crime-ridden neighborhoods.

This chapter addresses *affective conversions* that involve a reconfiguration of personhood through shifts of "affect" (Deleuze and Guattari 1994) or bodily felt intensity within the virtual space of deliverance rituals on township streets. Pentecostals turned secular places temporarily into religious ones, thus permitting, enabling, and sometimes forcing gang members to be vulnerable where they otherwise had to be in control. Intensities shifted when different values, interests, and identities crashed into each other and gave rise to an "excess" that could not be immediately grasped through language or cultural meanings.[1] The term "affective conversion" refers specifically to processes in which such intensities reach critical thresholds and result in confusion, loss of control, and a temporary state of pronounced vulnerability, particularly during parking-lot crusades.[2] This facilitated the actualization of men's potential that went beyond religious discourse and opened up a hinterland of nonrepresentational and prepersonal possibilities.

I argue that affect was vital for changing personhood from the enactment of an *ou* (pl. *ouens*), or street-smart man, to the subsequent enactment of a "born-again" gangster. During parking-lot crusades intensities of feeling were evoked by a "moral breakdown" (Zigon 2008, 165) when the sentiment of ingenuity that was learned in the informal economy on the streets directly contradicted an ou's perceived vulnerability in the face of God and his worldly evangelists. Rather than being a matter of mere rational reflection, the contradictions between the imperative to affect others, on the one hand,

and the imperative to be affected, on the other, opened up a nonrepresentational ground zero. Affect was experienced and given meaning through culturally coded emotions, such as shame and remorse, that were gradually turned into the "love" of a reformed Christian. Only after young men temporarily entered ritually constructed "spaces of virtuality" (Kapferer 2004), Pentecostal "love" was cultivated to be embodied as an ideally permanent sentiment, an emotional disposition that could be expressed, among other things, through secular social activism.

In the following, by means of a detailed case history, I will show that allowing vulnerability and giving up control, at least in relation to ministers and metaphysical powers, was vital for successful conversion. I show how personal transformation was retrospectively given meaning through an ethics of selfless giving and unconditional "love" that evolved in relation to a secularized world believed to be corrupted by gangsterism and moral downfall. Finally, the study shows that, in order to stay reformed, men had to perform ongoing work on the self. Becoming positive role models and leaders whom others could look up to and follow accomplished this most effectively. However, the conversion from street-smart ou to a man of "love" never entailed a complete break with the past, but rather a "transposition" similar to shifting a musical composition from one key to another while retaining the original structure. While reformed men emphasized selfless giving as the basis of personhood, they continued to rely on exchanges of favors, goods, and recognition through which they had defined themselves as ouens. At the same time, the outcomes for their social lives were radically different.

My discussion is based on ethnographic fieldwork with Afrikaans speakers in the Cape Flats, conducted intermittently between 2008 and 2015. The names of my research site and the protagonist in the case history have been changed to ensure their privacy.

GANGS IN THE CAPE FLATS

In South African cities, the rise of street gangs can be traced back to apartheid urban planning, economic exclusion, institutionalized racism, and the stigmatization of entire neighborhoods. In Cape Town, gangs mushroomed in the wake of social engineering projects that aimed to create racialized "group areas" during apartheid (1949–1994). Large numbers of people were expelled from the inner city and resettled in racially segregated townships on the urban outskirts. These townships trapped people in the Cape Flats lowlands and were inspired by Le Corbusier's modernist architecture, including high-density residential satellites linked with metropolitan nodes by railway lines and few access freeways. Where opportunities for employment, schooling, and entertainment were largely absent, some economically disadvantaged men sought success in an informal economy. Boys and young men created and transformed urban spaces through their involvement in homosocial male groups and illicit ventures (Pinnock 1984). This enabled them temporarily to acquire recognition, money, and a sense of dignity. In addition to taking over policing functions, gangs provided work in an informal economy that included trade in stolen goods, alcohol, and illicit drugs such as Mandrax, the sedative methaqualone.

In particular, urbanites classified as "Coloured" became subject to evictions. During apartheid this was a residual category that was used for those who did not easily fit other racial classifications. Although Coloured people were practically denied citizenship rights in the apartheid city, they were treated preferentially in comparison to blacks. Coloured group areas were furnished with two- and three-story multifamily brick-walled housing complexes. Here women became the unintended beneficiaries of racist legislation (Salo 2007). They were the preferential labor force in the city's waning textile industry. Coloured women with children also qualified for welfare grants, as well as access to public housing. In contrast, men were not entitled to the same kind of government support. Many men from impoverished Coloured group areas did not become patriarchal heads of families, particularly when caught up in the apartheid state's total institutions. For unruly boys, reformatories provided welfare nets in the face of poverty and, at the same time, constituted correctional facilities that sought to "normalize" them (Badroodien 2011, 305). In fact, they facilitated the formation of homosocial peer groups and became stepping-stones into prison. For the most marginalized, confinement turned into a rite of passage into manhood. Gangs provided relief from the infantilization and emasculation experienced by men in the colonial encounter in general, and particularly in the total institutions (Steinberg 2004).

The postapartheid city has been restructured in the wake of privatization, market liberalization, and economic differentiation. Although upwardly mobile families were able to leave the townships and urban redevelopment programs brought infrastructural improvements, socioeconomic segregation continued within the spatial grid laid out under apartheid (Besteman 2008). For the majority of people living in the Cape Flats, economic disparities increased and became more devastating in the face of new rights of citizenship. The disillusionment with the rise of democracy in the postapartheid city became perhaps most apparent through the increase in crime, violence, and drug misuse in the Cape Flats. Many young men and a few women continue to be more or less closely affiliated to streets gangs. As Standing (2006, 201) has argued, these gangs are deeply embedded in local communities and partly based on the idolization of local drug merchants and gang leaders. Their clan-like organization is still linked to loyalty and belonging among men.

THE MORAL ECONOMIES OF OUENS

Male gang members commonly self-identified as *ouens*, an Afrikaans word. An *ou*, literally "old" in English, was a street-smart man who gained respect through reciprocity. Gang members often characterized themselves in terms of what anthropologists have called "dividuals," that is, *dividable* persons made up through prior exchanges.[3] In the world of urban gangs, men ideally embodied this composite form of personhood through the disposition of *gedagte*, which translates literally as "thought," "understanding," or "mind." The semantics of the term nevertheless comprise more than cognition. The emotional disposition I refer to as "ingenuity" marked particular preferences with respect to economic inclusion and regard for others, and was associated with giving and receiving as well as the ability of a man to think of other's needs. From a Durkheimian perspective, gedagte was a social sentiment and constituted tendencies to respond emotionally in accordance with an internalized moral order.[4] Rather than being an end in itself, this represented an investment in future transactions from which ouens could benefit at some point when they were in need of resources.

Gang members used their wit to connect with others through reciprocal exchanges. This often took the form of a cunning navigation of the township, "hanging out" at street corners at the right time, taking the safest routes within and across gang territories, and exchanging favors with friends and local neighbors. In Dunefields, the exchange of gifts commonly took place on an edge that put the enactment of personhood at risk. As one gang member pointed out:

> Nothing is free man, nothing. We don't expect, but we expect something because that's the thing that keeps us alive here in Dunefields. That's why I say I can't do it with someone else's help also. I give him also, man, and I give him with the gedagte that when I have something this time, then he is there next time. Then he is there to defend that, if I need it. But if I don't

need it now, then I keep it to my brother who needs it, you know. That's the way it goes here. . . . You must be very careful what you say to guys like us. If you say, "Give me this pack of cigarettes, later I give you a 20 rand." Now you take the packet and later you don't come back. Then, I *moer* [hit] you, and after that it involves a lot of people, the law, the government, all that stuff. Why? Because I don't want to be a fool. Just leave it like that. If he at first place would have told me the truth, "Look here, I don't have the money." Then it wouldn't turn out like this. Sometimes you see the guys, they come here to use you. They want to use you. If this happens and it happens like that, tomorrow you walk in the street and you say he is a *naai* [fucker]. Why does he let somebody take his cigarettes, understand? Then I say I'm not a naai; I'm gonna kill you now. Then in the newspaper they're gonna write it's for the rand, but it's not for the rand, it's for the stuff he talks.

Although men like David could hardly afford to give without getting something in return in the face of poverty, it was not just the material good that was at stake. If the receiving party did not comply with the more or less explicit moral code of reciprocity, the giver could lose his status, since his gift was no longer perceived as such, but as a stolen good. Michael Taussig noticed that Marcel Mauss's notion of the "gift" alludes to the "impossible marriage between self-interest and altruism, between calculated giving and spontaneous generosity" (Taussig 1993, 94). It was this paradox that gave rise to men's perceived vulnerability in exchanges with others through which they hoped to foster resilience, recognition, and self-assurance on township streets. Over the course of fieldwork, I found that ouens' use of the term *gedagte* was contradictory and never fully captured actual forms of economic integration and exclusion. Openness to being affected by others was commonly seen as an obstacle and risk factor. After all, ingenuity could also be tied to deception and the propensity to take advantage of others for individual gain. If someone did not give the desired object or return a gift, their very identity as an ou was at stake.

Similar to the seemingly contradictory nature of gift exchange, the sentiment of ingenuity could swing toward or away from the receiving party. On the one hand, the relationship was characterized through attachment and what some men called "brotherly love" among gang members. On the other hand, it could involve the maximization of one's advantage at the expense of others. In Dunefields, narratives revolved around untrustworthy and treacherous men who were tied to a fear of being victimized. When David said "the guys, they come here to use you," he was referring to the corruption of the moral economy by those who turn the relationship into a source of personal gain and manipulation. The rampant individualism that was often part of gang life was externalized and associated with so-called *skollies*, or scavengers, coming from outside the local moral community. For men like David, the outrage and sense of indignation that came with abuse was not just about the loss of a material good. At stake was what Mauss ([1924] 1990) referred to as the "spirit" of a gift that in this case was nothing less than the very sentiment of gedagte that made gang members appear invulnerable in the face of rampant violence. When I started fieldwork, more than seventeen hundred people had been murdered in Cape Town over the previous year, the majority of whom were men from urban townships.[5]

RESTRUCTURING EMOTIONAL DISPOSITIONS

When I started my research, one of the few secular programs that provided a refuge for boys and young men involved in gangs had just closed its doors due to a lack of funding. In contrast, small Pentecostal churches seemed to be flourishing and were leading aggressive antigangsterism and drug abuse campaigns. Their deliverance rituals were referred to as "crusades" and reached out into gang territories, sometimes even into notorious drug houses. One of their strategies was to emphasize men's vulnerability and force them into a realization that their past actions had caused considerable suffering to themselves and others. The ritual practice provided alternatives to the rigid emotion management required to be successful in the informal economy. The stoic and dispassionate facial expression of an ou that signaled ingenuity on street corners could be released during services in which the dramatization of rapidly shifting emotional states was a currency for healing, change, and the presence of a higher power. The following case history is in many respects unique, but it points out the commonalities among "born-again" gangsters' experiences of conversion.

Thomas Fortune was an influential member of the Cisko Yakkie gang and had made a career as a "hit man" and a Mandrax merchant in Dunefields. One day, he was urged by a friend to attend a "crusade" organized by the Mighty Gospel Church. At the time, he identified as Muslim and only reluctantly agreed to join the event. A large white tent was erected temporarily on an open space between housing units. For Thomas, it was a door to another world. In an interview he described how the charismatic faith healer seemed to read his mind and addressed the downfalls of his life without addressing him directly. The next day, the minister switched his emphasis and seemingly pointed out the positive aspects of the gangster's life. When the minister pinned his gaze on him, Thomas looked away and sank into his seat, with his body temperature rising. The following day, he attended the third nightly ministry, which he described as follows:

> The third night, this man speaks about something that nobody knows about, and this man says, "Somebody on this side," and I am sitting on this side. And this man says, "Somebody on this side must come." And I think, "Go to hell, man, how can you know? It's only me and God that knows about this thing. How do you know about this thing? Not my mother nor my wife, nobody knows about it! I did it alone. So how can you know about it?" But this thing was eating me while I am sitting there. Hey, and I am telling you, the sweat is already running down. And I am sitting in the chair, sitting in the chair. And the man—and now you must know, the people are staying in front for prayer already. And then I am sitting. And then this man said, "There is one more person in this place. Just one more person, God is waiting for you." I sit, and this man says, "Your time is short. God wants to heal you, and he wants to save you out of all this." And that time, I was a gangster, hey. . . . I tell myself, "I am not going there." But I tell you, I don't know how I got to the front. I don't know how I got to the front. But I just knew I was in front afterward. And now I was really skeptical about this praying and touching you because, remember, I'm a Muslim still. So I used to hear how the people—they push you over and all that. "Tonight I am not going to touch you or do anything to you. You just lift your hands up and ask for forgiveness." I don't know how to pray, and this man says, "All you need to do is say is, 'Forgive me Lord for what I've done.'" Then I started to talk to God.

The ritual opened up a space in which Thomas was forced to reflect upon his past actions. This highly structured frame seemed to facilitate what Zigon (2008) has called a "moral breakdown," an experience that opens up largely unconscious moral dispositions to critical scrutiny and questions about "right" and "wrong." Such a breakdown may generate an ethical demand for resolution when a person perceives his or her conduct as problematic and is forced to reflect upon the consequences of past actions. From this perspective, ethics becomes a "stepping away" from a range of available moralities, a "conscious acting on oneself" that aims at becoming a morally more appropriate and acceptable person in a particular moment (Zigon 2009, 261). Thomas overcame his resistance and started to act on himself in new ways that were in accordance with the moral practices espoused by the Pentecostal community. However, this was not merely a matter of rational self-reflection. It has been argued that the body is central to Pentecostal religiosity (Csordas 1994b; Bialecki 2015; Brahinsky 2012). Among the men I encountered, the visceral experience of movement and intensity during the nightly ministries prompted the rapid deconstruction of the gendered disposition of gedagte, apparently compelling a need for ethical resolution.

The ritual offered a clearly structured internal set of practices that oriented attendees toward heaven and God. Thomas had to move his body, approach the minister, and lift his hands. This choreography evoked a series of culturally coded emotions such as guilt, shame, and remorse. The orchestration of memory, antecedent events and their interpretation, somatic experience, and bodily movement was a prerequisite for deliverance. The enactment of these dispositions was also related to the material infrastructures of the tent and the township parking lot, as well as those who were present in order to foster an emotionally mediated experience of moral breakdown. In a different religious context, Parish (1991, 333) observed that moral emotions work as "behavioural controls" because they are painful to experience and involve moral evaluations that alter the way people know themselves. In his narrative about the third nightly ministry, Thomas did not use the words "shame" or "guilt" and merely referred to a "thing" that was "eating" him, as well as the physiological response of sweat running down his face. Eventually, he raised his arms and asked for forgiveness for what he had done. That momentary intensity was channeled into a religiously meaningful experience that, however, did not immediately foster self-knowledge.

OPENING UP A VIRTUAL SPACE

Affective conversions entailed a temporary state of loss and uncertainty about how to enact personhood. There is no doubt that the deliverance ritual had a highly coded internal structure that is widely shared in Pentecostal and Charismatic Christianity across the globe (see Coleman and Hackett 2015). A vertical spatial order of heaven and hell formed the basis for a ritual that saved the believer from "evil forces" and fit in with normative emotional dispositions. However, men like Thomas did not follow a routine when they suddenly became affected in new ways that went beyond language and established religious codes. The deliverance ritual created what Kapferer (2004, 49) has called "virtuality" understood as a means for engaging immediately with the "ontological ground of being." This was not about reproducing the subjects needed to sustain a particular structure or the religious community. It inverted postapartheid urban space and opened up its virtual structure of possibility in which there was no sex, gender, class, or race. For Thomas this occurred through a breakdown of cultural codes related to township gang life, with its imperative to be ingenuous and invulnerable:

> Something came over me: it's like, it's like hot, but not a scary feeling. It was very peaceful, and it came over me. And I flew! I flew to the ground. And nobody touched me. Nobody touched me. After that, a nice feeling came over me. . . . Something hit me out of the ground and off my, off balance, and I, I was out for a few minutes, um. The people were actually scared because, they say, my body was going so up and down on the floor while I was lying there. And when I woke up, I was bewildered and I said, "Jy [you], jy, jy, jy, jy." And then one man came to fix me while I was there. He asked me if he can pray with me and, and I was still sitting. I said, "Yeah, you can pray with me." And he took me to a room and he asked me if I wanna be born again, saved, accept Christ Jesus as my personal savior. And you know, I was just in that state, I just said, "Yes, yes, yes, yes, yes." And then, when I came to my normal senses, I said, "Eh, why everybody call you brother now?"

Although the codes of global and African Charismatic Christianity determined the frame of the ritual, the internal ritual virtuality transcended representation. It corresponded to a prepersonal bodily intensity that changed Thomas's capacity to affect and be affected. This capacity has been called "affect" in Spinozist philosophy. Affect opens up the potential for new sensations, emotions, and ideas to arise. As Massumi pointed out, "Affect is the virtual as a point of view" (2002, 35). The term helped me to develop an awareness of human capacity that remains hidden in studies that focus on function and meaning. In contrast to properties, capacities have not been exercised yet. When they are exercised, they are not static states but dynamic events. As movement, transition, or becoming from one bodily state to the other, this may involve excess and creativity (Deleuze and Guattari 1994, 167–174). The "hit man" had the capacity to be vulnerable and affected by others all along, but it was only actualized through intensive differences generated by Pentecostal ritual.

The transmissions between affected and affecting bodies opened up a potential for change that was at odds with ingenuity as a marker of street-smart personhood on township streets. Thomas was momentarily affected by pure intensity without qualified emotion or cognition. He described a state of impaired coordination, paralysis of limbs and the entire body, inability to speak, numbness and tremors, and eventually loss of consciousness. The loss of control stood in stark contrast to how a leading gang member has to conduct himself on the streets. There was nothing that would sustain a gender identity or the stereotype of a skollie. Thomas was in a state of extreme vulnerability and embraced it. Counter to notions of the virtual in computing, this virtual event was real in the sense that the temporary loss of balance came with a loss of certainties that opened up a potential with a multiplicity of alternative social practices that were nonreferential to external social reality.

Similar to historically older forms of healing in southern Africa, affliction is central to becoming a "born-again" Christian at the Cape. Referring to a diasporic Ghanaian Pentecostal church, van Dijk (2007, 316) pointed out that vulnerability in this context is commonly pursued and desired as an outcome of action rather than something to be avoided. He claimed that the resulting "vulnerable agency" in relation to heavenly forces and church leaders safeguards morality and identity among Pentecostals. In a sense, the downfalls of gangsterism in the postapartheid city were a prerequisite for being touched by the Holy Spirit. Men like Thomas increased their agency and their very potential to act when they became open to being affected by the minister, the church members, and the metaphysical world they invoked. The virtual possibilities of vulnerability were nevertheless narrowed down when Thomas slowly came back to consciousness and was asked to pray by his new brothers and sisters. In his account, he gave no interpretation of the event and emphasized his absentmindedness when indicating that he hardly knew what the minister was talking about. He just said "yes" without being fully aware of what it meant to accept Jesus Christ. Intensive differences drove the flows of actions that were gradually channeled into a preestablished religious order. In order to be more than a single event, affective conversion also required ongoing work on the self and the learning of emotional dispositions that were meaningful to evangelical Christians.

BACK IN THE STREETS: "YOU ARE RUBBISH"

In the process of affective conversion, "born-again" gangsters inverted prior enactments of invulnerability. Once they left the ritual virtuality, they had to demonstrate their ability to "break" with the past and disconnect from drugs, gangsterism, and township streets. The deliverance ritual I have described was only the first step in moving out of the gang into the brotherhood of believers; it did not equal instant salvation. The ritual frame only opened up a moment to be vulnerable. This moment had to be followed by new social differentiations. There was no automatic integration into a new social collective and moral order, as outlined by classical ritual theory (Gennep [1909] 1960; Turner [1969] 1995). Thomas pointed out that he struggled to curb his drug habit and remained involved with the Cisco Yakkies after the event described earlier. The "break with the past" was curbed by the material structure of the township itself. In the Cape Flats, small neighborhood wards were rigidly compartmentalized and divided by precast concrete walls, highways, and vacant buffer zones. Young men could not move freely through the cityscape because outside their local moral community they were often perceived as gangsters or thugs who needed to be fended off by local residents. Actual gang members were extremely sedentary and often walked only a few streets within the perimeters of their territory. Within these high-density residential quarters, men typically hung out at street corners and yards, while respectable women, particularly mothers, were expected to remain inside the brick-stone homes (Salo 2007).

Thomas and other "born-again" gangsters had extreme difficulties in breaking with enactments of personhood that linked sentiments, streets, friendship networks, and drug houses just outside their doorsteps. For some of them it was a matter of weeks before they could no longer stand the intensity generated by the amused or demanding companions they had to pass on their way to often faraway church gatherings that could only be reached by minibus taxis. Ex-gangsters' commitment to change was continuously being put to the test in interactions with former friends and acquaintances. Within the radius of two blocks from my host's home in Dunefields, I encountered five young men who were not able to live up to the ideal of self-sufficiency and returned to street life after having identified as "born-again." Initially this was also the case with Thomas, who, weeks after "being touched," started to reengage in the enactment of an ou. He remembered how six months after he had been touched by the Holy Spirit, one of the members of the church came to visit him at the gang's hangout:

> We were drinking, smoking drugs. And this man come there. And this man tell me my fortune. And I looked at him this way, I was thinking this man is not scared even. I must just [clicks with his fingers] by the click of my fingers just kill people. We did! If I must order one of my, my guys now to shoot this man, he will shoot him, man! And here this man is telling me my life. He is still here. He is like insulting me here, man. And I tell him, "Na, my bru, moenie so gaan nie [my brother, don't go on like this]." And he tell me,

"Don't call me 'my bru!' I told you to change, but you don't want to change. You're *gemoers* [scum], you are rubbish." And I realized what is it about this man? This man can get hurt here. But he tell me that he wanna help. And there I experienced a different love. And I looked at this ou [man], and I was going to tell now what we are going to do. I looked at them and I say, "Who of you is loving me the way this man love me?" And since then I never looked back. I gave everything back to the gangs, money that was theirs, a car that was theirs. And I started my life from scratch over.

The indirect approach to addressing Thomas's downfall during the deliverance ritual was replaced by direct persuasion and blunt insult. It has been noted that Pentecostal counselors can be subtly judgmental or even aggressive toward those who do not want to receive their gospel (Burchardt 2013c). In this case, the use of the term *gemoers*, which could be translated into English as "scum" or "rubbish," was a serious defamation. At the Cape it is usually reserved for those who are presumed to be unwilling to better themselves, do not deserve any help, and are excluded from the moral economy of reciprocity. On the streets, the word is commonly accompanied by a sense of contempt; those who are humiliated in this way are commonly expected to express anger and retaliation. However, here the ambiguity of the missionary's performance, which could not be clearly read in terms of pre-established moral emotion scripts, seemed to give rise to a moment of doubt. Thomas emphasized that his uncertainty made him question the missionary's intentions and his gang brothers' allegiance. Again, his openness to being affected brought about a potential for change before another cultural script was evoked and recounted.

In retrospect, Thomas recast the prerepresentational potential of not knowing into language and a new emotional disposition. In his narrative, the encounter followed another Christian emotion script that to some degree countered the disposition of *ingenuity* and *sharpness*, at least with regard to self-gratifying individualism. The reformed gangster made sense of the event by emphasizing that the missionary was willing to risk his own life in order to save him. Thomas felt touched by the "love" of a fellow man who was willing to move into a position of vulnerability. This stood in stark contrast to the positive regard involved in tit-for-tat reciprocity in the profit-oriented informal economy. Here the personhood was enacted through selfless giving. The "love" Thomas referred to coincides with the notion of *agapē* used in Christian theology for compassion, charity, and forgiveness. Its blueprint as depicted in the New Testament is the fatherly love of God for humankind that is believed to save sinners. The underlying assumption here is that the object of God's love never does anything to merit it; hence the love is unconditional.[6] Although the missionary's performance was ambiguous and could by no means live up to this divine ideal, Thomas was affected in unexpected ways. He developed the sentiment of "love" in his own life and made it central to his subsequent engagement in a faith-based organization.

CIVIC ENGAGEMENTS: "WE NEED TO LIVE THE LIFE"

Affective conversions among "gangsters" were commonly accompanied by efforts to make up for the harm committed, rather than being a matter of millennial capitalism that promised salvation through the amassing of modern consumer goods. Before joining the congregation, Thomas had a relatively stable income through trade in stolen goods and Mandrax. For him, "breaking" with the informal economy first of all meant more financial strain and insecurity. He sought to make up for the crimes committed and joined a faith-based organization (FBO) called the Dream Factory that was dedicated to charitable acts in township schools. This could be seen as a form of restorative justice aimed at the restitution rather than retribution and punishment of an offender. However, among my research participants the restorative acts were never dedicated to particular victims of a crime or their families, as is the case in formal restorative practice (Johnstone and Van Ness 2007). They were dedicated to the "community" as a more abstract and overarching casualty of gang violence. Thomas's benefactor, the man who transformed his life by entering the drug den, was the same person who had founded the FBO. This former business administrator from a middle-class background left his career to support young people in township schools. In a similar vein, Thomas dropped out of the informal economy and exchanged his role as a gang leader for an unpaid position as youth educator. In his testimony he pointed out:

> Today, I see that there was no benefit to kill one another, to rob, to steal, and we do it in our own community, we hurt one another. And today I realize there is something greater and better to do for the community, and that's why I'm working with young people today. You can still change their minds. Our organization is a Christian-based organization. But we won't force Christianity down anybody. Because our lives, the way we live, must show the difference. So we don't force a religion down anybody's throat. . . . Our aim is

just to touch one life. It's not to give anything. We need to live the life. If we look at Jesus's life, he just lived the life, a normal life, and people saw the difference. So this is what we are trying to do.

Thomas emphasized that membership in the organization was not tied to a particular denomination. In fact, the staff and volunteers of the FBO were members of different churches. The FBO provided a platform for people with various church affiliations who nonetheless mostly identified as "born-again." Its agenda was explicitly secular in the sense that there was a distinction between the staff members' religious life and the domains in which they provided their services. Yet, Thomas stressed that the organization's success was based on prayers and its biblical foundation. As Burchardt (2013a) pointed out regarding FBOs in Cape Town, services with seemingly secular aims are based on discourses and practices that may ultimately aim at making conversion palatable through the moral, social, and financial benefits of "Pentecostal belonging." Most likely Thomas's dedication to Christ made the missionary endorse his participation in the Dream Factory. At the same time, it is safe to say that the reformed man's main objective was not to find followers for his church.

At the time of my research, the FBO provided tutoring and extracurricular activities at a local high school. According to the principal, about half of the learners had problems obtaining passing grades for their worst subjects, and some of them remained practically "illiterate" in classrooms crowded with up to fifty students. The core of the organization's program was constituted by monthly wilderness camps in which young men were taken out to hike and camp outside the city and leave the streets. Thomas emphasized that the poorest of the poor have no means to get their children to leave the townships, and he was thus hoping to provide an alternative to the mesmerizing appeal of gangs. Although it remains an open question to what extent such programs make a difference for the bulk of disadvantaged township youth, they seem to have long-lasting effects on their religiously inspired facilitators. It seems that sentiments were most effectively transformed when reformed men like Thomas had an audience to whom they could perform their new identity and teach by example. Through recognition, they had to become accountable for their actions. This was similar to men who developed "relational dignity" through involvement in civil society organizations, based on being cherished as leaders and role models (Reihling 2013). The successes of saving youth from crime, gangsterism, and drug abuse were largely unpredictable and probably scant in the face of rampant structural inequalities. However, former gang members could be sure that in the process they would "better" themselves, or at least not "backslide" into the informal economy.

It has been argued that Pentecostal churches in Africa may be more successful agents of change than civil society organizations because they collapse economic and personal development and are relatively independent of global development agencies (van Dijk 2012; D. Freeman 2012). In the case of the Dream Factory, the organization evolved out of affective conversions that were not necessarily determined by global cash flows, funding proposals, or formal employment. Thomas could not count on a salary and received only occasional stipends. His own financial situation and that of the organization were precarious for several years. He and other volunteers raised money from private donors, sometimes by asking for small donations at traffic lights. Thomas strongly believed that the Lord would provide a modest amount of money and emphasized that he was not tempted to re-enter the lucrative drug business. Restitution and maintaining reformation seemed to be a more meaningful currency than money alone. Thomas eventually married a member of his congregation, a female professional who, at times, contributed more to the household's financial resources than he did.

TRANSPOSITIONS OF URBAN PERSONHOOD

Affective conversions denote nonlinear processes of relatively sudden and unexpected changes in how enactments of personhood are valued and inscribed into the city. Reformed men sacralized urban spaces and thereby created intensities that facilitated the actualization of virtual potentials. These were real but largely invisible in the township. The camps erected on parking lots or vacant plots were literally part of what Burchardt (2013b) called Cape Town's "hidden religious topography." This also involved evangelical outreach into schools and drug houses that were by no means conceived as religious institutions. The very enactment of Pentecostal "love" spurned the blurring of boundaries between secular and religious places. While one was contingent on the informal economy of gangs and drugs, the other was tied to evangelical congregations and charity work. One was tied to substance abuse and interpersonal violence, the other to involvement in a form of civic activism that has become a unique feature of postapartheid development among the "urban poor" (Robins 2008).

Once a critical threshold was reached, affect could drive the conversion from street-smart to "born-again" gangsters. This conversion never represented a complete break with the past but rather a transposition—that is, old configurations of personhood were enacted in a different context with very different outcomes. Evidently, the men I encountered could never fully balance out the Pentecostal ideals of loving self-sacrifice and self-sufficiency. The very personhood of "born-again" gangsters was made up of externalized parts of others, such as goods, favors, and recognition. At the same time, it depended on individual achievement and navigation of the cityscape.[7] For the reformed men I encountered, composite personhood was the basis for individuality, since they had to connect with other "born-again" people to distinguish themselves from the gang brothers they had to leave behind. Thomas and other reformed ouens continued to enact ingenuity when they seized small opportunities to obtain donations on the streets or favors from other church members. Moreover, when Thomas worked with township youth, he depended on other people's appreciation and ongoing social affirmations of his identity as a reformed gangster. To make up for their misdeeds, ouens often had to commit themselves to role-modeling alternative behavior to be worthy of their following. The composite personhood of reformed men was based on spiritual rather than economic leadership and as such did little to change the poverty-sustaining secular political economy that partly led to its emergence. This nevertheless made a significant difference by keeping the reformed from backsliding into gangs.

The implicit coexistence and rupture between individualist and relational enactments of personhood complicate any notion of linear progression toward reformed men of "love." What "born-again" gangsters did was, after all, somehow similar to what they had done in their best moments as benevolent ouens. They enacted "open reciprocity," as David Graeber (2001) has called it, based on open trust and open credit rather than tit-for-tat exchange.[8] This commonly resulted in the giver's social and economic security over time. At some point, Thomas's benefactor offered him a job. For converts, individual agency was premised on social relationships. This resonated with findings across Africa that show how Pentecostals establish new communities of solidarity and care in times of distress.[9] Men like Thomas were "miraculously" able to make a modest living and, at least in part, overcame the dichotomy of selfless charity and self-absorbed accumulation that characterized Cape Town's urban market economy at the beginning of the twentieth century. In this sense, men's reformation based on mutuality was tied to ongoing interactions and affect that could not be fully codified in Pentecostal discourses or neat divisions between secular and religious places in the city.

Pentecostal ritual outreach enabled, encouraged, and forced (ex-)gang members to be vulnerable in an urban milieu in which it was dangerous to show tenderness. Conversion was only possible through men's continuing openness to being touched in relation to the evangelists, the community of "born-again" Christians, as well as God and his son Jesus Christ. The ability to be vulnerable without having to fear abuse from competitors in the informal economy seemed to be a major reason for men to convert. This may be a distinctive feature of conversions for young men involved in gangs in Cape Town. Vulnerability in conjunction with the emotional disposition of "love" marked a turning point. It complicated the claim that Charismatic Christianity in Africa became popular mainly because of its promise to deliver the believer from poverty.[10] For "born-again" gangsters it was affect and emotion that made them convert rather than capital. In fact, they left behind lucrative as well as potentially deadly opportunities to gain money and recognition through involvement in the gangs that have become ubiquitous in South African townships.

NOTES

1. Žižek, in *Organs without Bodies*, locates the notion of "excess" at the center of Deleuze's philosophy of becoming. He affirms an "irreducible excess of the problem over its solution" or of the "virtual over its actualizations" (2004, 50). From this perspective, the "reality of the virtual"—not to be confused with the unreal in media simulations—exceeds the actual world of observable things because it contains potentially infinite capacities to affect and be affected

2. Here I follow a Spinozist notion of "affect" of the sort developed by Deleuze and Guattari (1994) and Massumi (2002). As intensive difference, affect can only be registered in the body as an increase or decrease in its capacity to act, to affect, and be affected.

3. Strathern (1990) built the term upon the work of McKim Marriot, who used it to refer to South Asian notions of personhood that are opposed to the Enlightenment understanding of "individuals" in the sense of bounded and indivisible units. For a detailed discussion of the concept, see Fowler (2004).

4. See Durkheim (1912). Building on him, Radcliffe-Brown (1922, 233ff.) defined social sentiment as an "organized system of emotional tendencies centered around some object" and pointed out that "society depends for its existence on the presence in the minds of its members of a certain system of sentiments by which the conduct of the individual is regulated in conformity with the needs of the society."

5. Crime statistics recorded fifty-seven reported murders in Cape Town per 100,000 inhabitants in one year (2005/2006), which accounts approximately for the

figure given earlier if one takes into account a total population of about 3 million. See City of Cape Town (2009).

6. See Lewis (1960) for a discussion of the four types of love. He considered agapē, which he translated as "charity," to be more virtuous than other forms of love such as affection, friendship, and eros, which according to him are based on an individual's needs.

7. Robbins (2015, 179) argued that the co-presence of relational and individualist "value configurations" is common among evangelical Christians. Van Dijk (2001b), Daswani (2011), and Werbner (2011) also noted this for sub-Saharan Africa.

8. Graeber builds upon Sahlins's notion of "generalized reciprocity" tied to the virtues of altruism and generosity among people in close proximity (1972, 198). He distinguishes this from "closed reciprocity" that is more akin to short-term transactions of goods that in his opinion largely resemble the mode of market exchange.

9. See Dilger 2007; Dilger, Burchardt, and van Dijk 2010; and Burchardt 2013a.

10. See Gifford 1990; Maxwell 1998; Hasu 2012.

BIBLIOGRAPHY

Abaka, Edmund. 2005. *Kola Is God's Gift: Agricultural Production, Export Initiatives and the Kola Industry of Asante and the Gold Coast, c. 1820–1950.* Athens: Ohio University Press.

Ablon, Joan. 2002. "The Nature of Stigma and Medical Conditions." *Epilepsy and Behavior* 3 (6): 2–9.

Abu-Lughod, Lila. 1988. *Veiled Sentiments: Honor and Poetry in a Bedouin Society.* Berkeley: University of California Press.

Abu-Lughod, Lila, and Catherine A. Lutz. 1990. "Introduction. Emotion, Discourse, and the Politics of Everyday Life." In *Language and the Politics of Emotion*, edited by Catherine A. Lutz and Lila Abu-Lughod, 1–23. Cambridge: Cambridge University Press.

Abun-Nasr, Jamil. 1965. *The Tijaniyya: A Sufi Order in the Modern World.* London: Oxford University Press.

Acemoglu, Daron, Simon Johnson, and James A. Robinson. 2002. "An African Success Story: Botswana." In *In Search of Prosperity: Analytic Narratives on Economic Growth*, edited by Dani Rodrik, 80–119. Princeton, NJ: Princeton University Press.

Adebanwi, Wale. 2012. "Abuja." In *Capital Cities in Africa: Power and Powerless*, edited by Simon Bekker and Goran Therborn, 84–102. Cape Town: HRCS Press.

Adetona, Lateef. 2002. "NASFAT: A Modern Prayer Group and Its Contributions to the Propagation of Islam in Lagos." *World Journal of Islamic History and Civilization* 2 (2): 102–107.

Adogame, Afe. 1998. "Home Away from Home: The Proliferation of the Celestial Church of Christ (CCC) in Diaspora-Europe." *Exchange* 27 (2): 141–160.

Ahmed, Sara. 2004. "Affective Economies." *Social Text* 79, 22 (2): 117–139.

Ahmed, Sara. 2013. *The Cultural Politics of Emotion.* Edinburgh: Edinburg University Press.

Akukwe, Obinna. 2012. "Pastor Chris Oyakhilome's Theory of Alcoholism and Smoking." Accessed September 27, 2016. www.nigeriafilms.com /more/127-columnists/15964-pastor-chris-oyakhilome-s-theory-of -alcoholism-and-smoking.

Akyeampong, Emmanuel K. 1996. *Drink, Power, and Cultural Change: A Social History of Alcohol in Ghana, c. 1800 to Recent Times.* Oxford: James Currey.

Akyeampong, Emmanuel K. 2000a. "Africans in the Diaspora: The Diaspora and Africa." *African Affairs* 99 (395): 183–215. doi:10.1093/afraf/99.395.183.

Akyeampong, Emmanuel K. 2000b. "'Wo pe tam won pe ba' ('You Like Cloth but You Don't Want Children'): Urbanization, Individualism and Gender Relations in Colonial Ghana c. 1900–39." In *Africa's Urban Past*, edited by David Anderson, 222–234. Oxford: James Currey.

Akyeampong, Emmanuel K. 2015. "A Historical Overview of Psychiatry in Africa." In *The Culture of Mental Illness and Psychiatric Practice in Africa*, edited by Emmanuel Akyeampong, Allan G. Hill, and Arthur Kleinman, 24–50. Bloomington: Indiana University Press.

Alexander, Jocelyn, JoAnn McGregor, and Terence Ranger, eds. 2000. *Violence and Memory: One Hundred Years in the Dark Forests of Matabeleland, Zimbabwe.* London: James Currey.

Anderson, Alan. 2001. *African Initiated Christianity in the 20th Century.* Trenton, NJ: Africa World Press.

Appadurai, Arjun. 1990. "Disjuncture and Difference in the Global Cultural Economy." *Public Culture* 2 (2): 1–24.

ArchNet. 2002. "Abuja National Mosque." Massachusetts Institute of Technology. Accessed September 27, 2016. http://archnet.org/sites/703/media _contents/18822.

Arhin, Kwame. 1979. *West African Traders in Ghana in the Nineteenth and Twentieth Centuries.* London: Longman.

Asad, Talal. 1986. "The Idea of an Anthropology of Islam." The Center for Contemporary Arab Studies, Occasional Paper Series, Georgetown University, Washington, DC.

Asad, Talal. 2009. *Genealogies of Religion: Discipline and Reasons of Power in Christianity and Islam.* Baltimore: John Hopkins University Press.

Asad, Talal. 2014. "Thinking about Religion, Belief, and Politics." In *The Cambridge Companion to Religious Studies*, edited by Robert Orsi, 36–57. Cambridge: Cambridge University Press.

Asamoah-Gyadu, Kwabena. 2010. "Religious Education and Religious Pluralism in the New Africa." *Religious Education* 105 (3): 238–244.

Aschwanden, Herbert. 1989. *Karanga Mythology: An Analysis of the Consciousness of the Karanga in Zimbabwe.* Gweru: Mambo Press.

Ashforth, Adam. 1998. "Reflections on Spiritual Insecurity in a Modern African City (Soweto)." *African Studies Review* 41 (3): 39–67. doi:10.2307 /525353.

Ashforth, Adam. 2005. "Muthi, Medicine and Witchcraft: Regulating 'African Science' in Post-Apartheid South Africa?," *Social Dynamics* 31 (2): 211–242

Badroodien, Azeem. 2011. "From Boys to Men: The Education and Institutional Care of Coloured Boys in the Early Twentieth Century." *South African Review of Education* 17 (1): 7–26.

Barrett, David B. 1968. *Schism and Renewal in Africa: An Analysis of Six Thousand Contemporary Religious Movements.* London: Oxford University Press.

BBC News. 2016. *Zimbabwe Country Profile.* Accessed February 5, 2016. www .bbc.com/news/world-africa-14113249.

Beall, Jo, Owen Crankshaw, and Sue Parnell. 2002. *Uniting a Divided City: Governance and Social Exclusion in Johannesburg.* London: Earthscan.

Beatty, Andrew. 2014. "Anthropology and Emotion." *Journal of the Royal Anthropological Institute* 20 (3): 545–563. doi:10.1111/1467-9655.12114.

Becci, Irene, Marian Burchardt, and José Casanova, eds. 2013. *Topographies of Faith: Religion in Urban Spaces.* Leiden: Brill.

Becker, Jochen, Katrin Klingan, Stephan Lanz, and Kathrin Wildner, eds. 2013. *Global Prayers: Contemporary Manifestations of the Religious in the City.* Zurich: Lars Müller Publishers.

Beckford, Robert. 2011. *Dread and Pentecostal: A Political Theology for the Black Church in Britain.* Eugene, OR: Wipf and Stock.

Beckmann, Nadine, Alessandro Gusman, and Catrine Shroff, eds. 2014. *Strings Attached: AIDS and the Rise of Transnational Connections in Africa.* London: British Academy.

Bekker, Simon, and Goran Therborn, eds. 2012. *Capital Cities in Africa: Power and Powerless.* Cape Town: HRCS Press.

Berberich, Christine, Neil Campbell, and Robert Hudson. 2013. "Affective Landscapes: An Introduction." *Cultural Politics* 9 (3): 313–322.

Bergson, Henri. (1900) 1959. "Le rire. Essai sur la signification du comique." In *Oeuvres: Edition du centenaire,* 391–485. Paris: Presses Universitaires de France.

Bernstein, Jesse, and Moses Chrispus Okello. 2007. "To Be or Not to Be: Urban Refugees in Kampala." *Refuge: Canada's Journal on Refugees* 24 (1): 46–56.

Besteman, Catherine Lowe. 2008. *Transforming Cape Town.* Berkeley: University of California Press.

Bialecki, Jon. 2015. "Affect: Intensities and Energies in the Charismatic Language, Embodiment and Genre of a North American Movement." In *The Anthropology of Global Pentecostalism and Evangelicalism,* edited by Simon Coleman and Rosalind Hackett, 95–108. New York: New York University Press.

Biehl, João. 2013. *Vita: Life in a Zone of Social Abandonment.* Berkeley: University of California Press.

Biehl, João, and Peter Locke. 2010. "Deleuze and the Anthropology of Becoming." *Current Anthropology* 51 (3): 317–351.

Blackman, Lisa. 2012. *Immaterial Bodies: Affect, Embodiment, Mediation.* London: Sage.

Blanes, Ruy Llera. 2011. "Unstable Biographies. The Ethnography of Memory and Historicity in an Angolan Prophetic Movement." *History and Anthropology* 22 (1): 93–119.

Bloch, Maurice, and Jonathan Parry. 1982. "Introduction: Death and the Regeneration of Life." In *Death and the Regeneration of Life,* edited by Maurice Bloch and Jonathan Parry, 1–44. Cambridge: Cambridge University Press.

Bochow, Astrid, and Rijk van Dijk. 2012. "Christian Creations of New Spaces of Sexuality, Reproduction, and Relationships in Africa: Exploring Faith and Religious Heterotopia." *Journal of Religion in Africa* 42 (4): 325–344. doi:http://dx.doi.org/10.1163/15700666-12341235

Böhme, Gernot. 2013. *Athmosphäre: Essays zu einer neuen Ästhetik.* Frankfurt am Main: Suhrkamp.

Bourdieu, Pierre. 2010. *Distinction: A Social Critique of the Judgment of Taste.* London: Routledge.

Bowen, John R. 1989. "Salat in Indonesia: The Social Meanings of an Islamic Ritual." *Man* 24 (4): 600–619.

Bowen, John R. 1993. *Muslims through Discourse: Religion and Ritual in Gayo Society.* Princeton, NJ: Princeton University Press.

Bowen, John R. 2012. *A New Anthropology of Islam.* Cambridge: Cambridge University Press.

Bowie, Fiona. 2003. "An Anthropology of Religious Experience: Spirituality, Gender and Cultural Transmission in the Focolare Movement." *Ethnos* 68 (1): 49–72.

Brahinsky, Josh. 2012. "Pentecostal Body Logics: Cultivating a Modern Sensorium." *Cultural Anthropology* 27 (2): 215–238.

Brennan, Teresa. 2004. *The Transmission of Affect.* Ithaca, NY: Cornell University Press.

Brennan, Vicki L. 2010. "Mediating 'The Voice of the Spirit': Musical and Religious Transformations in Nigeria's Oil Boom." *American Ethnologist* 37 (2): 354–370.

Brenner, Neil. 2001. "The Limits to Scale? Methodological Reflections on Scalar Structuration." *Progress in Human Geography* 25 (4): 591–614.

Brodwin, Paul. 2003. "Pentecostalism in Translation: Religion and the Production of Community in the Haitian Diaspora." *American Ethnologist* 30 (1): 85–101.

Burchardt, Marian. 2009. "Subjects of Counselling: Religion, HIV/AIDS and the Management of Everyday Life in South Africa." In *AIDS and Religious Practice in Africa,* edited by Felicitas Becker and Wenzel Geissler, 333–359. Leiden: Brill.

Burchardt, Marian. 2010a. "Ironies of Subordination: Ambivalences of Gender in Religious AIDS Interventions in South Africa." *Oxford Development Studies* 38 (1): 63–82.

Burchardt, Marian. 2013a. "Access to the Social: The Ethics and Pragmatics of HIV/AIDS Support Groups in South Africa." In *Ethnographies of Social Support*, edited by Marcus Schlecker and Friederike Fleischer, 59–80. New York: Palgrave Macmillan.

Burchardt, Marian. 2013b. "Belonging and Success: Religious Vitality and the Politics of Urban Space in Cape Town." In *Topographies of Faith: Religion in Urban Spaces*, edited by Irene Becci, Marian Burchardt, and José Casanova, 167–187. Leiden: Brill.

Burchardt, Marian. 2013c. "'We Are Saving the Township': Pentecostalism, Faith-Based Organizations, and Development in South Africa." *Journal of Modern African Studies* 51 (4): 627–651.

Burchardt, Marian. 2014. "The Logic of Therapeutic Habitus: Culture, Religion and Biomedical AIDS Treatments in South Africa." In *Religion and AIDS Treatment in Africa: Saving Souls, Prolonging Lives*, edited by Rijk van Dijk, Hansjörg Dilger, Marian Burchardt, and Thera Rasing, 49–71. London: Ashgate.

Burchardt, Marian. 2015. *Faith in the Time of AIDS: Religion, Biopolitics and Modernity in South Africa*. Basingstoke: Palgrave Macmillan.

Burchardt, Marian, and Irene Becci. 2013. "Introduction: Religion Takes Place: Producing Urban Locality." In *Topographies of Faith: Religion in Urban Spaces*, edited by Irene Becci, Marian Burchardt, and José Casanova, 1–24. Leiden: Brill.

Burchardt, Marian, and Stefan Höhne. 2015. "The Infrastructures of Diversity: Materiality and Culture in Urban Space—an Introduction." *New Diversities* 17 (2): 1–13.

Burchardt, Marian, Monika Wohlrab-Sahr, and Ute Wegert. 2013. "'Multiple Secularities': Postcolonial Variations and Guiding Ideas in India and South Africa." *International Sociology* 28 (6): 612–628.

Burke, Jason, and Caty Enders. 2016. "Rev. Maramire vs. Robert Mugabe." *The Guardian*, July 11, 2016, accessed July 11, 2016. www.theguardian.com/world/2016/jul/11/zimbabwe-thisflag-protests-leader-calls-for-international-support.

Burke, Timothy. 1996. *Lifebuoy Men, Lux Women: Commodification, Consumption, and Cleanliness in Modern Zimbabwe*. London: Leicester University Press.

Burton, William F. P. 1961. "Luba Religion and Magic in Custom and Belief." *Annales du Musée Royal de l'Afrique Centrale, Sciences Humaines* 8 (35). Tervuren: Musée Royal de l'Afrique Centrale.

Buthali, Dabilani. 2003. "Methodological Aspects of Census, Quality Control Measures and Outcome." In *2001 Population and Housing Census Dissemination Seminar*, edited by Central Statistical Office, 40–56. Gaborone: Department of Printing and Publishing Services.

Butler, Judith. 2004. *Precarious Life: The Powers of Mourning and Violence*. London: Verso.

Butticci, Annalisa. 2013. "Crazy World, Crazy Faith! Prayer, Power and Transformation in a Nigerian Prayer City." In *Annual Review of the Sociology of Religion*. Vol. 4, *Prayer in Religion and Spirituality*, edited by Giuseppe Giordan and Linda Woodhead, 243–261. Leiden: Brill.

Cabrita, Joel. 2014. *Text and Authority in the South African Nazaretha Church*. London: International African Institute; Cambridge: Cambridge University Press.

Campbell, Colin. 1972. "The Cult, the Cultic Milieu and Secularisation." In *A Sociological Yearbook of Religion in Britain* 5, edited by Michael Hill, 119–136. London: SCM Press.

Carpenter, Robert T. 2004. "The Mainstreaming of Alternative Spirituality in Brazil." In *New Religious Movements in the Twenty-First Century: Legal, Political, and Social Challenges in Global Perspective*, edited by Phillip C. Lucas and Thomas Robbins, 213–282. New York: Routledge.

Cazarin, Rafael, and Mar Griera. 2018. "Born a Pastor, Being a Woman: Biographical Accounts on Gendered Religious Gifts in the Diaspora." *Culture and Religion* 19 (4): 451–70. doi:10.1080/14755610.2018.1534749.

Census Office. 2011. *2011 Population and Housing Census*. Gaborone: Government Printer.

Central Statistical Office. 2001. *2001 Population and Housing Census*. Gaborone: Government Printer.

Charlton, Sarah. 2014. "Public Housing in Johannesburg." In *Changing Space, Changing City: Johannesburg after Apartheid*, edited by Philip Harrison, Graeme Gotz, Alison Todes, and Chris Wray, 176–193. Johannesburg: Wits University Press.

Chinyowa, Kennedy. 2001. "The Context, Performance and Meaning of Shona Ritual Drama." In *Pre-colonial and Post-colonial Drama and Theatre in Africa*, edited by Losambe Lokangaka and Devi Sarinjeive, 3–13. Cape Town: New Africa Books.

Chiswick, Carmel U. 2008. *Economics of American Judaism*. New York: Routledge.

City of Cape Town. 2009. *Crime in Cape Town 2001–2008: A Brief Analysis of Reported Violent, Property and Drug Related Crime in Cape Town*. Cape Town: Strategic Development Information and GIS Department.

Clifford, James. 1997. "Diasporas." In *The Ethnicity Reader: Nationalism, Multiculturalism and Migration*, edited by Montserrat Guibernau and John Rex, 283–290. Oxford: Polity Press.

Cohen, Abner. 1981. *The Politics of Elite Culture: Explorations in the Dramaturgy of Power in a Modern African Society*. Berkeley: University of California Press.

Cole, Jennifer, and Christian Groes, eds. 2016. *Affective Circuits: African Migrations to Europe and the Pursuit of Social Regeneration*. Chicago: University of Chicago Press.

Coleman, Simon, and Rosalind I. J. Hackett, eds. 2015. *The Anthropology of*

Global Pentecostalism and Evangelicalism. New York: New York University Press.

Comaroff, Jean. 1985. *Body of Power, Spirit of Resistance: The Culture and History of a South African People*. Chicago: University of Chicago Press.

Comaroff, Jean. 2007. "Beyond Bare Life: AIDS, (Bio)Politics, and the Neoliberal Order." *Public Culture* 19 (1): 197–219. doi:10.1215/08992363-2006-030.

Comaroff, Jean. 2012. "Religion, Society, Theory." *Religion and Society: Advances in Research* 3 (1) : 5–34.

Comaroff, Jean, and John L. Comaroff. 1987. "The Madman and the Migrant: Work and Labor in the Historical Consciousness of a South African People." *American Ethnologist* 14 (2): 191–209.

Comaroff, Jean, and John L. Comaroff. 1991. *Of Revelation and Revolution*. Vol. 1, *Christianity, Colonialism, and Consciousness in South Africa*. Chicago: University of Chicago Press.

Comaroff, Jean, and John L. Comaroff. 2012. *Theory from the South, or, How Euro-America Is Evolving toward Africa*. Boulder, CO: Paradigm Publishers.

Corrigan, John. 2004. *Emotion and Religion: Approaches and Interpretation*. Oxford: Oxford University Press.

Corrigan, John, ed. 2008. *The Oxford Handbook of Religion and Emotion*. Oxford: Oxford University Press.

Crapanzano, Vincent. 2014. "Must We Be Bad Epistemologists? Illusions of Transparency, the Opaque Other, and Interpretive Foible." In *The Ground Between: Anthropologists Engage Philosophy*, edited by Veena Das, Michael Jackson, Arthur Kleinman, and Bhrigupati Singh, 254–278. Durham, NC: Duke University Press.

Csordas, Thomas J. 1990. "Embodiment as a Paradigm for Anthropology." *Ethos* 18 (1): 5–47.

Csordas, Thomas J. 1994a. *Embodiment and Experience: The Existential Ground of Culture and Self*. Cambridge: Cambridge University Press.

Csordas, Thomas J. 1994b. *The Sacred Self: A Cultural Phenomenology of Charismatic Healing*. Berkeley: University of California Press.

Csordas, Thomas J. 2002. *Body, Meaning, Healing*. New York: Palgrave Macmillan.

Dahl, Bianca. 2009. "The 'Failures of Culture': Christianity, Kinship, and Moral Discourse about Orphans during Botswana's AIDS Crisis." Special issue, *Africa Today* 56 (1): 23–43.

Dahl, Bianca. 2010. *Left Behind? Orphaned Children, Humanitarian Aid, and the Politics of Kinship, Culture, and Caregiving during Botswana's AIDS Crisis*. Chicago: University of Chicago Press.

Dale, B. Martin. 1995. *The Corinthian Body*. New Haven, CT: Yale University Press.

Daneel, Martinus. 1970a. *God of the Matopo Hills: An Essay on the Mwari Cult in Rhodesia*. The Hague: Mouton.

Daneel, Martinus. 1970b. *Zionism and Faith Healing in Rhodesia: Aspects of African Independent Churches.* The Hague: Mouton.

Daneel, Martinus. 1998. *African Earthkeepers: Interfaith Mission in Earth-Care.* Pretoria: University of South Africa Press, 1998. Republished in 2001 under the title *African Earthkeepers: Holistic Interfaith Mission.* Maryknoll, NY: Orbis Books.

Das, Veena. 1984. "For a Folk-Theology and Theological Anthropology of Islam." *Contributions to Indian Sociology* 18 (2): 293–300.

Das, Veena. 2007. *Life and Words: Violence and the Descent into the Ordinary.* Berkeley: University of California Press.

Daswani, Girish. 2011. "(In-)Dividual Pentecostals in Ghana." *Journal of Religion in Africa* 41 (3): 256–279.

Daswani, Girish. 2013. "On Christianity and Ethics: Rupture as Ethical Practice in Ghanaian Pentecostalism." *American Ethnologist* 40 (3): 467–479.

Daswani, Girish. 2015. *Looking Back, Moving Forward: Transformation and Ethical Practice in the Ghanaian Church of Pentecost.* Toronto: University of Toronto Press.

Davies, James. 2010. "Introduction. Emotions in the Field." In *Emotions in the Field: Psychology and Anthropology of Fieldwork Experience*, edited by James Davies and Dimitrina Spencer, 1–31. Stanford, CA: Stanford University Press.

Davis, Mike. 2006. *Planet of Slums.* London: Verso.

Debevec, Liza. 2012. "Postponing Piety in Urban Burkina Faso: Discussing Ideas on When to Start Acting as Pious Muslims." In *Ordinary Lives and Grand Schemes: An Anthropology of Everyday Religion*, edited by Samuli Schielke and Liza Debevec, 33–47. New York: Berghahn Books.

De Boeck, Filip, with photographer Marie-Françoise Plissart. 2004. *Kinshasa: Tales of the Invisible City.* Ghent-Amsterdam: Ludion.

De Boeck, Filip. 2007. "Death, the Occult and the City: Towards a Shadowgraphy of Urban Life in Central Africa." Presented at the Research Seminar on Anthropological Theory, Department of Anthropology, London School of Ecocnomics, March 8, 2007.

De Boeck, Filip. 2009. "At Risk, as Risk: Abandonment and Care in a World of Spiritual Insecurity." In *The Devil's Children: From Spirit Possession to Witchcraft: New Allegations That Affect Children*, edited by Jean S. La Fontaine, 129–150. Farnham, UK: Ashgate.

De Boeck, Filip. 2012. "Infrastructure: Commentary from Filip De Boeck. Contributions from Urban Africa towards an Anthropology of Infrastructure." *Cultural Anthropology Online*, November 26, 2012. www.culanth.org/curated_collections/11-infrastructure/discussions/7-infrastructure-commentary-from-filip-de-boeck.

De Boeck, Filip. 2013. "The Sacred and the City: Modernity, Religion, and the Urban Form in Central Africa." In *A Companion to the Anthropology of*

Religion, edited by Janice Boddy and Michael Lambek, 528–548. Oxford: Wiley.

De Boeck, Filip. 2015. "'Divining' the City: Rhythm, Amalgamation and Knotting as Forms of 'Urbanity.'" *Social Dynamics* 41 (1): 47–58.

De Boeck, Filip, and Sammy Baloji. 2016. *Suturing the City: Living Together in Congo's Urban Worlds*. London: Autograph ABP.

Debord, Guy. 1967. *Society of the Spectacle*. New York: Black and Red.

de Bruijn, Mirjam, and Rijk van Dijk, eds. 2012. *The Social Life of Connectivity in Africa*. New York: Palgrave Macmillan.

de Certeau, Michel. 1987. *La Faiblesse de Croire*. Paris: Éditions du Seuil.

De Craemer, Willy, Renée C. Fox, and Jan Vansina. 1976. "Religious Movements in Central Africa: A Theoretical Study." *Comparative Studies in Society and History* 18 (4): 458–475.

Deleuze, Gilles. 1990. *Expressionism in Philosophy: Spinoza*. Translated by M. Joughin. New York: Zone Books.

Deleuze, Gilles, and Félix Guattari. 1994. *What Is Philosophy?* New York: Columbia University Press.

Demart, Sarah. 2008. "Le 'combat pour l'intégration' des églises issues du Réveil congolais (RDC)." *Revue Européenne des Migrations Internationales* 24 (3): 147–165.

Demographia. 2015. *World Urban Areas: Built Up Urban Areas or World Agglomerations*. 11th annual edition.

Denzin, Norman. 1984. *On Understanding Emotion*. San Francisco: Jossey-Bass.

Desjarlais, Robert, and Jason C. Throop. 2011. "Phenomenological Approaches in Anthropology." *Annual Review of Anthropology* 40: 87–102.

Devisch, Renaat. 1996. "'Pillaging Jesus': Healing Churches and the Villagisation of Kinshasa." *Africa: Journal of the International African Institute* 66 (4): 555–586.

de Witte, Marleen. 2008. "Accra's Sounds and Sacred Spaces." *International Journal of Urban and Regional Research* 32 (2): 690–709.

de Witte, Marleen. 2011. "Touched by the Spirit: Converting the Senses in a Ghanaian Charismatic Church." *Ethnos* 76 (4): 489–509.

de Witte, Marleen. 2012. "Television and the Gospel of Entertainment in Ghana." *Exchange* 41 (2): 144–164.

de Witte, Marleen. 2015. "The Spectacular and the Spirits: Charismatics and Neo-traditionalists on Ghanaian Television." *Material Religion* 1 (3): 314–334. doi:10.2752/174322005778054050.

Dilger, Hansjörg. 2007. "Healing the Wounds of Modernity: Salvation, Community and Care in a Neo-Pentecostal Church in Dar es Salaam, Tanzania." *Journal of Religion in Africa* 37 (1): 59–83.

Dilger, Hansjörg. 2012. "Targeting the Empowered Individual: Transnational Policy-Making, the Global Economy of Aid, and the Limitations of Biopower in Tanzania." In *Medicine, Mobility, and Power in Global Africa: Transnational Health and Healing*, edited by Hansjörg Dilger, Abdoulaye

Kane, and Stacey A. Langwick, 60–91. Bloomington: Indiana University Press.

Dilger, Hansjörg. 2014. "Claiming Territory: Medical Mission, Interreligious Revivalism, and the Spatialization of Health Interventions in Urban Tanzania." *Medical Anthropology* 33 (1): 52–67.

Dilger, Hansjörg. 2017. "Embodying Values and Socio-religious Difference: New Markets of Moral Learning in Christian and Muslim Schools in Urban Tanzania." *Africa* 87 (3): 513–536. doi:10.1017/s0001972017000092.

Dilger, Hansjörg, Marian Burchardt, and Rijk van Dijk, eds. 2010. "Introduction – The Redemptive Moment: HIV Treatments and the Production of New Religious Spaces." Special issue, *African Journal of AIDS Research* 9 (4): 373–383.

Dilger, Hansjörg, Abdoulaye Kane, and Stacey A. Langwick, eds. 2012. *Medicine, Mobility, and Power in Global Africa: Transnational Health and Healing.* Bloomington: Indiana University Press.

Dilger, Hansjörg, and Dorothea Schulz. 2013. "Politics of Religious Schooling: Christian and Muslim Engagements with Education in Africa." Special issue, *Journal of Religion in Africa* 43 (4): 365–378.

Dilger, Hansjörg, Omar Kasmani, and Dominik Mattes. 2018. "Spatialities of Belonging: Affective Place-Making among Diasporic Neo-Pentecostal and Sufi Groups in Berlin's Cityscape." In *Affect in Relation: Essays on Affectivity and Subject Formation in the 21st Century*, edited by Birgitt Röttger-Rössler and Jan Slaby, 93–114. London: Routledge.

Dillon-Malone, Clive. 1978. *The Korsten Basketmakers: A Study of the Masowe Apostles, an Indigenous African Religious Movement.* Manchester: Manchester University Press.

Douglas, Mary. 1966. *Purity and Danger: An Analysis of Concepts of Pollution and Taboo.* New York: Routledge and Kegan Paul.

Dryden-Peterson, Sarah. 2006. "'I Find Myself as Someone Who Is in the Forest': Urban Refugees as Agents of Social Change in Kampala, Uganda." *Journal of Refugee Studies* 19 (3): 381–395.

Dumbe, Yunus. 2013. *Islamic Revivalism in Contemporary Ghana.* Huddinge, Sweden: Södertörns Högskola.

Duranti, Alessandro. 2010. "Husserl, Intersubjectivity and Anthropology." *Anthropological Theory* 10 (1–2): 16–35.

Durkheim, Émile. 1912. *The Elementary Forms of the Religious Life.* New York: Courier Dover Publications.

Durkheim, Émile. (1912) 2007. *Les formes élémentaires de la vie religieuse.* Paris: CNRS Éditions.

Eade, John. 2012. "Religion, Home Making and Migration across a Globalising City: Responding to Mobility in London." *Culture and Religion* 13 (4): 469–483.

Eliade, Mircea. 1959. *The Sacred and the Profane: The Nature of Religion.* New York: Harvest Books.

Ellison, C. G., and J. S. Levin. 1998. "The Religion-Health Connection: Evidence, Theory, and Future Directions." *Health Education & Behavior: The Official Publication of the Society for Public Health Education* 25 (6): 700–720.

Engelke, Matthew. 2002. "The Problem of Belief: Evans-Pritchard and Victor Turner on 'the Inner Life.'" *Anthropology Today* 18 (6): 3–8.

Engelke, Matthew. 2007. *A Problem of Presence: Beyond Scripture in an African Christian Church.* Berkeley: University of California Press.

Engelke, Matthew. 2010. "Past Pentecostalism: Notes on Rupture, Realignment, and Everyday Life in Pentecostal and African Independent Churches." *Africa* 80 (2): 177–199.

Englund, Harri. 2002. "Ethnography after Globalism: Migration and Emplacement in Malawi." *American Ethnologist* 29 (2): 261–286.

Escribano, Antonio Izquierdo, and Belén Fernández Suárez. 2006. "Panorama de la inmigración en España: Al alba del siglo XXI." In *Mediterráneo Económico: Procesos migratorios, economía y personas*, edited by Manuel Pimentel, 444–466. Almería: Instituto de Estudios de Cajamar.

Evans-Pritchard, Edward E. 1965. *Theories of Primitive Religion.* Oxford: Oxford University Press.

Fábos, Anita, and Gaim Kibreab. 2007. "Urban Refugees: Introduction." *Refuge: Canada's Journal on Refugees* 24 (1): 1–19.

Fanon, Frantz. 1961. "Colonial War and Mental Disorders." In *The Wretched of the Earth*, 181–291. New York: Grove Press.

Farías, Ignacio. 2011. "The Politics of Urban Assemblages." *City* 15 (3–4): 365–374.

Farnell, Brenda. 2000. "Getting Out of the Habitus: An Alternative Model of Dynamically Embodied Social Action." *Journal of the Royal Anthropological Institute* 6 (3): 397–418.

Farneth, Molly, Rachel Gross, and Schnable Youatt. 2009. "New Directions in the Study of Prayer: Scientific, Social Scientific, Ethnographic, and Theoretical Perspectives." Working Paper, Center for the Study of Religion, Princeton University.

Fassin, Didier. 2007. *When Bodies Remember: Experiences and Politics of AIDS in South Africa.* Berkeley: University of California Press.

Fassin, Didier. 2013. "On Resentment and *Ressentiment*: The Politics and Ethics of Moral Emotions." *Current Anthropology* 54 (3): 249–267.

Fassin, Didier, Matthew Wilhelm-Solomon, and Aurelia Segatti. 2017. "Asylum as a Form of Life: The Politics and Experience of Indeterminacy in South Africa." *Current Anthropology* 58 (2): 160–187.

Faubion, James D. 2009. "The Ethics of Fieldwork as an Ethics of Connectivity, or the Good Anthropologist (Isn't What She Used to Be)." In *Fieldwork Is Not What It Used to Be: Learning Anthropology's Method in a Time of Transition*, edited by James D. Faubion and George E. Marcus, 145–166. Ithaca, NY: Cornell University Press.

Favret-Saada, Jeanne. 1977. *Les mots, la mort, les sorts.* Paris: Gallimard.

Fiddian-Qasmiyeh, Elena. 2011. "Introduction: Faith-Based Humanitarianism in Contexts of Forced Displacement." *Journal of Refugee Studies* 24 (3): 429–439.

Fontein, Joost. 2015. *Remaking Mutirikwi: Landscape, Water and Belonging in Southern Zimbabwe*. Martlesham: Boydell and Brewer.

Förster, Till. 2016. "Envisioning the City in Africa: Anthropology, Creativity and Urban Culture." In *The Palgrave Handbook of Creativity and Culture Research*, edited by V. Glăveanu, 449–471. London: Palgrave Macmillan.

Fortes, Meyer. 1975. "Strangers." In *Studies in African Social Anthropology*, edited by Meyer Fortes and Sheila Patterson, 229–253. London: Academic Press.

Foucault, Michel. (1967) 1984. "Of Other Spaces: Utopias and Heterotopias." *Architecture/Mouvement/Continuité*, October 1984, 1–9.

Fowler, Chris. 2004. *The Archaeology of Personhood: An Anthropological Approach*. New York: Routledge.

Frahm-Arp, Maria. 2012. "Singleness, Sexuality, and the Dream of Marriage." *Journal of Religion in Africa* 42 (4): 369–383.

Freeman, Carla. 2012. "Neoliberal Respectability: Entrepreneurial Marriage, Affective Labour, and the New Caribbean Middle Class." In *The Global Middle Classes: Theorizing through Ethnography*, edited by Rachel Heiman, Carla Freeman, and Mark Liechty, 85–116. Santa Fe, NM: SAR Press.

Freeman, Dena, ed. 2012. *Pentecostalism and Development: Churches, NGOs and Social Change in Africa*. London: Palgrave Macmillan.

Freund, Bill. 2007. *The African City: A History*. Cambridge: Cambridge University Press.

Friedman, Jonathan. 1994. "The Political Economy of Elegance: An African Cult of Beauty." In *Consumption and Identity*, edited by Jonathan Friedman, 167–188. Chur: Harwood.

Fumanti, Mattia. 2013. "'Showing-Off Aesthetics': Looking Good, Making Relations and Being in the World in the Akan Diaspora in London." *Ethnos: Journal of Social Anthropology* 78 (2): 200–225.

Gade, Anna M. 2008. "Islam." In *The Oxford Handbook of Religion and Emotion*, edited by John Corrigan, 35–50. Oxford: Oxford University Press.

Galdos Urrutia, Rosario. 1985. "El declinar de la inmigracion y el crecimiento de la migracion interior en el País Vasco: 1971–1981." *Lurralde: Investigación y espacio*, no. 8: 183–188.

Garbin, David. 2013. "The Visibility and Invisibility of Migrant Faith in the City: Diaspora Religion and the Politics of Emplacement of Afro-Christian Churches." *Journal of Ethnic and Migration Studies* 39 (15): 677–696.

Gauntlett, David. 2011. *Making Is Connecting: The Social Meaning of Creativity, from DIY and Knitting to YouTube and Web 2.0*. Cambridge: Polity Press.

Geertz, Clifford. 1960. *The Religion of Java*. Chicago: University of Chicago Press.

Geertz, Clifford. 1973. "Religion as a Cultural System." In *The Interpretation of Cultures: Selected Essays*, 87–125. New York: Basic Books.

Gellner, Ernest. 1981. *Muslim Society*. Cambridge: Cambridge University Press.

Gemmeke, Amber B. 2008. "Marabout Women in Dakar: Creating Trust in a Rural Urban Space." Wien: Lit Verlag.

Gemmeke, Amber B. 2009. "Marabout Women in Dakar: Creating Authority in Islamic Knowledge." *Africa* 79 (1): 128–147.

Genette, Gérard. (1972) 1980. *Narrative Discourse: An Essay in Method*. Ithaca, NY: Cornell University Press.

Gennep, Arnold van. (1909) 1960. *The Rites of Passage*. London: Routledge.

Giddens, Anthony. 1992. *The Transformation of Intimacy in Modern Societies*. Cambridge: Polity Press.

Giddens, Anthony. 2004. *Modernity and Self-Identity: Self and Society in the Late Modern Age*. Cambridge: Polity Press.

Gifford, Paul. 1990. "Prosperity: A New and Foreign Element in African Christianity." *Religion* 20 (4): 373–388.

Gifford, Paul. 2004. *Ghana's New Christianity: Pentecostalism in a Globalizing African Economy*. Bloomington: Indiana University Press.

Glaser, Clive. 2000. *Bo-Tsotsi: The Youth Gangs of Soweto, 1935–1976*. Oxford: James Currey.

Glick Schiller, Nina, and Ayşe Çağlar, eds. 2011. *Locating Migration: Rescaling Cities and Migrants*. Ithaca, NY: Cornell University Press.

Gluckman, Max. 1972. *The Allocation of Responsibility*. Manchester: Manchester University Press.

Goffman, Erving. 1963. *Stigma*. Englewood Cliffs, NJ: Prentice-Hall.

Gondola, Charles-Didier. 2012. "Kisasa Makambo! Remembering the Future in the Congolese Urban Cauldron." *Perspectives: Journal du Réseau français des Instituts d'études avancées* 7:8–9.

Goodwin, Marc. 2011. "Adorno's Dilemma: On Difficult Writing and Sophistication in Anthropology Today." *Kroeber Anthropological Society Papers* 99/100 (1): 38–63.

Gordillo, Gaston. 2014. *Rubble: The Afterlife of Destruction*. Durham, NC: Duke University Press.

Gottschall, Marilyn. 2004. "Introducing Islam through Qur'anic Recitation." *Academic Exchange Quarterly* 8 (2): 35–39.

Graeber, David. 2001. *Toward an Anthropological Theory of Value: The False Coin of Our Own Dreams*. New York: Palgrave Macmillan.

Gregg, Melissa, and Gregory J. Seigworth. 2010. "An Inventory of Shimmers." In *The Affect Theory Reader*, edited by Gregory J. Seigworth and Melissa Gregg, 1–28. Durham, NC: Duke University Press.

Gusman, Alessandro. 2009. "HIV/AIDS, Pentecostal Churches, and the 'Joseph Generation' in Uganda." Special issue, *Africa Today* 56 (1): 67–86.

Gusman, Alessandro. 2013. "The Abstinence Campaign and the Construction of the Balokole Identity in the Ugandan Pentecostal Movement." *Canadian Journal of African Studies* 47 (2): 273–292.

Gusman, Alessandro. 2016. "Spiriti in diaspora: Rifugio e lotta spirituale nelle chiese pentecostali congolesi di Kampala." *Studi e Materiali di Storia delle Religioni* 82 (1): 17–33.

Gusman, Alessandro. 2018. "Stuck in Kampala: Witchcraft Attacks, 'Blocages', and Immobility in the Experience of Born-Again Congolese Refugees in Uganda." *Cahiers d'études africaines*, nos. 231-232: 793–815.

Hackett, Rosalind. 1989. *Religion in Calabar: The Religious Life and History of a Nigerian Town*. New York: Mouton de Gruyter.

Hall, David D. 1997. *Lived Religion in America: Toward a History of Practice*. Princeton, NJ: Princeton University Press.

Hammar, Amanda, JoAnn McGregor, and Loren Landau. 2010. "Introduction: Displacing Zimbabwe: Crisis and Construction in Southern Africa." Special issue, *Journal of Southern African Studies* 36 (2): 263–283. doi:10.1080 /03057070.2010.485779.

Harrison, Philip. 2014. "Materialities, Subjectivities and Spatial Transformation in Johannesburg." In *Changing Space, Changing City: Johannesburg after Apartheid*, edited by Philip Harrison, Graeme Gotz, Alison Todes, and Chris Wray, 2–39. Johannesburg: Wits University Press.

Harvey, David. 2008. "The Right to the City." *New Left Review* 53: 23–40.

Hasu, Päivi. 2012. "Prosperity Gospels and Enchanted Worldviews: Two Responses to Socio-economic Transformation in Tanzanian Pentecostal Christianity." In *Pentecostalism and Development: Churches, NGOs and Social Change in Africa*, edited by Dena Freeman, 67–86. Basingstoke: Palgrave Macmillan.

Haynes, Naomi. 2012. "Pentecostalism and the Morality of Money: Prosperity, Inequality, and Religious Sociality on the Zambian Copperbelt." *Journal of the Royal Anthropological Institute* 18 (1): 124–139.

Haynes, Naomi. 2014. "Affordances and Audiences: On the Difference Christianity Makes." *Current Anthropology* 55 (10): 357–365.

Headley, Stephen C. 2000a. "Afterword: The Mirror in the Mosque . . ." In *Islamic Prayer across the Indian Ocean: Inside and Outside the Mosque*, edited by David Parkin and Stephen C. Headley, 213–239. Richmond, UK: Curzon.

Headley, Stephen C. 2000b. "Sembah/Salat: The Javanisation of Islamic Prayer; the Islamisation of Javanese Prayer." In *Islamic Prayer across the Indian Ocean: Inside and Outside the Mosque*, edited by David Parkin and Stephen C. Headley, 169–212. Richmond, UK: Curzon.

Heald, Suzette. 2006. "Abstain or Die: The Development of AIDS Policy in Botswana." *Journal of Biosocial Science* 38 (1): 29–41.

Heiler, Friedrich. (1919) 1923. *Das Gebet: Eine religionsgeschichtliche und religionspsychologische Untersuchung*. Munich: Ernst Reinhardt Verlag.

Heiman, Rachel, Carla Freeman, and Mark Liechty, eds. 2012. *The Global Middle Classes: Theorizing through Ethnography*. Santa Fe, NM: SAR Press.

Henkel, Heiko. 2005. "Between Belief and Unbelief Lies the Performance of Salāt: Meaning and Efficacy of a Muslim Ritual." *Journal of the Royal Anthropological Institute* 11 (3): 487–507.

Herbrik, Regine, and Hubert Knoblauch. 2014. "Die Emotionalisierung der Religion." In *Sprachen der Emotion: Kultur, Kunst, Gesellschaft*, edited by Gunter Gebauer and Markus Edler, 192–210. Frankfurt am Main: Campus.

Hervieu-Léger, Danièle. 2002. "Space and Religion: New Approaches to Religious Spatiality in Modernity." *International Journal of Urban and Regional Research* 26 (1): 99–105.

Hirschkind, Charles. 2001. "The Ethics of Listening: Cassette-Sermon Audition in Contemporary Egypt." *American Ethnologist* 28 (3): 623–649. doi:10.1525/ae.2001.28.3.623.

Hirschkind, Charles. 2006. *The Ethical Soundscape: Cassette Sermons and Islamic Counterpublics*. New York: Columbia University Press.

Hochschild, Arlie. 1979. "Emotion Work: Feeling Rules and Social Structure." *American Journal of Sociology* 85 (3): 551–575.

Hollan, Douglas, and Jason C. Throop. 2008. "Whatever Happened to Empathy? Introduction." *Ethos* 36 (4): 385–401.

Holmes, Mary. 2010. "The Emotionalization of Reflexivity." *Sociology* 44 (1): 139–154.

Holmes Katz, Marion. 2013. *Prayer in Islamic Thought and Practice*. Cambridge: Cambridge University Press.

Hornberger, Julia. 2011. *Policing and Human Rights: The Meaning of Violence and Justice in the Everyday Policing of Johannesburg*. New York: Routledge.

Howell, Signe. 2007. *The Kinning of Foreigners: Transnational Adoption in a Global Perspective*. Oxford: Berghahn Books.

Hsu, Elisabeth. 2009. "Chinese Propriety Medicines: An 'Alternative Modernity'? The Case of the Anti-malarial Substance Artemisinin in East Africa." *Medical Anthropology* 28 (2): 111–140.

Hüwelmeier, Gertrud, and Kristine Krause, eds. 2010. *Traveling Spirits: Migrants, Markets and Mobilities*. New York: Routledge.

Iliffe, John. 1998. *East African Doctors: A History of the Modern Profession*. Cambridge: Cambridge University Press.

Illouz, Eva. 1997. *Consuming the Romantic Utopia: Love and the Cultural Contradictions of Capitalism*. Berkeley: University of California Press.

Inglis, Tom, and Susie Donnelly. 2011. "Local and National Belonging in a Globalised World: The Case of Contemporary Ireland." *Irish Journal of Sociology* 19 (2): 127–143.

Ingold, Tim. 2000. *The Perception of the Environment: Essays on Livelihood, Dwelling and Skill*. New York: Routledge.

Ingstad, Benedicte. 1994. "The Grandmother and Household Viability in Botswana." In *Gender, Work and Population in Sub-Saharan Africa,* edited by Aderanti Adepoju and Christine Oppong, 209–225. London: James Currey.

Jackson, Michael. 1983. "Knowledge of the Body." *Man* 18 (2): 327–345.

Jackson, Michael. 1996. "Introduction: Phenomenology, Radical Empiricism, and Anthropological Critique." In *Things as They Are: New Directions in Phenomenological Anthropology,* edited by Michael Jackson, 1–50. Bloomington: Indiana University Press.

Jackson, Michael. 1998. *Minima Ethnographica: Intersubjectivity and the Anthropological Project.* Chicago: University of Chicago Press.

Jackson, Michael. 2011. *Life within Limits: Well-Being in a World of Want.* Durham, NC: Duke University Press.

Jackson, Michael. 2012. *Lifeworlds: Essays in Existential Anthropology.* Chicago: University of Chicago Press.

Jacobson-Widding, Anita. 1989. "Notions of Heat and Fever among the Manyika of Zimbabwe." In *Culture, Experience and Pluralism: Essays on African Ideas of Illness and Healing,* edited by Anita Jacobson-Widding and David Westerlund, 27–44. Stockholm: Almqvist and Wiksell.

James, Paul. 2013. "Managing Metropolises by Negotiating Mega-Urban Growth." In *Institution and Social Innovation for Sustainable Urban Development,* edited by Harald Mieg and Klaus Töpfer, 217–232. New York: Routledge.

James, William. 2013. *The Principles of Psychology.* Redditch: Read Books.

Janson, Marloes, and Akintunde Akinleye. 2014. *The Spiritual Highway: Religious World Making in Megacity Lagos.* London: School of Oriental and African Studies, University of London.

Janson, Marloes, and Birgit Meyer. 2016. "Introduction: Towards a Framework for the Study of Christian-Muslim Encounters in Africa." *Africa* 86 (4): 615–619.

Jeater, Diana. 1993. *Marriage, Perversion, and Power: The Construction of Moral Discourse in Southern Rhodesia 1894–1930.* Oxford: Clarendon Press.

Jeater, Diana. 2007. *Law, Language, and Science: The Invention of the "Native Mind" in Southern Rhodesia, 1890–1930.* Portsmouth, NH: Heinemann.

Jenkins, Philip. 2011. *The Next Christendom: The Coming of Global Christianity.* 3rd ed. New York: Oxford University Press.

Jennings, Mark. 2015. "An Extraordinary Degree of Exaltation: Durkheim, Effervescence and Pentecostalism's Defeat of Secularisation." *Social Compass* 62 (1): 61–75.

Jensen, Steffen. 2008. *Gangs, Politics and Dignity in Cape Town.* Chicago: University of Chicago Press.

Jiménez Ramírez, Alfredo. 1981. *Llamamiento de Dios al Pueblo Gitano.* Jerez de la Frontera: Talleres Gráficos de Anfra.

Johnstone, Gerry, and Daniel Van Ness. 2007. "The Meaning of Restorative Justice." In *Handbook of Restorative Justice*, edited by Gerry Johnstone and Daniel Van Ness, 5–23. Portland, OR: Willan Publishing.

Jones, Carla. 2012. "Women in the Middle: Femininity, Virtues, and Excess in Indonesian Discourses of Middle Classness." In *The Global Middle Classes: Theorizing through Ethnography*, edited by Rachel Heiman, Carla Freeman, and Mark Liechty, 145–169. Santa Fe, NM: SAR Press.

Kalu, Ogbu. 2008. *African Pentecostalism: An Introduction*. Oxford: Oxford University Press.

Kanji, Aazneen. 1995. "Gender, Poverty and Economic Adjustment in Harare, Zimbabwe." *Environment and Urbanization* 7 (1): 37–56.

Kant, Immanuel. (1793) 2003. *Die Religion innerhalb der Grenzen der bloßen Vernunft*. Edited by Bettina Stangneth. Hamburg: Meiner.

Kanungo, N. Rabindra. 1982. *Work Alienation: An Integrative Approach*. New York: Praeger.

Kapferer, Bruce. 2004. "Ritual Dynamics and Virtual Practice: Beyond Representation and Meaning." In *Ritual in Its Own Right: Exploring the Dynamics of Transformation*, edited by Don Handelman and Galina Lindquist, 35–54. Oxford: Berghahn Books.

Katsaura, Obvious. 2016. "Enchanted Suburbanisms: Fantasy, Fear and Suburbia in Johannesburg." In *Routes and Rites to City: Mobility, Diversity and Religious Space in Johannesburg*, edited by Matthew Wilhelm-Solomon, Lorena Núñez, Peter K. Bukasa, and Bettina Malcomess, 163–189. Hampshire: Palgrave Macmillan.

Katz, Cindi. 2012. "Just Managing: American Middle-Class Parenthood in Insecure Times." In *The Global Middle Classes: Theorizing through Ethnography*, edited by Rachel Heiman, Carla Freeman, and Mark Liechty, 169–188. Santa Fe, NM: SAR Press.

Keane, Webb. 2003. "Semiotics and the Social Analysis of Material Things." *Language and Communication* 23 (3): 409–425.

Kgathi, Gositse L., Reofilwe Rio Saganabeng, and Tebogo E. Seretse. 2006. *Exploring Moral Issues, Form 2*. Cape Town: Heinemann Botswana.

Kihato, Caroline W. 2013. *Migrant Women of Johannesburg: Everyday Life in an In-Between City*. New York: Palgrave Macmillan.

Kirsch, Thomas. 2008a. "Religious Logistics: African Christians, Spirituality and Transportation." In *On the Margins of Religion*, edited by João de Pina-Cabral and Frances Pine, 61–80. Oxford: Berghahn Books.

Kirsch, Thomas. 2008b. *Spirits and Letters: Reading, Writing and Charisma in African Christianity*. Oxford: Berghahn Books.

Klaeger, Gabriel. 2009. "Religion on the Road: The Spiritual Experience of Road Travel in Ghana." In *The Speed of Change: Motor Vehicles and People in Africa, 1890–2000*, edited by Jan-Bart Gewald, Sabine Luning, and Klaas vam Walravenn, 212–232. Leiden: Brill.

Klaits, Frederick. 2010. *Death in a Church of Life: Moral Passion during Bots-wana's Time of AIDS*. Berkeley: University of California Press.

Knibbe, Kim, and Peter Versteeg. 2008. "Assessing Phenomenology in An-thropology: Lessons from the Study of Religion and Experience." *Critique of Anthropology* 28 (1): 47–62.

Knowles, Caroline. 2013. "Nigerian London: Re-mapping Space and Ethnic-ity in Superdiverse Cities." *Ethnic and Racial Studies* 36 (4): 651–669.

Knudsen, T. Britta, and Carsten Stage. 2014. *Global Media, Biopolitics, and Af-fect: Politicizing Bodily Vulnerability*. New York: Routledge.

Knudson-Cooper, Mary S. 1981. "Adjustment to Visible Stigma: The Case of the Severely Burned." *Social Science and Medicine. Part B: Medical Anthro-pology* 15 (1): 31–44.

Kobo, Ousman. 2009. "The Development of Wahhabi Reforms in Ghana and Burkina Faso, 1960–1990: Elective Affinities between Western-Educated Muslims and Islamic Scholars." *Comparative Studies in Society and History* 51 (3): 502–532.

Koić, Elvira, Pavo Filaković, Sanea Nađ, and Ivan Čelić. 2005. "Glossolalia." *Collegium Antropologicum* 29 (1): 307–313.

Kopytoff, Igor. 1971. "Ancestors as Elders." *Africa: Journal of the International African Institute* 41 (2): 129–142.

Krause, Kristine. 2014. "Pharmaceutical Potentials: Praying over Medicines in Pentecostal Healing." *Ghana Studies* 15–16: 223–250.

Kreibaum, Merle. 2016. "Their Suffering, Our Burden? How Congolese Refu-gees Affect the Ugandan Population." *World Development* 78: 262–287.

Lambek, Michael. 1990. "Certain Knowledge, Contestable Authority: Power and Practice on the Islamic Periphery." *American Ethnologist* 17 (1): 23–40.

Lambek, Michael. 2000a. "The Anthropology of Religion and the Quarrel between Poetry and Philosophy." *Current Anthropology* 41 (3): 309–320.

Lambek, Michael. 2000b. "Localising Islamic Performance in Mayotte." In *Islamic Prayer across the Indian Ocean: Inside and Outside the Mosque*, edited by David Parkin and Stephen C. Headley, 63–98. Richmond, UK: Curzon.

Lambek, Michael. 2012. "Facing Religion, from Anthropology." *Anthropology of This Century*, no. 4 (May). http://aotcpress.com/articles/facing-religion -anthropology/.

Lambertz, Peter. 2018. *Seekers and Things. Spiritual Movements and Aesthetic Difference in Kinshasa*. Oxford: Berghahn.

Landau, Loren. 2009. "Living within and beyond Johannesburg: Exclusion, Religion, and Emerging Forms of Being." *African Studies* 68 (2): 197–214.

Landau, Loren. 2010. "Loving the Alien? Citizenship, Law, and the Future in South Africa's Demonic Society." *African Affairs* 109 (435): 213–230.

Landau, Loren, and Veronique Gindrey. 2008. "Migration and Population Trends in Gauteng Province 1996–2055." Forced Migration Studies Pro-gramme Working Paper, Wits University, Johannesburg. Accessed June 5,

2019. http://urbanlandmark.org.za/newsletter/issue/0403/download/42
_LandauGindrey.pdf.

Lange, Isabelle. 2016. "To Heal the Body: The Body as Congregation among
Post-surgical Patients in Benin." In *Cosmos, Gods and Madmen: Frameworks
in the Anthropologies of Medicine*, edited by Roland Littlewood and Rebecca
Lynch, 93–115. Oxford: Berghahn Books.

Lanternari, Vittorio. 1983. *L'incivilimento dei barbari: Problemi di etnocentrismo
e d'identità*. Bari: Dedalo.

Lanz, Stephan. 2013. "Assembling Global Prayers in the City. An Attempt to
Repopulate Urban Theory with Religion." In *Global Prayers: Contemporary
Manifestations of the Religious in the City*, edited by Jochen Becker, Katrin
Klingan, Stephan Lanz, and Kathrin Wildner, 16–47. Zurich: Lars Müller
Publishers.

Larkin, Brian. 2004. "Degraded Images, Distorted Sounds: Nigerian Video
and the Infrastructure of Piracy." *Public Culture* 16 (4): 289–314.

Larkin, Brian. 2013. "The Politics and Poetics of Infrastructure." *Annual Review of Anthropology* 42:327–343.

Larkin, Brian, and Birgit Meyer. 2006. "Pentecostalism, Islam, and Culture:
New Religious Movements in West Africa." In *Themes in West Africa's History*, edited by Emmanuel Akyeampong, 286–312. Oxford: James Currey.

Last, Murray. 2011. "Another Geography: Risks to Health as Perceived in a
Deep-Rural Environment in Hausaland." *Anthropology and Medicine* 18 (2):
217–229.

Launay, Robert. (1992) 2004. *Beyond the Stream: Islam and Society in a West African Town*. Long Grove, IL: Waveland Press.

Lauterbach, Karen. 2014. "Religion and Displacement in Africa: Compassion
and Sacrifice in Congolese Churches in Kampala, Uganda." *Religion and
Theology* 21 (3–4): 290–308.

Leary, Michael E, and John McCarthy. 2013. "Introduction: Urban Regeneration, a Global Phenomenon," In *The Routledge Companion to Urban Regeneration*, edited by Michael E. Leary and John McCarthy, 1–14. Oxford:
Routledge.

Lefebvre, Henri. 1991. *The Production of Space*. Oxford: Blackwell.

Lefebvre, Henri. 1996. *Writings on Cities*. Oxford: Blackwell.

Lewis, Clive Staples. 1960. *The Four Loves*. New York: Harcourt Brace &
Company.

Lim, Chaeyoon, and Robert D. Putnam. 2010. "Religion, Social Networks,
and Life Satisfaction." *American Sociological Review* 75 (6): 914–933.

Little, Kenneth L. 1975. *African Women in Towns: An Aspect of Africa's Social
Revolution*. Cambridge: Cambridge University Press.

Litvak, Joseph. 1997. *Strange Gourmets: Sophistication, Theory, and the Novel*.
Durham, NC: Duke University Press.

Livingston, Julie. 2003. "Pregnant Children and Half-dead Adults: Modern

Living and the Quickening Life-cycle in Botswana." *Bulletin of the History of Medicine* 77 (1): 133–162.

Livingston, Julie. 2005. *Debility and the Moral Imagination in Botswana.* Bloomington: Indiana University Press.

Livingston, Julie. 2009. "Suicide, Risk, and Investment in the Heart of the African Miracle." *Cultural Anthropology* 24 (4): 652–680.

Loimeier, Roman. 1997. *Islamic Reform and Political Change in Nigeria.* Evanston: Northwestern University Press.

Loimeier, Roman. 2014. *Muslim Societies in Africa: A Historical Anthropology.* Bloomington: Indiana University Press.

Louveau, Frédérique. 2012. *Un prophétisme japonais en Afrique de l'Ouest: Anthropologie religieuse de Sukyô Mahikari (Bénin, Côte d'Ivoire, Sénégal, France).* Paris: Karthala.

Lovejoy, Paul. 1980. *Caravans of Kola: The Hausa Kola Trade 1700–1900.* Zaria, Nigeria: Ahmadu Bello University Press.

Löw, Martina. 2001. *Raumsoziologie.* Frankfurt am Main: Suhrkamp.

Luedke, Tracy J., and Harry G. West, eds. 2006. *Boarders and Healers: Brokering Therapeutic Resources in Southeast Africa.* Bloomington: Indiana University Press.

Luhmann, Niklas. 1986. *Love as a Passion: The Codification of Intimacy.* Cambridge, MA: Harvard University Press.

Luhrmann, Tanya. 2004. "Metakinesis: How God Becomes Intimate in Contemporary U.S. Christianity." *American Anthropologist* 106 (3): 518–528.

Lutz, Catherine A., and Lila Abu-Lughod, eds. 1990. *Language and the Politics of Emotion.* Cambridge: Cambridge University Press.

Lutz, Catherine, and Geoffrey M. White. 1986. "The Anthropology of Emotions." *Annual Review of Anthropology* 15: 405–436.

Lyon, Margot L. 1995. "Missing Emotion: The Limitations of Cultural Constructionism in the Study of Emotion." *Cultural Anthropology* 10 (2): 244–263.

MacGaffey, Wyatt. 1983. *Modern Kongo Prophets.* Bloomington: Indiana University Press.

MacGaffey, Wyatt. 1986. *Religion and Society in Central Africa: The baKongo of Lower Zaire.* Chicago: University of Chicago Press.

MacIntyre, Alasdair. (1981) 2007. *After Virtue: A Study in Moral Theory.* 3rd ed. Notre Dame, IN: University of Notre Dame Press.

Mahmood, Saba. 2001. "Rehearsed Spontaneity and the Conventionality of Ritual: Disciplines of 'Salat.'" *American Ethnologist* 28 (4): 827–853.

Mahmood, Saba. (2005) 2012. *Politics of Piety: The Islamic Revival and the Feminist Subject.* Princeton, NJ: Princeton University Press.

Malcomess, Bettina, and Matthew Wilhelm-Solomon. 2016. "Valleys of Salt in the House of God: (Re)territorialising Religion in the City." In *Routes and Rites to the City: Mobility, Diversity and Urban Space in Johannesburg,* edited by Matthew Wilhelm-Solomon, Lorena Núñez Carrasco, Peter K. Bukasa, and Bettina Malcomess, 31–60. Hampshire: Palgrave Macmillan.

Manyoni, Joseph. 1977. "Anthropology and the Study of Schism in Africa: A Re-examination of Some Anthropological Theories." *Cahiers d'études africaines* 17 (68): 599–631.

Marcus, George E., and Michael M. J. Fischer, eds. 1986. *Anthropology as Cultural Critique: An Experimental Moment in the Human Sciences.* Chicago: University of Chicago Press.

Marginson, Simon, Peter Murphy, and Michael Peters, eds. 2010. *Global Creation: Space, Mobility and Synchrony in the Age of the Knowledge Economy.* New York: Peter Lang.

Marshall, Ruth. 2009. *Political Spiritualities: The Pentecostal Revolution in Nigeria.* Chicago: University of Chicago Press.

Martinez, Francisco. 2014. "The Invisible City: Exploring the Third Something of Urban Life." *Culture Unbound* 6 (3): 647–669. doi:10.3384/cu.2000 .1525.146647.

Marzano, Michaela. 2007. *La philosophie du corps.* Paris: Presses Universitaires de France.

Massumi, Brian. 1987. "Notes on the Translation and Acknowledgements." In *A Thousand Plateaus*, edited by Gilles Deleuze and Felix Guattari, xvi–xix. Minneapolis: University of Minnesota Press.

Massumi, Brian. 2002. *Parables for the Virtual: Movement, Affect, Sensation.* Durham, NC: Duke University Press.

Massumi, Brian. 2015. *Politics of Affect.* Cambridge: Polity Press.

Massumi, Brian, and Joel McKim. 2009. "Of Microperception and Micropolitics." *Inflections* 3: 1–20.

Matsuoka, Hideaki. 2007. *Japanese Prayer below the Equator: How Brazilians Believe in the Church of World Messianity.* Lanham, MD: Lexington Books.

Mattes, Dominik, Omar Kasmani, and Hansjörg Dilger. 2019. "'All Eyes Closed': Dis/Sensing in Comparative Fieldwork on Affective-Religious Experiences." In *Analyzing Affective Societies: Methods and Methodologies*, edited by Antje Kahl, 265–278. London: Routledge.

Mauss, Marcel. 1968. *Oeuvres. 1. Les fonctions sociales du sacré.* Paris: Éditions de Minuit.

Mauss, Marcel. (1924) 1990. *The Gift: The Forms and Functions of Exchange in Archaic Societies.* Translated by W. D. Halls. London: Routledge.

Mauss, Marcel. (1934) 2004. "Les techniques du corps." In *Sociologie et Anthropologie*, 363–386. Paris: Quadriga and Presses Universitaires de France.

Maxwell, David. 1998. "'Delivered from the Spirit of Poverty?' Pentecostalism, Prosperity and Modernity in Zimbabwe." *Journal of Religion in Africa* 28 (3): 350–382.

Maxwell, David. 2008. "The Soul of the Luba: W. F. P. Burton, Missionary Ethnography and Belgian Colonial Science." *History and Anthropology* 19 (4): 325–351.

Mbembe, Achille, and Sarah Nuttall. 2008. "Introduction: Afropolis." In *Johannesburg: The Elusive Metropolis*, edited by Sarah Nuttall and Achille Mbembe, 1–36. Durham, NC: Duke University Press.

McCulloch, Jock. 2000. *Black Peril, White Virtue: Sexual Crime in Southern Rhodesia, 1902–1935.* Bloomington: Indiana University Press.

McDonald, David A. 2012. *World City Syndrome: Neoliberalism and Inequality in Cape Town.* London: Routledge.

McFarlane, Colin. 2011. "Assemblage and Critical Urbanism." *City* 15 (2): 204–224.

McGrail, Richard, Jesse Davie-Kessler, and Bascom Guffin, eds. 2013. *Affect, Embodiment, and Sense Perception.* A Cultural Anthropology curated online collection with author interviews. Accessed August 29, 2016. www.culanth.org/curated_collections/16-affect-embodiment-and-sense-perception.

McGregor, JoAnn. 2003. "Landscape and Memory in the Zambezi Valley, Northwest Zimbabwe." In *Social History and African Environments*, edited by William Beinart and JoAnn McGregor, 87–105. Oxford: James Currey.

Melhuus, Marit, and Signe Howell. 2009. "Adoption and Assisted Conception: One Universe of Unnatural Procreation. An Examination of Norwegian Legislation." In *European Kinship in the Age of Biotechnology*, edited by Jeanette Edwards and Carles Salazar, 144–161. London: Berghahn Books.

Meyer, Birgit. 1998a. "Commodities and the Power of Prayer: Pentecostalist Attitudes towards Consumption in Contemporary Ghana." *Development and Change* 29 (4): 751–776.

Meyer, Birgit. 1998b. "'Make a Complete Break with the Past': Memory and Post-colonial Modernity in Ghanaian Pentecostal Discourse." In *Memory and the Postcolony: African Anthropology and the Critique of Power*, edited by Richard Werbner, 182–208. London: Zed Books.

Meyer, Birgit. 2004a. "Christianity in Africa: From African Independent to Pentecostal-Charismatic Churches." *Annual Review of Anthropology* 33:447–474.

Meyer, Birgit. 2004b. "'Praise the Lord': Popular Cinema and the Pentecostalite Style in Ghana's New Public Sphere." *American Ethnologist* 31 (1): 92–110.

Meyer, Birgit. 2008. "Media and the Senses in the Making of Religious Experience: An Introduction." *Material Religion* 4 (2): 124–134.

Meyer, Birgit. 2009. "Introduction: From Imagined Communities to Aesthetic Formations: Religious Mediations, Sensational Forms, and Styles of Binding." In *Aesthetic Formations: Media, Religion, and the Senses*, edited by Birgit Meyer, 1–28. New York: Palgrave Macmillan.

Meyer, Birgit. 2010. "Aesthetics of Persuasion: Global Christianity and Pentecostalism's Sensational Forms." *South Atlantic Quarterly* 109 (4): 741–763.

Meyer, Birgit. 2011. "Mediation and Immediacy: Sensational Forms, Semiotic Ideologies and the Question of the Medium." *Social Anthropology* 19 (1): 23–29.

Meyer, Birgit. 2012a. "Mediation and the Genesis of Presence: Towards a Material Approach to Religion." Inaugural Lecture, University of Utrecht, October 19.

Meyer, Birgit. 2012b. "Religious and Secular, 'Spiritual' and 'Physical' in Ghana." In *What Matters? Ethnographies of Value in a Not So Secular Age*, edited by Courtney Bender and Ann Taves, 86–118. New York: Columbia University Press.

Meyer, Birgit. 2013. "Mediation and Immediacy: Sensational Forms, Semiotic Ideologies, and the Question of the Medium." In *A Companion to the Anthropology of Religion*, edited by Janice Boddy and Michael Lambek, 309–326. New York: Wiley.

Meyer, Birgit. 2015. *Sensational Movies: Video, Vision, and Christianity in Ghana*. Oakland: University of California Press.

Meyer, Birgit, and Dick Houtman. 2012. "Introduction. Material Religion: How Things Matter." In *Things: Religion and the Question of Materiality*, edited by Dick Houtman and Birgit Meyer, 1–23. New York: Fordham University Press.

Miescher, Stephan F. 2005. *Making Men in Ghana*. Bloomington: Indiana University Press.

Misago, Jean-Pierre, and Matthew Wilhelm-Solomon. 2016. "Expansion of Low-Cost Housing for All Is a Necessity for Inner-City Johannesburg." *Daily Maverick* (Johannesburg). June 3. www.dailymaverick.co.za /article/2016-06-03-op-ed-expansion-of-low-cost-housing-for-all-is-a -necessity-for-inner-city-johannesburg/#.V6G3RJN946g.

Mmegi. 2015. "Half of Batswana Are Middle Class—AfDB." November 13. www.mmegi.bw/index.php?sid=4&aid=801&dir=2011/May/Friday13/.

Mohr, Adam. 2012. "School of Deliverance: Healing, Exorcism, and Male Spirit Possession in Ghanaian Presbyterian Diaspora." In *Medicine, Mobility, and Power in Global Africa*, edited by Hansjörg Dilger, Abdoulaye Kane, and Stacey A. Langwick, 241–270. Bloomington: Indiana University Press.

Mohr, Adam. 2013. *Enchanted Calvinism: Labor Migration, Afflicting Sprits, and Christian Therapy in the Presbyterian Church of Ghana*. Rochester, NY: University of Rochester Press.

Mossière, Géraldine. 2007a. "Emotional Dimensions of Conversion: An African Evangelical Congregation in Montreal." *Anthropologica* 49 (1): 113–124.

Mossière, Géraldine. 2007b. "Sharing in Ritual Effervescence: Emotions and Empathy in Fieldwork." *Anthropology Matters* 9 (1): 1–14.

Mossière, Géraldine. 2010. "Mobility and Belonging among Transnational Congolese Pentecostal Congregations: Modernity and the Emergence of Socioeconomic Differences." In *Religion Crossing Boundaries: Transnational Dynamics in African and the New African Diasporic Religions*, edited by Afe Adogame and James Spickard, 63–86. Leiden: Brill.

Mottier, Damien. 2012. "Le prophète, les femmes, le diable: Ethnographie de l'échec d'une Église pentecôtiste africaine en France." *Sociologie* 3 (2): 163–178.

Moyer, Eileen, Marian Burchardt, and Rijk van Dijk, eds. 2013. "Counselling, Sexuality and Intimacy: Perspectives from Africa." Special issue, *Culture, Health and Sexuality* 15 (4).

Mukonyora, Isabel. 1998. "The Dramatization of Life and Death by Johane Masowe." *University of Zimbabwe Humanities Journal* 25 (2): 191–207.

Mukonyora, Isabel. 1999. "The Complementarity of Male and Female Imagery in Theological Language: A Study of the Valentinian and Masowe Theological Systems." PhD diss., University of Oxford.

Mukonyora, Isabel. 2006. "Women of the African Diaspora Within: The Masowe Apostles, an African Initiated Church." In *Women and Religion in the African Diaspora: Knowledge, Power, and Performance*, edited by Marie Griffith and Barbara Savage, 59–80. Baltimore: Johns Hopkins University Press.

Mukonyora, Isabel. 2007. *Wandering a Gendered Wilderness: Suffering and Healing in an African Initiated Church*. New York: Peter Lang.

Mukonyora, Isabel. 2012. "Religion, Politics and Gender in Zimbabwe: The Masowe Apostles and Chimurenga Religion." In *Displacing the State: Religion and Conflict in Neoliberal Africa*, edited by James Howard Smith and Rosalind I. J. Hackett, 136–162. Notre Dame, IN: University of Notre Dame Press.

Mukonyora, Isabel. 2015. "Four Ways into an African Sacred Wilderness." *Religion* 45 (2): 209–220.

Murray, Martin. 2011. *City of Extremes: The Spatial Politics of Johannesburg*. Durham, NC: Duke University Press.

Musanga, Terrence. 2015. "Intra-urban Mobilities and the Depiction of the City in Zimbabwean Fiction as Reflected in Valerie Tagwira's *Uncertainty of Hope* (2006)." *Journal of Black Studies* 46 (1): 102–116.

NASFAT. 2006. NASFAT *Prayer Book*. Ikeja: NASFAT.

Ncube, Mthuli, and Charles Leyeka Lufumpa. 2014. *The Emerging Middle Class in Africa*. New York: Routledge.

Nevin, Alice. 2014. "Instant Mutuality: The Development of Maboneng in Inner-City Johannesburg." *Anthropology Southern Africa* 37 (3–4): 187–201.

Newell, Stephanie. 2002. *Literary Culture in Colonial Ghana: "How to Play the Game of Life."* Bloomington: Indiana University Press.

Newell, Sasha. 2007. "Pentecostal Witchcraft: Neoliberal Possession and Demonic Discourse in Ivorian Pentecostal Churches." *Journal of Religion in Africa* 37 (4): 461–490.

Newell, Sasha. 2012. *The Modernity Bluff: Crime, Consumption, and Citizenship in Côte d'Ivoire*. Chicago: University of Chicago Press.

Nguyen, Vinh-Kim. 2009. "Therapeutic Evangelism: Confessional Technologies, Antiretrovirals, and Biospiritual Transformation in the Fight against AIDS in West Africa." In *AIDS and Religious Practice in Africa*, edited by Felicitas Becker and Wenzel Geissler, 359–379. Leiden: Brill.

Núñez, Lorena, and Brittany Wheeler. 2012. "Chronicles of Death Out of Place: Management of Migrant Death in Johannesburg." *African Studies* 71 (2): 212–233.

Nyamnjoh, Francis B. 2006. *Insiders and Outsiders: Citizenship and Xenophobia in Contemporary Southern Africa.* Dakar, Senegal: Codesria Books.

OED. 2014. *Oxford English Dictionary.* Oxford: Oxford University Press.

Ojo, Matthew A. 1997. "Sexuality, Marriage and Piety among Charismatics in Nigeria." *Religion* 27 (1): 65–79.

Ojo, Matthew A. 2006. *The End-Time Army: Charismatic Movements in Modern Nigeria.* Trenton, NJ: Africa World Press.

Okada, Mokichi. (1984) 1999. *Foundations of Paradise: From the Teachings of Meishu-Sama.* Torrance, CA: Johrei Fellowship.

Olabuénaga, José Ignacio Ruiz, and Cristina Blanco. 2009. *La inmigración vasca: Análisis trigeneracional de 150 años de inmigración.* Bilbao: Universidad de Deusto.

Olupona, Jacob. 2008. *Òrìsà Devotion as World Religion: The Globalization of Yorùbá Religious Culture.* Madison: University of Wisconsin Press.

Olupona, Jacob, and Regina Gemignani, eds. 2007. *African Immigrant Religious Communities in America.* New York: New York University Press.

Omata, Nahoiko. 2012. "Refugee Livelihoods and the Private Sector: Ugandan Case Study." Working Paper Series No. 86, Refugee Studies Centre, University of Oxford.

Oosterbaan, Martijn. 2009. "Sonic Supremacy: Sound, Space and Charisma in a Favela in Rio de Janeiro." *Critique of Anthropology* 29 (1): 81–104. doi:10.1177/0308275X08101028.

Oppong, Christine. 1981. *Middle Class African Marriage. A Family Study of Ghanaian Senior Civil Servants.* London: George Allen & Unwin.

Orsi, Robert A. 1985. *The Madonna of 115th Street: Faith and Community in Italian Harlem, 1880–1950.* New Haven, CT: Yale University Press.

Orsi, Robert A. 2005. *Between Heaven and Earth: The Religious Worlds People Make and the Scholars Who Study Them.* Princeton, NJ: Oxford University Press.

Orsi, Robert A. 2012. "Afterword. Everyday Religion and the Contemporary World: The Un-modern, or What Was Supposed to Have Disappeared but Did Not." In *Ordinary Lives and Grand Schemes: An Anthropology of Everyday Religion*, edited by Samuli Schielke and Liza Debevec, 146–161. New York: Berghahn Books.

Ossman, Susan. 2002. *Three Faces of Beauty: Casablanca, Paris, Cairo.* Durham, NC: Duke University Press.

Palmer, Gary B., and Debra J. Occhi, eds. 1999. *Languages of Sentiment: Cultural Constructions of Emotional Substrates.* Amsterdam: John Benjamins Publishing Co.

Parish, Steven M. 1991. "The Sacred Mind: Newar Cultural Representations of Mental Life and the Production of Moral Consciousness." *Ethos* 19 (3): 313–351.

Parish, Steven M. 1994. *Moral Knowing in a Hindu Sacred City: An Exploration of Mind, Emotion, and Self*. New York: Columbia University Press.

Parkin, David. 2000. "Inside and Outside the Mosque: A Master Trope." In *Islamic Prayer across the Indian Ocean: Inside and Outside the Mosque*, edited by David Parkin and Stephen C. Headley, 1–22. Richmond, UK: Curzon.

Parkin, David, and Stephen C. Headley, eds. 2000. *Islamic Prayer across the Indian Ocean: Inside and Outside the Mosque*. Richmond, UK: Curzon.

Parnell, Susan, and Edgar Pieterse, eds. 2014. *Africa's Urban Revolution*. London: Zed Books.

Parsitau, Damaris. 2009. "'Keep Holy Distance and Abstain Till He Comes': Interrogating a Pentecostal Church's Engagement with HIV/AIDS and the Youth in Kenya." Special issue, *Africa Today* 56 (1): 45–64.

Pauli, Julia. 2010. "The Female Side of Male Patronage: Gender Perspectives on Elite Formation Processes in Northwest Namibia." *Journal of Namibian Studies* 8: 27–47.

Peek, Philip M, ed. 1991. *African Divination Systems: Ways of Knowing*. Bloomington: Indiana University Press.

Pellow, Deborah. 1985. "Muslim Segmentation: Cohesion and Divisiveness in Accra." *Journal of Modern African Studies* 23 (3): 419–444.

Pellow, Deborah. 2002. *Landlords and Lodgers: Socio-spatial Organization in an Accra Community*. Westport, CT: Praeger.

Pew Forum on Religion and Public Life. 2012. *Faith on the Move: The Religious Affiliation of International Migrants*. Washington, DC: Pew Research Center. www.pewforum.org/files/2012/03/Faithonthemove.pdf.

Pieterse, Edgar. 2011. "Grasping the Unknowable: Coming to Grips with African Urbanisms." *Social Dynamics* 37 (1): 5–23.

Pieterse, Edgar, and Susan Parnell. 2014. "Africa's Urban Revolution in Context." In *Africa's Urban Revolution*, edited by Susan Parnell and Edgar Pieterse, 1–17. London: Zed Books.

Pile, Steve. 2005. *Real Cities: Modernity, Space and the Phantasmagoria of City Life*. London: Sage.

Pinnock, Don. 1984. *The Brotherhoods: Street Gangs and State Control in Cape Town*. Cape Town: D. Philip.

Pontzen, Benedikt. 2014. "Islam in the Zongo: An Ethnography of Islamic Conceptions, Practices, and Imaginaries among Muslims in Asante (Ghana)." PhD diss., Freie Universität Berlin.

Povinelli, Elizabeth A. 2011. *Economies of Abandonment: Social Belonging and Endurance in Late Liberalism*. Durham, NC: Duke University Press.

Povinelli, Elizabeth A. 2013. "The Social Projects of Late Liberalism." *Dialogues in Human Geography* 3 (2): 236–239. doi:10.1177/2043820613495784.

Prince, Ruth, Philippe Denis, and Rijk van Dijk, eds. 2009. "Christianity and HIV/AIDS in East and Southern Africa." Special issue, *Africa Today* 56 (1).

Promey, Sally, ed. 2014. *Sensational Religion: Sensory Cultures in Material Practice*. New Haven, CT: Yale University Press.

Pype, Katrien. 2009. "Historial Routes to Religious Television Fiction in Post-Mobutu Kinshasa." *Studies in World Christianity* 15 (2): 131–148.

Pype, Katrien. 2011. "Confession cum Deliverance: In/Dividuality of the Subject among Kinshasa's Born-Again Christians." *Journal of Religion in Africa* 41 (3): 280–310.

Pype, Katrien. 2012. *The Making of the Pentecostal Melodrama: Religion, Media, and Gender in Kinshasa*. New York: Berghahn Books.

Pype, Katrien. 2015. "The Heart of Man: Pentecostal Emotive Style in and beyond Kinshasa's Media World." In *New Media and Religious Transformations in Africa*, edited by Rosalind I. J. Hackett and Benjamin F. Soares, 116–136. Bloomington: Indiana University Press.

Quayson, Ato. 2014. *Oxford Street, Accra: City Life and the Itineraries of Transnationalism*. Durham, NC: Duke University Press.

Radcliffe-Brown, Alfred R. 1922. *The Andaman Islanders*. Cambridge: Cambridge University Press.

Rancière, Jacques. 2004. *The Politics of Aesthetics: The Distribution of the Sensible*. London: Bloomsbury.

Ranger, Terence. 1967. *Revolt in Southern Rhodesia 1896–7*. London: Heinemann.

Ranger, Terence. 2008. *Evangelical Christianity and Democracy in Africa*. Oxford: Oxford University Press.

Reader, Ian R. 1995. "Cleaning Floors and Sweeping the Mind: Cleaning as a Ritual Process." In *Ceremony and Ritual in Japan: Religious Practices in an Industrialized Society*, edited by Jan van Bremen and D. P. Martinez, 227–245. London: Routledge.

RebelGroup. 2016. "Johannesburg Inner City Housing Strategy & Implementation Plan 2014-2021: Strategy and Programmes." Johannesburg: RebelGroup.

Reckwitz, Andreas. 2012. "Affective Spaces: A Praxeological Outlook." *Rethinking History* 16 (2): 241–258.

Regenbogen, Arnim, and Uwe Meyer, eds. 2013. *Wörterbuch der Philosophischen Begriffe*. Hamburg: Meiner.

Reihling, Hans. 2013. "Positive Men: Searching for Relational Dignity through Health Activism in a South African Township." *Social Dynamics* 39 (1): 92–107.

Reihling, Hans. 2014. "Vulnerable Men: Gender and Sentiment at the Margins of Cape Town." PhD diss., Freie Universität Berlin.

Reihling, Hans. Forthcoming. "Affective Health and Masculinities in South Africa: An Ethnography of (In)vulnerability." New York: Routledge.

Ricoeur, Paul. 1967. *The Symbolism of Evil*. Boston: Beacon Press.

Riis, Ole, and Linda Woodhead. 2010. *A Sociology of Religious Emotion*. Oxford: Oxford University Press.

Rizzo, Matteo. 2017. *Taken for a Ride: Grounding Neoliberalism, Precarious Labour, and Public Transport in an African Metropolis*. Oxford: Oxford University Press.

Robbins, Joel. 2004. "The Globalization of Pentecostal and Charismatic Christianity." *Annual Review of Anthropology* 33: 117–143.

Robbins, Joel. 2006. "On Giving Ground: Globalization, Religion, and Territorial Detachment in a Papua New Guinea Society." In *Territoriality and Conflict in an Era of Globalization*, edited by Miles Kahler and Barbara F. Walter, 62–84. Cambridge: Cambridge University Press.

Robbins, Joel. 2009. "Pentecostal Networks and the Spirit of Globalization: On the Social Productivity of Ritual Forms." *Social Analysis* 53 (1): 55–66.

Robbins, Joel. 2013a. "Beyond the Suffering Subject: Toward an Anthropology of the Good." *Journal of the Royal Anthropological Institute* 19 (3): 447–462.

Robbins, Joel. 2013b. "Monism, Pluralism and the Structure of Value Relations: A Dumontian Contribution to the Contemporary Study of Value." *Hau: Journal of Ethnographic Theory* 3 (1): 99–115.

Robbins, Joel. 2015. "Dumont's Hierarchical Dynamism: Christianity and Individualism Revisited." *Hau: Journal of Ethnographic Theory* 5 (1): 173–195.

Robins, Steven L. 2008. *From Revolution to Rights in South Africa: Social Movements, NGOs and Popular Politics after Apartheid*. London: James Currey.

Robinson, Jennifer. 2010. "Living in Dystopia: Past, Present, and Future in Contemporary African Cities." In *Noir Urbanisms: Dystopian Images of the Modern City*, edited by Gyan Prakash, 218–240. Princeton, NJ: Princeton University Press.

Rosaldo, Michelle Z. 1980. *Knowledge and Passion: Ilongot Notions of Self and Social Life*. Cambridge: Cambridge University Press.

Rosaldo, Michelle Z. 1984. "Toward an Anthropology of Self and Feeling." In *Culture Theory: Essays on Mind, Self and Emotion*, edited by Richard A. Shweder and Robert A. LeVine, 137–157. Cambridge: Cambridge University Press.

Rosaldo, Renato. 1993. "Grief and a Headhunter's Rage." In *Culture and Truth: The Remaking of Social Analysis*, 1–21. Boston: Beacon Press.

Röttger-Rössler, Birgitt. 2004. *Die kulturelle Modellierung des Gefühls. Ein Beitrag zur Theorie und Methodik ethnologischer Emotionsforschung anhand indonesischer Fallstudien*. Münster: Lit Verlag.

Röttger-Rössler, Birgitt, and Hans J. Markowitsch, eds. 2009. *Emotions as Bio-cultural Processes*. New York: Springer-Verlag.

Röttger-Rössler, Birgitt, and Jan Slaby, eds. 2018. *Affect in Relation: Families, Places, Technologies*. London: Routledge.

Roy, Louis. 2003. *Mystical Consciousness: Western Perspectives and Dialogue with Japanese Thinkers*. Albany: State University of New York Press.

Russell, Aidan. 2011. "Home, Music and Memory for the Congolese in Kampala." *Journal of Eastern African Studies* 5 (2): 294–312.

Sahlins, Marshall David. 1972. *Stone Age Economics*. New York: Aldine de Gruyter.

Salazar, Carles. 2015. "Science, Religion and Forms of Life." In *Religion and Science as Forms of Life: Anthropological Insights into Reason and Unreason*, edited by Carles Salazar and Joan Bestard, 1–22. New York: Berghahn Books.

Salo, Elaine. 2007. "Mans is ma soe: Ganging Practices in Manenberg, South Africa and the Ideologies of Masculinity, Gender and Generational Relations." In *States of Violence: Politics, Youth, and Memory in Contemporary Africa*, edited by Edna G. Bay and Donald L. Donham, 148–178. Charlottesville: University of Virginia Press.

Samarin, William. 1972. *Tongue of Men and Angels: The Religious Language of Pentecostalism*. New York: Macmillan.

Sartre, Jean-Paul, and Justus Streller. 1962. *Das Sein und das Nichts*. Reinbek: Rowohlt.

Schapera, Isaac. 1933. "Premarital Pregnancy and Native Opinion: A Note on Social Change." *Africa: Journal of the International African Institute* 6 (1): 59–89.

Schatzberg, Michael. 2001. *Political Legitimacy in Middle Africa: Father, Family, Food*. Indianapolis: Indiana University Press.

Scheer, Monique. 2012. "Are Emotions a Kind of Practice (And Is That What Makes Them Have a History)? A Bourdieuian Approach to Understanding Emotion." *History and Theory* 51 (2): 193–220.

Scheer, Monique. 2015. "German 'Shouting Methodists': Religious Emotion as a Transatlantic Cultural Practice." In *Emotions and Christian Missions: Historical Perspectives*, edited by Claire McLisky, 45–72. Basingstoke: Palgrave Macmillan.

Scheper-Hughes, Nancy. 1994. "AIDS and the Social Body." *Social Science and Medicine* 39 (7): 991–1003.

Scheper-Hughes, Nancy, and Margaret M. Lock. 1987. "The Mindful Body: A Prolegomenon to Future Work in Medical Anthropology." *Medical Anthropology Quarterly* 1 (1): 6–41.

Schildkrout, Enid. 1970. "Strangers and Local Government in Kumasi." *Journal of Modern African Studies* 8 (2): 251–269.

Schildkrout, Enid. 1978. *People of the Zongo: The Transformation of Ethnic Identities in Ghana*. Cambridge: Cambridge University Press.

Schmidt, Elizabeth. 1992. *Peasant, Traders, and Wives: Shona Women in the History of Zimbabwe, 1870–1935*. Portsmouth, NH: Heinemann.

Schmidt, Elizabeth. 2013. *Foreign Intervention in Africa: From the Cold War to the War on Terror*. New York: Cambridge University Press.

Schmidt, Eric R. 2018. "The Influence of Religious-Political Sophistication on U.S. Public Opinion." *Political Behavior* 40 (1): 21–53. doi:10.1007/s11109-017-9390-z.

Schulz, Dorothea E. 2012. *Muslims and New Media in West Africa: Pathways to God*. Bloomington: Indiana University Press.

Schütz, Alfred. 1970. *Alfred Schütz on Phenomenology and Social Relations*. Edited by Helmut R. Wagner. Chicago: University of Chicago Press.

Seesemann, Rüdiger. 2011. *The Divine Flood: Ibrahim Niasse and the Roots of a Twentieth-Century Sufi Revival*. Oxford: Oxford University Press.

Selim, Nasima. 2018. "Learning the Ways of the Heart in Berlin: Sufism, Anthropology, and the Post-Secular Condition." PhD diss., Freie Universität Berlin.

Shoeb, Marwa, Harvey M. Weinstein, and Jodi Halpern. 2007. "Living in Religious Time and Space: Iraqi Refugees in Dearborn, Michigan." *Journal of Refugee Studies* 20 (3): 441–460.

Shouse, Eric. 2005. "Feeling, Emotion, Affect." *M/C Journal* 8 (6). http:// journal.media-culture.org.au/0512/03-shouse.php.

Simmel, Georg. (1903) 2006. *Die Großstädte und das Geistesleben*. Frankfurt am Main: Suhrkamp.

Simon, Gregory M. 2009. "The Soul Freed of Cares? Islamic Prayer, Subjectivity, and the Contradictions of Moral Selfhood in Minangkabau, Indonesia." *American Ethnologist* 36 (2): 258–275.

Simone, AbdouMaliq. 2004. "People as Infrastructure: Intersecting Fragments in Johannesburg." *Public Culture* 16 (3): 407–429.

Simone, AbdouMaliq. 2008. "People as Infrastructure." In *Johannesburg: The Elusive Metropolis*, edited by Sarah Nuttall and Achille Mbembe, 68–90. Durham, NC: Duke University Press.

Simone, AbdouMaliq. 2010. "The Social Infrastructures of City Life in Contemporary Africa." Discussion paper 51. Uppsala: Nordiska Afrikainstitutet.

Skosana, Ina. 2017. "Mayor's Claim – Undocumented Foreigners Make up 80% of Joburg Inner City – 'Absurd.'" *Africa Check*, September 7. Accessed June 23, 2019. https://africacheck.org/reports/mayors-claim-80-joburg -inner-city-residents-undocumented-foreigners-absurd/.

Slaby, Jan, Rainer Mühlhoff, and Philipp Wüschner. 2017. "Affective Arrangements." *Emotion Review* 14: 1–10.

Smart, Ninian. 1978. *The Phenomenon of Religion*. London: Mowbrays.

Soares, Benjamin. 2006. "Introduction: Muslim-Christian Encounters in Africa." In *Muslim-Christian Encounters in Africa*, edited by Benjamin Soares, 1–16. Leiden: Brill.

Soares, Benjamin. 2009. "An Islamic Social Movement in Contemporary West Africa: NASFAT of Nigeria." In *Movers and Shakers: Social Movements in Africa*, edited by Stephen Ellis and Ineke Van Kessel, 178–196. Leiden: Brill.

Social Issue Research Center. 2007. *Belonging*. Accessed September 27, 2016. www.sirc.org/publik/Belonging.pdf.

Solomon, Harris. 2011. "Affective Journeys: The Emotional Structuring of Medical Tourism in India." *Anthropology and Medicine* 18 (1): 105–118.

Solomon, Robert C. 1995. *A Passion for Justice: Emotions and the Origins of the Social Contract*. Lanham, MD: Rowman and Littlefield.

Sommers, Marc. 2001. "Young, Male and Pentecostal: Urban Refugees in Dar es Salaam, Tanzania." *Journal of Refugee Studies* 14 (4): 347–370.

Spronk, Rachel. 2009. "Media and the Therapeutic Ethos of Romantic Love in Middle-Class Nairobi." In *Love in Africa*, edited by Jennifer Cole and Lynn M. Thomas, 181–203. Chicago: University of Chicago Press.

Spronk, Rachel. 2014. "Exploring the Middle Classes in Nairobi: From Modes of Production to Modes of Sophistication." *African Studies Review* 57 (1): 93–114. doi: http://dx.doi.org/10.1017/asr.2014.7.

Srinivas, Smriti. 2008. *In the Presence of Sai Baba*. New Delhi: Orient Black Swan.

Standing, André. 2006. *Organised Crime: A Study from the Cape Flats*. Cape Town: Institute for Security Studies.

Starrett, Gregory. 1995. "The Hexis of Interpretation: Islam and the Body in the Egyptian Popular School." *American Ethnologist* 22 (4): 953–969.

Statistics South Africa. 2012. "Statistical Release P0351.4: Documented Immigrants in South Africa." Pretoria: Statistics South Africa. Accessed June 12, 2019. www.statssa.gov.za/publications/P03514/P035142012.pdf.

Steinberg, Jonny. 2004. *Nongoloza's Children: Western Cape Prison Gangs during and after Apartheid*. Braamfontein: Centre for the Study of Violence and Reconciliation.

Stephens, Don. 2012. *Ships of Mercy: The Remarkable Fleet Bringing Hope to the World's Forgotten Poor*. Lindale, TX: Mercy Ships.

Stewart, Kathleen. 2007. *Ordinary Affects*. Durham, NC: Duke University Press.

Stodulka, Thomas. 2015. "Emotion Work, Ethnography, and Survival Strategies on the Streets of Yogyakarta." Special issue, *Medical Anthropology* 34 (1): 84–97.

Stoler, Ann Laura. 2004. "Affective States." In *A Companion to the Anthropology of Politics*, edited by David Nugent and Joan Vincent, 4–20. Malden, MA: Blackwell.

Stoller, Paul. 2014. *Yaya's Story: The Quest for Well-being in the World*. Chicago: University of Chicago Press.

Stoller, Paul, and Cheryl Olkes. 1987. *In Sorcery's Shadow: A Memoir of Apprenticeship among the Songhay of Niger*. Chicago: University of Chicago Press.

Strathern, Marilyn. 1990. *The Gender of the Gift: Problems with Women and Problems with Society in Melanesia*. Berkeley: University of California Press.

Street, Alice. 2012. "Affective Infrastructure: Hospital Landscapes of Hope and Failure." *Space and Culture* 15 (1): 44–56.

Streib, Heinz, Astrid Dinter, and Kerstin Söderblom, eds. 2008. *Lived Religion: Conceptual, Empirical and Practical-Theological Approaches*. Leiden: Brill.

Stupart, Richard. 2016. "Is South Africa Home to More Than a Million Asylum Seekers? The Numbers Don't Add Up." *Africa Check*, August 15. Accessed February 24, 2017. https://africacheck.org/reports/south-africa-home-million-refugees-numbers-dont-add/.

Sundkler, Bengt G. M. 1961. *Bantu Prophets in South Africa*. London: International African Institute.

Svašek, Maruska. 2010. "On the Move: Emotions and Human Mobility." *Journal of Ethnic and Migration Studies* 36 (6): 865–880.

Taussig, Michael T. 1993. *Mimesis and Alterity: A Particular History of the Senses*. New York: Routledge.

Taylor, Charles. 2007. *A Secular Age*. Cambridge, MA: Harvard University Press.

Thrift, Nigel. 2004. "Intensities of Feeling. Towards a Spatial Politics of Affect." *Geografiska Annaler. Series B, Human Geography*, no. 86 (B): 57–78.

Throop, Jason C. 2010. "Latitudes of Loss: On the Vicissitudes of Empathy." *American Ethnologist* 37 (4): 771–782.

Throop, Jason C. 2012. "Moral Sentiments." In *A Companion to Moral Anthropology*, edited by Didier Fassin, 150–168. Malden, MA: Wiley Blackwell.

Ticineto Clough, Patricia, and Jean Halley, eds. 2007. *The Affective Turn: Theorizing the Social*. Durham, NC: Duke University Press.

Tissington, Kate. 2013. *Minding the Gap: An Analysis of the Supply of and Demand for Low-Income Rental Accommodation in Inner City Johannesburg*. Johannesburg: Socio-Economic Rights Institute.

Tlou, Thomas, and Alec C. Campbell. 1984. *History of Botswana*. Gaborone: Macmillan Botswana.

Topan, Faruk. 2000. "Swahili and Ismā'īlī Perceptions of Salāt." In *Islamic Prayer across the Indian Ocean: Inside and Outside the Mosque*, edited by David Parkin and Stephen C. Headley, 99–115. Richmond, UK: Curzon.

Triaud, Jean-Louis, and David Robinson, eds. 2000. *La Tijâniyya: Une confrérie musulmane à la conquête de l'Afrique*. Paris: Karthala.

Turner, Victor Witter. (1969) 1995. *The Ritual Process: Structure and Anti-structure*. Piscataway, NJ: Transaction Publishers.

Ukah, Asonzeh. 2007. "African Christianities: Features, Promises, and Problems." Working Paper, Department of Anthropology and African Studies, Gutenberg Universität, Mainz.

Ukah, Asonzeh. 2014. "Redeeming Urban Spaces. The Ambivalence of Building a Pentecostal City in Lagos, Nigeria." In *Global Prayers: Contemporary Manifestations of the Religious in the City*, edited by Jochen Becker, Katrin Klingan, Stephan Lanz, and Kathrin Wildner, 178–197. Zurich: Lars Müller Publishers.

Ukah, Asonzeh. 2018. "Charisma as Spectacle. Photographs and the Construction of a Pentecostal Urban Piety in Nigeria." In *Religion, Media and Marginality in Modern Africa*, edited by Felicitas Becker, Joel Cabrita, and Marie Rodet, 175–201. Athens: Ohio University Press.

UNDP, Ghana. 2007. *Offinso District: Human Development Report 2007. Vulnerability and the Attainment of the MDGs at the Local Level*. Accra: UNDP.

van Binsbergen, Wim M. J. 1981. *Religious Change in Zambia: Exploratory Studies*. London: Kegan Paul International.

van der Veer, Peter. 2013. "Urban Aspirations in Mumbai and Singapore." In

Topographies of Faith: Religion in Urban Spaces, edited by Irene Becci, Marian Burchardt, and José Casanova, 61–72. Leiden: Brill.

van Dijk, Rijk. 1997. "From Camp to Encompassment: Discourses of Trans-subjectivity in the Ghanaian Pentecostal Diaspora." *Journal of Religion in Africa* 27 (2): 135–169.

van Dijk, Rijk. 2001a. "Contesting Silence: The Ban on Drumming and the Musical Politics of Pentecostalism in Ghana." *Ghana Studies*, no. 4: 31–64.

van Dijk, Rijk. 2001b. "Time and Transcultural Technologies of the Self in the Ghanaian Pentecostal Diaspora." In *Between Babel and Pentecost: Transnational Pentecostalism in Africa and Latin America*, edited by André Corten and Ruth Marshall-Fratani, 216–234. Bloomington: Indiana University Press.

van Dijk, Rijk. 2007. "The Safe Suffering Body in Transnational Ghanaian Pentecostalism: Towards an Anthropology of Vulnerable Agency." In *Strength beyond Structure: Social and Historical Trajectories of Agency in Africa*, edited by Mirjam de Bruijn, Rijk van Dijk, and Jan Bart Gewald, 312–333. Leiden: Brill.

van Dijk, Rijk. 2009. "Social Catapulting and the Spirit of Entrepreneurialism: Migrants, Private Initiative, and the Pentecostal Ethic in Botswana." In *Traveling Spirits: Migrants, Markets and Mobilities*, edited by Gertrud Hüwelmeier and Kristine Krause, 101–117. New York: Routledge.

van Dijk, Rijk. 2010. "Marriage, Commodification and the Romantic Ethic in Botswana." In *Markets of Well-Being: Navigating Health and Healing in Africa*, edited by Marleen Dekker and Rijk van Dijk, 282–305. Leiden: Brill.

van Dijk, Rijk. 2011. "Cities and the Social Construction of Hotspots: Rescaling, Ghanaian Migrants, and the Fragmentation of Urban Spaces." In *Locating Migration: Rescaling Cities and Migrants*, edited by Nina Glick Schiller and Ayşe Çağlar, 104–122. Ithaca, NY: Cornell University Press.

van Dijk, Rijk. 2012. "Pentecostalism and Post-development: Exploring Religion as a Developmental Ideology in Ghanaian Migrant Communities." In *Pentecostalism and Development: Churches, NGOs and Social Change in Africa*, edited by Dena Freeman, 87–109. Hampshire: Macmillan.

van Dijk, Rijk. 2013. "Counselling and Pentecostal Modalities of Social Engineering of Relationships in Botswana." Special issue, *Culture, Health and Sexuality* 15 (supp. 4): 509–522. doi:10.1080/13691058.2013.825927.

van Dijk, Rijk. 2015a. "After Pentecostalism? Exploring Intellectualism, Secularization and Guiding Sentiments in Africa." In *Multiple Secularities beyond the West: Religion and Modernity in the Global Age*, edited by Marian Burchardt, Monika Wohlrab-Sahr, and Matthias Middell, 215–240. Boston: de Gruyter.

van Dijk, Rijk. 2015b. *Faith in Romance: Towards an Anthropology of Romantic Relationships, Sexuality and Responsibility in African Christianities*. Amsterdam: University of Amsterdam Press.

van Dijk, Rijk, Hansjörg Dilger, Marian Burchardt, and Thera Rasing, eds.

2014. *Religion and AIDS Treatment in Africa: Saving Souls, Prolonging Lives.* London: Ashgate.

Vásquez, Manuel. 2011. *More than Belief: A Materialist Theory of Religion.* Oxford: Oxford University Press.

Vásquez, Manuel A., and Kim Knott. 2014. "Three Dimensions of Religious Place Making in Diaspora." *Global Networks* 14 (3): 326–347. doi:10.1111/glob.12062.

Verlet, Martin. 2005. *Grandir à Nima (Ghana): Les figures de travail dans un faubourg populaire d'Accra.* Paris: Karthala.

Vieytez, E. Ruiz. 2010. *Pluralidades latentes: Minorías Religiosas en el País Vasco.* Barcelona: Icaria.

Vigh, Henrik. 2009. "Motion Squared: A Second Look at the Concept of Social Navigation." *Anthropological Theory* 9 (4): 419–438.

Wachholtz, Amy, and Usha Sambamoorthi. 2011. "National Trends in Prayer Use as a Coping Mechanism for Health Concerns: Changes from 2002 to 2007." *Psychology of Religion and Spirituality* 3 (2): 67–77.

Wanjiku Kihato, Caroline. 2014. *Migrant Women of Johannesburg.* Johannesburg: Wits University Press.

Watts, Carey Anthony. 2005. *Serving the Nation: Cultures of Service, Association and Citizenship.* Oxford: Oxford University Press.

Weeks, Sheldon G. 1993. "Reforming the Reform: Education in Botswana." *Africa Today* 40 (1): 49–60.

Weiss, Allen S. 1989. *The Aesthetics of Excess.* Albany: State University of New York Press.

Werbner, Richard P. 1985. "The Argument of Images: From Zion to the Wilderness in African Churches." In *Theoretical Explorations in an African Religion*, edited by Wim van Binsbergen and Matthew Schoffeleers, 253–286. London: Routledge and Kegan Paul.

Werbner, Richard P. 2004. *Reasonable Radicals and Citizenship in Botswana: The Public Anthropology of Kalanga Elites.* Bloomington: Indiana University Press.

Werbner, Richard P. 2011. *Holy Hustlers, Schism, and Prophecy: Apostolic Reformation in Botswana.* Berkeley: University of California Press.

Werbner, Richard, and Terence Ranger, eds. 1996. *Postcolonial Identities in Africa.* London: Zed Books.

Wetherell, Margaret. 2013. "Affect and Discourse—What's the Problem? From Affect as Excess to Affective/Discursive Practice." *Subjectivity* 6 (4): 349–368. doi:10.1057/sub.2013.13.

White, Bob W. 2005. "The Political Undead: Is It Possible to Mourn for Mobutu's Zaire?" *African Studies Review* 48 (2): 65–85.

Whyte, Susan Reynolds. 1997. *Questioning Misfortune: The Pragmatics of Uncertainty in Eastern Uganda.* Cambridge: Cambridge University Press.

Wikan, Unni. 1991. "Toward an Experience-Near Anthropology." *Cultural Anthropology* 6 (3): 285–305.

Wilhelm-Solomon, Matthew. 2015. "Dispossessed Vigils: Mourning and Re-generation in Inner-City Johannesburg." In *African Cities Reader 3: Land, Property and Value*, edited by Edgar Pieterse and Ntone Edjabe, 136–149. Cape Town: African Centre for Cities.

Wilhelm-Solomon, Matthew. 2017. "The Ruinous Vitalism of the Urban Form: Ontological Orientations in Inner-City Johannesburg." *Critical African Studies* 9 (2): 174–191. doi:10.1080/21681392.2017.1337520.

Wilhelm-Solomon, Matthew, Peter Kankonde, and Lorena Núñez. 2017. "Vital Instability: Ontological Insecurity in African Urban Space (editorial)." Special issue, *Critical African Studies* 9 (2): 141–151.

Wilhelm-Solomon, Matthew, Lorena Núñez, Peter K. Bukasa, and Bettina Malcomess. 2016. "Introduction." In *Routes and Rites to the City: Mobility, Diversity and Urban Space in Johannesburg*, edited by Matthew Wilhelm-Solomon, Lorena Núñez, Peter K. Bukasa, and Bettina Malcomess, 1–30. Hampshire: Palgrave Macmillan.

Williams, Bernard. 2011. *Ethics and the Limits of Philosophy*. New York: Taylor and Francis.

Winkler, Tanja. 2013. "Why Won't Downtown Johannesburg 'Regenerate'? Reassessing Hillbrow as a Case Example." *Urban Forum* 24 (3): 309–324.

World Health Organization. 2016. *World Health Statistics 2016: Monitoring Health for the SDGs Sustainable Development Goals*. Geneva: World Health Organization.

Wuaku, Albert Kafui. 2013. *Hindu Gods in West Africa: Ghanaian Devotees of Shiva and Krishna*. Leiden: Brill.

Zhang, Li. 2012. "Private Homes, Distinct Lifestyles: Performing the New Middle Class in China." In *The Global Middle Classes: Theorizing through Ethnography*, edited by Rachel Heiman, Carla Freeman, and Mark Liechty, 213–236. Santa Fe, NM: SAR Press.

Zigon, Jarrett. 2007. "Moral Breakdown and the Ethical Demand: A Theoretical Framework for an Anthropology of Moralities." *Anthropological Theory* 7 (2): 131–150.

Zigon, Jarrett. 2008. *Morality: An Anthropological Perspective*. Oxford: Berg.

Zigon, Jarrett. 2009. "Within a Range of Possibilities: Morality and Ethics in Social Life." *Ethnos* 74 (2): 251–276.

Žižek, Slavoj. 2004. *Organs without Bodies: Deleuze and Consequences*. New York: Routledge.

Zulu, Melekias, and Matthew Wilhelm-Solomon. 2015. "Tormented by Umnyama: An Urban Cosmology of Migration and Misfortune in Inner-City Johannesburg." In *Healing and Change in the City of Gold*, edited by Ingrid Palmary, Brandon N. Hamber, and Lorena Núñez, 135–148. Heidelberg: Springer International Publishing.

CONTRIBUTORS

ASTRID BOCHOW is a social anthropologist at the Georg-August Universität Göttingen, Germany. She does research and publishes on the family, youth, religion, and health in Kumasi, Ghana, and Gaborone, Botswana. Since September 2014, she has been principal investigator of the project "Social and Religious Activism: Health and Family in Law and Politics," funded by the German Research Foundation.

MARIAN BURCHARDT is professor of transregional sociology at the University of Leipzig and senior research partner of the Max Planck Institute for the Study of Religious and Ethnic Diversity in Göttingen. His research explores how power, diversity, and subjectivity play out in public space. He is the author of *Faith in the Time of AIDS* (2015) and coeditor of *Topographies of Faith: Religion in Urban Spaces* (2013). His work has appeared in *International Sociology,* the *Journal of Religion in Africa,* the *Journal of Modern African Studies*, and the *Journal of Southern African Studies.*

RAFAEL CAZARIN is a cultural sociologist at ISOR Rein Sociology of Religion at the Autonomous University of Barcelona. He has been appointed as a visiting researcher at the African Centre for Migration and Society, University of the Witwatersrand (2013) and the International Migration Institute, University of Oxford (2015). In 2018 he was awarded the Ivan Varga Prize for New Generation Scholars by the Research Committee in Sociology of Religion of the International Sociological Association. His work focuses on gender dynamics and processes of social transformation in religious contexts.

HANSJÖRG DILGER is Professor of social and cultural anthropology at Freie Universität Berlin, with a specialization in the anthropology of religion and medical anthropology. His research on Pentecostal churches and revivalist Muslim organizations in urban Tanzania has focused on the dynamics of moral and religious belonging, charismatic healing and body practices, and processes of spatialization and institutionalization in religiously diverse settings. Dilger is coeditor of the volume *Medicine, Mobility, and Power in Global Africa: Transnational Health and Healing* (2012).

ALESSANDRO GUSMAN (PhD, Social Anthropology) is Assistant Professor of Anthropology at the Department of Cultures, Politics and Society at the University of Turin. His research focuses on the presence of Pentecostalism in Uganda and, more recently, on Congolese churches in Kampala. Among his publications are the books *Pentecôtistes en Ouganda. Sida, moralité et conflit générationnel* (Karthala, 2018) and *Strings Attached: AIDS and the Rise of Transnational Connections in Africa* (Oxford University Press, 2014; coedited with Nadine Beckmann and Catrine Shroff) and the journal articles "The Abstinence Campaign and the Construction of the Balokole Identity in the Ugandan Pentecostal Movement" and "HIV/AIDS, Pentecostal Churches, and the 'Joseph Generation' in Uganda."

MURTALA IBRAHIM was born in Nigeria. He attended the University of Jos, where he received a BA in religious studies in 2008 and an MA in sociology of religion in 2012. He defended his PhD at Utrecht University. Ibrahim's PhD project is entitled "Sensation, Sight and Sound of Nigerian Religious Movements: A Comparative Study of Christ Embassy and Nasrullahi-Fathi Society (NASFAT)."

PETER LAMBERTZ is a postdoctoral research fellow with the Gerda Henkel Foundation based at the Institute for Asian and African Studies of the Humboldt University of Berlin. From 2016 to 2018 he was a postdoctoral fellow with the GHI Paris and the CREPOS in Dakar. He has been teaching at the Institute for Anthropological Research in Africa in Leuven, Belgium (IARA/KUL), and is visiting professor at the Catholic University of Kisangani (DRC). Peter holds degrees in history (ULB, Brussels) and global studies (Leipzig-Stellenbosch-Wroclaw), and a PhD in African Studies/Religious Studies (joint doctorate, Leipzig and Utrecht). His current research focuses on Congo's wooden *baleinières* river craft on the upper Congo River.

ISABELLE L LANGE is an assistant professor in anthropology at the London School of Hygiene and Tropical Medicine. Her research interests focus on identities surrounding personal senses of well-being, health care decision-making, and hospital environments. She also studies maternal health, focusing on questions of perceptions of quality of care and policy exchange, primarily in West and East Africa.

ISABEL MUKONYORA is Professor of religion at Western Kentucky University. Besides teaching classes on world religions and Christian theology, she conducts research on the effects of global Christianity, gender, and environmental issues. Her current book project is "100 Years of an African Diasporic Religious Thought," with a special focus on the history and ideas of the Masowe Apostles.

BENEDIKT PONTZEN is an anthropologist whose main areas of research are the ethnography and historiography of Asante, the anthropology of Islam and "traditional religion," especially in sub-Saharan Africa, and the anthropology of religion. Presently, he is a postdoctoral fellow at the University of Florida. He completed his PhD in anthropology at the Freie Universität Berlin in 2014. His thesis, "Islam in the Zongo," is an ethnography of lived Islam in its diversity as encountered among Muslims in Asante.

HANS REIHLING is a postdoctoral researcher at the University of Amsterdam and the Amsterdam Institute for Social Science Research. He is part of the Anthropology of Health, Care and the Body Program and the research project "Becoming Men: Performing Masculinities in Urban Africa." His research interests include morality, affect, embodiment, gender, and violence. He also works as a psychotherapist and is dedicated to bridging social science theory and practice in the mental health field.

RIJK VAN DIJK is a professor in the study of religion in contemporary Africa and its diaspora at the African Studies Centre, Leiden University. He coedited *The Quest for Fruition through Ngoma* (2000), with R. Reis and M. Spierenburg; *The Social Life of Connectivity in Africa* (2012), with M. de Bruijn; and *Religion and AIDS Treatment in Africa* (2014), with H. Dilger, M. Burchardt, and Th. Rasing. His current research is on Pentecostalism, consumerism, and marriage in Botswana.

MATTHEW WILHELM-SOLOMON is a lecturer at the Department for Social Anthropology at the University of Witwatersrand, Johannesburg. He completed his doctorate at the University of Oxford, which was an ethnographic study of HIV/AIDS treatment programs for displaced communities in northern Uganda. He is conducting ethnographic research in Johannesburg on themes of migration, religion, healing, health, and housing since 2011. His contribution to this volume is based on research funded by the "Salvaged Lives: A Study of Urban Migration, Ontological Insecurity, and Healing in Johannesburg" hosted at the African Centre for Migration and Society, at the University of the Witwatersrand, in partnership with the Freie Universität Berlin's Institute of Social and Cultural Anthropology. He is coeditor of the volume *Routes and Rites to the City: Mobility, Diversity and Religious Space in Johannesburg* (2016).

INDEX

Note: Page numbers in italics refer to illustrations

affective regenerations, 29, 31, 37, 49; and dislocation, 38; as embodied, 38; and hauntings, 40–41, 45, 49; and intimacy and mourning, 49–50; politics of, 31, 50; and the poor, 37; relations of care, 42; religious cleansings as, 41, 45–49; and religious symbols, 31–32, 38; rites as, 31–32, 37–38, 49–50; and urban regeneration, 37, 49; and urban spaces, 49–50; writing as, 50

affective routes and healing, 123–24; distance, uses of, 134–35; emotion and decision-making, 136–37; medical tourism, 136; patients seeking, 133–34; and social navigation, 136–37; villages, experiences of, 127–31, 135; villages *versus* cities, 121, 124, 134 36

affective trajectories, 14–15; and affective routes, 123; *versus* binary philosophies, 4, 18–19; and Christian salvation narratives, 227; conceptual goal of, 4; of Congolese refugees, 227, 240; and displacement, 59; emotional expression as, 53; and history, 15–16; literature informing, 2; and personal biographies, 16–17; and religion, 15, 186, 199; urban contexts of, 17–18

Africa, urban: affect, dynamics of, 1–3; characterizations of, 10; dispossession in, 10; dynamics of, 10–11; emotion, dynamics of, 1–3; history of, 9–10; population displacement, 10–11; postcolonial era, 10; precarity in, 2–3; religion in, 13–14, 17, 19; religion mediating emotions, 3–4; religious growth in, 114; scholarly approaches to, 3; scope of, 2, 25n1; sentiment, dynamics of, 2–3; spiritual movements in, 140–41, 156n5

Ahmed, Sara, 7, 144, 204–6

amplification, 102–5, 107

Angola, 141. *See also* Église Messianique Mondiale (EMM), Kinshasa

anthropology: of affect, 6–7; affective becoming of, 34–36, 42, 50; of be-

coming, 207; crisis of representation, 225; of emotions, 226; experience-near approach, 225–26; medical, 116n5; phenomenological approaches in, 225; problem of belief, 223; and religious authority, 99

Asad, Talal, 32

assemblage theory, 36

at*touch*ment, 142, 144–45, 150, 154–55

Basque Country, 161, 165–67, 170, 172

Benin: Cotonou, 120–21, 127, 130–32, 137n2; doctors in, 125; foreign aid reliance, 125; health indicators, 125, 137n3; social navigation in, 121–22

Biehl, João, 207

Bilbao, Basque Country, 161, 165–67, 170. *See also* Pentecostalism in Bilbao

Böhme, Gernot, 148

book overview, 1–2

botsetsi, 111–13, 115

Botswana: adoption in, 217–20; African Independent Churches, 209, 213; children and marriage in, 210–11, 213–17; economic boom, 203, 212, 220, 221n5; education, history of, 209–10, 213; education, moral, 213–15; family, attitudes toward, 214–15; Gaborone, 203–5, 207; and HIV/AIDS, 204; independence of, 212–13; the middle class in, 203–4, 212–13, 221n1, 221n5; Pentecostalism in, 207, 209, 212–14; population of, 204, 221n2

Botswana, Christianity in: benefits of, 207; denominations present, 208–9; and educated professionals, 212–13; education, role in, 16, 209–10, 213–16; and gender, 213; missionaries, 203, 208–10; Pentecostalism, 207, 209, 212–14; and poverty and death, 221n3

Botswanian educated professionals: anxieties over expectations, 215; and Christian education, 209–10, 213–16, 220; families of, 202–5; and gender roles, 204, 206, 209–10, 213; history of, 203–4, 210–12; and HIV/AIDS, 204, 219; and orphans, 217–18, 220; and Pentecostalism, 207, 209, 215, 217, 219–20; religious life of, 208–9; research methods and emotions, 208–9

Brazil, 139–41

Burke, Timothy, 55

Burton, William F. P., 148

Butticci, Annalisa, 163

capacities, 252

Cape Town: apartheid-era evictions, 245–46; Cape Flats, 246–47, 254; "Coloured" classification, 246; gangs, 243–47; *ouens*, 247–49, 251, 255, 259; Pentecostalism in, 243–44, 256–58; post-apartheid, 246–47; townships, 245–46; violence in, 249. *See also* affective conversions; Pentecostalism and Cape Town gang members

Cape York, 43, 46

Catholicism, 223, 231, 241n1

chapter overviews, 15–18, 20–25

Chinyowa, Kennedy, 47

Christ Embassy, 77, 79–80; and affect, bodily experiences of, 78–79, 88–91; churches, 84–85; emotional orchestration, 91–92; emotional practice at, 90; glossolalia, 92–94; and hope, 97; members of, 79; origins of, 79; Chris Oyakhilome, 79–80; services at, 86–88; songs of worship, 87–90; spatial practices, 94

Christianity: agapē concept, 255–56, 261n6; in Botswanian education, 209–10, 213–16, 220; buildings in Abuja, 83–85; Catholicism, 223, 231, 241n1; and Zimbabwe, 56–57. *See also* Botswana, Christianity in; Masowe Apostles; Mwari; Pentecostalism

cities: affective relations, impact on, 9; affective routes, 134–36; and amplification, 102–5, 107; circulation in, 12; and institutional survival, 106–7; and intensification, 12; life in, con-

tradictions of, 131; margins of, 53–54; as networks of sites, 12; and ontological insecurity, 12; as produced, 11, 132; refugees in, 228; regeneration of, 36–37, 49–50; and religion, 1–2, 9, 12–14; and religious innovation, 106; urban theory, 11–13, 36; *versus* villages, 121, 124, 134–36. *See also* Africa, urban

cleaning campaigns, Kinshasa public, 138–39, 156n2; Kin-la-poubelle joke, 150, 155, 158n23; as moral transformation, 144–45; photographs of, *140*; places targeted by, 149–51

cleaning rituals: Congolese, 145; Église Messianique Mondiale's, 142, 144–48, 155; houses, 147; Indian, 157n16; Japanese, 145–46; religious cleansings, 41, 45–49

Congolese churches, spread of, 229–30

Congolese refugees in Kampala: aid, competition for, 232; arrival experiences, 231; backgrounds of, 228; and Catholicism, 231; and family, 228–29; fear of conflict in diaspora, 238; language issues, 231, 239; legal issues, 228; life experiences of, 222, 227; life-worlds of, 223–24; numbers of, 228, 239; prior lives, disconnect from, 234; protective networks for, 229; and religious groups, 229; Western resettlement goals, 236. *See also* Pentecostalism and Congolese refugees

Cotonou, Benin, 120–21, 127, 130–32, 137n2

Csordas, Thomas J., 94

Dahl, Bianca, 217

Daneel, Marthinus, 63

dark buildings, Johannesburg, 29–30, 33; and affect, 46; government raids on, 51n5; hauntings of, 40–41, 45; negative associations with, 34–35; origins of, 30; research methods, 34–36; women in, 39–40. *See also* affective regenerations

Das, Veena, 226
de Boeck, Filip, 131, 135, 149–50
Deleuze, Gilles, 6, 30–31, 144
Democratic Republic of Congo, 145, 152–53, 159n31, 227–28. *See also* Congolese refugees in Kampala; Église Messianique Mondiale (EMM), Kinshasa; Kinshasa
Desjarlais, Robert, 225
Diamond Exchange, 39–42
dividuals, 247, 260n3
Douglas, Mary, 145
Duranti, Alessandro, 226

Église Messianique Mondiale (EMM), Kinshasa, 139; affect, theory of, 143–45; agricultural work, 148; and at*touch*ment, 142, 144–45, 150, 154–55; and Gernot Böhme's aesthetic theory, 148; and cemeteries, 152–53, *154*; cleaning (nettoyage) practices, 142, 144–48, 155; and crossroads, 150–51; flower arranging, 139, 146–49, 151; and haunted houses, 148; healing rituals, 141–42; Johrei centers and ritual, 142, 146–49, 156, 157n13; and local beliefs, 155; membership, 141; Messianiques, 138–39, 141, 143, 146–47, 155; *versus* Pentecostalism, 141–42, 145, 155; and political history, 152–54, 156; public outreach, 150; and the senses, 142, 156; sentiment concept, 143–44, 148; and Simbazikita market, 151; and space-making, 155; spirits and emotions, 144; spiritual atmosphere concept, 143–44, 147–49, 156, 157n13; successes of, 142; suffering, view of, 141; and unfortunate deaths, 151; and urban difficulties, 142, 145, 150, 154–55; and Zando market, 151; and Zen Buddhism, 145–46. *See also* cleaning campaigns, Kinshasa public
Eliade, Mircea, 67
embodiment, 94, 162–63, 191–94

emotion, 5–8; *versus* affect, 5, 78; as affect articulated, 5; affect becoming, 188; African, stereotyping of, 18–19; Sara Ahmed on, 7, 144, 205–6; colonial readings of, 18–19; cultural politics of, 205–7; definitions of, 94; encoding of, 1; and ethics, 5, 7; as methodological tool, 205; and objects, 205–6; orchestration of, 91–92; Pentecostal concepts of, 178–79; reflexivity of, 5; relational theories of, 7–8; religiously-inspired, 19; Eric Shouse's definition of, 78; and social fields, 205–6; sticky, 206
emotional practices, 90
emotional regimes, 6, 19
emotional repertoires of Pentecostalism, 163–64, 180; in Bilbao, 161–62, 168; elements unifying, 179; and emotional regimes, 161–62, 174–75, 177–79; and emotional resocialization, 168–69, 236; and emotions, concepts of, 178–79; and metakinesis, 164, 179; and migrants, 161–62, 179–80; reflexivity, use of, 179–80; and spiritual knowledge, 179; and urban domain, 19; uses of, 164
emotional resocialization, 168–69, 236
emotional socialization, 168
empathy, 226
epistemological sophistication, 99–102
ethnography, 226, 239
excess and Deleuzian becoming, 260
experience-near anthropology, 225–26

families, modern European, 206
Fanon, Frantz, 18
Fassin, Didier, 42
Fischer, Michael M. J., 225

Gaborone, Botswana, 203–5, 207
Gaie, Joseph, 213
gender: and *botsetsi* practice, 111–12; and Botswanian educated professionals, 204, 206, 209–10, 213; and cities,

Masowe Apostles, 52–53, 74; Christian God as Mwari, 64, 68–69; and city margins, 53–54; and displacement, 55; and emotion, 57–58, 62, 64, 74; and Gandanzara, 55, 65–66, 73; in Harare, 53–55, 60, 73, 75; historical and political contexts, 53–54, 58; and the Holy Spirit, 53–54, 59–60, 66–71; Johane Masowe Apostles Church, 72–74; liberation theology of, 64, 66–67, 73–74; and marginality, experiences of, 66; in Marimba, 72; name, meanings of, 54, 62, 67, 69; origins of, 54–55, 57; prayer, 55, 59–60, 62, 69–70; research on, 62; rituals of, 57, 68; and Second Chimurenga, 57; Shona roots of, 65; spiritual language of, 68–71, 74; and suffering, 68–69, 73–75; white robes of, 61, 65, 68–70, 75; wilderness and frontiers, 60, 64–65, 67–68, 73; women, 57, 70–71. See also Mwari

Massumi, Brian, 6, 78, 178, 188, 200n7, 252

Mauss, Marcel, 193, 248–49

medical tourism, 136

Meishu Sama (Mokichi Okada), 139, 143, 146, 150–51

Mercy Ships, 120; affect and networks, 17; and affective routes, 124; *Anastasis*, 120, 125–26, 134; in Benin, 119–20, 125; and faith, 133–34; goals of, 124; location selection, 124–25; patient social reintegration, 130–31; patient waiting periods, 121, 131; and social navigation, 124; and spatial affect, 126; spatial relations to cities, 125–26; and urban networks, 121; visitors to, 126–27. See also affective routes and healing

metakinesis, 164, 179

Meyer, Birgit, 82–83, 108, 198

middle class, global, 206

migrants: in Bilbao, 161, 165–68, 170–72; emotional repertoires of, 161–62,

179–80; Nigerian, 172, 181n6; pastors, 161, 166, 168, 171; in South Africa, 161, 172–73, 181n6; in Spain, 172, 181n6

moral breakdowns, 250

moral sentiments, 7

Musanga, Terrence, 58

Mwari, 52–53; as Christian God, 64, 68–69; in colonial Zimbabwe, 57, 63–64; creator view, 64; as ecological, 59, 65; and emotion, 68; and the Holy Spirit, 52–53, 64; and Masowe rituals, 53; mother view of, 64–65; Shona people and, 63–64; Voice of, 52, 54, 57, 64, 67–70

NASFAT, 80; and affect, bodily experiences of, 78–79, 89–92; dress code, 87; emotional orchestration, 91–92; emotional practice at, 90; and hope, 97; LailatulQadr practices, 91; members of, 79; mosques, 85–86; name of, 78; night vigils, 91; origins of, 80; prayer book recitations, 88–90; services at, 86–89; spatial practices, 94; zikr, 79, 89, 93–94

Nigeria, 82–83. See also Abuja

Nigerians, 172–73, 181n6

Otabil, Mensa, 113

pan-Africanism, 7, 173, 181n8

Parnell, Susan, 10

Pentecostalism: and adoption, 217, 219; African diaspora, 162; in Basque Country, 165–66; in Botswana, 207, 209, 212–14; in Cape Town, 243–44, 256–58; chastity, emphasis on, 214; continuity and discontinuity in, 227, 234; conversion rituals, 162; counseling, 207, 215; and cultural traditions, 112; and educated professionals, 209, 212–13; *versus* Église Messianique Mondiale, 141–42, 145, 155; emotional resocialization in, 168–69, 236; emotions in, 162–63, 179; and evil, 158n24,

170, 234; exuberance of, 163; and glossolalia, 92–94; growth of, 181n8; and the Holy Spirit, 91, 145; intellectualism in, 19; marriage views, 217, 220; membership in, 209; and middle-class lifestyles, 113; prayer camps, 108; and socio-economic sophistication, 101–2; sound and song, 162; and spiritual gifts, 169; spiritual knowledge, 179; success of, 91, 227, 260. *See also* Christ Embassy; emotional repertoires of Pentecostalism

Pentecostalism, religious sophistication in, 102; and biomedical knowledge, 110; and *botsetsi*, 111–13; and counseling, 110–11; and HIV/AIDS, 109–10; institutional, 106–9; spirit-sentiment distinctions, 111–14; as urban, 102; and *Vernunftreligion*, 114–15

Pentecostalism and Cape Town gang members: appeal to, 249; and the body, 251; outreach efforts, 244, 249, 255, 258; post-conversion, 254–59. *See also* affective conversions

Pentecostalism and Congolese refugees: and churches, refugee, 229–31, 240, 241n3, 241n5; churches as refuges, 224–25, 238–40; continuity and discontinuity, 227; conversions to, 231, 235, 238, 240, 241n12; deliverance sessions, 236–37; and demons, 235–36; Églises de Réveil, 229–30, 241n4; and emotional expression, 227, 240; as lived religion, 224; the past, breaks with, 234, 236, 239; and the problem of belief, 223, 237; research approach, 223–26, 239–40; and salvation-suffering-redemption narrative, 227, 241n5; and suffering, 234

Pentecostalism in Bilbao: born-again believers, 172; churches, 166; emotional knowledge in, 168; emotional regimes, 168–72; and emotional repertoires, 161–62, 168; knowledge, importance of, 167–71, 179; and mi-

grants, 167, 170, 172; networks of, 166; pastors, 161, 166–68, 170–72, 175; and prostitutes, 167; research methods, 164; and women, 170–71

Pentecostalism in Botswana: educated professionals, 207, 209, 215, 217, 219–20; in Gaborone, 203, 205; and the middle class, 212–13

Pentecostalism in Johannesburg: Bible school, 173, 175–77; and emotional regimes, 175, 177–78; and emotional repertoires, 161–62, 174–75, 177–78; knowledge, emphasis on, 175, 177, 179; migrant congregations, 173; migrant pastors, 161; pan-Africanism, 173; pastors, 160–61, 165, 173–75, 177–78; research methods, 164–65; school of marriage, 177–78; and spiritual knowledge, 177

Pieterse, Edgar, 3, 10, 30

Pile, Steve, 81

Povinelli, Elizabeth, 7

prayer: Congolese refugees and, 233; 'id prayers, 185, 196; of Masowe Apostles, 55, 59–60, 62, 69–70; Marcel Mauss on, 193; NASFAT prayer book recitations, 88–90; Pentecostal camps, 108. *See also salat* prayer

problem of belief, 223, 237

racism, 18

Reckwitz, Andreas, 78, 86, 143–44, 155, 157n12

refugees, 33, 227–29; in Uganda, 227–28. *See also* Congolese refugees in Kampala

relational theories of affect. *See* affect, relational theories of

religion: African, stereotypes of, 18; analytical methods, 32; anthropology of, 31–32; and belonging, 1; and cities, 1–2, 9, 12–14; and emotional encoding, 1; and emotional regimes, 6; lived, 224, 241n2; and refugees, 229; sensational, 105 religious buildings, 87. *See also* Abuja, religious buildings in

religious communities, 2, 8

religious experiences, 32, 192–93

religious expression, 8

religious innovation, 106–7

religious practices, 1, 8

religious sophistication, 98–99, 101; institutional, 106–9; as sentiment, 98–99, 101, 115; and *Vernunftreligion*, 114–15. *See also* Pentecostalism, religious sophistication in

religious symbols, 31–32, 38, 56, 141

rhythmanalysis, 11

Riis, Ole, 6, 171

rituals: as affective regenerations, 31–32, 37–38, 49–50, and community, senses of, 133; and hope, 133; and social regeneration, 37–38; and urban spatiality, 38. *See also* cleaning rituals

Rosaldo, Michelle, 6

Rosaldo, Renato, 223

salat prayer, 191; affective experiences of, 192–93; bodily postures of, 192; body and mind in, 193–94; and community, 195; as contested, 197; effects on practitioners, 194; and embodiment, 191–94; and identity, 191; importance of, 191, 194; and individuals, 199; as reproduction, 193; and the *sunna*, 191, 193, 197, 199; and the *umma*, 195; virtues associated with, 194–95; in zongos, 186–87, 190–91

salat prayer in Kokote Zongo: affects of, 16, 198–99; and community, 195, 198–99; the divine, relating to, 192–93; experience of, 191, 193–94; and identity, 191; physical unity during, 195, 201n26; and religious dissent, 195–98; virtues associated with, 194

Schapera, Isaac, 211

Scheer, Monique, 87, 90

Sekai Kyûseikyô (Church of World Messianity): founding of, 139; Meishu Sama, 139, 143, 146, 150–51; spiritual atmosphere concept, 143–44, 157n13; spread of, 139–41. *See also* Église Messianique Mondiale (EMM), Kinshasa

sensational religion, 105

sentiment: colonial readings of, 18–19; definitions of, 98; in Église Messianique Mondiale, 143–44, 148; moral, 7–8; relational theories of, 7–8; as representational, 7; and resentment, 8; social, 247, 260n4; and sophistication, 100–102, 107; and sophistication, religious, 98–99, 101, 115; *versus* spirit, 111–14; trajectories of, 99–100; urban dynamics of, 2–3

Shona language, 64, 67, 69

Shona people and culture, 47, 55, 64–65. *See also* Masowe Apostles; Mwari

Shouse, Eric, 78, 89

Sierra Leone, 122–23

Smart, Ninian, 61

social experience and uncertainty, 122–23

social navigation, 122–24. *See also* affective routes and healing

social sentiments, 247, 260n4

Solomon, Harris, 136

sophistication: epistemological, 99–102; institutional, 106–9; research on, in Africa, 100–101; as sentiment, 100–102, 107; socio-economic, 100–101; and urbanity, 100–101. *See also* religious sophistication

South Africa, 33, 172, 181n6. *See also* Johannesburg

space: and affect, 126; dwelling perspective of, 12; as produced, 11, 36; and spiritual movements, 155; in urban theory, 11–12; virtual, in affective conversions, 251–53

Spain, 161, 165–67, 170, 172, 181n6

spiritual movements, 140–41, 155, 156n5
Stewart, Kathleen, 7, 14, 16, 188
Street, Alice, 126
Sunnas (Islam), 190, 192, 194, 196–99

Taussig, Michael, 248
Throop, Jason, 7, 225
Tijaniyya Sufis (Islam), 190, 192, 196–99

Uganda, 227–29, 241n3. *See also* Congolese refugees in Kampala
urban regeneration, 36–37, 49–50
urban theory, 11–13, 36

Vernunftreligion, 100, 114–15
Vigh, Henrik, 36, 122–24
villages: *versus* cities, 121, 124, 134–36; experiences of, 127–31, 135; returns to, 134–35

Weber, Max, 114
Wetherell, Margaret, 14
Whyte, Susan Reynolds, 122
women: in dark buildings, 39–40;

Masowe Apostles, 57, 70–71; and Pentecostalism in Bilbao, 170–71
Woodhead, Linda, 6, 171

Zen Buddhism, 145–46
zikr, 79, 89, 93–94
Zimbabwe: Chimurengas, 56–58, 60; and Christianity, 56–57; colonial history of, 56–57; democratic elections, first, 57; Economic Adjustment Program, 58; the Great Depression, 54–55, 57; Harare, 53–55, 58–60, 73, 75; industrialization of, 55; informal settlements, clearance of, 10; Mwari in colonial era, 57, 63–64; post-2005 unrest, 33; violence, history of, 56–57. *See also* Masowe Apostles
zongos, in Ghana, 185, 190; affective regimes of, 186–87; and Asante society, 189–90; characterizations of, 200nn3–4; forgiveness, value of, 194–95; humility, value of, 194; name meaning, 189; religious practices of, 185–86; *salat* prayers, 186–87, 190–91. *See also* Kokote Zongo